The aesthetics of visual poetry
1914–1928

The aesthetics of visual poetry
1914–1928

WILLARD BOHN

THE UNIVERSITY OF CHICAGO PRESS

CHICAGO AND LONDON

The University of Chicago Press, Chicago 60637
The University of Chicago Press, Ltd., London

© Cambridge University Press 1986

All rights reserved. Originally published 1986
University of Chicago Press Edition 1993
Printed in the United States of America
01 00 99 98 97 96 95 94 93   6 5 4 3 2 1

ISBN 0-226-06325-9 (pbk.)

Library of Congress Cataloging-in-Publication Data

Bohn, Willard, 1939–
    The aesthetics of visual poetry, 1914–1928 / Willard
Bohn.
        p.   cm.
    Originally published: Cambridge : Cambridge University
Press, 1986.
    Includes bibliographical references and index.
    1. Visual poetry—History and criticism.   2. Poetry,
Modern—20th century—History and criticism.   I. Title.
PN1455.B6   1993
809.1'041—dc20   93-14501
                                                    CIP

TO MY WIFE, ANITA,

FOR BRINGING ME A NEW VISION OF "LE CHAT"

Contents

Acknowledgments *ix*

Introduction *1*

1

Music of the spheres *9*

2

The Futurist experience *29*

3

Apollinaire's plastic
imagination *46*

4

Toward a calligrammar *69*

5

Josep-Maria Junoy *85*

6

Modes of visual analogy
in Catalonia *103*

7

Joan Salvat-Papasseit *123*

8

The advent of Ultra *146*

9

Guillermo de Torre *172*

10

Marius de Zayas and
abstraction *185*

Notes *204*

Bibliography *219*

Index *226*

Acknowledgments

The following study was supported primarily by the National Endowment for the Humanities, which awarded me a Fellowship for College Teachers to complete the second half. Preliminary research for the Spanish and Catalan chapters was conducted under a grant-in-aid from the American Council of Learned Societies, which enabled me to consult valuable materials in Spain. Other sections were written during a residential fellowship at the Camargo Foundation and funded by two Organized Research Grants from Illinois State University. Preparation of the illustrations for publication was aided by an additional grant from the College of Arts and Sciences and from the Graduate School at the latter institution.

Earlier versions of several chapters appeared in the following publications and are reprinted, in revised form, with the kind permission of their editors: "Ardengo Soffici's *parole in libertà,*" *Pacific Coast Philology,* 11 (1976); "Free-Word Poetry and Painting in 1914: Ardengo Soffici and Guillaume Apollinaire," *Ardengo Soffici: l'artista e lo scrittore nella cultura del 900,* ed. Geno Pampaloni (Florence: Centro Di, 1976); "Circular Poem-Paintings by Apollinaire and Carrà," *Comparative Literature,* 31, No. 3 (Summer 1979); "L'Imagination plastique des calligrammes," *Que Vlo-Ve?* (Belgium), Nos. 29–30 (July–October 1981); "Some Aspects of Visual Poetry in Catalonia," *Comparative Literature Studies,* 18, No. 4, (December 1981); "Joan Salvat-Papasseit and Visual Form," *Kentucky Romance Quarterly,* 30, No. 1 (1983); "Guillermo de Torre and the Typographical Method," *Dada/Surrealism,* No. 12 (1983).

I would especially like to thank Elizabeth Wrigley, Director of the Francis Bacon Library, who aided my research in various ways and who granted permission to reproduce the manuscripts of Apollinaire's "Coeur couronne et miroir." I am grateful to Angela Maria Boneschi Mattioli for allowing me to include Carrà's *Festa patriottica* and to Dr. Massimo Carrà for permission to reproduce "Rapporto di un NOTTAMBULO milanese," by the same artist. To En Xavier Benguerel and Señora Gloria Videla de Rivero, who provided invaluable assistance in locating elusive publications, I extend my warmest thanks. Thanks also go to Professor Luis Monguió, for advice connected with Catalonia, and to Mr. and Mrs. Rodrigo de Zayas and Mrs. Virginia de Zayas, who graciously opened their home to me in Seville. I owe a special debt of gratitude to Señora Norah Borges de Torre for sharing her memories of Ultra with me and for providing access to numerous rare documents.

The following individuals were also of great help to me in my research:

Acknowledgments

Palmira Pueyo, Directora de la Biblioteca, Instituto Internacional, Madrid; Francisco Pérez-Serrano Marquínez, Director, Casa Municipal de Cultura "Zenobia y Juan Ramón," Moguer; Margarita Vásquez de Parga, Instituto Bibliografico Hispanico, Madrid; Manuel Revuelta Sañudo, Director, Biblioteca de Menéndez Pelayo, Santander; Martha Levrero de Kenny, Jefe de la Sección Referencia y Bibliografía, Biblioteca Nacional del Uruguay, Montevideo.

In Barcelona the staff of the Biblioteca de Catalunya and the Biblioteca Central were particularly accommodating. My efforts in Madrid were aided by librarians at the Biblioteca Nacional and the Hemeroteca Municipal, and the staff of the Bibliothèque national and Bibliothèque littéraire Jacques Doucet in Paris also helped with various problems. Special thanks go to Helga Whitcomb and the Interlibrary Loan staff at Milner Library, Illinois State University, who listened patiently to my extravagant requests and filled them promptly and efficiently. Joan Winters and the staff in the Circulation Department provided equally conscientious service and were consistently helpful. Renée Gernand and Mary Nevader, of Cambridge University Press, furnished invaluable editorial assistance. This volume has greatly benefited from their careful attention to detail. I am grateful finally to those anonymous individuals who heard one portion of the book or another presented as a paper and who offered their insights during discussion.

Introduction

For various reasons the critical response to visual poetry over the years has been disappointing. Although the genre has a long and varied history, from the *technopaegnia* of the ancient Greeks to the latest experiments with concrete poetry, it has received relatively little attention until recently[1] – this despite the fact that visual poetry is one of the hallmarks of our age, like jazz and abstract art. Certainly, for reasons connected with the nature of modern existence, it has flourished in the twentieth century as never before. In the process it has undergone some astonishing transformations (some of which this book examines), acquiring an unbelievable complexity – or simplicity – depending on the poet. Refined, redesigned, and redefined, visual poetry has been the object of countless schools and movements from 1914 to the present. As such it has spread to every corner of the globe, from Portugal to Japan, from Romania to Argentina. In view of its popularity and longevity, it is high time we began to recognize it as a significant art form. More important, it is time we began to try to understand it. As much as anything this is the goal of the present study, which is concerned with the production of aesthetic meaning. Although it concentrates on one fairly brief period, from 1914 to 1928, its conclusions about the nature of visual poetry are applicable to the entire genre.

From the inception of visual poetry, the critical reaction has been mixed. Beginning with Simonides of Keos in the fifth century B.C., critics have either stressed the similarities between poetry and painting or denied that they exist.[2] There does not appear to be any middle ground in this continuing debate. Either one accepts Horace's dictum *ut pictura poesis* ("in poetry as in painting") or one agrees with Lessing in the *Laokoön* that the two media are incompatible. Lessing based his argument on the fact that painting is a spatial art, whereas poetry is temporal. This is essentially the position taken by the great ballerina Tamara Karsavina, who, speaking of ballet, observed, "Each art is only powerful in its own domain, and once it seeks to embody the principles of other art it is doomed to failure."[3] My own view is that the creative artist functions best in a challenging atmosphere and that whatever serves as a challenge is legitimate. The poets studied here, for instance, were interested in seeing how the principles of painting could be applied to poetry. For them it was an interesting aesthetic problem to be explored again and again using a variety of approaches. As we shall see many of their solutions were ingenious, quite a few were brilliant, and all were interesting. In seeking to overcome precisely that dichotomy described by Lessing, they scrutinized

1

poetry and painting as no one had before.[4] Despite my belief in the power of this genre, the present book is not intended as an apologia for visual poetry. It is not meant to justify the numerous visual experiments discussed here, but to explain them. In the last analysis the poems are their own justification. The fact that they exist is enough.

For our purposes we can define visual poetry as poetry meant to be seen. Combining painting and poetry, it is neither a compromise nor an evasion but a synthesis of the principles underlying each medium. In its own way it is one of the most radical inventions (or reinventions) of our time. Michel Foucault describes the revolutionary import of visual poetry as follows:

> Ainsi le calligramme prétend-il effacer ludiquement les plus vieilles oppositions de notre civilisation alphabétique: montrer et nommer; figurer et dire; reproduire et articuler; imiter et signifier; regarder et lire.

> Thus the visual poem claims to abolish playfully the oldest oppositions of our alphabetic civilization: showing and naming; representing and telling; reproducing and articulating; imitating and signifying; looking and reading.[5]

Like Surrealism, visual poetry aims at a sort of "supreme point" where these antinomies cease to exist. It aims to abolish the dual perspective introduced by the written word. Not only is each letter a unit in a verbal chain; it belongs to a visual chain as well. As the reader deciphers the linguistic message, he retraces the visual message line by line. Thus the work exists simultaneously as poem and picture. How this happens is the subject of the present study, which among other things seeks to demonstrate the full potential of visual poetry. Not only is the genre an excellent vehicle for poetic inspiration; it is capable of many unsuspected nuances. In almost every case the visual dimension is an integral part of the poem, developing and expanding the verbal text. In the best poetry there is a constant dialogue between these two levels that increases the depth and breadth of our experience.

Critics have often observed that our century has placed great value on seeing and sight. Although the reasons for this are complex, we can rank the invention of the cinema as one of the leading factors. Destined to revolutionize modern consciousness, the early cinema emphasized the visual sign at the expense of everything else and introduced a radically new syntax. Not only was the word subordinated to the image; the way in which images were linked together was new and exciting. Audiences were attracted by the illusion of unmediated experience but also by the novelty of cinematic logic and sequence. In the early days of film every movie was an example of experimental cinema. Interestingly, the members of the avant-garde were passionate film buffs and even used cinematic effects in their works. While moving pictures were becoming ever more popular, still photography was also making progress. As newspapers and magazines began to proliferate, for example, they became increasingly oriented toward the visual. For one thing, there was a sharp increase in the number of photographic illustrations in periodicals around 1910.[6] For another, advertisements in the same publications began to incorporate more and more photographs. This development paralleled the rise of modern com-

Introduction

mercial advertising, which introduced an additional visual stimulus to everyday life. It is no accident, for example, that posters and billboards figure prominently in much of the early visual poetry.

For that matter, poetry in general was becoming more and more visual. As visual images proliferated at the social level, poets began to lay greater stress on the verbal image. Throwing off the Symbolist yoke, they rejected the latter's preoccupation with music in favor of a poetics that stressed the similarities between poetry and painting. Thus groups dedicated to the primacy of metaphor in poetry sprang up – groups such as the Imagists, the Ultraists, and the Surrealists. Arresting similes and vivid metaphors became the order of the day as poets vied with each other in their quest for the ultimate image. That there should be a renewed interest in visual poetry at this time is not surprising. For one thing, it was the logical outgrowth of the two currents – visual and verbal – I have just described. For another, it provided the perfect bridge between them. Although the invention of the typewriter would also seem to have been a necessary prelude to visual poetry, in fact it had little or no impact on the movement. Almost without exception the early poems were drafted as handwritten manuscripts. Not until e.e. cummings burst on the scene some nine years later did a visual poet compose on a typewriter. Only in the past thirty years has the machine come into its own as the favorite instrument of the Concretists and the Lettrists.

As much as anything, the rise of modern visual poetry reflects a new awareness of the printed page. For various reasons recent criticism has stressed the physical dimension of the text, seeing its words as autonomous entities. According to Jacques Derrida the written word is an object in its own right, its different meanings detached and deferred indefinitely.[7] Wolfgang Iser and others consider modern literature to be a series of self-conscious exercises designed to engage us in the process of reading. For Iser the increased emphasis on reader participation marks the demise of the classical quest for the meaning of the text, the significance of which is located in our interaction with the words on the page.[8] What characterizes modern literary experience, then, is the reader's attitude toward the printed page, the reader's consciousness of its formal qualities. The same observation applies to the text's attitude toward itself. In the twentieth century as never before, form calls attention to itself; the text flaunts its means even as it pretends to ignore them. Words no longer are perceived as transparent signs, but assume the shape and destiny of objects. To be sure, the current interest in the phenomenology of the written word has its roots in observations by earlier authors. So too the concept of the page as visual statement has had an interesting and varied history. As early as 1864 a young Stéphane Mallarmé strove to "peindre, non la chose, mais l'effet qu'elle produit" ("paint, not the thing, but the effect it produces").[9] This statement, which reveals the close affinity between his works and painting, was to culminate in a famous (if isolated) experiment with visual form thirty-three years later: *Un Coup de dés jamais n'abolira le hasard (A Throw of the Dice Will Never Abolish Chance)*. Describing the poem as a "simultaneous vision of the Page," Mallarmé noted the visual impact of the white spaces and stressed their rhythmic function:

> Les "blancs" en effect, assument l'importance, frappent d'abord; la versification en exigea, comme silence alentour, ordinairement . . . je ne

3

Aesthetics of visual poetry

transgresse cette mesure, seulement la disperse. Le papier intervient chaque fois qu'une image, d'elle-même, cesse ou rentre, acceptant la succession d'autres.

The white spaces indeed take on importance, are initially striking; ordinarily versification required them around like silence . . . I do not transgress this measure, only disperse it. The paper intervenes each time an image, of its own accord, ceases or withdraws, accepting the succession of others.[10]

Mallarmé's concept of visual silence, which creates a privileged space for the text and its individual images, has been adopted by a wide variety of authors since its appearance. Arguing that the blanks determine the type of reading the reader will perform on the text, Gérard Genette makes it the fundamental condition of poetry. For him the poeticity of a given work, its presence and intensity, depend on the *"margin of silence* which isolates it in the middle of ordinary speech."[11]

Not long after Mallarmé, between 1900 and 1904, Paul Claudel contributed a meditation on the printed page that partially synthesizes these two insights. "O mon âme!" he exclaimed. "Le poème n'est point fait de ces lettres que je plante comme des clous, mais du blanc qui reste sur le papier." ("Oh, my soul! The poem is not composed of these letters that I plant like nails, but of the white space that remains on the paper.")[12] The poem is not only black on white but white against black. By freeing the typographical characters from their background, which he forced into the foreground, Claudel prepared the way for the visual poets who were to follow. With his blessing – and Mallarmé's – they were free to twist letters into different shapes and to experiment with their placement on the page. Lecturing at the University of Geneva in those days, Ferdinand de Saussure added his authority to the growing visual trend by relating the latter to the reading process itself. "Nous lisons de deux manières," he remarked. "Le mot nouveau ou inconnu est épelé lettre après letter; mais le mot usuel et familier s'embrasse d'un seul coup d'oeil, indépendamment des lettres qui le composent; l'image de ce mot acquiert pour nous une valeur idéographique." ("We read in two ways: A new or unknown word is spelled out letter by letter, but a common, ordinary word is embraced by a single glance, independently of its letters, so that the image of the whole word acquires an ideographic value.")[13] These remarks, which stress the iconic shape of the written word, are part of a lengthy debate that took place in Europe during the early years of this century. One contingent, best exemplified by Ezra Pound, sought to develop an "ideogrammic method" that would retain traditional poetic forms but intensify their verbal imagery.[14] Another contingent, headed by Guillaume Apollinaire and the Italian Futurists, experimented with pictorial forms in an attempt to create "visual analogies" and "lyrical ideograms." Both factions strove to increase the visual impact of the poetic image and to provide the reader with a moment of epiphany.

If, as Jonathan Culler claims, "poetry lies at the center of the literary experience because it is the form that most clearly asserts the specificity of literature,"[15] visual poetry lies at the center of the *poetic* experience because it asserts the specificity of poetry. Not only does it differ from ordinary discourse about the world; it

4

Introduction

differs from fictional discourse, which is structured according to radically different norms. The specific features of visual poetry are those of poetry itself, dramatized according to the dictates of the visual imagination. Like the latter, visual poetry is a nondiscursive, presentational mode governed by ellipsis and parataxis. Like the latter, it is devoted to the cult of the image, which functions both as its support and its *raison d'être*. As one critic explains, "Figuration, spatialisation, visualisation du message poétique visent à remotiver le signifiant dans la relation analogique. . . . L'activité *littérale* tend alors à prendre le pas sur l'activité *littéraire* ou même dans les cas extrêmes à se substituer à elle." ("Figuration, spatialization, visualization of the poetic message aim at remotivating the signifier in the analogical relationship. . . . Thus *literal* activity tends to displace *literary* activity or even in extreme cases to replace it entirely.")[16] This accords with what we have noted previously about the primacy of the written word. Not only is the signifier no longer transparent; it becomes the main focus of the text. Following Roland Barthes we can identify visual poetry as a second-order semiological system in which language and image are articulated as follows:[17]

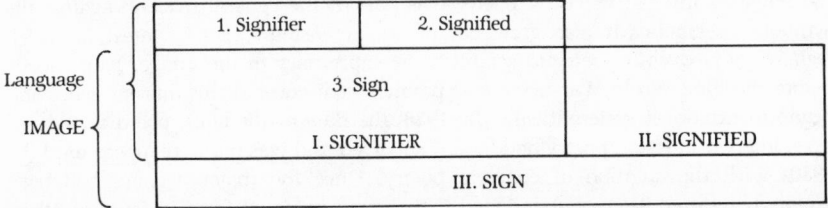

Unlike conventional poetry, visual poetry utilizes a dual sign. As such it comprises two sets of signifiers and signifieds – one verbal, the other visual. The linguistic sign, which constitutes a complete system in itself, functions as the first term of the visual sign, which expands to encompass a second signified at the visual level. In this manner the written word serves as the support for the visual message. Although the signifying system itself presents few problems, how the picture is related to the poem has been a matter of dispute for many years. Since this subject will be examined in detail in Chapter 4, let us simply note that visual poetry is a highly mimetic genre. Bridging the gap between the poet and the world, it codifies experience according to a series of formal conventions.

The poets whose work appears in these pages used such terms as "psychotype," "words at liberty," "figurative poetry," "ideograms," and "calligrams" to describe their compositions. Since these words are so localized, like the "topiary verse" of the Renaissance or "concrete poetry" of recent memory, the more general expression "visual poetry" is used here. Occasionally the term "figurative verse" occurs in connection with a poem that reproduces the shape of a specific object. I should add that the method employed in the following chapters is twofold. Rather than attempt to cover all the visual poetry of the period – which would require a dozen volumes – I have tried to identify the basic principles of the genre through the detailed analysis of individual poems. As such the book represents an exercise in applied aesthetics, although Chapters 3 and 4 explore structural typologies and erect a theory of visual poetry. This section, which includes a historical taxonomy and a

Aesthetics of visual poetry

discussion of metaphor and metonymy, furnishes a critical focus for the rest of the volume. In elaborating a grammar and syntax of visual poetry, which the succeeding chapters apply and develop, it provides a generic approach to the poetry as a whole. In general a reciprocal relationship exists between a given text and the principles governing its production. Just as each poem illustrates the rules underlying the signifying process, it cannot be understood without a firm grasp of visual poetics. Nor can one hope to understand the complex set of relations extending from the author to the text to the reader. Although I have tried to place the poems in their original context, this work is not meant to be an essay in literary history. At most I have emphasized certain similarities and differences while retaining some sense of continuity from one poet to the next.

The discussion begins, in Chapter 1, with the birth of modern visual poetry in Italy and France in 1914. Before that date pictorial effects were few and far between, and no attempt was made to exploit them. Although occasional examples can be found, such as Mallarmé's *Un Coup de dés*, Symbolism's obsession with musical analogy effectively discouraged visual experimentation. Among other things the renewed interest in visual poetry was part of the general reaction against the Symbolist aesthetic. It also grew out of an increasingly visual context in which technology vied with poetry to establish the supremacy of the image. Thus shortly before the First World War poets and painters rediscovered this ancient genre and began to explore it systematically. By 1928, the date of the latest poem considered here, interest in visual poetry had largely subsided and was not to reappear until the 1950s with the creation of concrete poetry. Once the major avenues had been explored, its practitioners abandoned their essays in visual form in favor of other, more provocative experiments. In particular the rise of Surrealism coincided with the genre's decline and captured the imagination, literally, of a whole generation of writers and artists. In this manner visual poetry succumbed to the same forces that had been responsible for its triumph. At the forefront of the avant-garde initially, it passed through the ranks and disappeared into historical oblivion.[18]

The history of visual poetry in general reflects the history and range of written scripts, which Jacques Derrida describes as follows: "L'histoire de la voix et de son écriture serait comprise entre deux écritures muettes, entre deux pôles d'universalité se rapportant l'un à l'autre comme le naturel et l'artificiel: le pictogramme et l'algèbre" ("The history of the voice and its writing is comprehended between two mute writings, between two poles of universality relating to each other as the natural and the artificial: the pictogram and algebra").[19] All visual poetry oscillates between these two poles, ranging from the concrete to the abstract, from the pictorial to the expressionistic. The model is equally valid whether we approach it from a diachronic perspective or seek to place it in a synchronic framework. In the twentieth century this principle is evident from the very beginning in the competition between the Italian Futurists and Guillaume Apollinaire. Not only do their works diverge along precisely these lines; they were the source of all subsequent experiments with visual form during this period. Indeed modern visual poetry in general stems from their fruitful competition.

This fact explains the rationale behind the selection of certain texts and the exclusion of others. Throughout the volume I have tried to address major currents of

Introduction

visual poetry, rather than minor ones, according to the polar model discussed above. I have made no attempt to include every development, since this study is not intended as a literary history. I have concentrated instead on areas of particular interest or on areas that present problems bearing on the genre itself. Above all, I have sought to elucidate fundamental processes through the examination of representative works. If a number of experiments have had to be omitted—notably those by the Dadas, the De Stijl group, and the Russian Cubo-Futurists—the principles underlying them are discussed in connection with other movements and other personalities. Thus the sections on Italian Futurism will interest readers familiar with Vassily Kamensky's typographical audacities or El Lissitzky's arrangements of Mayakovsky's poetry.[20] And those interested in, say, Pierre Albert-Birot or Vicente Huidobro will find other sections that shed light on these authors.

The absence of the Slavic poets, like the Dutch, was necessitated by a lack of linguistic competence. Given the complex interplay between verbal and visual elements, working with translations is inherently unsatisfactory. The Dada poets present difficulties of another order. Despite their indebtedness to Futurism and the modern French school, they do not accord the same importance to visual poetry. Admittedly, visual effects are fairly widespread in Dada publications, where they entertain the eye and signal a radical break with the past. The fact that these are entirely gratuitous, however, severely restricts their aesthetic function. Like the typographical effects in Hugo Ball's "Karawane"—perhaps the most familiar example—they are purely ornamental. At best they illustrate the divorce between signifier and signified that is one of the hallmarks of the movement.[21] Ceaselessly pointing to itself, Dada visual poetry is hopelessly narcissistic. Given these limitations, I have preferred to conduct a flanking maneuver rather than a frontal attack. The principle of ornamentation, for instance, is discussed in connection with other poets. And although Tristan Tzara's disciples are absent, the volume includes several examples of Barcelona and New York Dada. It is interesting that the two practitioners examined here (Junoy and de Zayas) were both professional artists, for ironically the only Dadaists to respect the integrity of the linguistic sign were the artists, whose verbal-visual collages reached their highpoint with the work of Kurt Schwitters. In this, however, they were following a trail blazed by the Futurists and Cubist painters who had experimented with similar works several years before.[22]

For reasons that remain unclear, visual poetry flourished in Italy, France, and Spain as nowhere else during this period. This fact explains why the present study focuses not just on European visual poetry but on that written in various Romance languages. The single exception, which is the subject of a separate chapter, is a work written in English. The first visual poem to appear in the United States, it represents an important bridge between the Old World and the New. Although specialists in the avant-garde have long been familiar with pictorial poetry in France and Italy—or have at least known of its existence—Spanish enthusiasm for the genre comes as a surprise. Indeed one of the most exciting moments during the preliminary research occurred when I realized how extensive the Spanish contribution was. Although twentieth-century *hispanistas* have always had a few visual poems at their disposal, the vast majority have been inaccessible. Buried in rare volumes and obscure reviews scattered across three continents, their very existence has remained unknown.[23] For the first time, then, we are in a position to evaluate Spanish achievements in this area and to compare developments in all three countries. Their common devotion to the cause of visual poetry provides yet another measure of Romance solidarity.

Except for Chapter 10, the chapters are arranged in chronological order. Since the major divisions occur along national and/or linguistic lines, however, this chronology is only approximate. Although the internal sequence remains undisturbed within each group, the groups themselves overlap to some extent. The first two chapters analyze some of the earliest visual poetry by Ardengo Soffici, Carlo Carrà, and Apollinaire. Chapter 1 juxtaposes a Futurist composition with a French poem to establish the basic parameters of the genre. Chapter 2 reconsiders Italian Futurism and the concept of "words at liberty." Chapter 3 examines Apollinaire's pictorial imagination and defines his contribution to the visual poetry tradition. In Chapter 4 Apollinaire's *calligrammes* serve as the pretext for a study of visual poetics based on Roman Jakobson's study of aphasia. The next five chapters trace the spread of visual poetry to Spain, first to Catalonia, where it thrived for more than a decade, then to Castile and Andalusia, where it was adopted by the Ultraist movement. Among the Catalan poets discussed are Josep-Maria Junoy, Joaquim Folguera, and Joan Salvat-Papasseit. The Castilian-speaking poets include Juan Larrea, Dámaso Alonso, and Guillermo de Torre. The final chapter follows visual poetry to the New World, where it was introduced by Marius de Zayas in New York. Transplanted from Europe to Latin America a few years later, it quickly took hold and spread throughout the Americas.

As much as anything, visual poetry's geographic diversity testifies to its obvious success. But what factors in particular have contributed to its popularity? To what does it owe its undeniable appeal? Perhaps the best answer is provided by Wendy Steiner in her penetrating study of interartistic aesthetics, *The Colors of Rhetoric*. In her estimation the different manifestations of this tradition, which includes visual poetry, represent an effort to combine presence with voice.[24] In particular, she notes, "the attempt to overreach the boundaries between one art and another is . . . an attempt to dispel (or at least mask) the boundary between art and life, between sign and thing, between writing and dialogue."[25] Nowhere is this process more evident than in visual poetry. Not only does it dissolve the traditional barriers between the reader and the text; it erases the boundaries between the text and the world. By defamiliarizing well-worn modes and habits, on the one hand, it sharpens the reader's sensibility and encourages participation in the creation of the poem. Not only is the link between signifier and signified revitalized; the reader himself is integrated into the work. By eroding the distinction between art and nature, on the other hand, visual poetry instills new life into the text. Here its fundamental task is to remotivate the signifier. Bridging the gap between the object and its reflection, it creates an unmistakable presence and gives the composition an immediate voice. Thus in the end visual poetry's popularity stems from its role as a dual sign. Reflecting the primary modes of human perception – sight and sound – it appeals to us because these are the norms of existence itself.

1

Music of the spheres

The year 1914 was decisive in the history of the European avant-garde. In the months preceding the First World War artists and writers experimented with a wide variety of forms in an attempt to exhaust the expressive possibilities of their respective disciplines. Among the most radical genres invented and feverishly explored during this period were visual poetry and verbal painting – poetry that appealed to the eye and painting that appealed to the ear. Thus Apollinaire invented (or reinvented) the figurative poem, which reproduced the form of objects to make a picture. And Carlo Carrà, in addition to writing typographical poetry, co-invented the word-painting. In 1914 their paths crossed in a manner that was to be highly beneficial to both when the Futurists came to Paris in the spring. Together with Giovanni Papini, Carrà found lodging in the offices of Apollinaire's review, *Les Soirées de Paris*, and came to know the poet quite well.[1]

Spheres of influence

Given the mutual admiration and understanding that existed between the two men, it is perhaps not surprising that each created a circle-shaped work at about the same time. Apollinaire's first visual poem, "Lettre-Océan" ("Ocean-Letter"), was published in *Les Soirées de Paris* on June 15, 1914. A reproduction of Carrà's work, executed in July, appeared in *Lacerba* on August 1, 1914, with the title *Dipinto parolibero (Festa patriottica) (Free-Word Painting – Patriotic Celebration)*. A collage made of tempera and pasted papers on cardboard, it consists largely of phrases cut out of newspapers or added in white paint, blended together in a harmonious color scheme. As I have shown elsewhere, Apollinaire's poem was in fact the source of Carrà's composition.[2] This explains the high degree of resemblance between them, which until recently had been unremarked.[3] Both have the same geometrical configuration. The lines of poetry in the poem, like the phrases and painted papers in the collage, form a series of concentric circles radiating outward from a circular center, from which extend a number of symmetrical "spokes." The same can be said of the principal techniques employed. Both works exploit the visual properties of written language to create ideogrammatic compositions in which the formal configuration reinforces the linguistic message and vice versa. If they are essentially pictures formed of words, they are also literary works the structure and spatial relations of which are determined by the physical properties of the text, by the

9

LETTRE-OCEAN

Je traverse la ville net en avant
et je la coupe en **Z**

J'étais au bord du Rhin quand tu partis pour le Mexique
Ta voix me parvient malgré l'énorme distance
Gens de mauvaise mine sur le quai à la Vera Cruz

Les voyageurs de *l'Espagne* devant faire
le voyage de Coatzacoalcos pour s'embarquer
je t'envoie cette carte aujourd'hui au lieu

Juan Aldama

Correos
Mexico
4 centavos

TPIRANGA

REPUBLICA MEXICANA
TARJETA POSTAL

11 45
29 -5
11
Rue des Batignolles

de profiter du courrier de Vera Cruz qui n'est pas si
Tout est calme ici et nous sommes dans l'atten
des événements.

U. S. Postage
2 cents 2

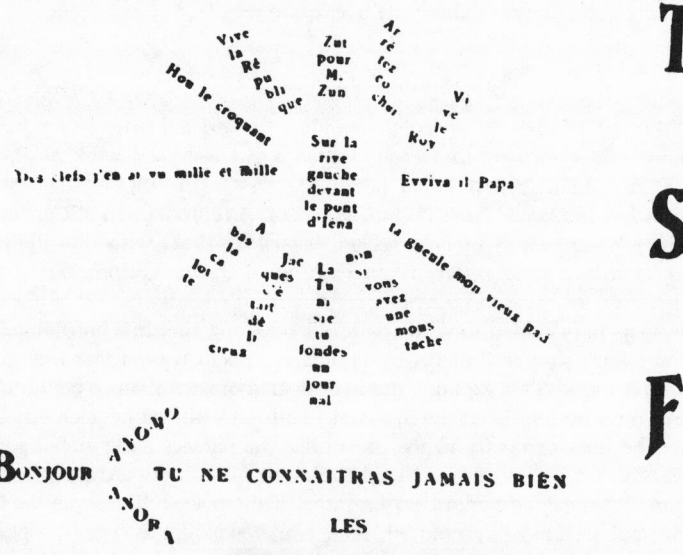

Bonjour **T**U NE CONNAITRAS JAMAIS BIEN

LES

Mayas

Figure 1. Guillaume Apollinaire

10

Te souviens-tu du tremblement de terre entre 1885 et 1890 on coucha plus d'un mois sous la tente

BONJOUR MON FRÈRE ALBERT à Mexico

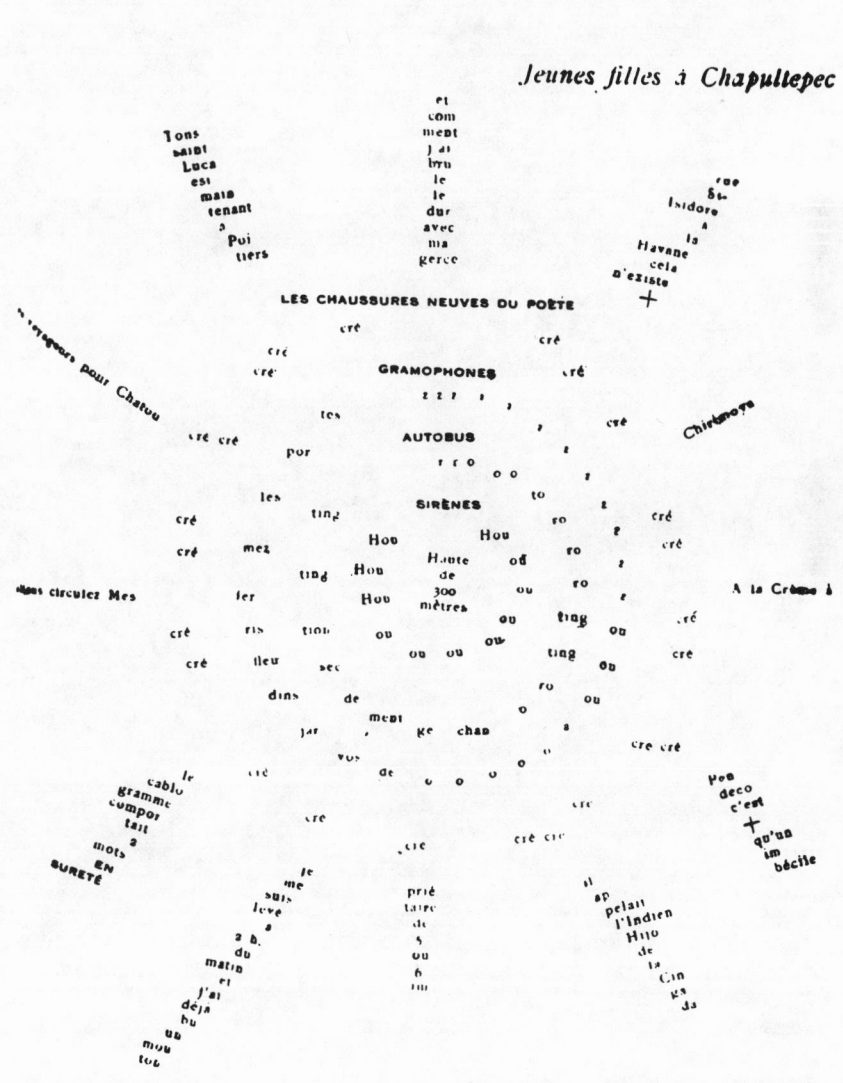

Jeunes filles à Chapultepec

Guillaume Apollinaire

11

Figure 2. Carlo Carrà, *Festa patriottica*

12

Music of the spheres

juxtaposition of the words on the page (or canvas). Perception and conception, image and metaphor tend to merge into one indivisible whole. In this context the compositions represent extreme examples of concrete metaphor.

As if these similarities were not enough, the works have a common subject matter. Both are schematic representations of patriotic demonstrations/celebrations taking place in a public square in a large city (Paris and Milan). In seeking to render the atmosphere of these gatherings, both depend heavily on sight and sound. The evocation of the physical surroundings (people, objects, signs, etc.) is complemented by the reproduction of the auditory dimension: assorted noises, political slogans, and bits of conversation. The gramophones in Apollinaire's work are playing a song with the words "De vos jardins fleuris fermez les portes" ("Close the gates to your flower gardens"). The snatches of music in the poem are matched by a fragment of sheet music pasted to the collage and by assorted references to an "orchestra" and "canzoni" ("songs"). Similarly, the sounds made by Apollinaire's new shoes ("cré cré"), the phonograph's scratchiness ("zzzz"), and the bus's motor ("rro oo to ro ro ro") correspond to Carrà's onomatopoeic "crucra crucra," "bree bree," " cric crac," "zzzz," and the sounds of various vehicles ("Trrrrrrrrrrrrr," "traaak tatatraak"). More important, both works situate near their centers factory sirens that make the sound "Hou ou ou . . . Hou Hou Hou" in one case and "HUHUHUHUHUHUHUH" in the other. The political slogans are particularly interesting. With Carrà we encounter the exclamations "EEVVIIIVAAA IL RÈÈÈ ("LLOONNNGG LIIVE THE KIIING"), "EVVIVAAA L'ESERCITO" ("LOOONG LIVE THE ARMY"), various "EEVVIVAAA" 's and one "ABBA . . . SSOOoo" ("DOWN WIth"). With Apollinaire we find "Vive la République" ("Long live the Republic"), "Vive le Roy" ("Long live the King"), "A bas la calotte" ("Down with the clergy"), and oddly "Evviva il Papa" ("Long live the Pope").

From the foregoing it is clear that the painting and poem are closely related. The subject matter, structure, sirens, and political slogans of one have been borrowed largely from the other. At first glance it appears that Apollinaire was influenced by Carrà. The cry "Evviva l'Esercito" certainly conforms to Futurist politics as outlined in the "Programma politico futurista" (one of the signers of which was Carrà), which demanded "una più grande flotta e un più grande esercito" ("a larger navy and a larger army")(*Lacerba*, October 15, 1913). Moreover, the phrase occurs almost verbatim as the title of an article by Agnoletti: "Viva l'esercito" (*Lacerba*, October 15, 1914). Similarly, Apollinaire's "Vive le Roy" seems to echo Carrà's "Evviva il Rè" (a reference to Victor Emmanuel III), which, when translated to a French setting that had not known a king in nearly a hundred years, appears to make little sense. The explanation is undoubtedly twofold: Apollinaire's reference is to his friend Pierre Roy, who shortly thereafter collaborated with him on a booklet of visual poetry, and to the French Monarchist party. The old-fashioned spelling *roy* is particularly appropriate in the mouth of an old-fashioned political faction. In addition it functions as a satirical comment, indicating that in Apollinaire's opinion the Royalist party was outdated and hopelessly out of touch with the modern age.

Apollinaire's swipe at the clergy, "A bas la calotte," is consistent with the Futurist policy of *anticlericalismo* (*Lacerba*, October 15, 1914). But in this case how are we to interpret his "Evviva il Papa" in the same poem? The fact that the

13

Aesthetics of visual poetry

exclamation is in Italian would seem to indicate Futurist influence, but the sentiment itself is inconsistent with Futurist anticlericalism. And if Apollinaire uses Italian, Carrà incorporates several French words into his collage: "beau," "aujourd'hui," "mouche," "carreau" ("beautiful," "today," "fly," square"), among others. From other evidence it seems that this line probably has nothing to do with Futurism. For one thing, Apollinaire occasionally liked to insert lines of (non-Futurist) Italian into his poetry, much like T. S. Eliot and Ezra Pound.[4] For another, it recalls the ambiguous praise of "Zone" (1912): "L'Européen le plus moderne c'est vous Pape Pie X" ("The most modern European is you, Pope Pius X") (*Po*, p. 39). The conclusive proof, I think, is furnished by a newly discovered calligram representing a "canon . . . dominé par un soleil de victoire" ("a cannon dominated by a victory sun"), which Apollinaire hurriedly composed as a dedication on a copy of *Alcools*.[5] Dated August 10, 1914, the "sun" component is modeled on "Lettre-Océan" and has a circular center from which rays radiate outward in every direction. Snatches of "La Marseillaise" are mingled with fragments of conversation and two political slogans: "Vive la République" and "Bojé Krani Tsaria" ("God Save the Tzar"–also a hymn).[6] There is no question of Russian influence here. Rather this line represents an exclamation by a Russian residing in Paris and summarizes Russian patriotism in the face of the war. It is probably also a salute by Apollinaire to Russia as France's ally. Just as Russian sentiments are expressed in Russian, the feelings of the Italian people are expressed by the Italian slogan in "Lettre-Océan" during a demonstration. Apollinaire establishes the poles of this demonstration by giving us two sets of opposing slogans: catholicism versus anticlericalism, royalism versus republicanism.

Elsewhere in "Lettre-Océan" the influence of Futurism is quite marked and has been indicated by more than one critic. Following the audacities of Apollinaire's *Antitradition futuriste* (1913), this should come as no surprise. Apollinaire never attempted in any case to disguise his debt to the Futurists in his early visual poetry, which after "Lettre-Océan" evolved into a distinct genre of its own, the calligram. One month after "Lettre-Océan" appeared, Apollinaire published an article about this poem by Gabriel Arbouin who cited the precedence of experiments by eight different Futurists.[7] Writing in *Paris-Midi* (July 22, 1914) with a view toward differentiating his figurative poetry from that of the Renaissance, Apollinaire himself stated, "Il y a juste la même différence qu'entre telle voiture automobile du XVIe, mue par un mouvement d'horlogerie, et une auto de course contemporaine" ("There is exactly the same difference as between a toy automobile of the sixteenth century, powered by clockwork springs, and a modern racing car.")[8] His audience would have immediately recognized the allusion to Marinetti's *Fondazione e manifesto del futurismo* (*Foundation and Manifesto of Futurism*) (1909), the most famous sentence of which was: "Un automobile da corsa . . . è più bello della Vittoria di Samotracia" ("A racing car is more beautiful than the *Victory of Samothrace*"). It is interesting that, reviewing his visual poetry in 1918, Apollinaire chose to insert his experiments into the context of the free-verse movement: "Quant aux *Calligrammes*, ils sont une idéalisation de la poésie vers-libriste" ("As for *Calligrammes*, the poems are an idealization of poetry in free verse").[9] His insistence that the principle behind this poetry was identical to that underlying the *vers libre* again reveals his indebted-

14

Music of the spheres

ness to Futurism and allies him to Marinetti, for the predominant form utilized by literary Futurism was that of "free words" (*parole in libertà*), invented in 1912 by Marinetti by analogy with free verse. As expressed in the article "Dopo il verso libero le parole in libertà" ("After Free Verse, Free Words") (*Lacerba*, November 15, 1913) and elsewhere, the free-word technique was designed to replace free verse, from which it had issued. Because Apollinaire's first experiments in this area follow those of the Futurists by a good two years, his comment probably should be considered a paraphrase of Futurist doctrine. Both he and Marinetti regarded their new genres as steps toward complete literary liberation, differing from free verse only in their degree of freedom.

❖❖❖❖❖❖❖

For the Futurists, the invention of the *parole in libertà* led to the development of what they called *l'immaginazione senza fili* ("the wireless imagination"), a free form of expression that, like wireless telegraphy, was no longer tied to traditional, cumbersome modes of communication. "Per immaginazione senza fili," wrote Marinetti, "io intendo la libertà assoluta delle immagini o analogie, espresse con parole slegate e senza fili conduttori sintattici" ("By wireless imagination I mean the absolute freedom of images or analogies, expressed in words which are untied and without the connecting wires of syntax") (*L'immaginazione senza fili e le parole in libertà*, May 11, 1913). The metaphor of wireless telegraphy dominates the imagery of literary Futurism and is the key to understanding much of its doctrine. Thus the letters T S F (*télégraphie sans fil* "wireless telegraphy") in "Lettre-Océan" may well indicate Futurist influence. The Futurists wished to communicate more quickly and more economically than was possible with traditional literature in order to revitalize the author–reader relationship. To accomplish these ends a new grammar was needed, and it is no accident that the very first item of the first literary manifesto reads, "Bisogna distruggere la sintassi, disponendo i sostantivi a caso, come nascono" ("It is necessary to destroy syntax, arranging the nouns at random just as they are born") (*Manifesto tecnico*, May 11, 1912).

The Futurists accordingly invented a number of stylistic devices to replace conventional syntax and to produce a telegraphic style. Several of these are to be found in "Lettre-Océan." Reflecting the Futurists' use of mathematical signs ($+$, $-$,:, $=$, $>$, $<$) to indicate relationships, Apollinaire writes, "Pendeco c'est $+$qu'un imbécile" and "rue St. Isidore à la Havane cela n'existe $+$." Similarly, just as the Futurist *Sensibilità numerica* requires the notation in Arabic numerals of dimensions, weights, volumes, and speeds, Apollinaire peppers the poem with quantitative figures in phrases such as "Haute de 300 mètres" ("300 meters high"). "Je traverse la ville / nez en avant / et je la coupe en 2" ("I am crossing the city / nose first / and I cut it in 2"), he writes at the beginning, using a stylized boldface numeral to give the impression of a nose in profile.[10] Two of the best known Futurist techniques, onomatopoeia and expressive typography, are likewise to be found in the poem, though they are employed more conservatively than in the *parole in libertà*. Apollinaire limits the function of onomatopoeia, as we have seen, to reproducing actual physical sounds (sirens, motors, etc). This is only one of many types of Futurist onomato-

15

Aesthetics of visual poetry

poeia and corresponds to what Marinetti termed *onomatopea diretta imitativa elementare realistica* ("realistic, elementary, imitative, direct onomatopoeia") (*Lo splendore geometrico e meccanico e la sensibilità numerica*, March 18, 1914). It does not approach the complexity of a typical Futurist text, which also includes *onomatopea indiretta complessa e analogica, onomatopea astratta*, and *accordo onomatopeico psichico* ("analogical, complex, and indirect onomatopoeia"; "abstract onomatopoeia"; and "psychic, onomatopoeic agreement").

In like manner, the expressive typography of "Lettre-Océan," though probably Futurist inspired, is devoid of Futurist pyrotechnics. Typographical experimentation is limited primarily to the use of boldface Roman type, small capitals, and large capitals. There is also considerable use of slightly undersized type. The poem contains two examples of italics and four instances of words in oversized (boldface) type, including the title. In the latter category, the words "**MON FRÈRE ALBERT**" are slightly stylized. Although Apollinaire introduces four parallel wavy lines in three separate places, we see none of the brackets and tabular categories typical of Futurism. In general the lines are arranged in an orderly, symmetrical fashion. Individual words and phrases exhibit a uniform type and font, although these may change from section to section. There are none of the typographical gradations common to Futurism whereby a single word may employ six different sizes of type or a given vowel may be multiplied a dozen times to express the intonation, facial expression, or gestures of the speaker (*ortografia libera espressiva* – "free expressive orthography"). Ironically, Apollinaire's expressive typography is really not very expressive.[11] This has the effect of distancing his typographic achievements from those of Futurism and tends to ally them with Cubism. In the last analysis, despite considerable typographical variation throughout the poem, individual differences tend to be minimal. There is a distinct emphasis on harmony and composition that is not characteristic of the *parole in libertà*. The poem has considerable texture, but not the jagged edges of Futurist poetry.

The most startling aspect of "Lettre-Océan" is undoubtedly the revolutionary way in which the lines are arranged on the page, that is, its pictorial aspect. Unlike Apollinaire's subsequent calligrams, this poem is not truly figurative, but schematic. It does not attempt to render the actual appearance of objects and events, but presents them in a geometric, diagrammatic fashion. This fact is of paramount importance, since the Futurists developed precisely the same sort of visual poetry in the months immediately preceding the creation of Apollinaire's poem. "Lettre-Océan" thus represents a transitional phase between the *parole in libertà* and the later calligrams. In pre-1914 Futurist poetry most of the typographical effects are not pictorially oriented, but are concerned with sounds and/or relationships. In late 1913 and 1914 one encounters a tendency toward the use of brackets to classify ideas and sensations into different categories, a form Marinetti baptized *tavole sinottiche di valori lirici* ("synoptic tables of lyric values"). The few representational poems are not really pictorial, but schematic, and proceed according to *analogy* (the essence of poetry according to Futurists).[12]

In March 1914 Marinetti called attention to the emergence of a new form of analogy, the *analogia disegnata* ("visual analogy"), singling out for praise Cangiullo's poem "Fumatori II" ("Smoking 2nd Class") (*Lacerba*, January 1, 1914). Can-

Music of the spheres

giullo had taken the word *fumare* ("to smoke"), lengthened it to "FUUUUUMARE," and made each successive letter larger than the one before so that the word appeared to expand. According to Marinetti this funnel-shaped word "esprimeva le lunghe e monotone fantasticherie e l'espandersi della noia-fumo durante le ore trepidanti di un viaggio in treno" ("expressed the long monotonous reveries and the expansion of the tedium smoke during the anxious hours of a train trip") (*Lo splendore geometrico*). It is important to note that Marinetti expressly condemned *figurative* poetry in the same manifesto, insisting that Futurist poems retain their abstract, analogical nature.[13] Although 1914 Futurist poetry represents an advance over previous models, adding the concept of the visual analogy, it remains true to its original principles. Marinetti described the new form thusly: "Le parole in libertà . . . si trasformano naturalmente in *auto-illustrazioni*, mediante l'ortografia e tipografia libere espressive, le tavole sinottiche di valori lirici e le analogie diseg-nate" ("Words at liberty are naturally transformed into *self-illustrations* by means of free expressive orthography and typography, synoptic tables of lyric values, and visual analogies") (*Lo splendore geometrico*). Excluding the first category, this is an excellent description of the visual elements and analogical processes at work in "Lettre-Océan."

"Lettre-Océan"

Apollinaire's poem was presumably written a few weeks before its publication, and it is probably safe to assume that its facsimile postmark indicates the date of composition: May 29, 1914. Parenthetically, the fact that the author signed and dated his first visual poem testifies to the close ties between the *calligram* and painting.[14] In addition to the Futurist influence noted previously, the presence of analytical and synthetic Cubism is also evident.[15] At least as far back as "Zone" (1912) Apollinaire began to imitate the Cubist painters who decomposed an object into its parts, seen from different angles, and regrouped them in two-dimensional patterns (simultanism). In "Lettre-Océan" he juxtaposes radically disparate objects, images, and lines to form a psychovisual collage constituting a faithful impression of contemporary reality. The distortions of the traditional space–time nexus wrought by recent advances in communication (telephones, telegraphy) and trans-portation (airplanes, automobiles) are reflected by comparable fragmentation and distortion in the poem. In a sense, as Daniel Delbreil remarks, the poem celebrates our modern victory over space and time.[16]

   "Lettre-Océan" 's most obvious parallel is with the accomplishments of syn-thetic Cubism. Braque and Picasso introduced letters, words, *papiers collés* ("pasted papers"), and other objects into their paintings in an attempt to incorporate bits of everyday reality chosen for their aesthetic, not their utilitarian, value. As Apollinaire himself says in *Les Peintres cubistes*, "On peut peindre avec ce qu'on voudra, avec des pipes, des timbres-poste, des cartes postales ou à jouer, des candélabres, des mor-ceaux de toile cirée, des faux cols, du papier peint, des journaux" ("One can paint with whatever one wants, with pipes, stamps, postcards or playing cards, candelabras, pieces of oilcloth, false collars, wallpaper, newspapers").[17] Significantly, two postage stamps and a postcard have been introduced into "Lettre-Océan." More importantly,

17

Aesthetics of visual poetry

the poem consists largely of scraps of everyday reality – from the sirens, bus, gramophones, and new shoes, on the one hand, to the numerous snatches of conversation, on the other. This is probably what M.-J. Durry is referring to when she says, "Papiers collés presque toute la "Lettre-Océan' " ("Almost all of 'Lettre-Océan' is pasted papers").[18] Georges Schmits finds another analogy:

> Certaines de ces bribes de conversation sont amputées comme le sont d'un coup de ciseaux les papiers collés des cubistes; mais elles se reconstituent facilement:
>> [En voi]ture les voyageurs de Chatou
>> [Pro]priétaire de 5 ou 6 im[meubles]
>> allons circulez Mes[sieurs].

> Certain bits of conversation are amputated like the pasted papers of the Cubists; but they can easily be reconstructed:
>> [All a]board passengers for Chatou
>> [Land]lord of 5 or 6 buil[dings]
>> move along every[body][19]

On the most basic level, Apollinaire and Picasso were performing analogous experiments with form, mixing verbal and pictorial elements in their works (although in different proportions). Both were in effect painting with words – whence the title of Apollinaire's projected volume of visual poetry, *Et moi aussi je suis peintre* (*And I Too Am a Painter* – Correggio's response to a painting by Raphael). Michel Butor views this project as "une réponse poétique à la prise de possession de la lettre et du mot par la peinture cubiste" ("a poetic response to Cubist painting which had taken over letters and words").[20] This description also fits "Lettre-Océan" perfectly.

Apollinaire was fond of contrasting the inherent successiveness of music and literature with the immediacy and simultaneity of painting. In his article "Simultanisme-Librettisme," published in the same issue of *Les Soirées de Paris* as "Lettre-Océan," he indicates how he meant his startling new poem to be approached. Whereas in his earlier simultanist poetry he had tried to "habituer *l'esprit* à concevoir un poème simultanément comme une scène de la vie" ("accustom the *mind* to conceive a poem simultaneously like a scene from life"), he now wished to "[habituer] *l'oeil* à lire d'un seul regard l'ensemble d'un poème, comme un chef d'orchestre lit d'un seul coup les notes superposées dans la partition, comme on voit d'un seul coup les éléments plastiques et imprimés d'une affiche" ("accustom the *eye* to read a whole poem with a single glance, as an orchestra conductor reads the different ranks of notes in a score simultaneously, as one sees the plastic and printed elements of a poster all at once") (my italics). The change in emphasis from the mind to the eye, from simultaneous *conception* to simultaneous *perception*, was a large step to take. Nevertheless, "Lettre-Océan" was a logical development of processes explored previously in "Lundi rue Christine" ("Monday Christine Street") and "Les Fenêtres" ("The Windows"), representing a more determined effort to achieve simultaneity in poetry. If Apollinaire's reference to a conductor recalls Mallarmé's *Un coup de dés* (*A Throw of the Dice*), which, conceived as "une partition" ("a score"), employs "une vision simultanée de la Page" ("a simultaneous vision of the

18

Music of the spheres

Page"), the basic analogy is not to music, but to painting. In singling out the "éléments plastiques" of a poster for imitation, Apollinaire is following up a long-standing interest in posters as a theoretical source of poetry.[21]

As Butor notes, "Lettre-Océan" possesses "une puissance plastique frappante" ("a striking plastic power"). The eye is free to wander over its surface at will as in a painting, attracted by one feature, then by another, perceiving (and enjoying) the various patterns and contrasts.[22] As it was originally printed, on two opposite pages, "Lettre-Océan" was clearly conceived as an aesthetic whole. In particular it is noteworthy for the symmetry of its elements and the parallels between them. The two wheel-and-spoke patterns are balanced against each other but differ in size and detail. Visually, the smaller pattern is a condensed version of the larger. It presents a simplified statement that the latter takes up and develops in more detail. Similarly, the large expanses of open space in the larger wheel counterbalance the confined, dense field of type at the upper left-hand corner, in a dialogue between freedom and constraint. In like manner the two wheels, which threaten to roll (or expand) off the page, are contained by horizontal lines of type, continuing the dialectical opposition mentioned previously. The visual sign reinforces the linguistic sign in an extremely direct, concrete fashion. Visual cues prepare us for various manifestations of the basic dialogue as they appear in the text, where known is contrasted with unknown, personal with impersonal, near with far. Related structures of large versus small and circular versus linear are likewise mirrored by the visual and verbal text. Finally, we are introduced to the spatial relations of the poem via the visual, diagrammatic configuration of the large wheel, which serves to chart the open regions ahead. As Roger Shattuck remarks, one receives an "impression of the distribution of the world in space, of distances which at the same time separate and link together remote places."[23] In "Lettre-Océan" France is balanced against Mexico, everyday banality against exoticism, safety against danger, Parisian politics against those in Meso-America, separation against unification. The immensity of the distance bridged by wireless telegraphy, linking the two continents, contrasts with that covered by the Pont d'Iéna, connecting the left and right banks of the Seine.

Remembering "Lettre-Océan"'s status as a poster-poem, we are first struck by six phrases in heavy boldface type that function as "headlines": "**LETTRE-OCÉAN**," "**REPUBLICA MEXICANA, TARJETA POSTAL**," "**T S F**," "**MAYAS**," and "**MON FRÈRE ALBERT**" ("**OCEAN-LETTER**," "**MEXICAN REPUBLIC, POSTCARD**," "**WIRELESS TELEGRAPHY**," "**MAYAS**," and "**MY BROTHER ALBERT**"). These fragmentary cues, perceived simultaneously like those of a poster, immediately establish the boundaries of the poem. We know its purpose, destination, and the basic form it will take; it will be a telegraphic letter connecting the author with his brother Albert in Mexico. Once the basic motifs have been established, the eye proceeds to recognize the pictorial elements in the poem, that is, to consider it as a painting. Next comes the process of actually reading the work. From poster to painting to poem, simultaneous perception leads to similtaneous conception once the text has been decoded.

"Lettre-Océan" is by far the most complex of Apollinaire's visual poems and summarizes his poetic achievement between 1912 and 1914. The title is borrowed from post-office terminology and designates a type of mail that was exchanged at

Aesthetics of visual poetry

sea between outgoing and incoming ships.[24] Here it is used in a broader sense to describe a letter sent across the ocean, ostensibly by telegraph. Apollinaire's name at the end is also the signature to his letter. In reality, however, the poem is a sort of Cubist collage, incorporating one or more of Albert's postcards to him. The final achievement represents a synthesis of the correspondence between the two brothers and an evocation of their physical surroundings (Paris and Mexico City). Just as Apollinaire introduces the Eiffel Tower to symbolize Paris, he evokes several symbols of Mexico – for example, "chirimoya" (a tropical fruit resembling the custard-apple) and *"Jeunes filles à Chapultepec"* (*"Girls at Chapultepec"*). The latter is probably the title of a picture postcard received from Albert depicting the famous Chapultepec gardens and presidential palace. The arrow reading "Bonjour / anomo / anora / tu ne connaîtras jamais bien les **MAYAS**" ("Hello / anomo / anora / you will never know the **MAYAS** well") seems to symbolize the Maya, who in turn symbolize Mexico. Private references abound, some of which may never be deciphered. If, as Schmits shows, Apollinaire makes a pun on "Mayas" (Indians and breasts), the references to *anomo* and *anora* remain totally cryptic.[25]

A glance at the poem reveals that it consists of three distinct figurative poems (four counting the arrow) linked together by theme and concept: a postcard, a bunch of keys on a ring, and the Eiffel Tower transmitting a telegraphic message. The last is not immediately discernible and emerges as something of a shock. One suddenly recognizes, on reading the central notation "Haute de 300 mètres," that one is not looking *at* a wheel but *down upon* the tower from *above*. The abrupt shift in perspective – perhaps the poem's greatest surprise – is exhilarating, for the numerous scattered fragments suddenly join together in a meaningful pattern. The "postcard" presents two disconnected halves of a dialogue between Apollinaire and his brother, framed at the top and divided in the middle by four parallel wavy lines representing cancellation marks (possibly doubling as radio waves). Apollinaire's initial remarks are followed, in the lower half, by a faithful evocation of a Mexican postcard from Albert that probably reproduces the actual message on one such card. The postmark reading "Rue des Batignolles" undoubtedly records its arrival in Paris from Mexico, since Apollinaire himself normally frequented the Blvd. Saint-Germain post office. The card bears two postage stamps – a United States two-cent stamp (carmine, with a portrait of George Washington) and a Mexican four-centavo stamp (also carmine, with a portrait of Juan Aldama, a Mexican patriot executed in 1811). This indicates that it was sent or given to someone leaving Mexico for the United States on the French liner *Espagne*, someone who remailed it upon reaching his destination.

The reference to "Ypiranga" is connected with Albert's message, both reflecting political events of the period. As a result of two separate incidents at Veracruz and Tampico in 1914, the U.S. Atlantic Fleet blockaded these ports to prevent the unloading of the arms and ammunition President Huerta was importing from Germany:

> The German ship *Ypiranga* . . . was approaching Veracruz with a cargo
> of two hundred machine guns and 15,000,000 rounds of ammunition
> for Huerta. The *Ypiranga* could not be seized, but the port facilities of

Music of the spheres

Veracruz could [and were, on April 21, 1914, resulting in the deaths of 19 Americans and 300 Mexicans]. Meanwhile the *Ypiranga* turned around, sailed south, and without hindrance unloaded its cargo [at Coatzacoalcos].[26]

This explains why the "courier de Vera Cruz n'est pas sûr" ("mail from Vera Cruz is uncertain") and why the oceanliner is leaving from Coatzacoalcos instead of Veracruz. It also indicates that the "gens de mauvaise mine sur le quai à la Vera Cruz" ("ominous-looking persons on the dock in Vera Cruz") are members of the United States Marines. Finally, the message sent by Albert, "Tout est calme ici" ("Everything is calm here"), corresponds to the message received by Apollinaire on the opposite page: "La cablogramme comportait 2 mots EN SURETÉ" ("The cablegram consisted of 2 words IN SAFETY"). Apollinaire constantly worried about his brother's safety in the midst of the never-ending Mexican revolution and must have received many reassurances like these. A recently published postcard from Albert shows that much of the worry was justified.[27] Apollinaire's anxious characterization of Mexico as "ce sacré pays d'Indiens et d'érotisme sanglant" ("that damned country full of Indians and bloody eroticism") summarizes the image conveyed by the present poem.[28]

It is generally assumed that, like its neighbor, the small circle-poem is a representation of the Eiffel Tower broadcasting telegraphic messages. This interpretation is supported by the observation that its center is situated "sur la rive gauche devant le pont d'Iéna" ("on the Left Bank opposite the Jena Bridge") – the location of the Eiffel Tower – and by the letters T S F conspicuously posted in the margin. Nevertheless, this is probably not the case. For one thing, in the manuscript the letters **T S F** are placed exactly in the middle of the space between the two circles and thus have no particular association with the small circle.[29] The shift to the left was apparently the decision of the typographer, who, faced with a full page on the right and a middle disappearing into the binding, shoved the letters into the only space available. For another thing, the center originally read "la foule" ("the crowd"). What we obviously have is a *poème-conversation* in which "le poète au centre de la vie enregistre en quelque sorte le lyrisme ambiant" ("the poet at the center of life records so to speak the surrounding lyricism")("Simultanisme-Librettisme"). Thus, as Margaret Davies implies, the center of the poem is occupied by *the poet* (Apollinaire) standing somewhere between the Pont d'Iéna and the Eiffel Tower.[30] The poem's shape is a perfect diagram of the spatial relations in this, and every, conversation-poem and illustrates Apollinaire's description above. One more important point should be made: The form of the figure seems to be that of a bunch of keys on a ring. This impression is strengthened by the shape of several of the verses and by the line "Des clefs j'en ai vu mille et mille" ("I have seen thousand and thousands of keys"). The most protuberant verse, it serves as the starting point of the poem and carries a disproportionate amount of weight. Although it probably has nothing to do with St. Peter, as Schmits claims, it does furnish an ironic commentary on the four political slogans, each of which claims to be the "key" to an ideal society. In "La Clef" ("The Key") (*Po*, pp. 553–5), the poem from which this line is borrowed, it functions in an identical manner.

21

Aesthetics of visual poetry

The resemblance of the small circle-poem to "Lundi rue Christine" (*Po*, pp. 180–2) is made even more striking by the fact that several lines seem to be left over from the earlier poem, especially "Jacques c'était délicieux" ("Jacques, it was delicious") and "La Tunisie tu fondes un journal" ("In Tunisia you are founding a newspaper"). However, these remarks refer to more recent events, recounted by Apollinaire in his column "La Vie anecdotique" (*Mercure de France*, May 1, 1914). His friend Jacques Dyssord, who had recently started a newspaper in Tunis, sent him a copy containing several "delicious" anecdotes. Besides the allusion to Pierre Roy, there are two additional private references: "Zut pour M. Zun" ("Phooey on M. Zun") and "ta gueule mon vieux pad" ("shut your trap, pal"). Georges Schmits astutely interprets the former as a sour commentary on Henri-Martin Barzun, who in a heated dispute culminating in Apollinaire's "Simultanisme-Librettisme," accused the latter of stealing Simultanism, Dramatism, and Orphism from him. "Pad" is identified as "une réduction populaire de 'padre' avec le sens de 'petit père' " ("a popular reduction of *padre* meaning 'pal' "). Interestingly, both manuscripts reveal that the phrase originally read "ta gueule mon vieux Bar" ("shut your mouth, Bar"). Added to "Zun" it was apparently too transparent an allusion for Apollinaire, who modified the letters on the proofs (unless "pad" is a simple misprint). To maintain the lines' identity as snatches of conversation, Apollinaire injects a certain amount of slang. Such words as "croquant" ("clodhopper, hick") and "zut" ("phooey") are immediate clues that this is spoken language. In this context the key-ring structure, with Apollinaire in the middle, is particularly appropriate. If the spoken phrases (sound waves) are all receding from the poet, they are also converging toward the center where he is standing – to which they become fastened forever as soon as they are captured by the recording process ("enregistrement") of the ear.

The final ideogram depicting the Eiffel Tower as a telegraph station 300 meters in the air (as indeed it was) embodies a more sophisticated version of simultanism. Like "Les Fenêtres" (*Po*, pp. 168–9), it is a *poème simultané* in which the poet's visual and/or aural impressions of a given scene are mingled with the thoughts passing through the mind at the same time. Besides the factory sirens and other noises at the center, the auditory dimension is filled out with street cries and snatches of conversation.[31] To the shouts of the bus driver ("changement de section" – "transfer point"), who is leaving for Chatou, are added the cries of a gendarme ("allons circulez Messieurs" – "keep moving, folks") and those of a street vendor – recorded in manuscript A as "A la crème à la crème fromage à la crème" ("With cream, with cream, cheese made with cream"). The most vivid conversational fragment is "et comment j'ai brûlé le dur avec ma gerce," uttered by an underworld character and containing two particularly savory slang expressions. *Brûler le dur* means "to ride the rails" (without a ticket), and *gerce* means "mistress" or "prostitute."[32] The image is that of a pimp and his girl.

Among Apollinaire's random thoughts – sent as messages – "Toussaint Luca est maintenant à Poitiers" informs his brother of the whereabouts of an old friend. "Je me suis levé à 2 h. du matin et j'ai déjà bu un mouton" ("I got up at 2 A.M., and I have already drunk a sheep") may refer to a bottle of Mouton wine.[33] In the *poèmes simultanés* Apollinaire commonly adds yet another dimension to expand the scope of the action. He will suddenly cut either to historical events or to geographically

22

Music of the spheres

dispersed events occurring at the same time as the action in Paris. With the location of the poem as its center, the action radiates outward in concentric circles to encompass the *arrondissement*, the city, the nation, the continent, and the whole world. This is the situation in the present ideogram, in which the implicit structure of the *poème simultané* is rendered visible. References to the past are brief and include the "tremblement de terre entre 1885 et 1890." Geographically we proceed from Paris to the suburb of Chatou (where Apollinaire's mother lived) and then, via Poitiers, to Havana and eventually to Mexico, our final destination. The line "rue St.-Isidore à Havane cela n'existe +" ("St. Isidore Street in Havana no longer exists") refers to the Cuban red-light district in the Calle San Isidro, which had recently been closed down.[34] The Mexican references have already been discussed, except for "il appelait l'Indien Hijo de la Cingada," which is a misspelled Spanish obscenity: "he called the Indian Son of a Whore." As I have shown elsewhere "Pendeco" should actually be spelled "pendejo," a slang expression for a hopeless moron, someone who is "plus qu'un imbécile."[35] Apollinaire delights in citing this pungent Mexicanism, which is followed by its own definition.

The visual form of the large wheel is particularly effective, as has been noted. Philippe Renaud thinks Apollinaire borrowed it from "la représentation symbolique des ondes hertziennes, sans doute déjà popularisée en 1914" ("the symbolic representation of radio waves, doubtless already popularized by 1914").[36] Given the poem's Mexican context, it may also refer to the Aztec calendar stone preserved in the National Museum, which resembles a giant sun. To Daniel Delbreil and Françoise Dininman it suggests an aerial view of a huge sundial in which the shadow marking the hour is cast by the Eiffel Tower. The same authors note that in 1912 the International Conference on Time designated the French capital as the location from which the international hour would be transmitted. Henceforth the rest of the world would dance to Paris's tune, making the city and the tower a symbolic axis mundi. These considerations may have influenced Apollinaire when he came to design his poem, but the configuration is consistent with his own artistic evolution as well. Apart from his use of the circle as an important thematic structural principle or his related preoccupation with circular myth (e.g., Ixion, Icarus, and Christ), Apollinaire's personal and poetic vision had long utilized circle patterns in an intimate psychological context. In his important analysis of poetic form in *Alcools*, Jean-Claude Chevalier concludes that "dès le moment pourtant des premiers poèmes, le cercle est un élément fondamental d'organisation" ("from the moment of his very first poems, the circle is a fundamental element of organization").[37] Among the various recurring forms that he isolates – forms that recall the obsessive metaphors of Charles Mauron – Chevalier discerns one figure of particular interest: *l'ombilic*. A central point surrounded by a circle, the "umbilicus" configuration is precisely that of the large wheel in "Lettre-Océan." Jean Levaillant, in an article on the spatiality of *Calligrammes*, detects a related but separate structural figure: the circle and the line.[38] The symbolism of this figure is evident, springing from the unconscious depths of the poet's sexuality, and finds its archetypal expression in the last two lines of "Tour" ("Tower"), inspired by Robert Delaunay: "La Tour à la Roue / S'adresse" ("The Tower addresses / the Ferris Wheel")(*Po*, p. 200).

Citing this poem, Levaillant emphasizes Apollinaire's need to orient his space

Aesthetics of visual poetry

according to fixed coordinates and his tendency to choose a high vantage point in order to dominate it. In "Tour," as he says, "nous sommes . . . au centre de l'univers traversé par toutes les lignes de forces, humaines et cosmiques" ("We are at the center of the universe, where all the lines of force converge, human and cosmic"). Needless to say, these characteristics are all found in "Lettre-Océan." For one thing, the large wheel has a vertical center (the Eiffel Tower), thus duplicating the circle–line opposition. And from the top of the tower Apollinaire can look out in every direction along twelve axes extending to the distant horizon. In this way he is able to impose order on his environment, both immediate and global, and to take possession of the world around him.[39] Apollinaire's 1913 description of the "fourth dimension" in painting provides an excellent description of the spatiality of the large wheel: "Elle figure l'immensitè de l'espace s'éternisant dans toutes les directions à un moment déterminé. Elle est l'espace même, la dimension de l'infini." ("It represents the immensity of space extending forever in every direction at any given moment. It is space itself, the dimension of the infinite.")[40] As a simultanistic *tranche de vie* in which time and space are momentarily frozen, the large wheel begins to take on the appearance of a full cosmology. And since the Eiffel Tower at the center possesses the power to actuate the fourth dimension, it becomes a superb mechanical symbol of the creative artist.

Festa patriottica

From a letter to Gino Severini we know that Carrà originally titled his composition *Festa patriottica–poema pittorico*.[41] A glance at the collage, however, shows that the change in designation from *poema pittorico* ("pictorial poem") to *dipinto parolibero* ("free-word painting") was well advised. If Carrà's intention was avowedly to "unire in armonia visiva e complessa immagini poetiche . . . con elementi propri della pittura" ("unite in a complex visual harmony poetic images and actual pictorial elements"),[42] *Festa patriottica* is more a painting than a poem. In his letter to Severini, Carrà stresses the plastic and abstract character of this composition: "Io ho abolito ogni rappresentazione di figura umana perchè volevo darne *l'astrazione plastica del tumulto cittadino*" ("I have eliminated any reference to the human figure because I wanted to create *a plastic abstraction of civic tumult*") (my italics). Thus, despite a wealth of concrete detail, the emphasis is on the general rather than the particular. This is entirely in accord with Futurist doctrine, dating back to 1910 (*La pittura futurista, manifesto tecnico*), which preferred evoking an *état d'âme* ("state of mind") to portraying a single localized experience. Carrà uses piercing rays of sound, interrupted by vivid patches of color, to paint a picture of a celebration rather than of people celebrating. The title itself, *Festa patriottica*, is deliberately generic, and the subject of the celebration is never specified.

This last statement must be reiterated in the face of the oft repeated assertion that *Festa patriottica* is a political work. Thus Max Kozloff, calling it a "celebration of war," claims that "this work was expressly designed to exacerbate the volatile political climate of an Italy internally vacillating between the adversaries in a war known to be imminent."[43] Unfortunately, this simply is not true. Nor is the collage a piece of propaganda "in favor of intervention on the side of the Allies."[44] For one

24

Music of the spheres

thing, we have Carrà's own testimony that its subject is simply "civic tumult." For another, detailed analysis fails to turn up a single reference to war – or to violence of any kind.[45] Likewise, there is no mention of the Allies. If there are occasional foreign words, this is a typical cosmopolitan feature of Futurist poetry and painting and is not politically motivated here or elsewhere. The fact that the *papiers collés* were nearly all snipped out of poems published in *Lacerba* makes it possible to identify their sources.[46] This in turn permits us to reconstruct incomplete phrases and to determine exact meanings by consulting the original context. Thus, for example, the sounds "traak tatatraak" are taken from Marinetti's "Correzione" ("Correction"), where they represent the backfiring of a car as it slows down. Like "TRrrrrrrrrrrrrr" and "TRRRRRR" (speeding-car noises from the same poem), they have nothing to do with gunfire but are merely traffic noises of a public square.

Since the cries "Evviva il Rè" and "Evviva L'Esercito" are really not war oriented either, simply reflecting general patriotic feelings, Kozloff in effect pins most of his argument on Carrà's prominent use of "the German word 'TOT' (dead), in headline newsprint." If his characterization is correct, this could represent a collective (if ungrammatical) death wish directed toward Germany and Austro-Hungary. However, Carrà does not use German words anywhere else in *Festa patriottica* – or in his previous works. And the symbol "**TOT**" is part of Futurist iconography, dating back to 1909 (but never connected with death). A glance at the 1914 *Corriere della Sera* reveals that **TOT** was the name of a prominently advertised antiheartburn pill manufactured in Milan. Carrà is obviously using these three letters (borrowed, incidentally, from Soffici's "Passeggiata") to represent a large poster. In confirmation of this interpretation one has only to look diagonally across the painting to the other side. Balanced against the antacid logo, in large letters (upside down) there is the name "Odo[l]," widely advertised as "il miglior dentifricio del mondo" ("the best toothpaste in the world"). The closest we come to politics is the small, upside-down Italian flag at the bottom inscribed "Trieste Italiana Milano." This is a reference to the Irredentist party, which first became prominent in 1878 for advocating the incorporation into Italy of neighboring areas with large Italian populations, such as Trieste. But the reference is fleeting and not easily deciphered (being upside down), lost as it is in a wealth of associations and competing for attention with several large signs. The same is true of the tiny, half-buried notation "[A]ustria Ungh[eri]a" near the Odol sign. Juxtaposed with "[C]ORRIER[E] DELLA SERA," it probably represents a newspaper headline.

Festa patriottica is thus exactly what it pretends to be, a patriotic celebration on a national holiday corresponding to the Fourth of July or Bastille Day. It is characterized by an atmosphere of joyful exuberance, not militancy, which is evidenced in form and content alike. The phrase "grugniti di folle eccitate" ("grunts of excited crowds") at the upper right is balanced by the capsule summary "[h]urrrrrrrrrrraaaaaaahhh (penetrante gioioso)" ("hurrrrrrrrrrraaaaaaahhh, piercing joyful") in the upper left-hand corner. Similarly, the work is peppered with evocative "Evviva"'s and "urrah"'s which echo enthusiastically back and forth across the collage. The bits of music and the orchestra lend a cheery air to the occasion, as do the flags and bright colors. The broken patches of red, yellow, and green reproduce the colors of the Italian flag and by the variety of their

Aesthetics of visual poetry

shifting patterns emphasize the constant commotion in the square. Carrà summarizes his intentions near the Odol sign with the single phrase "ritimi pittorici" ("pictorial rhythms"). His use of color clearly follows the criteria established in his 1913 manifesto *La pittura dei suoni, rumori, odori* (*The Painting of Sounds, Noises, Smells*), in which he demands:

> 1. I rossi, roooossssi roooooooosssissssimi che griiiiiiidano.
> 2. I verdi, i non mai abbastanza verdi, veeeeeerdiiiiiisssssimi, che striiiiiiiidono; i gialli non mai abbastanza scoppianti; i gialloni-polenta; i gialli-zafferano; i gialli-ottoni.
> 3. Tutti i colori della velocità, della gioia, della baldoria, del carnevale più fantastico, dei fuochi d'artifizio, dei café-chantants e dei music-halls.

> 1. Reds, rrrrreds,, the rrrrreddest rrrrreds that shouuuuuuut.
> 2. Greens, that cannot be greener, greenest of greeeens, that screeee-eeeam; yellows as violent as can be; polenta yellows, saffron yellows, brass yellows.
> 3. All the colors of speed, of joy, of carousing, of the most fantastic carnivals, of fireworks, of café-chantants, and of music halls.

Another phrase in the collage refers to a related program set forth in the same manifesto, summarized here as "suoni rumori odori pesi calore" ("sounds noises smells weights heat"). Carrà uses color and line to express the plastic equivalent of these sensations. Similarly, he arranges words and letters meticulously to produce their poetic equivalent. Sounds and noises mingle with terms indicating heat and weight (quantity). Olfactory impressions, such as "flatulenze," combine with snatches of conversation, for example, "e poi dice solo Rosina mi può far contento" ("and then he says only Rosina can make me happy"). By far the most common word in the collage is, appropriately, "echi" ("echoes"). Often occurring in a repetitive series, it not only represents the various echoing sounds in the "piazza," but gives the impression of an open space surrounded by tall buildings. "Questo ribollimento e turbine di forme e di luce sonore, rumorose e odoranti" ("This bubbling and whirling of forms and light, composed of sounds, noises, and smells"), to borrow a phrase from the manifesto quoted above, has its origin in the 1910 *Manifesto tecnico*, which calls for "dinamismo universale" in painting and states that two forces tend to destroy the concreteness of form: light and motion. The complete absence of concrete form in *Festa patriottica*, resulting from the broken color and constant motion, represents the conclusion of a long chain of experiments in this direction.

The initial impact of Carrà's picture is almost blinding and strikes the viewer with the force of an explosion. Temporarily disoriented by the whirling mass of blurred colors and forms, we succumb to a sort of pictorial vertigo. Spiraling out from the center, the composition is a "rousing work that seems to go off like a siren."[47] In fact, the factory siren is the most important metaphor in the painting and assumes a structural role. Serving simultaneously as a symbol of the emotional climate and the skeleton of the actual composition, it provides a great unifying

Music of the spheres

force. The viewer's initial impression of chaos is soon dispelled by the observation that the painting is highly ordered. The analogy is not to music here, as has been suggested, but to poetry. It suffices to recall Carrà's references to "poetic images," the influence of Apollinaire's poem, and the work's original status as a *poema pittorico*. By "immagini poetiche" Carrà presumably means images evoked poetically by means of the written word. Thus each word or group of words is meant to suggest an image. The subject and emotional tone are established immediately by the first expression to catch the eye: "EEVVIIIVAAA IL RÈÈÈ." We are faced at once with a loud, enthusiastic patriotic mass demonstration. From there the eye travels to "**TOT**," which discloses the presence of large posters in the celebration, and on to "**STRADA**" ("**STREET**"), an indication that the celebration is out-doors, probably in a city environment. In this way the eye is directed to the top and upper left-hand corner, where – exactly as if it were the opening section of a poem – the remaining major themes (images) are quickly established. "**SOLE SCROTO SBADIGLIO**") ("**SUN SCROTUM YAWNING**") stresses the sun's size and power, whereas *"sole bruciaticcio"* (*"burning sun"*) intensifies its heat and adds the smell of burned matter. "Sghiiiignazzare tutti i colore delle nostre affiches interne ubbriachi" ("Drunkards all the colors of our inner posters guffffaw") evokes the brightly colored posters and intimates that the crowd has been drinking. Except for the allusion to the public "orchestra" playing in the square, the remaining references fall under the general heading of "città moderne" ("modern cities"): "forme geometriche," "strada," and "200 rumori" ("geometric forms, street, and 200 noises"). Elsewhere in the painting we find a matching notation: "illogicità della città." If Apollinaire emphasizes modern communications, Carrà stresses modern forms of transportation. Both by name and by sound there are references throughout to trains, streetcars, bicycles, and automobiles. There are also several references to modern technology, including "volontà di Edison" ("Edison's determination") and "lucelettrica" ("electriclight").

The center of the spiral contains some highly important information: "AU-DACIA ROMPICOLLISMO / **ITALIA** / aviatore / battere il record / eliche perforanti" ("AUDACITY DAREDEVILISM / **ITALY** / aviator / beat the record / piercing propellers"). One suddenly realizes that, like Apollinaire's large wheel, Carrà's painting has a vertical center. At its apex – far above the celebrating crowd – a daredevil pilot is trying to set a new aviation record of some sort. The words "eliche perforanti" evoke the loud noise of the airplane's propellers and the piercing spirals of the sirens. They may also refer to acrobatic stunts by the pilot. In any case the airplane is clearly connected with the celebration below and contributes to the festive atmosphere. Among other things, it is now evident that we are viewing the spectacle *through the pilot's eyes*, high in the air and traveling at a rapid speed. This provides an explanation for the extremely flat perspective of the painting. In fact not only is the perspective two-dimensional; it is oriented from the center of the spiral facing out. Most of the words are focused on the center: Below the center they are upside down, and on both sides they are arranged vertically. This means that they can be read only by someone inside the spiral who is directly facing them. Carrà's centralist perspective, which contributes to the general appearance of disorder, is markedly different from the perspective of

27

Aesthetics of visual poetry

"Lettre-Océan," in which the words tend to adhere to the horizontal and remain upright. The latter is designed for the reader rather than the participant. With Carrà the reverse is true. Although Apollinaire's work is easier to read, Carrà's is more logical. Finally, it should be noted that the spinning motion and blurred forms of the celebration can now be explained in other terms. If formerly Carrà's spiral was seen to be a purely abstract representation of collective emotion, it is now offset by the possibility of a realistic visual interpretation: The landscape below is distorted because it represents the view from a high-flying, circling airplane. Of course, the two interpretations are not mutually exclusive. In neither instance does this diminish the forcefulness of the spiral composition, a form considered particularly dynamic by the Futurists.

From the foregoing discussion it is evident that *Festa patriottica* exemplifies better than any other Futurist work the celebrated dictum "Noi porremo lo spettatore nel centro del quadro" ("We will put the viewer in the center of the picture") (*Manifesto tecnico*). Significantly, Carrà claimed to have invented this idea, although this was disputed by Boccioni. In any case the interaction of the colors (based on a *complementarismo congenito* – "congenital complementariness" – analogous to free verse), the multiple impressions of motion, and the centralist perspective create an atmosphere of activity difficult to escape. The net effect is that of a rhythmic environment surrounding the viewer, actively involving him in the painting. Like Cubism, Futurism abolished the role of the viewer as passive observer. As Marianne W. Martin remarks, *Festa patriottica* is the most Futurist of all Carrà's works.[48] Ironically, it marks the end of the first phase of Futurist painting and the end of Carrà's career as a Futurist. Although he executed a few more drawings and collages in this style, he soon turned to Metaphysical painting and then to Mythic Realism. Apollinaire himself perfected a style of visual poetry that was less fragmentary than "Lettre-Océan." Consisting of short lyrical phrases molded into the shape of simple figures, it allowed him more leeway for personal expression.

2

The Futurist experience

From a certain point of view the history of the European avant-garde can be seen as a continual quest for aesthetic freedom. From another it represents a broader phenomenon stemming from social conditions. If the avowed intention of the avant-garde has been to revolutionize artistic expression, it has also sought to revolutionize modern consciousness, to alter our attitudes toward ourselves and our perceptions of the world around us. Seen in this light, the attempt to free language into new modes of signification acquires additional meaning. In the production of the text, for example, there is no longer a clear distinction between aesthetic and pragmatic concerns. Subjective cognition leads to objective verification. Behind every personal statement lies a political program. Herbert Marcuse traces the origins of this dual focus to a common concern with language, with a desire to liberate the word:

> There is the inner link between dialectical thought and the effort of avant-garde literature: the effort to break the power of facts over the word, and to speak a language which is not the language of those who establish, enforce, and benefit from the facts.[1]

Nowhere are the ideological implications of the avant-garde enterprise more apparent than in Italian Futurism, dedicated to the principle of *parole in libertà*. Of all the modern movements Futurism is by far the most programmatic. In manifesto after manifesto its politics are spelled out in detail and correlated with its artistic endeavors. At both levels the Futurists sought to overthrow the established order, which they perceived to be weak and ineffectual, and to replace its senseless veneration of the past (*passatismo*) with a program for the future. Rebelling against bourgeois conventions, they strove to free Italy from its historical chains and to revitalize Italian culture. These concerns are particularly evident in the renewal of literary form through visual poetry. In the first place, poetry itself – even traditional poetry – is essentially a subversive genre. Liberated from the constraints that discursive order imposes on it, the word is free to combine with others in a hundred unforeseen ways. In the second place, whereas ordinary poetry is nondiscursive, visual poetry is antidiscursive. In the radicalness of its pictorial language lies the ultimate rebellion against the power structure. Since the visual world exists outside discourse, the word is powerless to intervene. In all three works that form the subject of this chapter, the action takes place in a cafe – that bastion of modern subversive activity. Although they

Aesthetics of visual poetry

share a similar subject matter and outlook, visually they are distinct from one another. Each illustrates a different aspect of Futurist visual activity, ranging from the abstract to the concrete, from the conceptual to the figurative. Despite their obvious differences, which reflect the aesthetic preferences of their creators, they remain true to the Futurist ideal. Each in its own way seeks to "break the power of facts over the word." Indeed, in keeping with its visual orientation, each seeks to break the power of words over the poem. In the absence of verbal mediation, visual poetry succeeds in restoring the immediacy of experience and the integrity of individual consciousness.

Introspection and representation

Before creating *Festa patriottica* Carlo Carrà experimented with the idea of a circular composition in a little-known collage drawing entitled "Rapporto di un NOTTAMBULO milanese" ("Report by a Milanese NIGHT OWL"). Not only does this work form an important bridge between the circular poem and the circular painting; it represents an interesting artistic achievement in its own right. Like "Lettre-Océan," as we shall see, it is both a *poème-conversation* and a *poème simultané*. Seated in a cafe in the Galleria Vittorio Emanuele II in Milan at 4:30 A.M. Carrà records snatches of conversations going on around him and juxtaposes his private thoughts with a description of the scene. One line reads "MERRRDE" in reference to Apollinaire's manifesto *L'Antitradition futuriste* published the year before.[2] Other traces of the French poet can be seen in the parallel wavy lines at the top, which are taken from "Lettre-Océan" (Figure 1, Chapter 1). Originally intended to represent cancellation marks on the postcard, they have been reduced here to graphic signs with a largely plastic function. In addition one phrase is taken from the same poem: "ta gueule mon vieux" ("shut your trap, pal"). Like Apollinaire's "ta gueule mon vieux pad" it represents part of a conversation overheard in a public place. Inserted surreptitiously into the drawing, these references are meant to acknowledge the painter's debt to his friend in Paris.

The work itself, however, is resolutely Futurist. Again illustrating the famous phrase "Noi porremo lo spettatore nel centro del quadro" ("We will put the viewer in the center of the picture"),[3] Carrà's drawing spirals in on itself before exploding in every direction like a supernova. The radical reversal from contraction to expansion, from concentration to dispersion, is due to a ripple effect governing the various modes of perception. At the center of the drawing, seated at one of the numerous "tavolini" ("small tables") in the cafe, the artist records the myriad sense impressions converging on him from every angle. These do not stop when they reach him, however, but continue to radiate out in wider and wider circles. They approach the painter only to recede immediately into the distance. Based on the concentric model of sound waves, the composition spatializes Carrà's perceptions and projects them outward onto the viewers gathered around it. At the same time, since we identify with the artist in the process of reconstructing his experience, we find ourselves at the center of the picture along with him. Interiority and exteriority alternate in an endless dialectic reflecting the tension between contraction and expansion. More than anything the drawing impresses us with its dynamism – perhaps the chief Futurist tenet. Before we even begin to decipher it, we perceive that everything is in

30

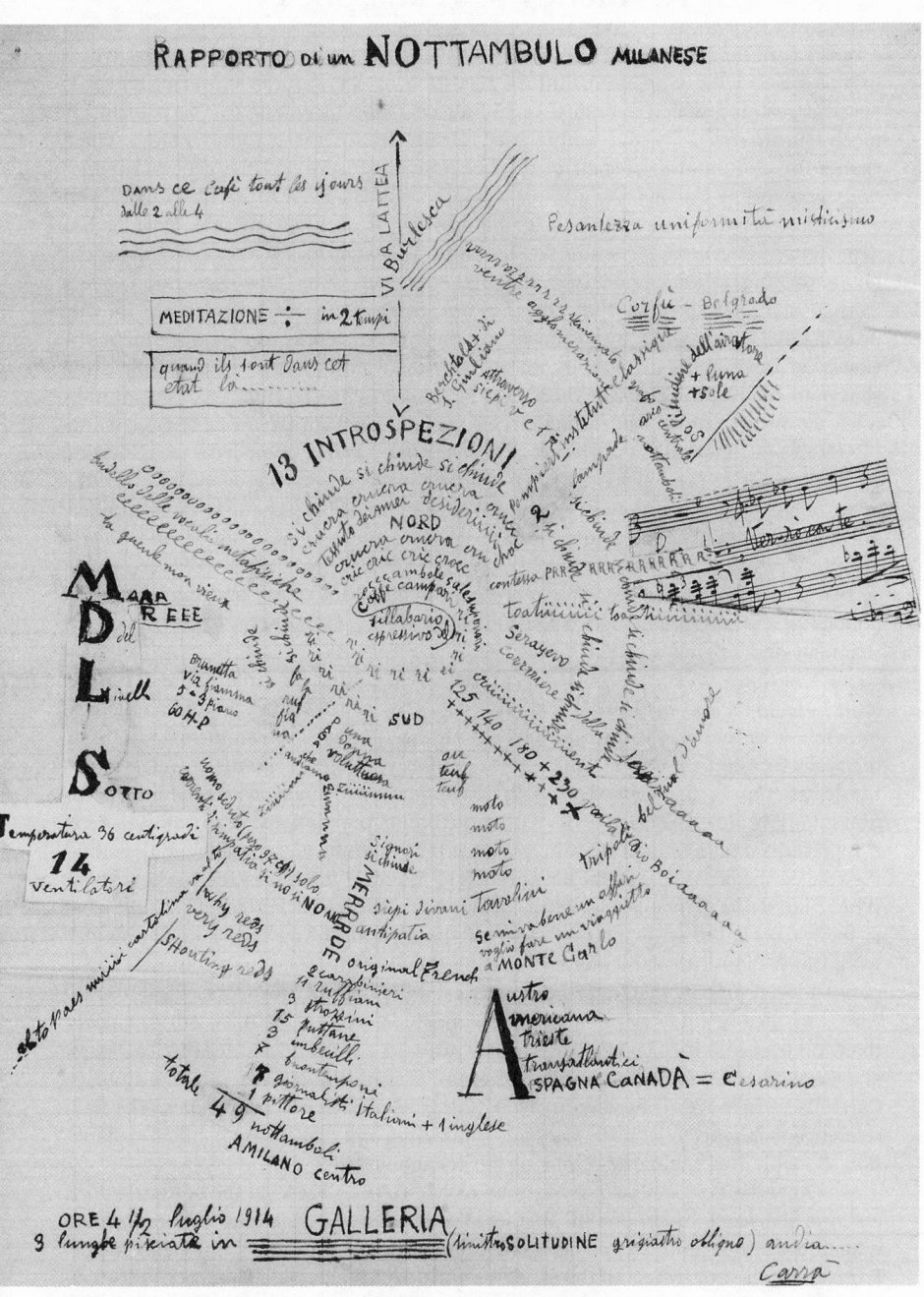

Figure 3. Carlo Carrà

31

Aesthetics of visual poetry

a state of motion as sense impressions interpenetrate each other in an endless whirl. In this respect the work is a faithful rendition of the Futurist universe, which is never at rest and which is unified by numerous forces traversing it. This principle is nicely summarized by the ambiguous refrain "moto moto moto moto," which evokes the continual *movement* of the boisterous drinkers and the general *commotion* surrounding Carrà.

The viewer's first approach to the drawing is necessarily visual. Once he has determined its general structure, his attention is drawn to several words in particular, according to various artistic and literary conventions. One convention, taken from poster art, specifies that the size and intensity of the lettering are directly proportional to a word's importance. Another, borrowed from poetry, requires the viewer to begin with the title. A third, associated with circular forms, obliges the viewer to read in a clockwise direction. Beginning with the title, then, which indicates the time and place of the action, we proceed clockwise to encounter the words "**CORFÙ – BELGRADO,**" a piece of sheet music, and a giant letter **A** sheltering an assortment of proper nouns. From the title we learn that the work will take the form of an objective report of nocturnal activity in Milan. The first group, underlined four times for the printer, establishes an international context and certain expectations. Whatever the eventual subject, it will somehow involve Greece and Serbia. The second configuration represents a snatch of music and introduces the notions of entertainment and conviviality. Someone, somewhere, is playing an instrument and singing a song.

The third, which presents several problems, expands the international context to include Spain and the New World and evokes two of the Futurists' abiding themes. As symbols of modernity, for example, the "transatlantici" ("oceanliners") exemplify their glorification of power and speed. Similarly, "Trieste" seems to refer to the Irredentist party – also evoked in *Festa patriottica* – which advocated the incorporation into Italy of neighboring areas with large Italian populations. Read in this fashion it represents a nationalistic slogan, its concern with unification paralleling the unifying role of the oceanliners. But how are we to interpret the rest of the configuration? What underlying principle caused the artist to group these words together, and what is their association with the first letter of the alphabet? The reader of Carrà's day would have had little difficulty recognizing this as a variation on a common newspaper advertisement. Headquartered in Trieste, the Linea Austro-Americana ("South American Steamship Line") employed an almost identical emblem. Boasting no fewer than "38 transatlantici," it advertised departures for North and South America, Spain, and Canada. Following the practice of visual synecdoche pioneered by the Cubists, Carrà uses the advertising logo to evoke the general idea of a newspaper. The final reference to "Cesarino" ("Little Caesar") is puzzling and may have a political explanation. Possibly it is the name of one of the oceanliners.

Our attention is now drawn to the word "**GALLERIA**" at the bottom, which restricts the scene of action still further. We are not just in Milan; we are inside a magnificent entertainment center containing coffee houses and fashionable shops. From there the eye travels to the expression "**Sotto Livello Del Maaareee**" ("**Below SSSeeeaaa Level**"), which is strange, to say the least. According to two earlier versions the scene takes place some 36 meters below sea level.[4] But since Milan is

The Futurist experience

120 meters *above* sea level, the words introduce a discordant note – and a puzzle – into the proceedings. The final phrase to catch our eye, **"13 INTROSPEZIONI,"** brings us back to the starting point. This is the form that the work will take: a discrete series of introspective glimpses. Despite our initial impression – a previous version even reads "18 Introspezione nell' **IO**" ("18 Introspections of **MYSELF**") – Carrà is determined not to be personal.[5] Instead the drawing presents a series of vignettes of life in the Galleria in the early morning.

Since "Rapporto di un NOTTAMBULO" is a form of poetry, it reflects the conventions of this genre. Beginning at the upper left, we learn that the action takes place in a cafe and that it will take the form of a meditation expressed in two different rhythms. The first and third phrases – rendered in the "original French," as an English journalist tells us later – are spoken by French tourists who regard the proceedings with a jaundiced eye. "Quand ils sont dans cet état là" ("When they are in that state") refers to the general drunkenness of the clientele and is echoed by other French phrases across the room. "Au teuf teuf" ("on the choo-choo"), one character remarks humorously, while on the right another character verbally abuses the artists of the Institut Classique, who are a bunch of pompous fools ("pompiers"). On the left yet another Frenchman is becoming quarrelsome as he tells his companion to shut up ("ta gueule mon vieux"). The drawing itself is superimposed on a vertical axis running from "NORD" to "SUD." At the top the notation "VIA LATTEA Burlesca" ("Comical MILKY WAY") probably refers to the numerous lights reflected in the glass dome covering the Galleria. Beyond the panoply of artificial stars, "attraverso siepi vetri" ("beyond [the] barriers [and the] window-panes"), a full moon hangs in the sky like a lone airplane silhouetted against the dawn ("solitudine dell'aviatore + luna + sole").

These two references illustrate a process common to Futurism that occurs again and again in Carrà's drawing – the destruction of normal syntax. Abolishing articles, conjunctions, and other nonessential words, Carrà strings isolated nouns together to create a telegraphic style. Here as elsewhere the goal of *l'immaginazione senza fili* ("the wireless imagination") is to escape the confines of grammar in order to communicate directly and forcefully. In addition to copious examples of expressive typography, the painter uses a mathematical shorthand to indicate relationships. Thus the division sign $\div$ signifies "divided into," and the plus sign $+$ stands for the word "and." Other Futurist devices include onomatopoeia and free expressive orthography (*ortografia libera espressiva*), which registers the intonation, facial expression, and gestures of the speaker. In the former category the animated state of the people sitting on the center level ("grado centrale") is represented by a mechanical whirring sound, "rrrrrrrrrrrrrrr." This is an example of what F. T. Marinetti termed *onomatopea indiretta complessa e analogica*, in which the relation of sound to object is analogical. By contrast the two streams of o's and e's emerging from the circles at about two o'clock are an example of *onomatopea astratta*, whose relation to its subject is considerably more tenuous. Like "crucra crucra cru," "cric cric cric crocc" was suggested by "Lettre-Océan," where similar noises are produced by the poet's new shoes. In an earlier version Carrà identifies these sounds with passing footsteps.[6] This is an example of *onomatopea diretta imitativa elementare realistica*, which seeks to reproduce the actual sound.

Aesthetics of visual poetry

There are numerous instances of orthographical distortion, from "**Maaar-eee,**" which reproduces the flat intonation of the speaker and the vast expanse of the sea, to "teatriiiiiiiiiiiii" and "MERRRDE." The second example evokes the rows of bright lights outlining the front of the theaters, whereas the third suggests the speaker with his lip curled in disgust. Like "Criiiiiiiiiiiiiient" ("screeeeeeeeeeeeee-eam"), the phrase "tessuto dei miei desideriiiii" ("tissue of my desiiiiires") reflects the acuteness of the speaker's emotion. One also encounters the principle of *sensibilità numerica,* which requires the recording in Arabic numerals of dimensions, weights, volumes, and speeds. Carrà covers the drawing with quantitative notations, including "14 ventilatori" ("14 fans") and "choc 2 lampade," which originally read "le choc de deux lampade" ("the shock of two lamps").[7] The sequence "125 140 180 + 230 voilà" represents someone adding up a bill in response to the request "PAGA che andiamo" ("PAY so we can go"). From the fact that the temperature is 36 degrees centigrade (97 degrees Fahrenheit) we know it is a scorching night. Even the people sitting in the cafe are described in quantitative terms. Among the 49 night owls there are 2 carabinieri, 11 pimps, 3 moneylenders, 15 whores, 3 imbeciles, 7 good-time Charlies, 7 Italian journalists, 1 Englishman, and 1 painter (Carrà). Nevermind that these add up to 50 people; they include a man sitting alone who weighs 97 kilograms (213 pounds) and a voluptuous prostitute strolling among the tables ("una donna voluttuosa/fa la ruffiana"). Carrà gives her vital statistics as follows: "Brunette/No. 5 Flame Street/3rd floor/60 H-P." Besides the street name, which testifies to her professional ardor, the last figure is particularly amusing. In 1914 a 60-horsepower automobile was a powerful machine built as much for speed as for comfort.

The physical setting itself is evoked with great economy of means like a series of rapid brush strokes. In addition to the individuals sitting at the tables, Carrà gives us glimpses of various objects in and around the cafe. Some of these are seen only in passing – the picture postcard of the Alps at the lower left, for example, or the blurred outline next to it painted with "Why reds/very reds/Shouting reds." Apparently uttered by the English journalist, the latter phrase is both descriptive and programmatic. Besides evoking a specific form, it refers to Carrà's 1913 manifesto *La Pittura dei suoni, rumori, odori (The Painting of Sounds, Noises, Odors),* which calls for vivid colors, including "I rossi, rooooossssssi roooooooosssisssssimi che griiiiii-dano" ("Reds, rrrrreds, the rrrrreddest rrrrreds that shouuuuuuut"). Other subjects, such as the posters and signs at the center of the drawing, leap out at the viewer and seize his attention. Thus "Caffè" and "Campari" clearly advertise two popular beverages available at the cafe. The expression "rocccambole sale superiori," however, presents several problems. For one thing, *rocambola* is a vegetable known as a sand leek or Spanish garlic. For another, with a slight change "sale superiori" can mean either "upper auditoriums" or "excellent salt." To add to the confusion a character called Rocambole was the swashbuckling hero of a series of novels by Ponson du Terrail. If we can reject the first interpretation as inappropriate to the cafe setting, either of the latter two is possible. Rocambole may be the name of a condiment or, as seems more likely, the hero of a movie playing upstairs in the Galleria. In either case what interests Carrà is the array of signs, which constitute a "sillabario espressivo" ("expressive primer"). As such they embody a number of

The Futurist experience

elementary principles that make them a valuable resource for modern poetry and painting.

This brings us back to the question of proper nouns, which play such a prominent role in the drawing. In addition to those mentioned previously. two examples are particularly interesting: "Corrrrrieri della Seeeeraaaaa" and "Serayevo." At this point several things begin to fall into place. These lines can only refer to newspaper headlines about the assassination of the Archduke Franz Ferdinand on June 28, 1914, at Serajevo. Our suspicion is confirmed, moreover, by an earlier version of the drawing that includes references to two papers: "supplemento *Il Secolo* / supplemento *Corriere della Sera*" juxtaposed with the notation "Corfù Belgrado Ulster / ca pète."[8] Clearly, Carrà considers the assassination to be the latest in a series of international incidents building up to an inevitable cataclysm ("ca pète"). Sitting at his table with a copy of the *Corriere della Sera* before him–an "extra" edition occasioned by unexpected events–he scans the headlines and exclaims, "125 140 180 + 230 voilà Avo Boiaaaaaaa." This time the series of numbers parallels the increasing likelihood of war, which will be a victory for the "Grim Reaper." Once we understand what is involved we can proceed to decipher the reference at the top (above the "introspezione") to "Berchtold + di S. Giuliano." The first name refers to Count Leopold Berchtold, an Austrian politician who was in favor of intervention in the Balkans. Regarding an Austro-Serbian war as inevitable, he used Serajevo as a pretext to invade the neighboring country. The Marchese Antonino di San Guiliano was the Italian minister of foreign affairs, who favored a policy of neutrality in the conflict. Not surprisingly, both names often figured in the headlines, as they do here.

It remains to call attention to the auditory dimension of the "Rapporto," which, in accordance with Carrà's manifesto, is quite marked. As the artist tells us himself, the different voices represent "sympathetic [and] yes no yes NO NO antipathetic currents" running through the crowd. Most of the conversations are fragmentary, although one utterance manages to remain intact. Among the examples we have not yet examined, an anonymous person–perhaps Carrà himself–observes that he will have enough money to make a trip to Monaco if a business deal works out. Elsewhere someone sings about a count and a countess, and another voice chimes in with a verse in praise of "Tripoli bel suol' d'amore" ("Tripoli fair land of love"). To this must be added the general babble of voices noted previously and the generous amounts of onomatopoeia, especially the sound of footsteps spiraling out from the center. Throughout the work the refrain "si chiude" echoes from one side of the room to the other. It is closing time, and the waiters are impatient to go home. The final exclamation is truncated as Carrà steps through the doorway. All we hear is the first half of *andiamo* ("let's go") before he is gone. And yet the story is not quite over. Among other things, the phrase "budello delle vocali metafisiche" gives us occasion to pause. To be sure there is a triple pun here centered on the word *bordello*, meaning both "brothel" and "uproar." Not only is there an "uproar of metaphysical vowels" in the cafe, the constant hubbub resembles the indiscriminate intercourse of a house of prostitution. The fact that *budello* itself designates the intestines, however, alerts us to an underlying malaise. Not only is the cafe inhabited by an assortment of unsavory characters; Carrà compares their conversation to an attack of flatulence.

Aesthetics of visual poetry

This observation plus the concluding lines place the drawing in a different perspective. Continuing in the same bawdy vein, the artist signs and dates his composition while noting that he has emptied his bladder three times during his stay. If this is a humorous example of "numerical sensibility," the emphasis on bodily functions reinforces our previous impression. The drawing is not meant to be a charming portrait of a typical cafe scene. The final line describes the Galleria's "sinistro SOLITUDINE grigiastro obliquo" ("grim, grayish, oblique SOLITUDE") and gives us a glimpse of Carrà. Thematically this section mirrors a statement at the upper right in which the general atmosphere is characterized by "pesantezza uniformità misticismo" ("oppressiveness monotony mysticism"). This finally explains why the scene takes place "below sea level." Beneath the Galleria's glass dome, the heavy atmosphere and subdued lighting remind Carrà of an aquarium. All about him mouths open and close in a stream of meaningless vowels like the silent gapings of so many fish. The entire drawing is framed by these two sections in which the solitude of the aviator prefigures the artist's personal solitude at the end. If these gloomy observations are intended to describe the cafe, in fact they tell us more about Carrà. Exhausted after a night of drinking, he is overcome by melancholy and a sense of heaviness. Surrounded by the dregs of humanity, he feels lonely and pessimistic about the future of the human race. On another level, certainly, his pessimism is related to recent political events that threaten to engulf the world in war. Reading the newspapers has only confirmed his opinion of human nature, exemplified by the unparalleled stupidity of the world's leaders. Seen in this perspective, the cafe represents a microcosm of the world at large. Carrà's special target is the world of international politics, which despite its pretentions is subject to the same raw passions and calculated vices as the people sitting in the cafe. Among other things, "Rapporto di un NOTTAMBULO milanese" is an iconoclastic exercise designed to expose the corrupt foundations of power. In freeing the word from its accustomed servitude, Carrà wished to shatter bourgeois illusions both about the nature of language and about the nature of the political process.[9]

Classicism and anarchy

As a member of the Futurists, Ardengo Soffici was unique. A "classiciste parmi les anarchistes" according to one critic,[10] he tended to be more rational, more conservative than his fellow artists and poets. Of all the painters in the group, for example, Soffici was the most highly influenced by Cubism, an eminently rational movement. This is immediately evident if one compares his painting entitled *Lines and Volumes of a Street* (1912) with Umberto Boccioni's *The Street Enters in the House* (1911). The former is a static, highly ordered example of analytic Cubism in which planes and volumes are decomposed and juxtaposed to form a totally abstract work. The latter is representational and charged with energy and motion in accordance with the Futurist aesthetic of dynamism. We see about the same thing in Soffici's *Simultaneità di Donna Carretto Strada* (*Simultaneity of Donna Carretto Street*), published in the January 15, 1914, issue of *Lacerba*. Another street scene, it differs from the first by the inclusion of a few recognizable objects, by the presence of more motion, and by the juxtaposition of several fragmented signs. One can be reconstructed to

The Futurist experience

read "PENSI [ONE]"("PRIVATE HOTEL"), and the letters "RAG" are probably taken from "RAGIONIERE" ("Accountant"). Although more Futurist influence is noticeable here, the overwhelming influence is that of synthetic Cubism.

Throughout Soffici's association with *Lacerba* one notes a paradoxical contrast between theory and practice.[11] Through his articles he became one of the principal theoreticians of Futurism, but his own works remained essentially cubist in inspiration. Thus in his article "Il soggetto nella pittura futurista" ("The Subject in Futurist Painting"), published in *Lacerba* on January 1, 1914, Soffici makes the excellent point that "ogni nuovo soggetto comanda al pittore un nuovo senso plastico e perciò un nuovo stile" ("every new subject demands a new plastic sense and thus a new style from the painter") – this by way of justifying Futurist aesthetics. Thus radically new subjects such as airplanes, trains, music halls, and circuses must be depicted in a radically new (i.e., Futurist) manner. Paradoxically, following this closely reasoned defense of the need for innovation, Soffici chose to portray two traditional, even conservative, topics in the very next issue (January 15, 1914) – a deserted city street and a glass of water. The former is represented by *Simultaneità di Donna Carretto Strada*, the latter by the poem "Bicchier d'acqua" ("A Glass of Water"). Soffici's first attempt at *parole in libertà* seems quite futuristic on the surface. Certainly it represents a radical departure from the conventions of his previous poetry. Although it lacks the copious quantities of onomatopoeia and mathematical signs advocated by Marinetti, we note a sprinkling of foreign words – "amarillo" ("yellow"), "affiches" ("posters"), "spring" – and expressive typography. Furthermore, it contains Futurist punctuation: Full stops tend to be indicated by blank spaces.

The special typographical effects are rudimentary, consisting for the most part of occasional words (the names of colors) printed in large black capitals. At one point Soffici employs a large typographical bracket. At another he spreads a five-word string of capitals across the page horizontally:

> Perpendicolarmente la nullità della
> notte sonno a picco blu-di-prussia iu silenzio
> **SILENZIO** SILENZIO SILENZIO SILENZIO SILENZIO
> fino al vertice metafisico d'oltre i pianeti

Perpendicularly the nullity of the night sheer Prussian blue sleep in silence SILENCE SILENCE SILENCE SILENCE SILENCE as far as the metaphysical vertex beyond the planets.

In describing the perpendicular lines of the glass, Soffici uses three metaphors: night, sleep, and silence. These in turn are characterized by the absence of light, of motion, and of sound. Thus he chooses the common denominator of *absence* to express the static, pure, absolute quality of the glass.[12] He glimpses a bit of infinity in the eternally frozen waterglass, whence the reference to the "vertice metafisico" ("metaphysical vertex") in the last line. The decrescendo effect of the third line is particularly well suited to the subject. The progressive decrease in size of "silenzio" functions in two entirely different ways, presenting both an aural and a visual analogy. Read aloud – or even silently – this line has a special auditory dimension.

BICCHIER D'ACQUA

Parole in libertà.

In un pollice di trasparenze circolari
cristallo   miracolo disciplinare di molecole
sentinelle fronte all'infinito circostante   un
mondo   Globi angoli plaghe d'imper-
sonalità   vedi   stagni d'acromia al taglio
degli orizzonti in partenza solitudini d'etere
     Perpendicolarmente la nullità della
notte sonno a picco blu-di-prussia iu silenzio

SILENZIO SILENZIO SILENZIO SILENZIO SILENZIO

fino al vertice metafisico d'oltre i pianeti
     Poi strie bianche virgole di pla-
tino ondulazioni di gelo nevi in abbandono pa-
gine vuote d'alba senza speranze senza rosa di
ciminiere di tetti   Ma subito accanto
un'equatore d'occhi di fuoco   portici d'oro
d'amore penne di sole   Gli orienti in
fiore le sirie carovane d'amarillo dei ricordi verso
la mecca delle gioventù de' popoli
Siamo sulla terra   Rotazione di pri-
smi nella serenità dell'acqua

IRIDE

VIOLETTO ROSSO ARANCIONE GIALLO VERDE AZZURRO INDACO VIOLETTO

Sciaguattio di felicità mascherata degli es-
seri degli elementi delle stagioni delle civiltà
     VIOLETTO come in cuori profondi
di assassini dormire dormire delle passioni col
vino le glorie vomitate sullo strascico postumo
delle stelle   **ROSSO** profumo elettrico
della carne baciata estate d'affiches sulle guance
delle città senza vergogna   **ARANCIONE**
mare del sud in amore strade notturne gonfie
di calcoli al ritmo prostituto delle serenate
     GIALLO labbra dell'ironia nel no-
vembre dei cimiteri strazio di un cielo sugli au-
tunni teatrali delle vetrate   **VERDE**
stemperamento velenoso di gemme bagno dell'a-
nima nell'aritmetica dei viaggi delle traversate
sguardi di pupille giovani verso la vita fuoco
complementare   **AZZURRO** eternità
dell'intelligenza migrazione delle nostalgie nel
cerchio degli assoluti senza cuore
INDACO rifluire rumoroso del sangue delle velocità delle guerre nei misticismi prostrati golfo
stazione dell'esistenza allucinata in pressione
di partenza   **VIOLETTO ULTRAVIO-
LETTO NERO** voluttà morte promessa spring
scoppio uragano meccanico di nuove primavere
     Un mondo   E un giro liquido
d'ali ebbre d'aria   Sfera pirotecnica
della fantasia al caffè.

Figure 4. Ardengo Soffici

The Futurist experience

The reader interprets the string of repetitions as a multiple echo. As this dies away to nothing, the final absence of sound corresponds to the "absence" of the glass. Furthermore, the optical effect of this line gives an additional spatial dimension to the passage. Possessing an illusionary perspective, the verse seems to move away from us, traveling from left to right, until it disappears. The distance symbolized by this typographical shift corresponds in turn to the infinite space between us and the metaphysical vertex (which presumably is the source of the universe).[13]

Despite an initial impression of confusion, the poem is actually quite orderly and proceeds in a logical manner. The typographical effects and blank spaces are symmetrically arranged, so that the blacks and whites provide a counterpoint to the poem. Visually it even looks something like a glass. The main difficulty arises from Soffici's use of highly impressionistic language to convey the effect made on him by the glass of water. His imagery and diction are reminiscent of the hallucinatory poetry of Rimbaud, who seems to have been the major influence on this poem. Soffici begins by describing the glass of water as seen from above. Its circular forms and thick base suggest infinity, impersonality, and solitude to him. The same sort of associations are evoked by a frontal view in the next stanza, which, as we have seen, takes us "oltre i pianeti" ("beyond the planets"). The third stanza brings us back to earth, where Soffici concentrates on the delicate light patterns in the glass. The upper part of the glass (which is half full of water) is painted in cold white tones, the lower half in warm yellows. Suddenly the angle of vision shifts slightly so that the water functions as a prism. Concentrating on the prismatic spectrum, Soffici devotes the last half of the poem to the associations each color has for him, for example,

> **ROSSO** profumo elettrico
> della carne baciata estate d'affiches sulle guance
> delle città senza vergogna . . . .

RED electric perfume of kissed meat summer of posters on the cheeks
of the shameless cities . . . .

This process is clearly borrowed from Rimbaud's sonnet "Voyelles" ("Vowels"), in which the "naissances latentes" ("latent births") of each vowel are described in a similar fashion. Traveling through the color spectrum, we finally come to violet, ultraviolet, and black (death), which would seem to be the end of the journey. However, the poem ends on a note of rebirth: From death we emerge into an explosion of spring. The last line returns us to the author, who is composing the poem in a coffee house: "Sfera pirotecnica della fantasia al caffè" ("Pyrotechnical sphere of fantasy at the cafe").

From the foregoing description it is clear that "Bicchier d'acqua" is primarily a cubist, not a futurist poem. The composition, subject matter, and style are plainly those of Cubism. We see none of the polemics, dynamism, or radical discontinuity characteristic of Futurism, nor do we encounter any Futurist themes. Indeed the very concept of the "still life" – which is what informs this poem – is antithetical to the Futurist aesthetic. It is instructive to glance at Soffici's article in the next issue of *Lacerba* (February 1, 1914) entitled "Chicchi del grappolo" ("A Bunch of Grape Seeds"), for in discussing "uno dei più importanti principi della nostra nuova estet-

Aesthetics of visual poetry

ica" ("one of the most important principles of our new aesthetic"), that is, the principle of artistic deformation, he chooses the glass in "Bicchier d'acqua" to illustrate his remarks. According to Soffici the Futurist artist's (or poet's) perception of his subject is affected (1) by its surroundings, (2) by the accidents of light and shadow, and (3) by the associations it evokes. Thus

> l'emozione ch'esso gli procura modifica nella sua fantasia il rapporto delle parti che lo compongono. Per rappresentarlo egli dovrà dunque tradurre questa visione particolare, commossa, lirica, alterando perciò lo schema astratto generale della pura geometria.

> the emotion that this arouses modifies in his imagination the relations between the parts that compose it. To represent the subject he must thus express this lyrical, moving, special vision, altering the general abstract arrangement of pure geometry.

This, then, is the process Soffici used in his poem, a process that by 1914 was hardly revolutionary. His description is an excellent definition of Cubism rather than Futurism.

The February 15 issue of *Lacerba* contains another free-word poem by Soffici that makes an interesting contrast with the painting *Simultaneità di Donna Carretto Strada*. Entitled "Passegiata" ("Promenade"), it reproduces a walk through the streets of Florence and represents an advance over Soffici's previous works. Among other things it is more dynamic, depicting a stroll rather than a fixed view, and embodies several Futurist themes. Typographically the poem is also more adventurous, going so far as to include facsimile signs and advertisements. Still, it does not begin to match the typographical audacity of recent poems by Carrà, Marinetti, and others, which were becoming increasingly visual. The Futurists in general were entering a new phase in which they sought to ally poetry and painting. As we have seen, their experiments with typographical poetry quickly gave way to others involving typographical painting. Among the first examples of this genre, Soffici's *Al buffet della stazione* (*In the Railway Cafe*) appeared in the same issue of *Lacerba* as Carrà's *Festa patriottica* (August 1, 1914). Curiously, it has nothing in common with any of its predecessors. Both of Carrà's works are circular abstractions and juxtapose verbal fragments in an asyntactical setting. On the contrary, Soffici's work is frankly pictorial, and his verbal syntax is largely preserved. A brilliant example of synthetic Cubism, it is simultaneously a free-word painting and a free-word poem. Conceived as a still life set in a railroad station, *Al buffet della stazione* is composed almost entirely of linguistic elements.

On the left we see the outlines of an espresso coffee machine, on the right part of a newspaper – both of which are filled with words. These forms are juxtaposed with a single diagonal line representing the edge of the table where Soffici is seated. There is extensive use of expressive typography, the formal value of which is at least as important as its semantic value. In the latter category one notes the presence of several posters advertising, among other things, an aperitif ("**BYRRH**") and a hair tonic called "**CHININA-MIGONE**."[14] We see that coffee costs 25 centesimi, the newspaper 5 centesimi. There is one bizarre detail: The spout of the coffee machine reads "**CICCA SPENTA**" and is thus a "cigarette butt" and a

AL BUFFET DELLA STAZIONE

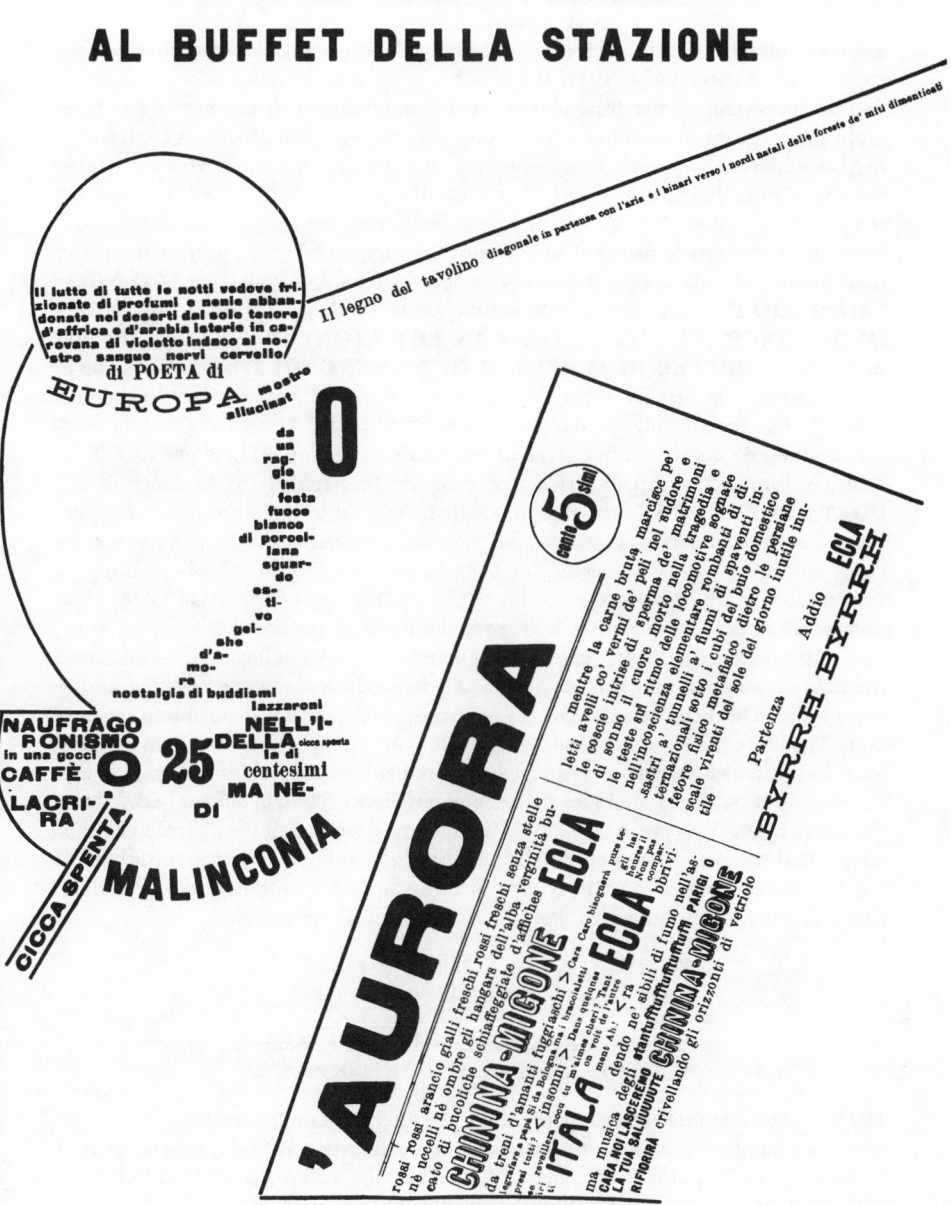

Figure 5. Ardengo Soffici

Aesthetics of visual poetry

spout simultaneously. The eye is drawn first to the biggest, blackest letters on the page: "[L] ' **AURORA**" ("**THE DAWN**"). This is both the name of the newspaper and an indication of the time of day, which is described in the next three lines. From there the eye travels to the next most prominent word, "**MALINCONIA**" (" **MELANCHOLY**"), which forms the base of the coffee machine. This establishes the tone: bitter loneliness mixed with misanthropic cynicism. These emotions are magnified by the setting, as we picture a dingy railroad station cafe strewn with cigarette butts, nearly deserted in the early morning. The lower part of the coffee machine is particularly effective in portraying the situation: "**NAUFRAGO NELL' IRONISMO DELLA** cicca spenta in una gocciola di **CAFFÈ LACRIMA NERA DI MALINCONIA**"("**CASTAWAY IN THE IRONY OF THE** cigarette butt in a drop of **COFFEE BLACK TEAR OF MELANCHOLY**"). Both the drop of coffee and the cigarette butt function as objective correlatives here – as devices that objectify the melancholy of the anonymous "naufrago" ("castaway"), who presumably represents the author. This impression is strengthened by a group of bold-face words near the top of the coffee machine that record the presence of a " **POETA di EUROPA,**" who must be Soffici. Dazzled by a festive sunbeam glancing off a piece of crockery ("fuoco bianco di porcellana"), the latter observes the cafe's colorful clientele consisting of beggars and prostitutes ("Geïshe d'amore"). Surrounded by the dregs of society, like Carrà in "Rapporto di un NOTTAMBULO milanese," Soffici sips his coffee and reads the morning paper.

Throughout the work there are scattered references to locomotives and train tracks in keeping with the railroad motif. Otherwise the remainder evokes the sordidness of love. This is the main theme of the newspaper, which is divided into two sections. The first consists of a dialogue – half in Italian, half in French – between two runaway lovers, which Soffici overhears. Speaking of her husband, whom she has just left, the woman says, "Dans quelques heures il se reveillera cocu tu m'aimes cheri?" ("In a few hours he will wake up a cuckold do you love me dear?"). But the man is more concerned that she has remembered to bring along the family jewelry. The sordidness of the dialogue is made even more evident by its juxtaposition with two verses from the climactic duet of *La Traviata* ("Parigi, O cara," Act III, Scene 6):

PARIGI O CARA NOI LASCEREMO
LA TUA SALUUUUUTE REFIORIRÀ.

OH MY DARLING WE WILL LEAVE PARIS
YOUR HEALLLLLTH WILL THRIVE AGAIN.[15]

The form "saluuuuute" attempts to render the effect of a prolonged high note in the opera. Evoking the pathos of the lovers' reunion, when Alfredo returns to find Violetta in the last stages of consumption, the lines serve to contrast faithfulness with adultery, true love with base passion, sublimity with crassness. The newspaper's second section evokes the "fetore fisico metafisico" ("metaphysical physical stench") of existence in general and love in particular: "mentre la carne bruta marcisce pe'letti avelli co' vermi de' peli nel sudore e le coscie intrise di sperma de' matrimoni di sonno" ("while the raw meat rots on the beds tombs with hairy worms in the sweat and thighs soaked with the matrimonial sperm of sleep"). The

The Futurist experience

newspaper itself begins and ends with a glimpse of the dawn, which frames the central meditation on love and degradation. The first three lines describe the reddening of the morning sky and the emergence of the sun from "the hangars of the dawn." The last few lines chart the sun's progress as it begins its climb into the sky. Its ascension is reflected on the green shutters of the building across the street, which thus function as a sort of "staircase": "scale virenti del sole del giorno inutile inutile" ("verdant stairs of the sun of the useless useless day"). Like "Rapporto di un NOTTAMBULO milanese," the work ends with the author's departure. Uttering a clipped goodbye, he steps out the door and leaves us to stare at a wall full of posters.

As noted, *Al buffet della stazione* resembles Carrà's drawing in a number of respects. If anything its vision is even bleaker, its tone more despairing, than the cynical observations of the earlier composition. At the center of both works lies a pessimistic view of the world anchored in contemporary reality. That Soffici chooses to denounce love in particular suggests that he is recovering from an unhappy love affair. Whatever the source of his mordant commentary, it is important to note that it accords with official Futurist doctrine, which banished sentiment from the poetic arena. Heading a long list of sentimental themes that had contributed to the decadence of modern Italy, love was condemned as a feminine strategy designed to sap vigor and virility. Just as the Futurist platform wished to free art and literature from this debilitating theme, it sought to liberate Italian men from an illusion that had emasculated them for centuries. Seen in this light, the subversive nature of Soffici's composition becomes clear. Disguised as a simple aesthetic statement, its hatred of the status quo is directed at two targets: culture and society.

It remains to say a word about the artistic inspiration underlying *Al buffet della stazione.* If the idea of a cafe still life was already present in "Bicchier d'acqua," it took a painter (and a fellow Futurist) to put Soffici on the right road. This person was Carlo Carrà, who published a poem in *Lacerba* on July 1, 1914, entitled "Cd'hArcOUrFÉ." An evocation of the Café d'Harcourt in Paris, it was accompanied by a clever collage, also by Carrà, which he called *Sintesi circolare di oggetti (Circular Synthesis of Objects).* The latter is a splendid example of synthetic Cubism and, like the poem, represents a cafe still life. Moving from left to right, we see the edge of a table, a glass of liquor, a seltzer bottle with siphon, and part of a newspaper the name of which (in large, black letters) is partially visible. Except for the glass these components are identical to those in *Al buffet.* The same is true of the placement of the two principal objects. The seltzer bottle and the coffee machine are to the left of their respective newspapers, both of which occupy the lower right-hand corner. Not only are the first two objects closely related; one seems to be modeled on the other. The fact that the spout of the siphon consists of a cigarette glued to the collage finally explains why the spout of Soffici's coffee machine reads "**CICCA SPENTA.**" Among other things, the latter feature is meant to acknowledge the artist's debt to his Futurist colleague.

Given Soffici's predilection for Cubist aesthetics, it is not surprising that he patterned *Al buffet della stazione* on this particular work. Although Carrà is generally considered to have been the most talented (and the most representative) of the Futurist painters, by mid-1914 he had exhausted the possibilities of Futurism and

Figure 6. Carlo Carrà, *Sintesi circolare di oggetti*

The Futurist experience

was about to leave the group. During this period he executed a brilliant series of cubist collages, including *Sintesi circolare*, which compare favorably with those of Picasso and Braque. Carrà's response to French models paralleled similar concerns by Soffici, whose debt to his contemporaries in France was greater and long standing. Temperamentally a Cubist, as we have seen, Soffici was incapable of embracing Futurism to the extent of a Marinetti or a Boccioni. In his best works, such as *Al buffet* and "Bicchier d'acqua," the conflict between these two artistic tendencies is resolved.[16] Since Soffici was primarily a painter, he composed his poetry according to artistic criteria. In both his figurative and his non-figurative poems there is a strong appeal to the eye. Structural elements, colors, shapes – all are ordered in such a way as to constitute a visual language independent of, but related to, the linguistic message.

3

Apollinaire's plastic imagination

Although Apollinaire's reputation as poet, novelist, and art critic has greatly increased in the years since his death, critics have persisted in condemning his visual poetry. The spectrum of opinion ranges from "jeu inoffensif" ("harmless game") to "assez puérile" ("rather childish") and "absurdité visuelle" ("visual nonsense").[1] Typically, Apollinaire's efforts are dismissed with the observation that the genre was basically stillborn because it had no imitators (in fact there were a great many imitations, beginning with "Rapporto di un NOTTAMBULO milanese" and *Festa patriottica*). Even during Apollinaire's lifetime, critical reaction was largely unfavorable. Although the response of the avant-garde was enthusiastic, the attitude of friendly critics was frankly guarded.[2] Elsewhere the comments were more acerbic, and most critics shared the opinion of Félicien Fagus, who, citing visual poems by Panard and Rabelais, objected, "Mais c'est vieux comme le monde la machine de ce vieux farceur d'Apollinaire" ("But this is as old as the hills, this ridiculous gadget of Apollinaire's") (*Paris-Midi*, July 20, 1914).

Despite the historical resistance to the calligram, recent critics have begun to recognize the complexity of inspiration underlying its deceptively simple exterior, among them Michel Foucault. Regarding the calligram as a tautological construct, Foucault focuses on its existence as a dual sign, noting that it "se sert de cette propriété des lettres de valoir à la fois comme des éléments linéaires qu'on peut disposer dans l'espace et comme des signes qu'on doit dérouler selon la chaîne unique de la substance sonore" ("uses that capacity of letters to signify both as linear elements that can be arranged in space and as signs that must unroll according to a unique chain of sound").[3] Although his concept of the calligram as tautology is mistaken, as we shall see in Chapter 4, in its role as semiotic double agent Apollinaire's picture-poem possesses undeniable visual appeal. In addition to the great aesthetic interest that it offers the modern reader-viewer, the calligram represents a highly original contribution to the visual tradition. Moreover, the extensive history of visual poetry, which Fagus held against Apollinaire, only proves the validity of the genre. Replying to his accuser two days later, Apollinaire advanced much the same argument by tracing the pictographic principle back to the origins of written language. His defense was twofold:

M. Fagus a raison: dans ma poésie, je suis simplement revenu aux principes puisque l'idéogramme est le principe même de l'écriture. Ce-

46

Apollinaire's plastic imagination

Que mon
Flacon
Me semble bon!
Sans lui
L'ennui
Me nuit,
Me suit.
Je sens
Mes sens
Mourants,
Pesants.
Quand je la tiens,
Dieux! que je suis bien!
Que son aspect est agréable!
Que je fais cas de ses divins présents!
C'est de son sein fécond, c'est de ses heureux flancs
Que coule ce nectar si doux, si délectable,
Qui rend tous les esprits, tous les cœurs satisfaits.
Cher objet de mes vœux, tu fais toute ma gloire.
Tant que mon cœur vivra, de tes charmants bienfaits
Il saura conserver la fidèle memoire.
Ma muse à te louer se consacre à jamais,
Tantôt dans un caveau, tantôt sous une treille,
Ma lyre, de ma voix accompagnant le son,
Répétera cent fois cette aimable chanson:
'Règne sans fin, ma charmante bouteille;
Règne sans cesse, mon flacon.

Figure 7. Charles–François Panard (1674–1765), "Que mon flacon me semble bon!"

pendant, entre ma poésie et les exemples cités par M. Fagus, il y a juste la même différence qu'entre telle voiture automobile du XVIᵉ, mue par un mouvement d'horlogerie, et une auto de course contemporain. Les figures uniques de Rabelais et de Panard sont inexpressives comme les autres dessins typographiques, tandis que les rapports qu'il y a entre les figures juxtaposées d'un de mes poèmes sont tout aussi expressifs que les mots qui le composent. Et là, au moins, il y a, je crois, une nouveauté [*Paris-Midi*, July 22, 1914].

M. Fagus is right: in my poetry I have simply returned to basic principles since the ideogram is the fundamental principle of writing. How-

Aesthetics of visual poetry

Easter-wings.

LOrd, who createdst man in wealth and store,
     Though foolishly he lost the same,
          Decaying more and more,
               Till he became
                    Most poore:
                    With thee
               O let me rise
          As larks, harmoniously,
     And sing this day thy victories:
Then shall the fall further the flight in me.

My tender age in sorrow did beginne:
     And still with sicknesses and shame
          Thou didst so punish sinne,
               That I became
                    Most thinne.
                    With thee
               Let me combine
          And feel this day thy victorie:
     For, if I imp my wing on thine,
Affliction shall advance the flight in me.

Figure 8. George Herbert

ever, the difference between my poems and the examples he cites is like
that between a toy automobile of the sixteenth century, powered by
clockwork springs, and a modern racing car. The solitary shapes by
Rabelais and Panard lack expressiveness, like the other typographical
drawings, whereas the relations between the juxtaposed figures in one
of my poems are as expressive as the words that compose it. And this at
least, I think, is a new invention.

Coinciding with the first calligrammatic experiments, Apollinaire's remarks offer
precious insight into the nature and function of his visual poetry. It is important to
note that he insists on both the modernity and the uniqueness of the calligram. This
tends to support his subsequent claim, on at least two occasions, that he had
invented a brand new genre of poetry.[4] The following section, which concentrates
on the initial calligrams, is devoted to a detailed comparison with the Western
visual poetry tradition.[5] Not only will this comparison corroborate Apollinaire's
claim; it will reveal his contributions to the visual tradition.

Apollinaire's plastic imagination

Repetition and renewal

If the boundary between statement and style is often difficult to discern, in visual poetry it is practically invisible. Situated at the intersection of legibility and visibility, the calligram exploits the visual properties of written language and the semantic possibilities of visual form. For the sake of convenience most of Apollinaire's innovations can be said to involve "form" rather than "content." This is not to deny the importance of his achievements in the latter category. A brief glance at the calligrammatic subject matter reveals that his contribution was crucial. As Alain-Marie Bassy rightly observes, Apollinaire was the first to use visual poetry for strictly lyrical purposes.[6] Traditionally, this genre was reserved for religious or philosophical poets, and it is no accident that many of the early works assume the form of altars, wings, and eggs. For that matter, even Mallarmé's *Un Coup de dés n'abolira jamais le hasard* (*A Throw of the Dice Will Never Abolish Chance*) is essentially restricted to the realm of metaphysical speculation. And though the Futurists freed visual poetry from these subjects, their own visual poems contain little that can properly be called lyrical. Mostly they chant the strident glories of technology, the city, and war, since women and love were banished from the Futurist program. Apollinaire, on the contrary, is an unabashed lyrical poet. In the calligrams, as elsewhere, he is skilled in the use of nuance and inflection. His relations with women form a constantly recurring leitmotif. Above all, he is a master of the personal statement and the intimate presentation. In short, had Apollinaire brought nothing else to visual poetry, his emphasis on lyric themes would have been enough to ensure him a place of honor in the history of the genre.

It is equally instructive to examine Apollinaire's choice of formal elements, for these too depart radically from the traditional norms. As he himself noted, the calligrams are more visually expressive than their antecedents. Though the reasons for this will become apparent as we progress, the flexibility and freshness of form is related to the new freedom of subject matter. Within the fairly rigid confines of the printer's art, the calligrams present an astonishing variety of shapes: from the simple lines of everyday objects to visual ballets of complicated counterpoint. Typically, the poems swirl into themselves, swoop into the air, or advance toward the reader. There is a surprising amount of movement, in direct opposition to traditional figurative poetry, which is entirely static. Margaret Davies explains the situation as follows:

> En prenant à l'art visuel ses moyens pour remplir l'espace, l'image risque de perdre de ses effets mobiles de transformations et de métamorphoses dans le temps. Elle tend à devenir statique, figée.
>
> Il me semble que l'évolution du calligramme démontre précisément les efforts qu'Apollinaire a déployés pour vaincre ce problème.

> In assuming visual art's means of filling space, the image risks losing its kinetic power of transformation and metamorphosis in time. It tends to become static, fixed.
>
> It seems to me that the calligram's evolution precisely demonstrates Apollinaire's efforts to overcome this problem.[7]

49

Aesthetics of visual poetry

Additional expressiveness is provided by the poem's distinctive texture. As P.-M. Adéma has pointed out, the photographic reproduction of calligrams in the poet's own handwriting was a major innovation. Previously limited by typographical possibilities, visual poetry was now free to expand and grow. Apollinaire's poems immediately acquire greater plasticity; his graphic notation becomes more supple and more subtle. It has also been suggested that the "imperfect" (handwritten) state of these poems reflects the antiliterary stance of the calligrams in general, which derive much of their inspiration from graffiti, posters, and so forth.[8] Certainly we are much more aware of Apollinaire's presence, of his personality, in the handwritten calligrams. There is a greater intimacy between the poet and the reader, who no longer have to communicate via the intermediary of typographical characters. By preserving the text in its original state, Apollinaire provides us with a visual record – often humorous or whimsical – of his hesitations and enthusiasms.

Mention should be made of another sort of texture that appears in figurative poetry for the first time and that is linguistic rather than visual. As Michel Décaudin remarks, "Apollinaire utilise avec la plus grande liberté non le vers, mais la phrase, le mot, voire la lettre seule" ("Apollinaire freely employs not verses but phrases, words, even individual letters").[9] Traditionally, visual poetry uses individual verses as its building blocks. Although Mallarmé's prismatic subdivisions of the Idea in *Un Coup de dés* and the telegraphic style of the Futurists prepared the way, Apollinaire was the first to apply this technique consistently to figurative verse. In part it corresponds to his growing insistence on the aesthetic, existential, and psychological function of artistic discontinuity as a reflection of modern experience.[10] But it is equally true that Apollinaire is guilty of deliberate obscurantism. By placing a number of stumbling blocks in the reader's way he forces him to *earn* the calligram by inscribing himself in the economy of the poem. In the process of decoding the visual and verbal message(s) the reader must participate in the structures of signification that govern the text. The act of reading thus replicates the original act of creation. In this, of course, Apollinaire belongs to a large group of modern writers and artists who require a participatory commitment from the reader-viewer. Indeed for Wolfgang Iser this principle is inseparable from modern cultural experience and its preoccupation with process.[11] From the foregoing it is clear that visual poetry seeks to revolutionize not only the concept of writing, but that of reading as well. This subject will be considered in more detail toward the end of the chapter.

Beginning with the Russian Formalist Victor Shklovsky's observation that "the entire history of scripts illustrates the struggle between ornamental and representational principles," Peter Mayer has constructed a visual typology that we shall adapt to our own purposes.[12] In a brief but cogent discussion of the ways in which language may acquire a visual dimension, he differentiates between "framed writing" and "shaped writing."

> (1) *Framed writing*, which has a longer history than shaped writing, consists of one or more words encompassed by a line drawing. The linguistic message is contained by the pictorial outline. Ardengo Soffici uses this device in *Al buffet della stazione* where the coffee machine and the newspaper are outlined in ink.

50

Apollinaire's plastic imagination

(2) *Shaped writing*, on the contrary, produces its own pictorial form without recourse to artistic aids. It consists entirely of linguistic elements and includes three sub-types.

(a) *Solid forms*, by far the most common type of figurative poetry in the West, are notable for their linguistic density. A solid body of words, the text consists of a vertical series of horizontal verses whose individual lengths are varied to produce pictorial contours without the aid of outline. The various eggs, altars, and wings of pre-modern visual poetry are all exercises in solid form, as well as Panard's and Rabelais' bottles. Assuming that Soffici's "Bicchier d'acqua" is meant to depict a glass of water, which seems likely, it belongs to this category.

(b) *Outlined forms* (both closed and open) are notable for their linguistic plasticity. Here the text is reduced to one or more lines that reproduce the contours of a given object. The closed forms tend to enclose large amounts of open space but may have a few additional words in their interior.

(c) *Distorted letters* derive their effect from their own plasticity. A calligraphic form *par excellence*, the shape of the work is determined by one or more individual letters which are distorted in a pictorial fashion. This type of shaped writing is widespread in Turkey and the Arabic countries. It is also common in advertising.

This classification, which is capable of providing a visual typology of the calligram, applies only to figurative poetry. It is of little use in analyzing works like the *parole in libertà*. To account for the visual acrobatics of the *analogia disegnata* we must add another category:

(d) *Dislocated letters* retain their normal typographical identity but operate independently in the linguistic sequence. Their significance derives from the difference that separates them from their fellows – whether in size or in placement on the page. Canguillo's expanding FUMARE [see Chapter 1] belongs to this category as does the vanishing *silenzio* in Soffici's "Bicchier d'acqua."

On the basis of this typology we can isolate yet another contribution by Apollinaire to the visual poetry tradition – one that was destined to have major implications. Whereas pre-Apollinarian figurative verse in the West utilizes either framed writing or solid forms (with very few exceptions), the early calligrams depend on outlined forms. If there are occasional flirtations with solid compositions, notably the *cravate* ("necktie") in "La Cravate et la montre" and the *figue* ("fig") in "La Figue l'oeillet et la pipe à opium," the overwhelming emphasis is on the newer genre. Not until 1915 does the solid form begin to gain ground, and even then Apollinaire continues to favor the other, probably because it more nearly approximates the experience of drawing. Initially, then, Apollinaire approaches visual poetry, not from the perspective of literary tradition, but from that of artistic tradition.

Aesthetics of visual poetry

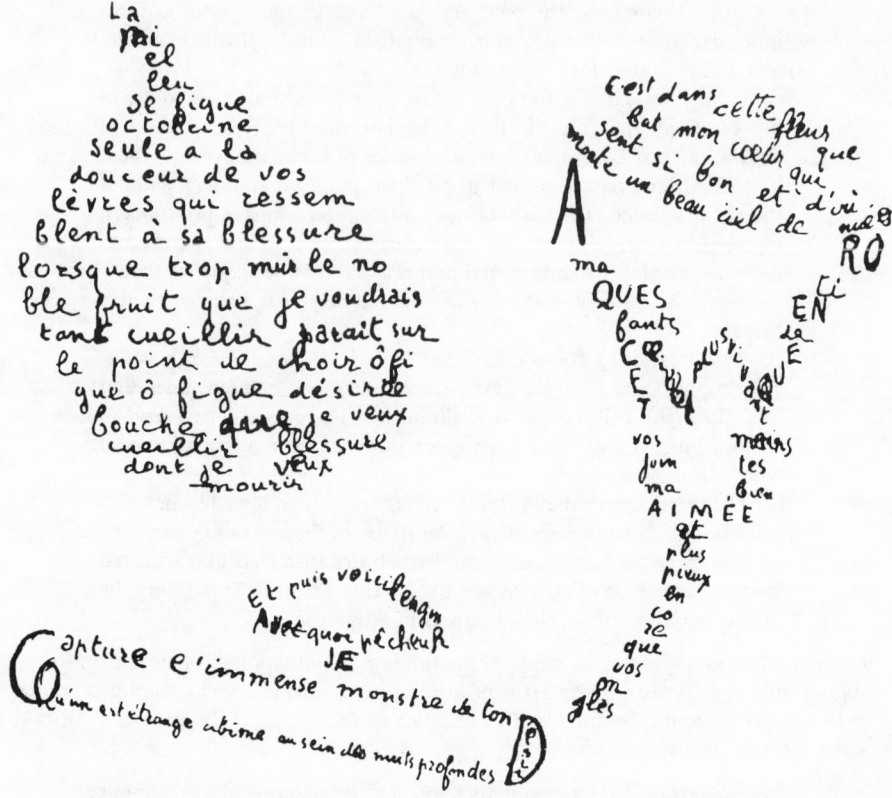

Figure 9. Guillaume Apollinaire, "La Figue l'oeillet et la pipe à opium"

Despite Bassy's claim, it is not true that Apollinaire used solid and outlined forms indiscriminately. On the contrary, he was well aware of their differences. The former emphasizes the volume, weight, or uniform texture of an object. The latter is often used neutrally to indicate contours and patterns but may also connote grace, delicacy, and fragility. For example, the *figue* is given a solid form, but the *oeillet* ("carnation") accompanying it is depicted in outline. Similarly, the solidity of the cannons and monuments (Eiffel Tower, Notre Dame, etc.) contrasts with the fragile outlines of the hearts and mirrors. The same differentiation of form may even exist within a single calligram. Thus Lou's *palmier* ("palm tree') has a solid trunk, but its delicate fronds are drawn in outline. At first glance the solid form of Léopold Survage's *lunettes* ("eye glasses") appears to contradict everything we have said, for their fragility can scarcely be questioned.[13] The answer seems to be that they are *dark* glasses, like those on the statue in Giorgio de Chirico's *Portrait of Guillaume Apollinaire*. The solid form merely indicates their opacity. This convention occurs in

Apollinaire's plastic imagination

Madeleine

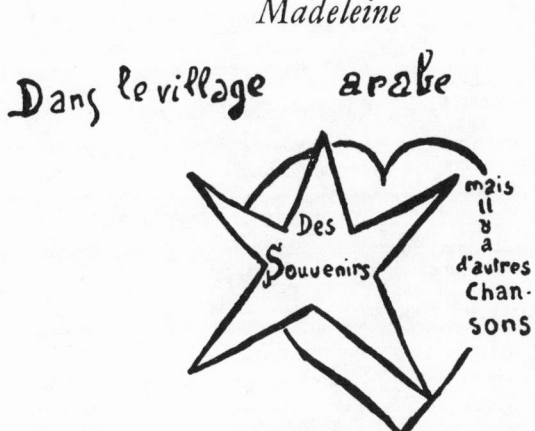

Figure 10. Guillaume Apollinaire, "Madeleine" (excerpt)

other calligrams, such as the *cravate* where it is meant to represent the solid color of an object (cf. Lou's dress in her portrait in "Poème du 9 février 1915," *PO*, p. 409).[14]

From what we have seen, the main lines of Apollinaire's calligrammatic development are clear. Beginning with outlined forms in 1914, he progresses to solid forms early in 1915. Shortly thereafter, in June 1915, he introduces two additional types of calligram in *Case d'armons*. The first, a sort of peripheral experiment, is identical to what Mayer calls framed writing. Deriving its shape from a line drawing, the framed calligram occurs in poems as diverse as "Madeleine," "Les Profondeurs" ("The Depths") (*Po*, p. 607), and "L'Horloge de demain" ("The Clock of Tomorrow") (*Po*, p. 682). The second, which has been called constructivist and expressionist, could also be termed futurist or abstract (by analogy with abstract art). Essentially a Futurist invention, this form consists of visual poetry employed in a nonpictorial manner. Its appropriation by Apollinaire eventually led to the creation of the name "*calligramme*."[15] Since his poetry was no longer purely figurative, Apollinaire decided to replace his original *idéogrammes lyriques* by a term emphasizing "beautiful writing." Rejecting such terms as *schématogramme* and *morphogramme* for the same reason, I have preferred to follow Apollinaire's usage.

Apollinaire describes the last major innovation in his reply to Fagus. Whereas traditional pictorial poetry consists of "figures uniques" ("solitary shapes"), his own poems contain multiple figures arranged in unified compositions. "Les rapports qu'il y a entre les figures juxtaposées d'un de mes poèmes," he says, "sont tout aussi expressifs que les mots qui le composent" ("The relations between the juxtaposed figures in one of my poems are as expressive as the words that compose it"). This is a truly revolutionary invention. Although "Lettre-Océan" is clearly indebted to the *parole in libertà*, there is surprisingly little Futurist influence in the rest of the

LA CRAVATE ET LA MONTRE

A Edouard Férut

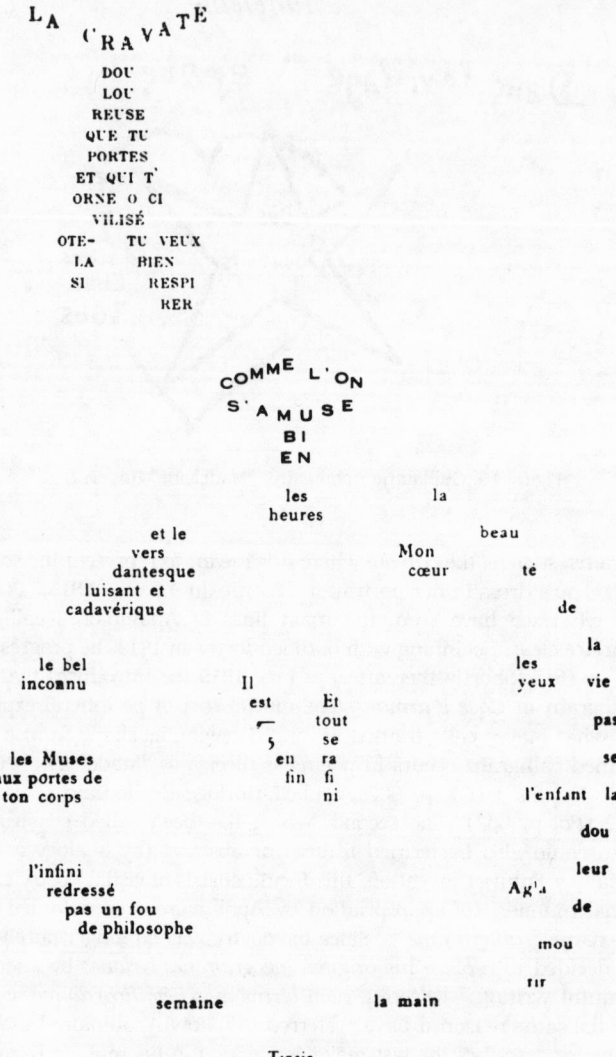

Figure 11. Guillaume Apollinaire

54

Apollinaire's plastic imagination

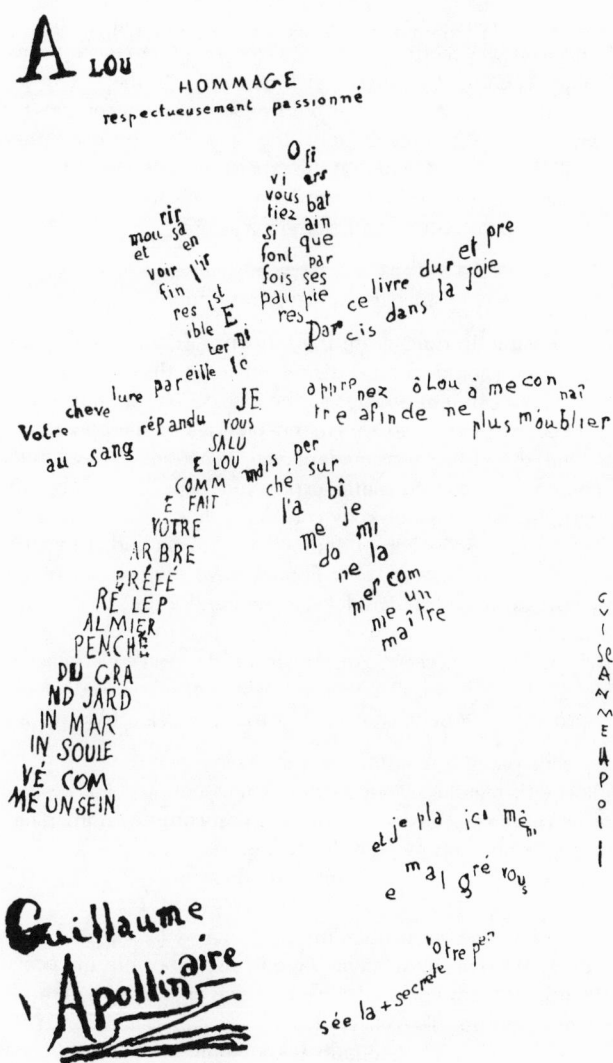

Figure 12. Guillaume Apollinaire

calligrams. To be sure, some of the abstract calligrams make use of the *analogia disegnata* (cf. "Du coton dans les oreilles," *Po*, p. 287), but this device is conspicuously absent from the initial examples published in *Les Soirées de Paris*. All of these, even "UN CIGARE allumé que fume" ("A LIGHTED CIGAR that is smoking") ("Paysage") (see Figure 15), represent a radical advance over the crude notation of the visual analogy. Contrasting the *parole in libertà* with the calligram in 1914, Gabriel Arbouin singled

Aesthetics of visual poetry

out the essential difference: "Devant de pareilles productions [futuristes], on restait encore indécis. Après la 'Lettre-Océan,' ce qui s'impose et l'emporte c'est l'aspect typographique, précisément *l'image*, soit *le dessin.*" ("In the face of similar Futurist efforts, one remained undecided. After 'Lettre-Océan,' what compels recognition and carries the day is the typographical appearance, precisely the *image*, the *drawing*"[my italics].)[16] Apollinaire did not abandon the experiments of "Lettre Océan," as has been charged; he refined them according to the dictates of the ideogram and painting. It was a question of aesthetic evolution rather than rejection.[17]

Ideogram, sign, and symbol

Although it is possible to exaggerate the influence of the Chinese ideogram on the calligram, this idea should not be dismissed altogether. As Ernest Fenollosa remarked in 1907, in a brilliant booklet on the ideogram and Chinese poetry, "Chinese notation . . . is based upon vivid shorthand pictures of the operations of nature."[18] This means that the entire written language functions as "concrete poetry" (the term is Fenollosa's). Ideogrammatic expression depends on the juxtaposition of several pictographic signs, which may combine to form a sentence or a single word. Moreover, "in the process of compounding, two things added together do not produce a third thing but *suggest some fundamental relation between them.* For example, the ideogram for a 'messmate' is a man and a fire" (my italics).[19] A similar principle would seem to be at work in the calligram, which Apollinaire tells us depends on "figures juxtaposées." And we recall the poet's insistence on the expressive function of the "rapports" between these figures. Indeed Bassy has demonstrated this process in "Coeur couronne et miroir" ("Heart Crown and Mirror").[20]

> Mon Coeur pareil à une flamme renversée
> Les Rois QUi MeuRent Tour A touR Renaissent au coeur des poèteS
> Dans ce miroir je suis enclos vivant et vrai comme on imagine
> les anges et non comme sont les reflets
>   Guillaume Apollinaire

> My Heart like an overturned flame
> The Kings WHo are DyiNg One By onE Are reborn in the poets' heartS
> In the mirror I am enclosed alive and real as one imagines
> the angels and not like reflections
>   Guillaume Apollinaire

Following the order specified in the title and the alchemical formula *formatio, reformatio, transformatio*, we witness Apollinaire's double metamorphosis. Bassy's indentification of the *mirror* as a mandorla (a halo surrounding the body) provides the key to the ideogrammatic code. *On the basis of the figures alone*, taken as pictographic symbols, the reader-viewer is able to discern the double progression (1) man→king→saint and (2) love→power→spirituality. We do not need the text to follow the progressive elevation of the poet-Apollinaire. Although the written message recapitulates and develops the visual message, specifying that it is a matter of apotheosis via poetic creation, the basic drama of transcendence is enacted visually.

Apollinaire's plastic imagination

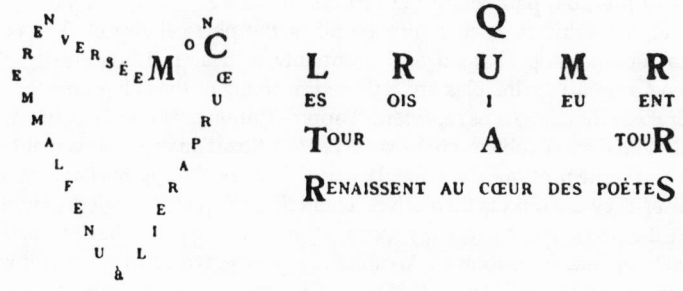

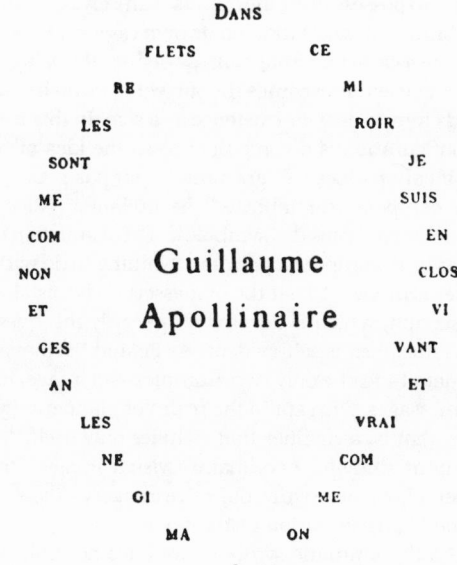

Figure 13. Guillaume Apollinaire, "Coeur couronne et miroir"

By establishing a visual hierarchy corresponding to an abstract system of values, Apollinaire suggests fundamental relations between the three categories. Using visual language, he makes a number of complex statements: (1) Mere brute existence is not enough; (2) transcendence of this state is possible; (3) transcendence of this state is desirable; (4) acquisition of power and prestige is an improvement but is not sufficient; (5) a saint is more valuable than a king; (6) the ultimate goal involves refinement and purification; and so on. Interestingly, the structure of "Coeur couronne et miroir" is identical to that of the Chinese sentence. Both depend on a linear series of pictograms. Take the notion of elevation, moreover, which is the major structural principle of Apollinaire's poem. In Chinese the sentence "the sun rises in the east" is rendered by three characters, each of which contains the sign for the sun. The astonishing thing is that as it passes from one character to the next, this

57

Aesthetics of visual poetry

sign *rises in position*, paralleling the process in nature.[21] In Apollinaire's poem the increase in the value of each figure parallels the physical rise of the poet: from village to mountaintop chateau and eventually to heaven. Undoubtedly, this and other ideogrammatic principles are reflected in many of the calligrams.

For Bassy the calligrams represent "l'appropriation poétique d'Apollinaire sur les choses. Ce sont d'autres objets, créés par le poète à titre d'analogon de la réalité, afin de permettre au verité poétique d'occuper l'espace" ("the poetic appropriation of things by Apollinaire. They are objects themselves, created by the poet as analogues with reality to permit the poetic word to occupy space").[22] In this connection he demonstrates the prominence of magic symbols in Apollinaire's poetry, where they are cultivated for their "pouvoir initiatique" ("initiatory power"). The power they confer on the poet, he declares, is superior to possession of the objects themselves. From this he concludes that the calligram constitutes a meditation on its own essence. Stressing its conceptual origins and its existence as a virtual image, Bassy defines the calligram as a pure signifier. Ceaselessly signifying itself, it becomes the subject of its own discourse. Unfortunately, his argument leads him to deny its existence as a *sign*. In this connection he postulates that the visual configuration is divorced (1) from the idea of representation and (2) from that of signification. "Les calligrammes n'ont pas pour fonction de représenter des objets ou de composer un tableau," he exclaims. "Rien à voir avec l'art du peintre. . . . Mais ce ne sont plus des symboles." ("The function of the calligrams is not to represent objects or to compose a painting. Nothing to do with the painter's art. . . . But neither are they symbols.") That the first assertion is mistaken will become evident in the following section, which is devoted to precisely this question. That the second proposition is also mistaken is self-evident. As Roland Barthes and Umberto Eco have demonstrated in detail – to cite only two examples – an image, indeed *any* image, contains a variety of messages.[23] Except in the realm of photography there is no such thing as a pure signifier, that is, a signifier that signifies only itself.[24] From this fact one deduces the necessity of studying Apollinaire's visual imagery from every conceivable angle. Symbol, metaphor, metonymy, objective imagery – these and other visual modes structure the reader's interpretation of the text.

Among the calligrammatic symbols, we have no difficulty in recognizing that the *couronne* symbolizes kingship, whereas the *coeur* is a time-honored symbol of love. Similarly, the *oeillet* is historically associated with the image of the Poet, which is why the Douanier Rousseau repainted his portrait of Apollinaire when he discovered he had included gillyflowers instead of carnations. And the *salamandre* in "Les Profondeurs" (*Po*, p. 607) is a perfect symbol of indestructability, for according to legend the salamander has the capacity to live in the midst of fire: "Cadence/ Cirque/Tout un monde neuf parait/Dans l'univers/Un peu plus animal mais + pur/le glace/le feu" ("Rhythm/Circus/A whole new world appears/In the universe/A little more animalistic but purer/ice/ fire"). In heraldry and Christian symbolism the salamander represents faith and courage.[25] Here it symbolizes France in particular and humanity in general, which, dragged into the infernal "depths" of the First World War, will emerge unscathed. Indeed this trial by fire will serve as a means of purification and renewal. Written in 1918, the poem is clearly prophetic.[26]

Even the swastika in "Coup d'éventail . . . " ("Rap of a Fan . . . ") (*Po*, p. 643), which is a magic token, functions as a symbol in the context of the poem. More

Apollinaire's plastic imagination

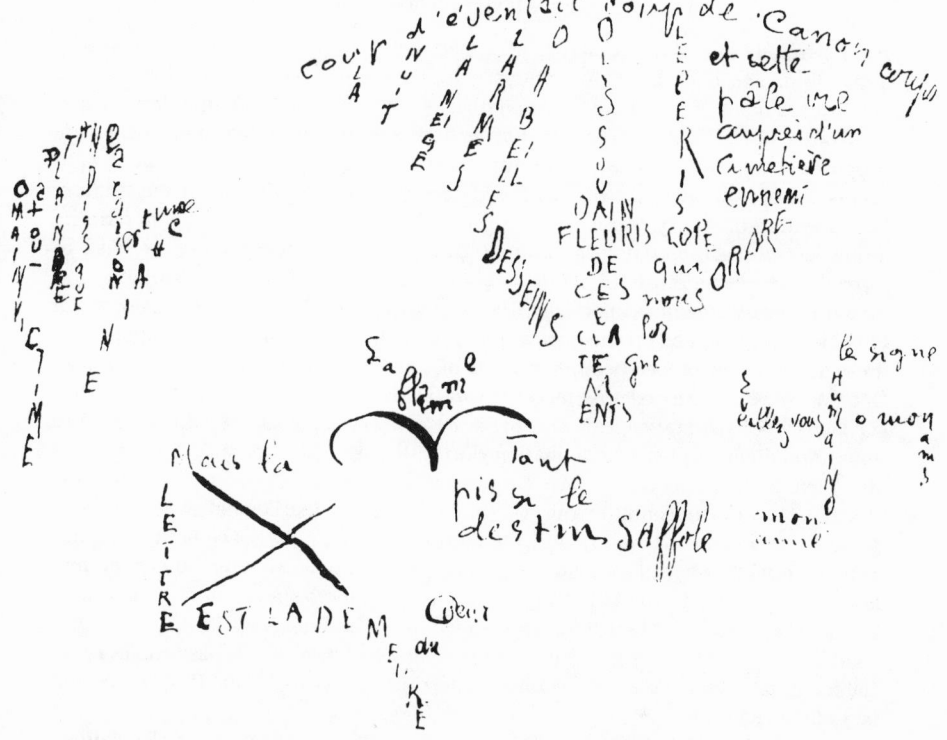

Figure 14. Guillaume Apollinaire, "Coup d'éventail"

precisely, it is magic token and symbol simultaneously. From the first point of view, the swastika (from Sanskrit: *su,* "well," and *asti,* "to be") is an extremely ancient good-luck charm. This accords with Apollinaire's comment to Jean-Yves Blanc, to whom the poem was addressed, that "le svastica marque la douceur bienheureuse" ("the swastika represents blissful happiness") (*Po,* p. 1144). Furthermore, this reading makes a certain amount of sense. As a magic charm the swastika protects Apollinaire from the dangers of the war, represented by the "coup de canon" ("cannon shot") and the "éclatements" ("bursts") of the *éventail.* However, its magic value is not much help in understanding the figure's verbal message: "EVEillez-vous O mon amie / le signe HUMAIN O mon amie" ("AWaken O my friend / the HUMAN sign O my friend"). The key to deciphering these lines lies in the swastika's *symbolic* value, for this figure is also a universal symbol of the sun.[27] Here it signals the coming of dawn, whose rosy hues banish the horrors of night warfare evoked in the *éventail.* The poem thus ends on a positive, even optimistic, note. The rising of the sun, marking the traditional hour of awakening, also seems to symbolize Apollinaire's faith in a radiant future for humanity. As such it makes an excellent "signe humain."

59

Aesthetics of visual poetry

Composition as explanation

If the symbolic role of the calligram is beyond doubt, the same is true of its status as a painting. For one thing, as various critics have commented, the influence of Cubism is evident everywhere.[28] For another, Apollinaire chose the title *Et moi aussi je suis peintre* (*I Too Am a Painter*) for his first collection of calligrams, which were supposed to appear in color. It is symptomatic, moreover, that all the initial calligrams (except "Il pleut") were composed according to the principle of the still life. First and foremost they consist of a number of related objects juxtaposed to form an aesthetic composition. There is nothing gratuitous in the process. On the basis of form and composition, each figure is chosen from among many possibilities and placed in a predetermined position. The emphasis is on the visual relations between the objects as much as on the objects themselves. In good cubist fashion Apollinaire drops the illusion of perspective in favor of total sensory awareness of the whole. Once we have recognized this fact, we can divide the calligrams into (1) still lifes, (2) landscapes (or cityscapes), and (3) portraits. These categories will continue to shape Apollinaire's plastic imagination during the next four years. In 1914 the still lifes include such poems as "La Cravate et la montre" ("The Necktie and the Watch"), "Coeur couronne et miroir," and "La Mandoline l'oeillet et le bambou" ("The Mandolin the Carnation and the Bamboo") (*Po*, p. 209). The notion of landscape governs "Voyage" (see Figure 18, Chapter 4), in which a train "meurt au loin dans les vals et les beaux bois frais" ("dies away in the distance among the valleys and the cool woods"), "Lettre-Océan" (a cityscape), and not surprisingly "Paysage." Finally, as an example of portraiture, "Montparnasse" (*Po*, p. 736) assembles seven characters in a group portrait against a backdrop including Victor Hugo's tree and the Café du Rotonde.

Pierre Albert-Birot (the director of *SIC*) and others have occasionally claimed that Apollinaire did not care about the appearance of his calligrams.[29] The manuscripts, proofs, and printed poems all reveal, however, that he went to great lengths to obtain the perfect composition. Significantly, Albert-Birot's experience was limited to "Il pleut" ("It's Raining") – the only calligram to appear in *SIC* – whose typographical realization was a masterpiece. Even the epistolary calligrams, which were written hastily and under trying conditions, demonstrate surprising aesthetic coherence. In "Coup d'éventail . . . ", for example, the *main* ("hand") on the left is balanced by the swastika's "signe HU*MAIN*" on the right. In turn, the square form of the swastika recurs in the *lettre*, which bills itself as "LA DEMEURE du Coeur" ("THE RESIDENCE of the Heart"). Directly above this last word is the outline of the top of a heart. In form and orientation it corresponds to the much larger *éventail*. Thus several forms are balanced against each other to produce a pleasing composition. Among the earlier calligrams, the figures in "Paysage" are related by a different principle but are every bit as coherent. Apparently consisting of four unrelated images, "Paysage" bears an astonishing resemblance to Fernand Léger's *Les Fumeurs* (*The Smokers*) (1911), which juxtaposes precisely the same four elements. In the foreground we see a man smoking a cigar (or possibly a pipe), enveloped in clouds of smoke. The background consists of houses and small trees. Moreover, according to the conventions of painting, three-dimensional distance is

60

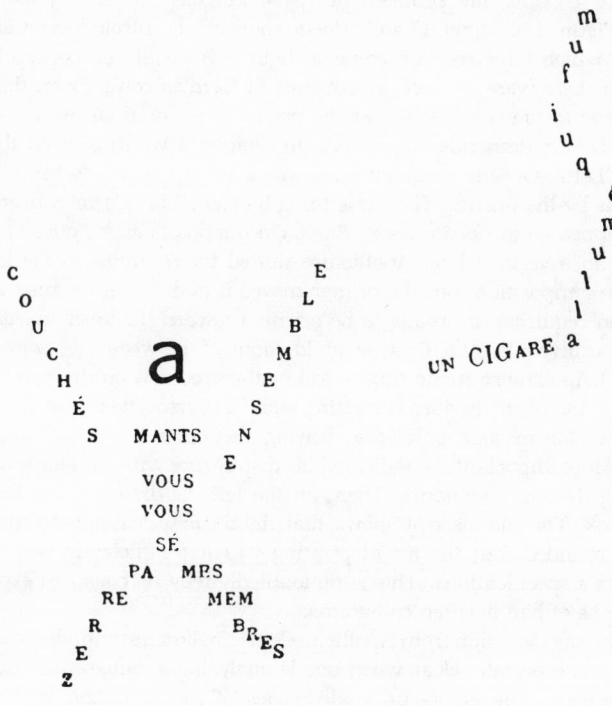

Figure 15. Guillaume Apollinaire, "Paysage"

Aesthetics of visual poetry

rendered as height on the canvas. The background occupies the top half of the picture, the foreground the bottom half–exactly as in "Paysage." Whether or not the calligram reflects Léger's influence (Apollinaire singles out *Les Fumeurs* for praise in *Les Peintres cubistes*), it was clearly composed according to the principle of the landscape.[30] Utilizing the insights of Roman Jakobson, we can identify this principle as visual metonymy (which depends on contiguity). "Coup d'éventail. . ." on the other hand, was constructed according to the principle of metaphor (which depends on similarity). Note that we are speaking only of the visual relations among the various figures. Clearly, our understanding of the calligram would benefit from an art historian's systematic analysis. What, for example, are the compositional structures of modern painting? How are these related to those of the calligram? Is the number 3, so prominent in the early poems, favored by any of Apollinaire's artist friends? What about the principle of triangular composition governing works like "Coeur couronne et miroir"?[31]

Although answers to these questions are slow in coming, one can observe Apollinaire tackling the problem of visual language in such poems as "Lettre-Océan" (Figure 1, Chapter 1) and "Coeur couronne et miroir," the manuscripts and proofs of which have recently come to light.[32] From plastic conception to plastic expression there were numerous problems of form to solve. From the composition on the page to the composition at the printer's, the original inspiration was often modified by the demands of printing. In Chapter 1 we discovered that the letters **T S F** in "Lettre-Océan," originally situated between the two "wheels," were shifted to one side by the printer. The same thing happened to "Coeur couronne et miroir" when it appeared in *Les Soirées de Paris*. On the proofs each figure appeared under the other in a vertical line. Apollinaire shifted the *couronne* to the left to make a triangular composition, but the printer moved it to the right because of the printing convention requiring an image to be oriented toward the inner margin. (A similar reversal occurred in "La Cravate et la Montre" between *Les Soirées* and *Calligrammes*.) Apollinaire made three additional corrections on the proofs, all of them concerning the *coeur*. Besides correcting a spelling error, he changed the preposition "A" to "à" for reasons of clarity, leaving the other letters as capitals or small capitals. More important, he indicated his displeasure with the shape of the heart by redrawing its upper contours. Then, on the left, he drew a heart to show how it should look. The manuscript shows that the *coeur* was supposed to be fatter and perfectly rounded, but the art of printing was not sufficiently developed to meet Apollinaire's specifications. This is undoubtedly why he began to experiment with photographs of handwritten calligrams.

That any deviation from Apollinaire's original manuscript distorts the meaning of a poem is especially clear when one is analyzing a calligram's visual configurations. Moreover, the errors or inadequacies of interpretation by printers in *Les Soirées* and *Calligrammes* have been compounded by successive generations of editors. Partly this is due to the limitations of photography. Even in the *Oeuvres poétiques*, "La Mandoline l'oeillet et le bambou" (*Po*, p. 209) contains three serious errors. Two of these occur in the line "ô batailles la terre trembla comme une ma doline." In the original manuscript it reads, "ô batailles la terre tremble comme une mandoline" ("o battles the earth trembles like a mandolin").[33] The third letter of "mandoline"

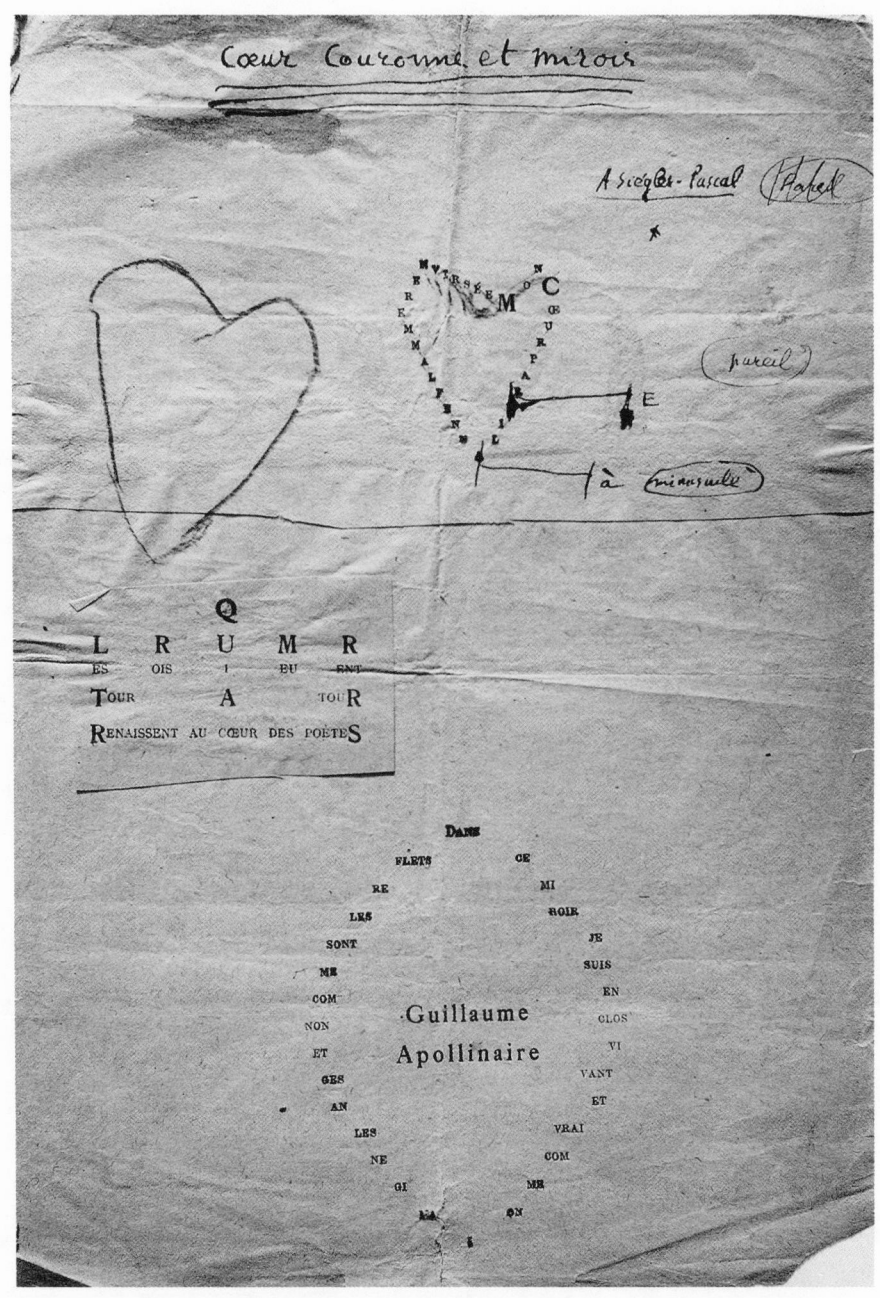

Figure 16. Guillaume Apollinaire, corrected proofs of "Coeur couronne et miroir"

was not picked up by the photoengraving process because it was too faint. The third error concerns the triangular composition of the calligram, which should be rotated clockwise some 30 degrees until the *oeillet* is vertical. Thus the focus of the composition changes from the *bambou*, which is no longer its base, to the carnation, which represents its vertical axis. As the hypotenuse of a right triangle, it quite properly sums up (synthesizes) the other two sides – visually and textually.

That such a distortion can have serious repercussions is demonstrated by Bassy's reading of "Coeur couronne et miroir," based on the poem's shape. In *Calligrammes* (1918) and in the *Oeuvres poétiques* it forms a triangle oriented toward the bottom of the page. From this Bassy deduces that it is a magic sign or *pantacle*, derives the formula *formatio, reformatio, transformatio*, and applies it to this and other calligrams. As we have seen, however, the original version in *Les Soirées* faces a different direction. Furthermore, it and subsequent versions are isosceles triangles, whereas the triangular *pantacle* cited by Bassy is equilateral. Either of these discrepancies is enough to discredit his theory. Fortunately (and unexpectedly), the manuscript comes to his rescue. As originally conceived, the figures do indeed form an equilateral triangle pointing toward the bottom of the page. Unlike the version in *Calligrammes*, the *miroir* is centered perfectly on the other two forms. The 1918 version thus represents an attempt by Apollinaire to restore the poem to its original shape. The manuscript also reveals that the small capitals were supposed to be lower-case letters and that the *coeur* was to read, "Mon Coeur pareil *à une* flamme renversée." The invention of the small capitals was apparently yet another distortion by the printer.

Theory and practice

It remains to relate Apollinaire's plastic imagination to the theory and practice of simultanism, for there is little doubt that the visual poetry grew out of the same background as "Les Fenêtres" and "Lundi rue Christine." Despite obvious differences, the *calligramme*, the *poème simultané*, and the *poème-conversation* embody the same basic concept. This is what Apollinaire himself says in "Simultanisme-Librettisme." It is no accident, moreover, that the article appeared in the same issue of *Les Soirées de Paris* as "Lettre-Océan" (June 15, 1914). Just as the calligram illustrates some of the premises of the article, the latter provides a theoretical context for the poem.[34] In this capacity it functions as a *défense et illustration* of the calligram in general:

> On a donné ici des poèmes où cette simultanéité existait dans *l'esprit* et dans *la lettre même* puisqu'il est impossible de les lire sans concevoir immédiatement la simultanéité de ce qu'ils expriment, poèmes-conversation où le poète au centre de la vie enregistre en quelque sorte le lyrisme ambiant.
>
> Et même *l'impression* de ces poèmes est plus simultanée que la notation successive de M. Barzun.
>
> C'est ainsi que si on a tenté (*L'Enchanteur pourrissant*, "Vendémiaire," "Les Fenêtres," etc.) d'habituer *l'esprit* à concevoir un poème simultanément comme une scène de la vie, Blaise Cendrars et Mme Delaunay-Terck ont fait une première tentative de simultanéité écrite

Apollinaire's plastic imagination

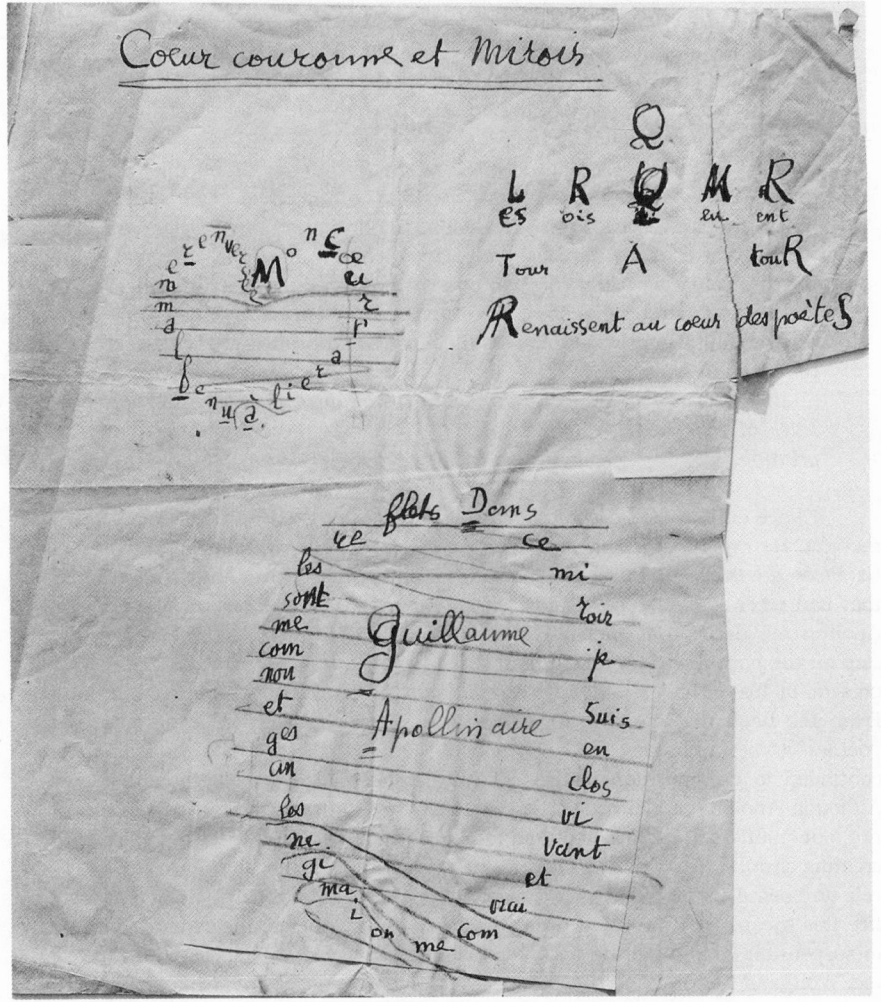

Figure 17. Guillaume Apollinaire, manuscript of "Coeur couronne et miroir"

où des contrastes de couleurs habituaient *l'oeil* à lire d'un seul regard l'ensemble d'un poème, comme un chef d'orchestra lit d'un seul coup les notes superposées dans la partition, comme on voit d'un seul coup les éléments plastiques et imprimés d'une affiche. . . .

Ici même, après s'être efforcé de simultanéiser *l'esprit* et *la lettre* des poèmes . . . on s'efforcera aussi de faire faire un pas à cette question de *l'impression* nouvelle.

Aesthetics of visual poetry

I have presented here poems where simultaneity existed in *spirit* and in *the letter* since it is impossible to read them without immediately conceiving the simultaneity they express, conversation-poems in which the poet at the center of life records, so to speak, the surrounding lyricism.

And even the *printing* of these poems is more simultaneous than M. Barzun's successive notation.

Thus I have tried (with *The Putrescent Enchanter*, "Vendémiaire," "The Windows," etc.) to accustom *the mind* to conceive a poem simultaneously like a scene from life, Blaise Cendrars and Mme Delaunay-Terck have made a first attempt at written simultaneity where contrasting colors accustomed *the eye* to read a whole poem with a single glance, as an orchestra conductor reads the different ranks of notes in a score simultaneously, as one sees the plastic and printed elements of a poster all at once. . . .

In these very pages, after trying to simultanize *the spirit* and *the letter* of the poems . . . I will also try to tackle the question of new *printing*.

I have emphasized certain words here to show the evolution of Apollinaire's thought. He explains that, in inventing the calligram, he was following the lead of *La Prose du transsibérien*, a collaborative effort by Cendrars and Sonia Delaunay that had recently combined visual ("simultanéité écrite") and textual simultanism. Apollinaire's decision to appeal to the eye as well as to the mind was a necessary step on the path toward total simultanism. Significantly, these two tendencies were present in his earliest simultanist experiments, although in different proportions. From the beginning his twin goals were to "simutanéiser l'esprit et la lettre des poèmes" ("to simultanize the spirit and the letter of the poems"). As long as he continued to use traditional forms, it was impossible to achieve the latter goal. Although Apollinaire claimed to have partially simultanized the printing (by omitting punctuation?), the lines still had to be read successively. Of necessity the role of creating simultaneity was relegated to the mind, which could be trained to "concevoir un poème simultanément" ("conceive a poem simultaneously"). In actual practice this means that the mind proceeds cumulatively, holding the various elements in suspension while ordering and reordering them in a continual search for meaning. Wolfgang Iser describes the process as follows: "We look forward, we look back, we decide, we change our decisions, we form expectations, we are shocked by their nonfulfillment, we question, we muse, we accept, we reject; this is the dynamic process of recreation."[35] The reader thus relies on the process of anticipation and retrospection to guide the search for a consistent interpretation. Only at the conclusion of the poem do the various semantic elements coalesce to form a conceptual gestalt, according to the patterns of expectation that have accumulated. Textual simultanism is thus an a posteriori process. It differs in degree rather than in kind from traditional operations involved in reading. By contrast visual simultanism relies on an a priori process.

In developing the calligram Apollinaire was finally able to realize a long-standing dream: to simultanize the letter of his poetry. For the first time the

66

Apollinaire's plastic imagination

printing was truly simultaneous. But though the visual configuration could be apprehended instantly, the lines of poetry still had to be deciphered one by one. If anything, the process of reading was more time-consuming than before. Not surprisingly, a number of critics have been disturbed by the seeming contradiction here. Bassy has gone so far as to deny that the calligrams possess any simultaneity at all.[36] How, indeed, are we to resolve the persistent conflict between the verbal and the visual elements? Does not the "long temps de difficile déchiffrement" ("long period of difficult deciphering") (M.-J. Durry) automatically preclude any sort of meaningful simultanism? The answer seems, in fact, to be no – no more than it does in the *poème simultané*, which is often just as tortuous. Moreover, the verbal–visual "conflict" proves to be illusory, for in reality *simultanism does not depend on immediate comprehension.*[37] At least this is true of total simultanism, which we define as the fusion of visual and textual simultanism. We can envisage the process of reading a calligram as follows. (1) The reader perceives the visual form(s) and extracts one or more visual messages instantaneously. (2) Retaining these in his mind, he submits the text to the operations outlined above. The dialectics of this process, however, are considerably more complex than in the *poème simultané*. There is a constant dialogue between the various elements on three different levels: visual–visual, visual–textual, and textual–textual. Like simultaneous poetry, the calligram is largely a poetry of conceptualization. Most of the images are formed in the mind's eye rather than on the page. Unlike simultaneous poetry, the calligram is also a poetry of visualization. Among other things, its visual dimension gives it greater immediacy and greater impact than in traditional poetry and provides a richer reading experience. The absence of linguistic mediation not only frees the reader from the constraints of discursive logic; it encourages us to experience the visual forms *as form.*

As noted previously, visual poetry seeks to alter our concept of reading as well as of writing. In its role as a dual sign it forces us to *look* at the text before we read it, that is, to acknowledge its physical authority. By calling attention to its physical premises, visual poetry insists on the autonomy of the text, on its integrity as an expressive form. And just as the existence of visual poetry makes it impossible to ignore the physical appearance of the text, it prevents us from regarding the text as a transparent vehicle for a larger message. Reading is no longer conceived as a mechanical operation performed on a passive text, but is seen to be a series of interpretive acts designed to overcome the resistance of the written word. For Iser the production of meaning in a literary work is a function of the dialectical structure of reading. Pursuing a strategy of defamiliarization, the text challenges the reader's norms and expectations in order to trigger the imagination.[38] This process is governed in particular by the principle of indeterminacy, which manifests itself in contradictions, negations, and blanks. Visual poetry, with its emphasis on fragmentation and spatial forms, seeks to provide just such a reading experience. "Lettre-Océan" is an especially good example, but this is true of all the calligrams.

In every case the reader is shocked and disoriented by their physical appearance, which defies traditional literary values. Conceived as discontinuous exercises, the calligrams are spread out against the page like pieces of a jigsaw puzzle. Exposed for all to see, their verbal blanks are made manifest at the visual level,

67

Aesthetics of visual poetry

where they are finally concretized. These indeterminacies play a key role in the production of meaning in both the visual and the verbal text. In ascertaining the former the reader takes his cue from the physical gaps that shape letters into words, words into figures, and figures into larger configurations. In deducing the latter he struggles to overcome the physical barriers of the text that impede verbal signification. These difficulties make the reader conscious of the reading process itself, which Iser identifies as the ultimate literary experience. The final gestalt depends heavily on the spatialization of the text. On the one hand, the visual shapes focus the imagination, specifying the shape, style, and perspective of the primary object. To the extent that the visual component dominates the text, the latter can be said to have a concrete gestalt. On the other hand, the shapes activate the reader's imagination, which, as its etymology attests, is a highly visual phenomenon. Functioning as visual stimuli, they encourage the reader to create a series of mental images and to relate them to those of the text. Ultimately, the calligrams speak to consciousness itself, the operations of which call for the articulation of the Image.

4

Toward a calligrammar

The previous chapter examined the calligram from the reader's perspective and studied its innovative visual effects. The present chapter analyzes the calligram from the inside out. By focusing on the figurative examples – Apollinaire's chief contribution to the visual tradition – it attempts to establish the parameters of his art and to expose the foundations of the creative process. As we dissect the verbal and visual images one by one, we will observe this process in action. In a picture-poem the network of action, reaction, and interaction is far more complex than in traditional poetry. Instead of the linear relationships typical of the latter form, the various components form a three-dimensional structure. We have seen previously that relationships exist (1) between visual and nonvisual images (visual–textual), (2) between visual images (visual–visual), and (3) between nonvisual images (textual–textual). In seeking to determine the relational structures governing Apollinaire's imagination, the analysis here will draw heavily on Roman Jakobson's study of the two polar figures of speech: metaphor and metonymy.[1]

As Jakobson demonstrated, human discourse is invariably either metaphoric or metonymic (or a combination of the two). The development of discourse takes place along two different semantic lines: One topic may lead to another through *similarity* ("the metaphoric way") or through *contiguity* ("the metonymic way"). Thus in a series a given topic/statement/image must either resemble its neighbor or be associated with it in some manner. These are the two basic modes of communication. That metonymy plays an important part in Soffici's *Al buffet della stazione* (Figure 5, chapter 2) is easy to demonstrate. An inventory of its elements reveals that many of them are related by physical contiguity. The same is true of Carrà's two works, the metonymic bias of which is quite marked. In all three, bits of conversation, objects, and posters correspond to a specific setting whose boundaries determine what is to be included. Each poem reflects its physical surrounding and creates a unified context. In the cafe texts, for example, the coffee machine, cigarette butts, and newspapers all belong to the code "cafe." In *Festa patriottica* (Figure 2, Chapter 1) the flags, crowds, and band music situate the work in a public square and establish its patriotic premise. In their role as metonymic signs these elements serve to naturalize the text, to establish its *vraisemblance*. "Lettre-Océan" is even more metonymic, although the type of contiguity involved varies from section to section. Even "Bicchier d'acqua" (Figure 4, Chapter 2), which is primarily metaphoric, is structured by a metonymic series of colors positioned in the text according to their physical contiguity in the spectrum. At the same time examples of metaphor abound in these works, from the

Aesthetics of visual poetry

"naufrago" ("castaway") in Soffici's cafe to the posters that "scream" back at the crowd in *Festa patriottica*. On the visual plane we can cite Apollinaire's keyring, which is related to the political slogans of which it is composed according to the principle of similarity. Jakobson himself notes that a competition between metaphor and metonymy is manifest in any symbolic process. Usually one mode predominates (poetry is inherently metaphoric, prose is essentially metonymic), but this varies according to period and style. Cubist painting is highly metonymic. Since the calligram combines cubism with lyric poetry, it will be interesting to see which form triumphs, to what degree it is dominant, and under what circumstances.

At the start we should note that there are 133 figurative calligrams extant. These are combined in various fashions to form a total of 52 poems, varying from the extremely simple to the extremely complex.[2] This means that almost all the calligrams are part of a group. In fact there are only 11 free-standing images in the entire collection. Apollinaire clearly wanted us to view his calligrams in terms of a broader context, not as isolated phenomena. Of the 52 poems, 36 are purely figurative, 14 are mixed (visual and nonvisual), and 2 can be classified either way.[3] Most of the mixed poems were written at the front in 1915 and doubled as letters, accounting for half the figurative poetry that year. These were exceptional circumstances, however, and the pure form is clearly the norm. With one exception the poems can be dated without much difficulty. "L'Oiseau et le bouquet" belongs to the 1916–18 period, but the exact year is unknown. The general history of the calligram is illustrated by the table below. A "poem" may be either a single calligram or a group of calligrams. By "calligram" I mean any combination of words and figurative elements forming a distinct picture.

	1914	1915	1916	1917	1918	NO DATE	TOTAL
Poems	16	18	6	8	3	1	52
Calligrams	46	48	12	19	6	2	133

The rise of the calligram was limited to the first two years, as the table shows, and its fall occupied the last three. The pioneering achievements of 1914 were consolidated, quantitatively and qualitatively, by the developments of 1915. But beginning in 1916, following his lengthy convalescence from a head wound, Apollinaire began to direct his attention elsewhere. Although he continued to dabble with the calligram from time to time, his initial enthusiasm had abated.

The verbal foundation

Since the calligrams have usually been viewed with mistrust, there has never been a systematic survey of their visual imagery, though generalizations abound.[4] One school of thought holds that the picture represents the primary verbal metaphor. Thus we read that "in figured verse the shape of the poem is the main metaphor of the poem."[5] Another believes that it represents the tenor of the primary metaphor so that "gramma et schéma ont le même point de départ – non l'object métaphorique

70

Toward a calligrammar

mais le support de la métaphore" ("gramma and schema have the same point of departure – not the metaphoric vehicle but the tenor of the metaphor").[6] This appears to be the position of Francois Rigolot, who claims that the calligram depends on a "motivation analogique des signifiants" ("analogical motivation of the signifiers") that removes it from the realm of communication and increases its ludic value.[7] Yet another school asserts that the poem's shape represents the primary object described in the poem. This is Michel Foucault's position: The text repeats the drawing, which depicts what the text says. For him the calligram's distinctive feature is the tautological relationship uniting verbal and visual images.[8] Unfortunately, as we shall see, things are not quite so simple. For one thing, much of the poetry does not employ metaphor at all. For another, many of the visual images do not recur in the verbal text. In a recent issue of *Poétique* Jean Gérard Lapacherie argues that the specific property of the calligram is, in fact, its semantic plurality (*polysémie*), [9] which can never be grasped by the reductive approaches mentioned previously. In attempting to describe the calligram's complex mechanisms, we shall take this statement as our guide.

The notion of a primary verbal image in general would seem to reflect one of two possible ideas: either greater functional value or greater positional value. The first definition gives the following results:

CALLIGRAMS	VISUAL IMAGE
43	Duplicates the most important verbal image
37	Duplicates a verbal image of average importance
2	Duplicates a verbal image of less importance
51	Duplicates no verbal image whatsoever
133	

The second definition applies to the very first image in the poem, regardless of its linguistic function. Eliminating pronouns, the visual image duplicates the initial verbal image in only fifty-nine calligrams (four of which consist of a single image). Almost all of these belong to the 1914–15 period. If the verbal–visual relationship is extended to include various associations, in addition to duplication, the count rises to sixty-four in the first case and eighty-five in the second. In short, although there is a tendency toward visualization of the initial and/or most important image, especially during the first two years, the concept of the primary verbal image does not adequately describe the calligrammatic process.

The same holds true for generalizations about metaphor – the tenor–vehicle structure of which can also be applied to the metonymic couple. In theory the two terms are interchangeable: If *A* equals *B*, then *B* must equal *A*. In practice it is usually possible to determine which term is the source of the other. Alain-Marie Bassy differentiates between them on the basis of *comparant* versus *comparé* (comparer versus compared). The same distinction exists between subject and object. Take the calligram of the night sky in "Voyage," for example: "La douce nuit lunaire

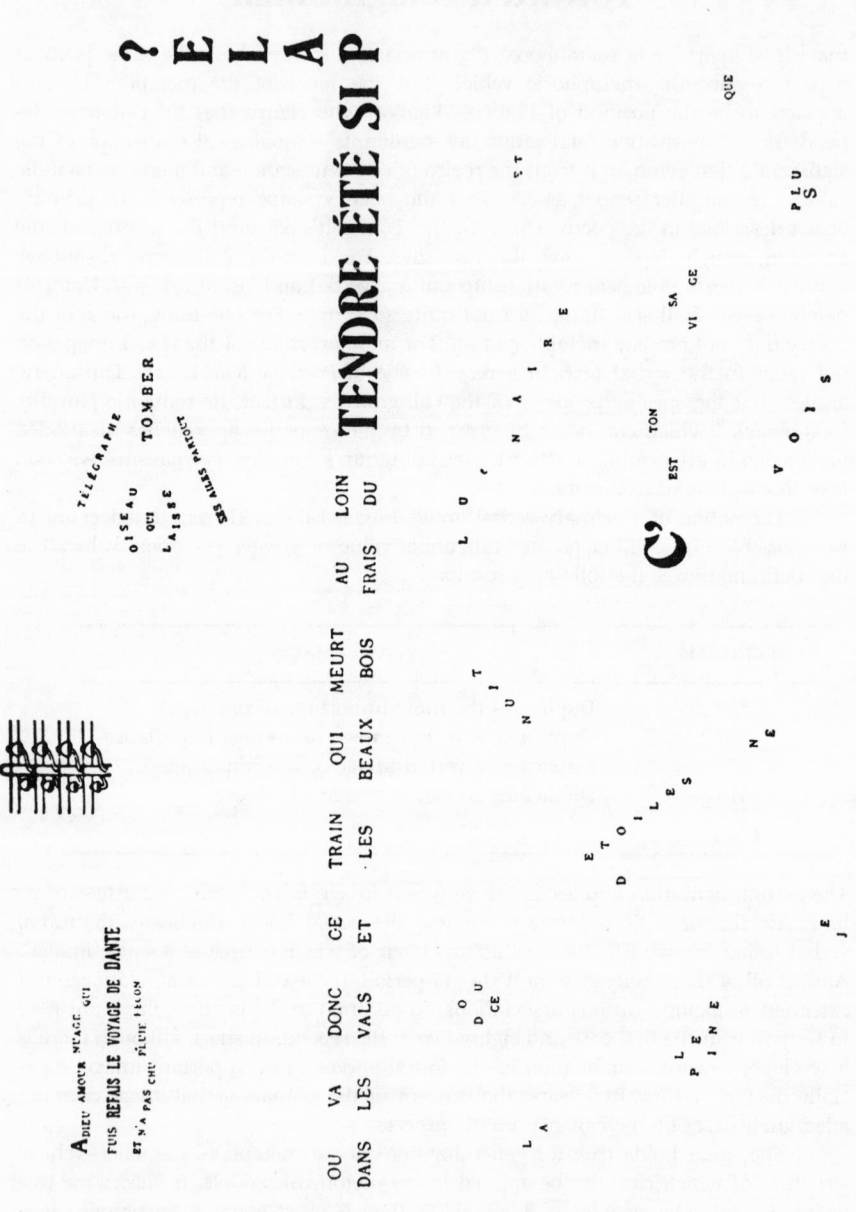

Figure 18. Guillaume Apollinaire, "Voyage"

Toward a calligrammar

et pleine d'étoiles C'est ton visage que je ne vois plus" ("The gentle lunar evening filled with stars is your face which I no longer see"). Marie Laurencin's face is clearly the subject of the comparison (tenor), whereas the sky is the object (vehicle). Apollinaire has simply reversed the terms. Of the eighty-two cases in which the visual image repeats a verbal image, 56 percent involve verbal metaphors, and 39 percent verbal metonyms. There does not seem to be any significant difference between tenors and vehicles, as the following table shows:

VERBAL METAPHOR		VERBAL METONYM		ISOLATED
TENOR	VEHICLE	TENOR	VEHICLE	IMAGE
13	33	16	16	4

Although Apollinaire exhibits a preference for metaphoric vehicles, which account for 40 percent of the visual imagery, he frequently ventures into the other three areas as well. The absence of a linguistic monopoly here is significant. It means that the calligrams cannot be reduced to a simple formula, as some critics would like to believe. A slightly different distribution characterizes the fifty-one cases in which the visual image does *not* duplicate a verbal image:

VERBAL METAPHOR		VERBAL METONYM		ISOLATED
TENOR	VEHICLE	TENOR	VEHICLE	IMAGE
7	2	20	15	7

Once again there is no significant variation between tenor and vehicle. In contrast to the metaphoric preference of the first group, there is a marked metonymic bias here (69 percent), peaking in 1915. From this we can infer the existence of two polar tendencies in the calligrams. On the one hand, there is a tightly structured body of poetry organized around the principle of resemblance. On the other, there is a group of loosely structured poems that depend on the principle of association. Between these two extremes lie an infinite number of poetic possibilities.

Of the sixty-seven verbal metonyms anchoring the visual image to the linguistic text, twenty-six are extended metonyms and three are implicit metonyms (e.g., the heart in "De toi depuis longtemps," *Po*, p. 413). Among the fifty-five metaphoric anchors there are six similes, nine extended metaphors, and thirteen implicit metaphors. Apollinaire clearly prefers concise metaphoric statements of identity to diffuse comparisons. Although metaphoric tenors and vehicles normally share a given characteristic, a few exploit similar functions (like the ring of keys in "Lettre-Océan") (Figure 1, Chapter 1) or physical resemblance (like the heart in "Coeur couronne et miroir") (Figure 13, Chapter 3). And although most of the metonymic couples depend on physical proximity, several additional types of contiguity are evident. For example,

Aesthetics of visual poetry

"Lettre-Océan" and "La Petite Auto"(*Po*, p. 208) exploit temporal proximity. In the former, actions and images are simultaneous; in the latter they are sequential. Some poems, including "Lettre-Océan," also contain examples of psychological proximity in which the poet's memories, thoughts, and sensory impressions are recorded in their original contiguity. Other metonyms are functional in nature (e.g., the bottle in "Montparnasse," *Po*, p. 736), and still others rely on categorical proximity. Evolving from genus to species, the carnation in "La Figue l'oeillet et la pipe" (Figure 9, Chapter 3) begins as a "fleur" and ends as an "oeillet" ("carnation"). In the letter to Lou dated June 21, 1915 (*Po*. p. 479), the ivy proceeds in the opposite direction: "Lierre herbe de la fidelité / Lierre herbe de la tendresse" ("Ivy plant of fidelity / Ivy plant of tenderness"). But the most unusual form of metonymy is that existing between cause and effect. The rarest form as well, it is illustrated by the marvelous little man with widespread arms and legs in "Paysage" (Figure 15, Chapter 3): "Amants couchés ensemble vous vous séparerez mes membres" ("Lovers sleeping together my members you will separate yourselves"). Properly speaking, this calligram belongs to a subtype based on stimulus and response.[10]

Although a detailed study of the verbal imagery cannot be undertaken here, two-thirds of the calligrams contain three or more verbal images. Most of these (fifty-one poems) are grouped according to a mixture of metaphor and metonymy, although there are twenty-six purely metonymic and twelve purely metaphoric poems. From a compositional standpoint, the mixed form is generally more viable than the pure. The metonymic strain is normally too amorphous, the metaphoric strain too rigid. The hybrid variety permits a high degree of expressiveness, yet gives Apollinaire enough flexibility to follow the various strands of his inspiration. Two structures are worthy of note – one circular, the other linear. The first involves an excellent means of reinforcing primary imagery. It is present in the *bouteille* (*"bottle"*): "Petite bouteille où Monsieur Baty conserve l'antique nectar" ("Little bottle in which Monsieur Baty keeps the ancient nectar") (*Po*. p. 736). And in the oranges in "Poème du 9 février 1915" (*Po*, P. 409): "Les oranges de Baratier sont les meilleurs de la France. Elles ont la saveur de ta chair chaude comme le soleil semblable à ces oranges." ("Baratier oranges are the best in France. They taste like your flesh hot as the sun which resembles these oranges.")

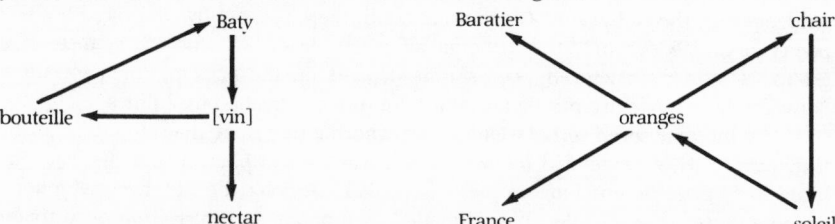

In the first poem the implicit metaphor "nectar" – or rather its tenor "vin" – is paired metonymically with the other two images. Generated by the second term, it refers back to the *first* image and thus completes the chain. In this way Apollinaire enhances his imagery and avoids metonymic diffuseness. The second excerpt is a good example of circular metaphor (cf. this process in the *figue* Figure 9, Chapter 3).

Toward a calligrammar

Based on the tautology oranges =chair =soleil =oranges, it leaves the reader with a richer vision of these fruits and a sense of nature's harmony. The other structure combines metaphor and metonymy in a linear chain. In "Visée" (*Po*, p. 224), for example, Apollinaire takes a series of metaphors and connects them metonymically like so many vertebrae:

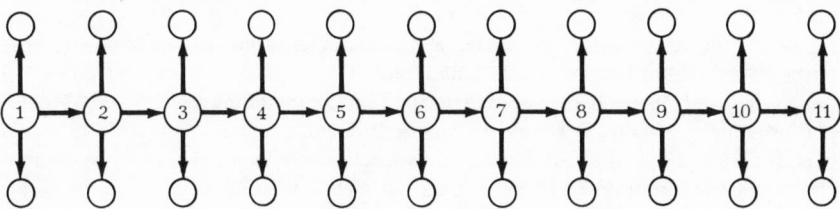

Enumerating eleven elements of the wartime landscape before him, he pauses to link each one to a pair of metaphors. A similar structure informs the *montre* (Figure 11, Chapter 3), in which each of the metaphors on the dial belongs to the numerical (metonymic) sequence 1–12. In both cases the process of composition is quasi-mechanical.

Visual metaphor versus visual metonymy

Returning now to the verbal–visual rapport, we apply the same rules as in the purely verbal realm. Not only can we speak of visual metaphor and visual metonymy, we can continue to use the same model: (verbal) tenor ⟶ (visual) vehicle. As before, other images may intervene or impinge on either term without altering this relationship. The following diagram of the calligrammatic process illustrates the options that are available:

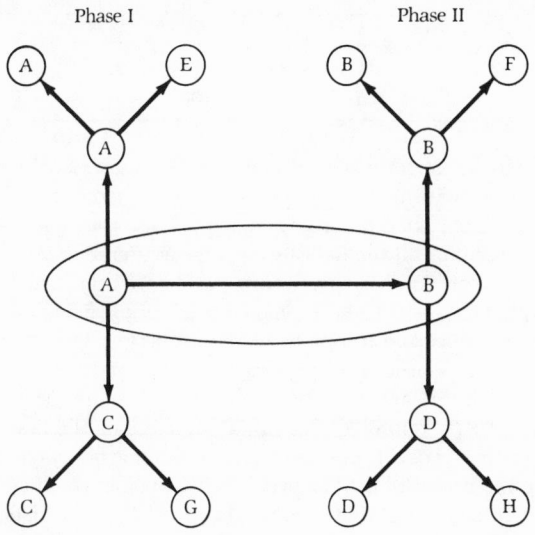

Aesthetics of visual poetry

The large oval represents the boundary between the verbal and the visual text. The verbal image at the center is divided into tenor (A) and vehicle (B). Each of these may in turn generate one of two matching images at the visual interface. It may simply duplicate itself (top), or it may attract a vehicle (bottom). This process can then be repeated at the visual level to produce a whole cluster of calligrams. From this it is evident that a first-generation visual image can originate in one of four ways. It may reproduce the verbal tenor or vehicle, or it may act as a vehicle itself to one of these terms. The portion labeled Phase I illustrates the dynamics of an isolated verbal image. By itself, Phase II corresponds to the functioning of an implicit verbal meta-phor/metonym. Finally, it should be stressed that this model has a definite verbal bias. It assumes that the visual imagery always has a verbal origin, which is demon-strably false in a number of cases. A glance at the *montre* (Figure 11, Chapter 3), for example, reveals that it could have been conceived only visually. Arranged in linear fashion, one line under another, the words would make no sense. Arising spontane-ously or suggested by another calligram, a visual image may (1) duplicate itself verbally or (2) generate a verbal vehicle via metaphor/metonymy. Either of these may then function as tenor or vehicle at the purely verbal level. Thus to adapt the diagram to visually generated poetry we need only reverse the direction of the arrows. We are left with a total of eight ways in which a figurative poem can take form.

If verbally the ratio of primary metonyms to primary metaphors is about even (67:55), visually it is more than 3:1. In making the transition from verbal to visual, and vice versa, Apollinaire clearly prefers to think in terms of contiguity rather than similarity. Among other things, metonymy offers a relative freedom of choice, whereas metaphor is apt to be too restrictive. The distribution by year is as follows:

	1914	1915	1916	1917	1918	NO DATE	TOTAL
Visual metaphor	–	5	2	3	1	1	12
Visual metonym	7	21	2	7	2	–	39
Total	7	26	4	10	3	1	51

The year 1915 was decisive for both visual metaphor and visual metonymy, which are closely associated with the war poetry. In *Case d'armons*, for example, virtually every calligram is constructed according to one of these principles. Statistically, they account for 54 percent of all the figurative poetry written that year.

The great majority of these poems appear to have been visually generated. For one thing, Apollinaire seems to have wanted a pictorial survey of life at the front. Typically, they reproduce the trappings of the artillery or visual stimuli connected with the war: cannons, helmets, boots, aerial torpedos, and so forth. For another, the verbal message is almost always subservient to the picture. The history of visual metaphor, born in 1915, reinforces our initial impression. The first example depicts an aerial torpedo and reads, "J'entends chanter l'oiseau le bel oiseau rapace" ("I hear the bird singing the beautiful bird of prey" ("2ᵉ Cannonier conducteur," *Po*, p. 215). The second is identical, except that it substitutes "siffler" ("to whistle") for "chanter" ("Premier Cannonier conducteur"). The third portrays the front line: "Pourquoi la

Toward a calligrammar

Premier canonnier conducteur
Je suis au front et te salue
Non non tu n'as pas la berlue
Cinquante-neuf est mon secteur

J'entends siffl$_{er}$ l'oiseau
Le
bel oiseau rapa^{ce}

```
                              O      C
                              M      H
                              O      E
Je v$^{ois}$ de l$_{oin}$     N  A  R
la   c$_{athédra}$$^{le}$     NDRE
                              BILLY
```

Figure 19. Guillaume Apollinaire, "Premier Cannonier conducteur"

chère couleuvre se love de la mer jusqu'à l'espoir attendrissant de l'Est" ("Why the dear snake coils from the sea to the moving hope of the East") ("Loin du pigeonnier," *Po*, p. 221). For purposes of comparison let us examine a typical example of visual metaphor in "l'Oiseau et le bouquet." Depicting a bird in flight, one figure reads, "Un chant d'amour je viens du paradis et j'y retournerai" ("A love song I come from paradise and I will return there"). As the verbal tenor is metamorphosed into the visual vehicle, it follows the sequence literal $\longrightarrow$ figurative. The song is the subject, the bird its metaphorical representation. Curiously, this process is reversed in Apollinaire's first three visual metaphors. Here the verbal term is figurative, and the visual term literal. In other words, we are dealing with a *visual tenor* and a *verbal vehicle*. This means that the original order of composition was the reverse. Taking images from the battle zone around him, Apollinaire paired them with verbal animal metaphors (vehicles).[11] From this it is evident that visual metaphor originated at the pictorial, not the linguistic, level.

Like its verbal cousin, visual metaphor normally pairs its images on the basis of shared characteristics. Although there are no instances of functional links here, a few examples exploit physical resemblance (e.g., the snake in "Loin du pigeonnier," *Po*, p. 221). Where visual metaphor differs significantly from its verbal model is in the enormous gap between tenor and vehicle. Often it takes an act of faith to make the connection. Actually, the problem lies in the quality of the metaphoric process here: By definition, only one of the terms is ever stated verbally. By its very nature, visual metaphor is implicit. It is up to the reader to identify the other (visual) term according to the particular graphic code adopted by the poet. For the poem to work, this image must be readily decipherable. Unfortunately, a number of Apollinaire's

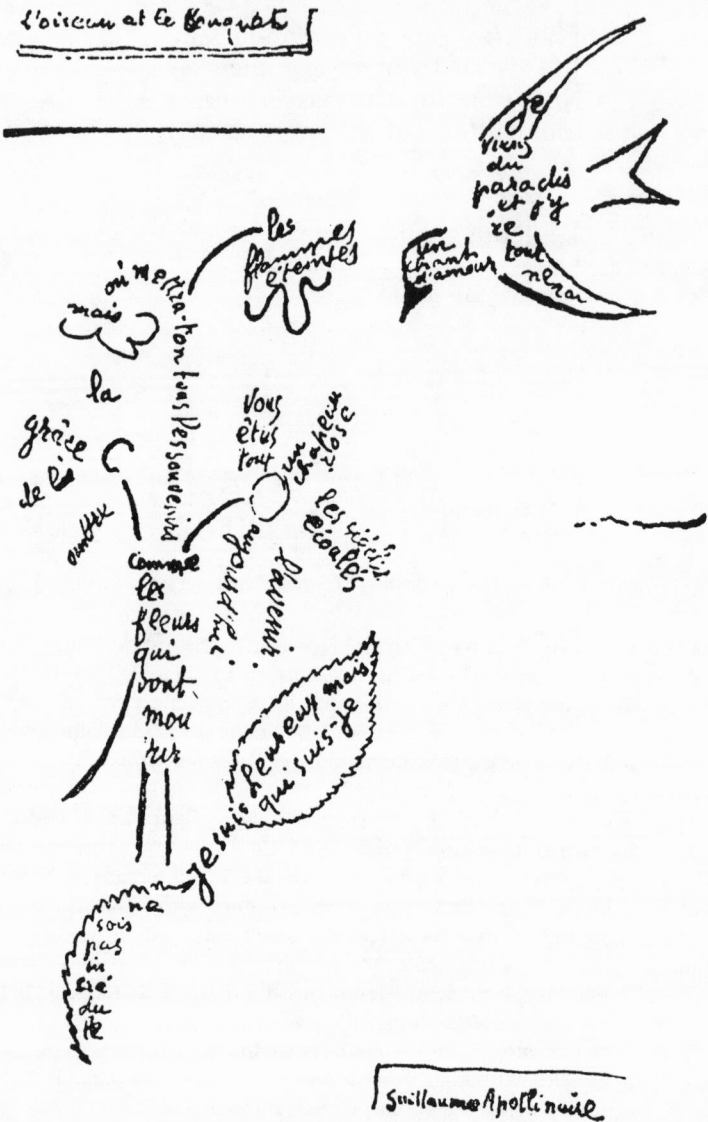

Figure 20. Guillaume Apollinaire, "L'Oiseau et le bouquet"

pictures are difficult to make out. Although the *oiseau* offers no problem, identification of the aerial torpedos and the front line is a laborious process. The likeness is extremely crude in the first case and only hinted at in the second. Other calligrams are even more obscure. Consider the swastika in "Coup d'éventail" (Figure 14, Chapter 3),

Toward a calligrammar

which reads, "Eveillez-vous ô mon amie le signe humain ô mon amie" ("Awaken O my friend the human sign O my friend"). In Chapter 3 we saw that Apollinaire is evoking the sun, whose universal symbol is the swastika. What differentiates this poem from previous examples is the absence of a verbal tenor. There is no reference anywhere to the sun, which leaves us with a hermetic puzzle. This is an example of *implicit visual metaphor* in which one term is completely missing. The situation becomes even more complex when the remaining term starts to disintegrate.

If Apollinaire's visual metaphors suffer from obscurity, his visual metonyms are generally more coherent. Unlike the former, they display a marked preference for a verbal metonymic base (74 percent) – divided fairly evenly between tenors and vehicles. In turn the great majority of these belong to larger (verbal) image clusters, of which half are metonymic and half metonymic/metaphoric. This ratio is twice that of the verbal group as a whole. Significantly, some 41 percent of the poems (sixteen works) are *entirely metonymic*, confirming the existence of the metonymic pole detected earlier. The figure for *entirely metaphoric* poetry is only 17 percent (two works). However, these statistics are limited to groups of at least three verbal images. If we take into account single images and tenor–vehicle couples, the figures rise to 87 and 50 percent, respectively. Thus, where metonymic or metaphoric principles govern the verbal–visual rapport, they tend to perpetuate themselves at the verbal level. There are other differences between verbal and visual metonymy as well. Whereas the former is overwhelmingly based on physical proximity, fully half the visual metonyms exploit functionality. The various pipes ("Fumées," 210, and "Je fume en pensant," *Po*, p. 797) exist to facilitate the act of smoking. The function of the *enveloppe* in "Coup d'éventail" (Figure 14, Chapter 3) is to enclose the "lettre." The purpose of the *montre* (Figure 11, Chapter 3) is to measure the passing of "les heures" and, ultimately, "la vie." Although some of these choices may be gratuitous, their numerical strength testifies to a unity of vision. Moreover, this is artistic rather than literary, since no such pattern exists at the purely verbal level. Functionalism is clearly related to physical appearance. Actually, given the primacy of the visual image here, the situation is the reverse. It is the picture that evokes the verbal description of its function. The entire process hinges on Apollinaire's attitude toward the calligrammatic object. In general he is not content with a simple portrait, but insists on a *definition*. In defining an object in terms of its function, he passes from the realm of aesthetics to that of metaphysics.

The final peculiarity of Apollinaire's visual metonymy is the relatively high incidence of implicit structures (25 percent). Whereas primary verbal metonymy is almost always explicit, *implicit visual metonyms* abound. Some are functional; others rely on physical proximity. In some the verbal–visual connection is extremely tenuous; in others it is merely indirect. Thus the marvelous poem "Pablo Picasso" incorporates three blank spaces (negative calligrams) shaped like a pipe, a bottle, and a violin without specifying that these objects occur in Picasso's paintings. Here the missing link is accessible to the average reader, but this is not true of an epistolary calligram in the form of Notre Dame included in "Premier canonnier conducteur" (Figure 19, Chapter 4): "O mon cher André Billy." In this case one has to know that André Billy was living in Paris at the time.[12] The structure is thus: André Billy ⟶ (Paris) ⟶ Notre Dame. In "As-tu connu la putain de Nancy" (*Po*,

Aesthetics of visual poetry

p. 214) the gap is even more difficult to bridge. Arranged to form a bugle (which at first looks like a cannon), the words seem to have no connection with the picture. The poem reads, "As-tu connu la putain de Nancy qui a foutu la xxxxxx à toute l'artillerie" ("Did you know the whore from Nancy who gave the xxxxxx to all the artillery"). To decipher the link here one has to be familiar with French military songs and their obscene variations. In Apollinaire's unit, for example, these lines were sung to the tune of reveille, a *bugle* call sounded at daybreak to awaken the troops. If the progression putain de Nancy $\longrightarrow$ (song) $\longrightarrow$ (military) $\longrightarrow$ (reveille) $\longrightarrow$ (bugle call) $\longrightarrow$ bugle seems circuitous to us, for Apollinaire it was instantaneous.

Group dynamics

The preceding sections have attempted to analyze the individual calligram in all its complexity. Great as this is, it pales into insignificance when we note that most of the calligrams are integrated into much larger structures. There is no mistaking Apollinaire's intentions. For one thing, few of the figurative poems are meant to be entirely self-supporting. Eighty percent of the calligrams are deliberately juxtaposed with other calligrams, forming a total of thirty-one figurative groups. For another, we recall that Apollinaire stressed the importance of the intercalligrammatic bond in his reply to Fagus in 1914. As we saw in Chapter 3, the calligrams are invariably grouped according to one of several pictorial principles. There are thirteen still lifes, eleven landscapes (including cityscapes and seascapes), and seven portraits. Although their chronological distribution is unremarkable, Apollinaire favors objects over persons by a large margin. If, as we remember, an individual calligram can originate in eight different ways, then a group of n calligrams has 8^n possible paths of origin. This means that "Coeur couronne et miroir," for example, has 512 possibilities at its disposal. Clearly, the potential for group diversity is immense and the likelihood of repetition small. At the level of the microstructures we are presented with a bewildering number of choices, making evolutionary studies virtually impossible. Fortunately, we can examine the compositions from a different point of view. A macrostructural analysis, concentrating on the imagery, allows us to explore the group dynamics of figurative poetry in general.

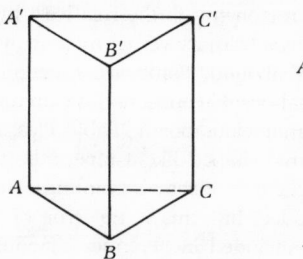 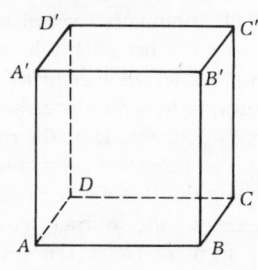 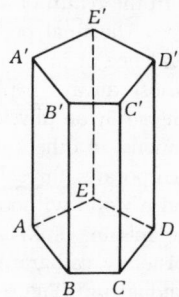

The above diagrams represent groups of three, four, and five calligrams, respectively. The letters $A, B, C, \ldots, E$ designate their verbal components, whereas

80

Toward a calligrammar

$A', B', C', \ldots, E'$ denote their visual components. Each letter and its prime constitute an individual calligram composed of a verbal tenor and a visual vehicle. There are thus five planes of interaction (semantic surfaces) in the first instance, six in the second, and seven in the third, according to the formula $p = n + 2$. In each group one plane is entirely verbal, another is entirely visual, and the rest are verbal–visual. In addition we can differentiate between planar and linear interaction. In the former the vertical planes are formed by juxtaposing (comparing) one calligram with another. Each subgroup is then juxtaposed with the rest to form an interrelated complex. The horizontal planes are generated by homogeneous verbal or visual images and undergo a similar juxtaposition. The same horizontal and vertical distinctions exist at the linear level, where interaction is between individual images. Once point-to-point relations are established (inter- and intracalligrammatic), the relationships themselves are juxtaposed. In this connection one can distinguish three types of linear interaction based on the strength of the imagistic bond: primary (vertical), secondary (horizontal), and tertiary (diagonal). The third (e.g., AC') is much weaker than the other two but cannot be completely disregarded. In "Coeur couronne et miroir" there are three primary lines ($l_1 = n$), six secondary lines ($l_2 = 2n$), and six tertiary lines $[l_3 = n(n - 1)]$ – a total of fifteen different relationships involving six images.

At this point we can complete our survey of Apollinaire's calligrams with a brief three-dimensional analysis. Although the verbal–visual links have been studied in detail, for example, it remains to consider them in a group setting. Let it be said at the outset that they do not fit any one pattern. Not only do the vertical bonds vary from one poem to the next; they are rarely homogeneous within a single group. This means that in a given work the images on either horizontal plane usually belong to several different categories. In the case of "Coup d'éventail" (Figure 14, Chapter 3), for instance, there are four different types of visual image. Statistically, initial appearances are deceiving. Forty-two percent of the compositions have duplicate visual and verbal imagery, whereas 19 percent introduce new imagery from one plane to the next. Only 29 percent of the works exhibit any consistent rhetorical pattern, however, and these are divided into projected verbal metaphor (four groups), visual metonymy (three groups), and projected verbal metonymy (two groups). Once we begin to differentiate between tenors and vehicles, the fragmentation becomes overwhelming. Clearly, there is no point in searching the vertical structures further. We must look elsewhere if we expect to locate the principle underlying the group calligrams.

This leaves the visual and verbal planes, which can be classified according to their metaphoric and metonymic constituents. Dividing them into pure and mixed categories on this basis gives the following results:

	VERBAL PLANE				VISUAL PLANE		
	METAPHORIC		METONYMIC				
	TENORS	VEHICLES	TENORS	VEHICLES	METAPHORIC	METONYMIC	TOTAL
Groups	2	1	16	5	4	23	51

Aesthetics of visual poetry

As the table reveals, the two planes are amazingly cohesive. Not only is each figurative group united by metaphor/metonymy on at least one level; the intraplanar bonds are entirely homogeneous. With one exception, *in each composition the horizontal verbal and/or visual links are exclusively metaphoric or exclusively metonymic.* Inexplicably, "Le Troisième Poème secret" (*Po*, p. 624), which is not listed, mixes metaphor and metonymy in both planes. In fact the visual and the verbal sequences are identical: atoll $\longrightarrow$ coral $\longrightarrow$ flower. At the verbal level Apollinaire's insistence on homogeneous horizontal ties even extends to the tenor–vehicle model. Where a group is interconnected via verbal images, the linkage (metaphoric or metonymic) passes through all the tenors or through all the vehicles. The table, incidentally, gives a false impression of the metonymic balance here. Tenors and vehicles are chosen about equally until 1917, when the former take over entirely. Statistically, metonymy triumphs over metaphor in the figurative groups by a huge margin (86 vs. 14 percent). This ratio remains constant from one plane to the other. In addition 68 percent of the compositions are linked verbally, and 100 percent are connected visually. This means that some two-thirds of the works are linked on *both* planes. The high degree of horizontal reinforcement indicates that Apollinaire was striving to establish a collective identity, a collective meaning, for each group. The year 1914 marks the beginning and the highpoint of this procedure. The first year's compositions are more numerous (twelve) and have a greater frequency of reinforcement (75 percent) than those of any other year. Finally, we should note that when only one plane is "coherent," that is, bounded by linked images, the composition must have originated at the same level. According to this criterion, the ten *un*reinforced works all have visual origins.[13]

We have noted that metaphoric links are extremely rare on either one of the planes. Since in principle group metaphor is no more difficult than group metonymy, their proportions are due solely to the quality of Apollinaire's inspiration. It is important to note that horizontal visual metaphor depends entirely on physical appearance. For metaphoric relations to exist between two objects they must have the same *shape*. In "Coup d'éventail" (Figure 14, Chapter 3), for instance, the hand, the fan, and the heart share one shape, and the envelope and the swastika share another. The two existing manuscripts of "Lettre-Océan" (Figure 1, Chapter 1) reveal that, as originally conceived, this poem revolved about the two wheel-and-spoke patterns, another example of horizontal visual metaphor.[14] If it is theoretically possible to duplicate visual metaphoric relations on the verbal plane (e.g., pictures of a wheel and the sun, which are then equated verbally), this does not happen with Apollinaire. What one does find occasionally is a series of horizontal verbal metaphors projected onto the visual plane. This is a totally different process. Thus in "Coeur couronne et miroir" (Figure 13, Chapter 3) the crown proclaims that poets and kings have identical hearts. The three images of this metaphoric statement are then projected (metonymically and literally) onto the visual plane as a portrait of Apollinaire, a crown, and a heart. Visually this group is perfectly coherent. The poet and the king continue to share a common heart, which is positioned between them. Since similarity of shape is lacking, however, this is not horizontal visual metaphor. The relational pattern is *verbal* (verbal metaphor made manifest) and can originate

82

Toward a calligrammar

only at that level. If verbal metaphoric thinking is undeniably a visual process, it remains a literary, not an artistic, experience.

Therefore, relations on both planes can be the same only if they involve metonymy. At least this is what one finds in Apollinaire. And since most visual images duplicate verbal images, the tenor–vehicle model is helpful in detecting significant patterns. Basically, there are two sorts of metonymic parallels. Some works depend on a perfect one-to-one correspondence between the visual imagery and the verbal tenors or vehicles. Thus in "Voyage" (Figure 18, Chapter 4) the visual series cloud + bird + train + night sky is repeated at the verbal vehicular level. Tight structures such as this are relatively common, occurring in some 40 percent of the cases (eight groups). In other works vertical duplication is lacking, but parallelism exists nonetheless. In the first Léopold Survage group (*Po*, p. 675), for example, the visual sequence spectacles ⟶ book is reflected in the choice of verbal vehicles: vision ⟶ canons of beauty. Just as glasses can be used to read a book, one's personal vision is what determines aesthetic canons. This and other loose structures account for 60 percent of the metonymic parallels (twelve groups). The prevalence of horizontal metonymy in general has already been demonstrated. As with the individual calligrams, physical proximity is the most common unifying principle. On the visual plane several groups exploit psychological proximity, whereas categorical proximity occurs in a few works at the verbal level. Typically, Apollinaire juxtaposes several unrelated objects in a particular manner to form a painting. Thus in "Paysage" (Figure 15, Chapter 3) he portrays a man smoking a cigar in his front yard. The fact that the work is divided into four separate calligrams makes no difference. Here, as elsewhere, visual unity is imposed from without via a pictorial frame.

Thesis, antithesis, synthesis

In light of Jakobson's analysis of metaphor and metonymy outlined at the beginning, how are we finally to understand the calligrams? How are they related to French poetry in general, and what do they teach us about Apollinaire's imagination? Precise answers to these questions would require us to determine the frequencies of the tropes (1) in the rest of Apollinaire's poetry and (2) in the broader poetic tradition. Without these statistics, we can still formulate a number of conclusions. As Jakobson had predicted, there is an active competition between metaphor and metonymy in the calligrams. It is evident in the polarization of the poetry into two opposite camps and permeates every structure we have examined. Since metonymy emerges as the victor in every case, it is clearly the governing principle here. Yet the polar model does not tell the whole story, for on several occasions the contest is almost a draw. Thus verbal primary metaphors and metonyms are present in roughly equal amounts. And though there are some purely metaphoric or metonymic verbal image clusters in the individual poems, most of the clusters are mixed. For that matter, many of the verbal–visual links are also mixed. From this perspective Gérard Genette's remarks on Proust apply equally well to the calligrams: "Loin d'être antagonistes et incompatibles, métaphore et métonymie se soutiennent et

83

Aesthetics of visual poetry

s'interpénetrent" ("far from being antagonists and incompatible, metaphor and metonymy support and interpenetrate each other").[15] This is especially true of the verbal imagery. The fact that the ratio of metaphor to metonymy seems perfectly normal here suggests that the verbal component is relatively traditional. Indeed critics have been quick to point out that many calligrams are composed of alexandrines and/or octosyllabic lines. In the last analysis, then, the calligram is basically a hybrid genre. To the extent that it is metaphoric, it incorporates the traditional bias of lyric poetry. To the extent that it is metonymic, it reflects the influence of Cubism. Each genre's influence is felt most strongly on the corresponding calligrammatic level (verbal or visual). Moreover, just as the metaphoric trend represents a continuation of Symbolism, the metonymic trend constitutes a reaction against this movement.

Where Apollinaire departs from tradition, clearly, is at the visual level – which represents a radical innovation in itself. Visually the calligrams are overwhelmingly metonymic, both horizontally and vertically. Not only is metonymy the principal visual trope; it also binds the group calligrams together. Its existence on the visual plane is so pervasive that it provokes a parallel response on the verbal plane. Above all, Apollinaire's approach to the calligram is visual and metonymic. In his preoccupation with the object and with the architecture of the group he mirrors the concerns of the Cubist painters. In his desire to push metaphor and metonymy as far as they will go – to the brink of incoherence and beyond – he prefigures the Surrealists. In all probability the great majority of the calligrams originated at the visual level. Certainly the birth of visual metaphor occurred in this manner, and the pattern is well established elsewhere. This means that the visual component is at least as important as the verbal. It also means that the origins of this poetry are artistic, not literary. Like the painters and sculptors around him, Apollinaire thinks by means of the shapes he creates. Any study of the calligrams that ignores the fundamental role of visual thinking is doomed to be incomplete. For this reason I have suggested several models to relate the visual imagery to the verbal. By isolating Apollinaire's compositional structures, it becomes possible to grasp the calligram in all its complexity. In fact an understanding of the function of metaphor and metonymy reveals a certain basic *simplicity*. These insights transcend the limitations of any one author, time, or place to encompass figurative poetry in general.

5

Josep-Maria Junoy

It is generally recognized that the Spanish avant-garde grew out of earlier movements in France and Italy. This phenomenon was particularly evident in Catalonia, which reacted against the political hegemony of Castile by strengthening its traditional ties with these two countries. During the first phase, between 1916 and 1924, Catalan writers experimented with Italian Futurism and drew heavily on French literary cubism.[1] Agustí Esclasans, one of the original participants, later recalled the enthusiastic reception these movements received: "Qui de nosaltres, els joves, l'any 1919, no jurava pel nom sagrat d'Apollinaire de la mateixa manera que una estona abans havia jurat pel nom sagrat de Marinetti? Del futurisme al cubisme literari per anar a raure al dadaïsme, tota una llarga sèrie d'entusiasmes i de fantasies." ("Among the young men who were active in 1919, was there one of us who did not swear by the sacred name of Apollinaire, as he had sworn by the sacred name of Marinetti before that? From Futurism to literary cubism and finally dadaism: one long series of enthusiasms and fantasies.")[2] Although the nature of this influence varied from writer to writer, one of its earliest signs was the emergence of visual poetry in Barcelona. To be sure, there had been a local visual tradition of sorts, but it had died out some years before. The last known example occurs in Rafel Nogueras Oller's *Les tenebroses* (Barcelona: Plaça del Teatre, 1905), which includes a poem in the shape of an "S." Written in praise of life and its pleasures, this work is in fact entitled "Una esse." Curiously, the shape and title seem to have no connection with the subject matter. This fact plus the heavy, solid form of the poem link it to an ancient liturgical tradition going back to the Middle Ages. As a vehicle for devotional poetry, the shape was meant to enhance the verbal message while remaining totally subservient to it.

Artists and art

The earliest practitioner of the new visual poetry in Catalonia was Josep-Maria Junoy. The first issue of his review, *Trocos* (*Pieces*) – later changed to *Trossos* when J. V. Foix became the director – included three examples. Appearing in 1916, it contained a total of seven poems by Junoy celebrating various artists whose work was being exhibited at the Galeries Dalmau. These included Pierre Ynglada, Albert Gleizes, Hélène Grunhoff, Serge Charchoune, Josep de Togores, Xavier Nougués, and Umberto Boccioni.[3] Five more visual poems appeared the following year. In 1920

Aesthetics of visual poetry

PIERRE YNGLADA

Jardi a la francesa

Estança de Racan

Maduixes en crema d'Isigny

i

del distant Japó

un

Herbari Lineal

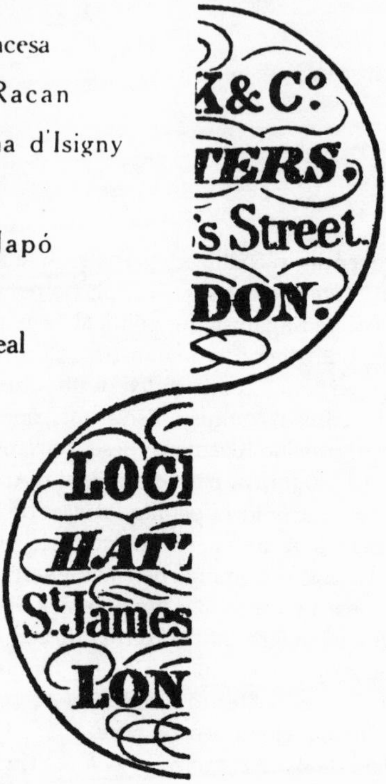

Figure 21. Josep-Maria Junoy

most of Junoy's visual poetry was collected in *Poemes i cal·ligrames* (Barcelona: Llibreria Nacional Catalana), which featured a preface by Apollinaire. Although Guillermo Díaz-Plaja claims that these works represent Apollinarian inspiration carried to its logical consequences,[4] in fact they borrow heavily from Futurism. Among other things one finds the same preoccupation with geometric forms – spirals, parabolas, zigzags – as in Italy. Futurist thematics are also very much in evidence. Although the term *cal·ligrama* comes from Apollinaire, Junoy's version does not resemble its French prototype. Predominantly abstract, it rejects the figurative bias of the latter, its fascination with objects, and its pictorial structure.

Interestingly, the first poem resembles neither one of its antecedents. Nor does it conform to the visual typology elaborated in Chapter 3. Entitled "Pierre Ynglada," it juxtaposes seven unrhymed lines of poetry (arranged conventionally) with a beautifully textured hat label reading, "Lock & C? / Hatters / St. James Street /

London." The latter has been sliced in two vertically and its left half displaced downward until it barely touches the upper half, forming a pleasing S-shaped curve. The label itself is an excellent example of framed writing, in which the verbal text is contained by a visual frame. To the extent that it embraces the horizontal lines, the same can be said of the entire poem. Placed to one side, however, it does not actually enclose the text but seems to accompany it like an emblem. Clearly, this is a hybrid genre of Junoy's devising in which decoration is juxtaposed with denotation, ornamentation with verbalization, and dislocation with enumeration. Above all, the poem's visual configuration testifies to its originality. Junoy's love of texture, evident here as throughout his work, provides a tactile dimension that reflects the author's playful humor. These characteristics differentiate his work from that of other visual poets and give it a distinct personality.

The lines of poetry themselves read as follows: "Classic French garden/Stanza by Racan/Strawberries in cream from Isigny/and/from distant Japan/a/Lineal Herbarium." This apparently banal composition is actually rather complex. Since there are no verbs in the poem, for example, the relationship between its components must be inferred by the reader. These in turn are remarkably static. Isolated on the page, the four images recall the frozen groups of unrelated objects in Giorgio de Chirico's paintings. Although it is tempting to picture them as a still life or a landscape, their structure remains stubbornly sequential. Moreover, the source of their unity is verbal rather than visual. Clearly, the work is meant to be a portrait of Ynglada, who contributed artwork to *Troços* and who was a close friend of Junoy's. (The 1920 version, in *Poemes i cal·ligrames*, is simply titled "Un amic" – "A friend.") More precisely, it is a portrait of the artist as a young aesthete. Like a classic French garden or limpid verses by the seventeenth century poet Racan, Ynglada's art embodies a highly developed sense of formal beauty. The artist himself is blessed with a superior aesthetic sensibility trained in the classic mode. Like Junoy he is a connoisseur of the finer things in life.

To complete the portrait we must add the rich sensuality of the strawberries and cream and the exoticism of the Japanese herbarium. It is significant that the cream comes not from just any place but from Isigny, a village in Normandy famous for its dairy products. A symbol of quality, it testifies to the refined taste of the artist (and the poet). Besides exoticism, the Japanese herbarium conveys the notion of precision and order, since the dried plants in a lineal herbarium are arranged by genus and species. Actually, this image is not as arbitrary as it seems, for Ynglada often drew groups of animals modeled on museum exhibits (several of which appear in *Troços*). All these traits are finally combined in the hat label, which provides a visual summary. If the first three objects evoke the French qualities of the artist, who affected the name Pierre instead of the Catalan Pere or the Castilian Pedro, the English label is a punning reference to his surname, Ynglada. We also know that he was a passionate admirer of England and France, and had lived in each country for several years.[5] Although the label undoubtedly evokes Ynglada's penchant for British hats, it has several other associations. In Spain, for example, a British hat is an exotic artifact, a symbol of wealth and elegance. It should be added that Lock & Co. were the oldest and most prestigious hatters in London. Like Isigny they symbolize quality and taste. In addition the simple unadorned style of British

Aesthetics of visual poetry

headgear reflects a basic conservatism, in keeping with the tenets of British fashion. The net impression is one of simple elegance. The poem begins and ends with this (visual) statement.

If the use of labels was pioneered by the Cubist painters (and authorized by Apollinaire), the idea of defining human subjects in terms of physical objects derives from Francis Picabia, who resided in Barcelona during much of 1916. The five objects in "Pierre Ynglada" have a common purpose and a common style. From a structural perspective they are grouped according to the principles of horizontal and vertical metaphor. Just as each object serves as a metaphor for the artist and his work, each participates in the global theme "elegance." As such they have a common signified. Although the objects are not without metonymic associations, as metaphors they derive their power from shared characteristics. Not only do they resemble Pierre Ynglada, they resemble each other. Presided over by a conspicuous visual metaphor, the poem consists of a single tenor (Ynglada) linked to multiple vehicles. In 1920 Junoy added the image of a "maillot de circ" ("circus tights") and replaced Racan's stanza with the words "Alexandrí Niquelat." Neither of these choices was especially felicitous. The latter may refer to the last Tzar, Nikolai Aleksandrovich, recently executed by the Bolsheviks. Or Junoy may have been thinking of Nicolas Alexandre (1654–1728), who authored a *Dictionaire botanique et pharmaceutique*. Either figure is consistent with the themes of elegance and order. The idea of a circus performer in tights, however, introduces a discordant note. It is no longer a question of rarity and refinement but of popular entertainment.

The next poem, "Jongleurs d'Héléne Grunhoff," is filled with vitality. The body of the text is arranged in a single horizontal line that zigzags across the page like a flash of lightning. Although this pattern may duplicate the design of Grunhoff's painting, its shape is probably attributable to Junoy. At first glance the line appears to depict the path of a ball as it passes from one juggler to another. Closer scrutiny reveals several problems with this interpretation, including the fact that the ball should describe an arc, not a zigzag. From this we conclude that the line reproduces the rhythm of several balls passing between the jugglers and only vaguely suggests their trajectories. Masquerading as an outlined form, it turns out to be a visual analogy. Taking the sentence rather than the word as his basic unit, Junoy utilizes dislocated words instead of letters. The analogical process remains the same. In both cases the linguistic function is transferred to the visual level. Verbally and visually language is conceived as an analytical tool for isolating basic principles. Like the previous work, "Jongleurs" is remarkable for its typographical texture. The reader's attention is drawn initially to the word, "ÁN I M A ," its gigantic boldface letters strung out between the peaks of the zigzag. It then shifts to another inscription below in Gothic boldface: "𝕹𝖔𝖇𝖑𝖊 𝖎 𝖁𝖊𝖍𝖊𝖒𝖊𝖓𝖙." These three terms establish the character of Grunhoff's art, the forcefulness and elegance (nobility) of which proceed directly from her soul. All the typographical indications point to the latter as the source of her inspiration. This suggests that her paintings are highly emotional, that they speak the language of the soul.

The rest of the text reads, ("arc lamp's raw light nourishing a/mass of polyhedric narration/with a tyrannical/and confused dynamism/bristling with vermillion – black/and gold shoe polish"). At this point the verbal message causes the

Josep-Maria Junoy

JONGLEURS
D'HÉLÈNE GRUNHOFF

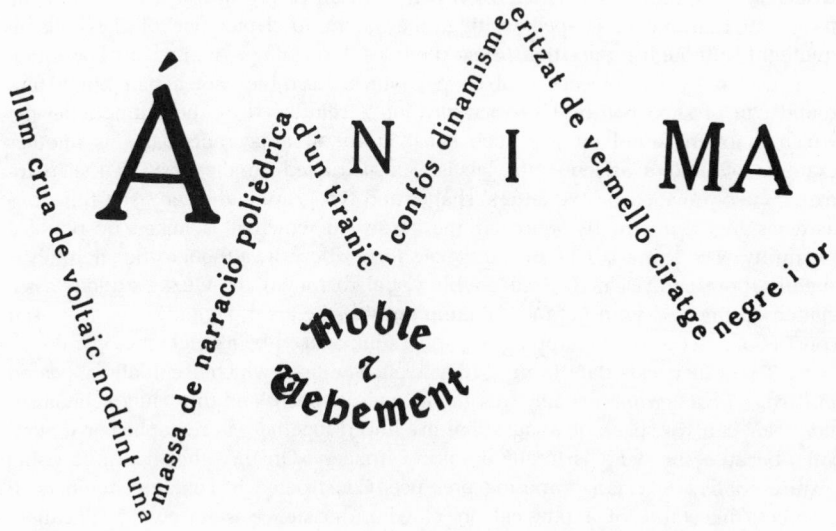

Figure 22. Josep-Maria Junoy

reader to reevaluate the visual configuration. Judging from the first line, the zigzag form has a realistic basis after all. If it represents several balls passing between two jugglers, it just as surely depicts an electric discharge passing between the poles of an arc lamp. Depending on our point of view it is either a visual analogy or an outlined form – or both. Although the polyhedron lends a tinge of Cubism to the composition, as a symbol of raw energy the arc lamp is closely associated with Futurism. Both images appear to have a metaphorical relation to the text. Although the arc lamp could conceivably refer to the painting's dazzling light, it probably describes Grunhoff's brilliant inspiration. Seen in this perspective the image represents an attempt to modernize the traditional symbol for inspiration in which light is equated with creative "illumination." It also suggests that the "mass of polyhedric narration" is the painting itself, which is conceived in terms of Cubist discourse. That it is "nourished" by the arc lamp indicates that it has its source in the latter object, which, as artistic inspiration, springs from the artist's very soul.

The mention of "dinimisme" puts a Futurist seal on the work for once and for

89

all. Junoy's initial concept of "vehemence" is translated not only by this term, but by the harsh light of the lamp. It is intensified by the adjective "tirànic" and by the vigorous participle "eritzat" ("bristling"). These aggressive images contrast with the noble solidity of the polyhedric mass and the artist's nourishing presence. The poem's visual effects are thus echoed by the verbal text. The only objective facts at our disposal are the painting's title, "Jongleurs," and its primary colors: red, black, and gold. Without a doubt it is a lively work full of energy and painted in bright colors. That the latter are compared to shoe polish indicates that Grunhoff has given the work a smooth, shiny finish. It also recalls the words **"𝕹oble i 𝖁ehement."** the distorted letters of which form an ellipse near the bottom of the page. An example of shaped writing, they seem to depict one of the balls in midflight, although its position *below* the lines is puzzling. Another interpretation is suggested by the object's oval shape, which resembles not a ball but a flat, round can of shoe polish. This identification is reinforced by the Gothic lettering, which is often found on just such cans. From all appearances this is another example of Junoy's affection for labels. Reconstructed on the basis of the metonymic cues provided by the letters' shapes and typography, the can itself functions as a visual metonym. Its source is the *ciratge* to which it is linked by physical proximity. The same is true of the zigzag form above it, although the situation is slightly more complicated. As a double visual metonym the zigzag exploits associations connected with (1) the arc lamp and (2) the art of juggling. The text itself consists of a series of overlapping metaphors introduced by a single metonym.

Two other texts date from 1916 as well. The first, which eventually appeared in *Poemes i cal·ligrames*, is only marginally a visual poem and thus eludes classification. Nor can we speak of images that are linked together via metaphor or metonymy, because the work is totally devoid of imagery. On the other hand, its visual texture confers a certain imposing presence. Constructed of concrete signifiers, it assumes the status of a physical object whose existence is its own justification. Entitled "Art poètica," the poem features a large Z at the top of the page linked to a large A at the bottom by a vertical column of dots. Despite the absence of a verbal text several observations are in order. First, the fact that there are exactly twenty-seven dots suggests that the sequence represents the Catalan alphabet. Second, the title indicates that these are meant to function as a manifesto the concerns of which are spelled out letter by letter, dot by dot. The key to deciphering Junoy's baffling poem involves a journey along Jakobson's metonymic way. Just as letters are the foundation of (written) language, language is the basis of human thought. Ultimately, all intellectual endeavor depends on the alphabet – either written or phonetic – for its formulation and expression. The present work is intended not only as a commentary on language but as a critique of culture as well. That Junoy has reversed the normal order of the alphabet signifies that he is protesting traditional values in both domains, which must be turned upside down. Thus the new aesthetics demands a radical restructuring of art involving its most basic elements. There is need for a new artistic language that will reflect new modes of consciousness. Rejecting the end product of a long tradition (Z), Junoy proposes to lead us to new beginnings (A) by standing art on its head. Seen in this perspective, "Art poètica" functions as a visual metonym by virtue of its linguistic basis. If the date can be

Josep-Maria Junoy

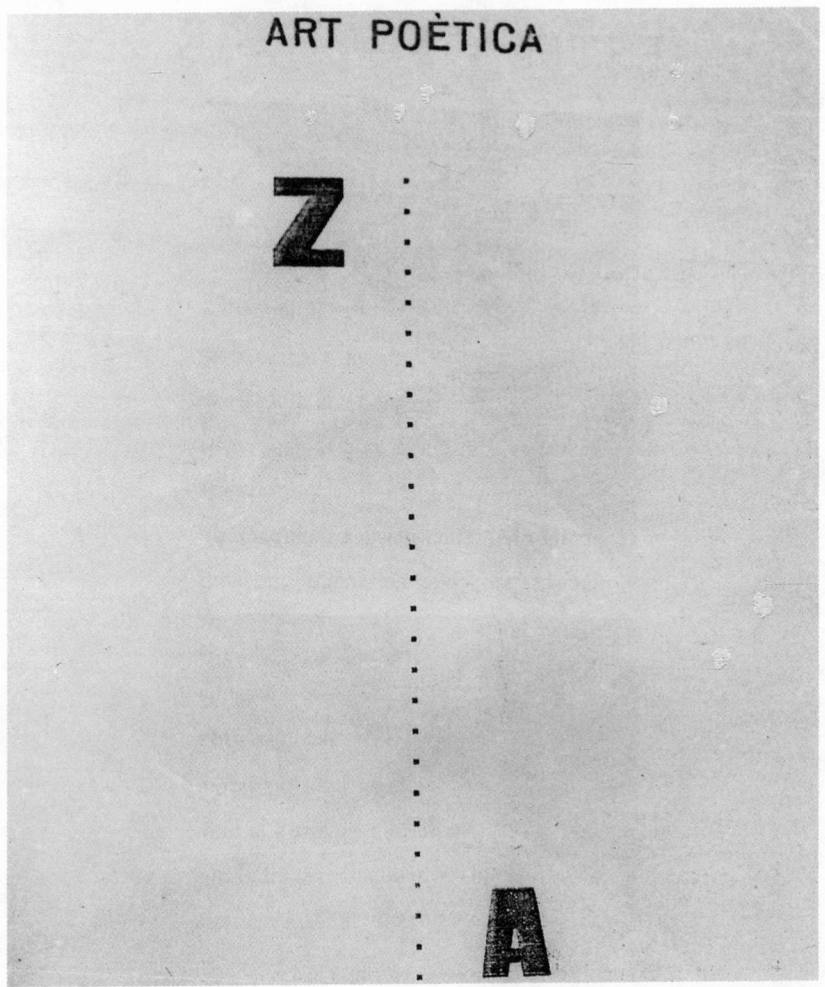

Figure 23. Josep-Maria Junoy

trusted, it is also the earliest known example of alphabet poetry, a genre that rose to prominence under Dada and Surrealism.[6] Antedating Louis Aragon's notorious poem "Suicide" by a full four years, it grew out of much the same background and embodied a similar philosophy of language.

"Estela angular" ("Angular Wake") is yet another type of visual poem. Commemorating Umberto Boccioni's recent death on the battlefield, it comprises seventeen lines of unpunctuated prose compressed into two right triangles placed one beneath the other. These are carefully aligned with one another but have somewhat different dimensions. Each triangle forms the lower right-hand half of a rectangle

91

Aesthetics of visual poetry

ESTELA ANGULAR

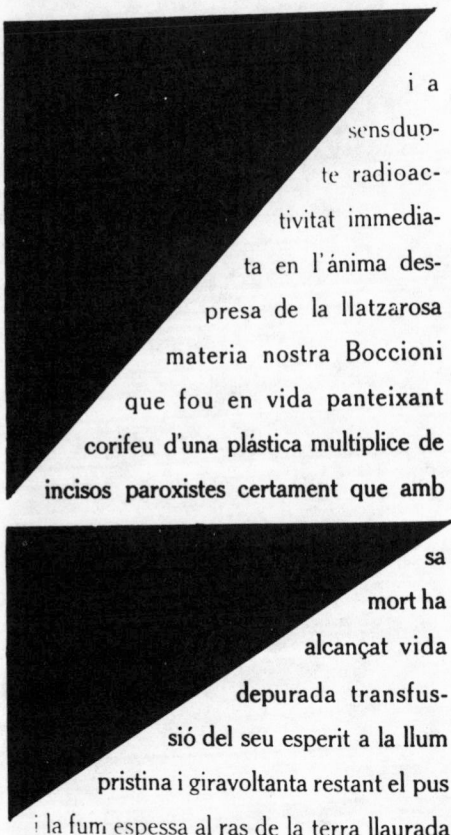

i a
sens dup-
te radioac-
tivitat immedia-
ta en l'ánima des-
presa de la llatzarosa
materia nostra Boccioni
que fou en vida panteixant
corifeu d'una plástica multíplice de
incisos paroxistes certament que amb

sa
mort ha
alcançat vida
depurada transfus-
sió del seu esperit a la llum
pristina i giravoltanta restant el pus
i la fum espessa al ras de la terra llaurada

Figure 24. Josep-Maria Junoy

that is divided in two by its hypoteneuse. In each case the superior half of the rectangle is painted solid black in mourning for Boccioni, Once again Junoy asserts his independence by utilizing a hybrid genre. Combining framed and shaped writing, the poem consists of solid verbal forms that mirror the solid visual forms above them. The latter attempt to embrace the verbal elements with only partial success. The work's contours are thus partially pictorial and partially linguistic. In terms of artistic composition the poem is forceful and intensely angular, like the sculptor himself. The same can be said of its solidity, which is equated with Boccioni and which furnishes an important visual theme. Like "Pierre Ynglada," "Estela angular" is essentially a portrait. In both poems the author establishes his subject's character by a combination of visual and verbal strategies. In conventional narrative, as Roland Barthes

Josep-Maria Junoy

observes, character is created "lorsque des sèmes identiques traversent à plusieurs reprises le même Nom propre et semblent s'y fixer" ("when identical semes traverse the same proper name several times and appear to settle upon it").[7] In visual poetry identical semes traverse not multiple instances of the subject's name so much as multiple projections of his name onto the metaphoric axis. On both the visual and the verbal level the subject is equated with various objects that serve as simulacra. As with narrative, the construction of character depends on consistency-building operations that the reader performs on the different versions of the subject.

This explains the prevalence of metaphor in poems that aim at visual portraiture. In the present work, as in "Pierre Ynglada," the human tenor is paired with multiple metaphoric vehicles that comment on his character. As before there is a certain amount of visual metonymy, associated here with the unmistakable color of mourning. Although the two black triangles suggest the finality and suddenness of Boccioni's death, they also suggest the influential (angular) wake left by his passage through life. In this context, it should be noted that one of the alternative meanings of *estela* is "stele." Visually and functionally the poem does indeed answer this description, but there the resemblance ends. The metaphoric and metaphysical value of the text outweighs its commemorative function:

> i a sensdupte radioactivitat immediata en l'ánima despresa de la llatza-rosa materia nostra Boccioni que fou en vida panteixant corifeu d'una plástica multiplice de incisos paroxistes certament que amb sa mort ha alcançat vida depurada transfusió del seu esperit a la llum pristina i giravoltanta restant el pus i la fum espessa al ras de la terra llaurada

> detached from our miserable matter, the soul undoubtedly has immediate radioactivity. Boccioni was a living and breathing coryphée of multiplex plasticity and paroxysmic clauses, whose death has enabled him to attain a purified life (the transfusion of his spirit with pristine, fluttering light), while pus and clouds of smoke cover the plowed earth.

The Futurist cult of modernity (and energy) is reflected in the image of the radioactive soul. If Junoy chooses to emphasize this aspect of Boccioni's work, the theme of force—first stated in the visual text—is continued in the "paroxysmic clauses" that evoke (metonymically) the latter's passionate manifestos. Similarly, the theme of Boccioni's influence, which is implicit in the wake/trail image, is restated by the central metaphor. As one of the founders of Futurism, Boccioni resembles the *koryphaios*, or "leader," of the chorus in ancient Greek tragedy. Otherwise the poem proceeds via a series of polar images. Following a pattern of repetition and reinforcement, body is opposed to soul, life to death, corruption to purity, and earth to heaven. In addition a visual–verbal contrast exists between the *darkness* of the black triangles and the *light* of the Holy Ghost, seen here in its traditional guise as a fluttering dove. The final image of tilled fields suggests that the "wake" in question may be that of a tractor rather than a boat (*estela* also means "furrow" or "track"). The poem thus ends on a slightly optimistic note. If the landscape is bare and forlorn, the plowed furrows hold the promise of eventual renewal. Once again the author is referring to Boccioni's influence and its (re)generative power.

Aesthetics of visual poetry

Figure 25. Josep-Maria Junoy, "Sacarina i mentol en espiral"

Later themes

In 1917 Junoy published a poem entitled "Sacarina i mentol en espiral" ("Saccharin and Menthol in a Spiral") in the September issue of *Troços*. Dedicated to Nijinsky and dated June 1917, it incorporates three different abstract forms. Extending diagonally across the page in huge boldface letters is the word "**DELTOÏDES.**" The title itself forms a spiral in the upper left corner, and the lower right is occupied by a fanlike arrangement of eight lines terminating in the letters "F A N G D I V I" ("D I V I N E M U D"). In its orientation the fan's 45 degree arc corresponds to the lower half of the upper right quadrant of a circle. Without the dedication we could never decipher this interesting composition, which turns out to be a portrait of Nijinsky, who spent much of 1917 in Spain. In June (the date of the poem) we know that he danced with the Ballets Russes at the Gran Teatre del Liceu de Barcelona, which is undoubtedly where Junoy saw him.[8] Visually and verbally the images are

Josep-Maria Junoy

remarkably cohesive. The spiral title, which is modeled on Bètuda's "Looping the Loop" (*Lacerba*, April 1, 1914),[9] is a classic example of a visual analogy. Employing dislocated syllables rather than letters, it revolves in a counterclockwise direction to bring the reader into contact with the second visual shape, which leads him in turn to the third. Reading is thus conceived as a series of graceful gestures whose momentum parallels that of the text, which parallels that of its subject. Since the Futurists prized the spiral as a symbol of energy, this figure probably refers to Nijinsky's reputation as a dynamic dancer. In addition, viewed from a realistic perspective, it suggests the latter's grace and balance as evidenced in a series of pirouettes. The hyphens between each syllable, for example, introduce the idea of deliberate regularity and testify to Nijinsky's perfect control. If the spiral evokes his grace, the diagonal "**DELTOÏDES**" suggests his power. Slicing boldly across the page, it represents the beginning of a great leap (*grand jeté*) as he launches himself into space. Like the first figure, it is a simple visual analogy. The same is true of the third figure, whose letters "F A N G D I V I" appear to depict the final phase of Nijinsky's leap. Leaping into the air, the dancer (who was famous for his *ballon)* seems to float there forever before descending to earth in a graceful arc.

Like "Pierre Ynglada" and "Estela angular," "Sacarina" is a portrait of a distinguished artist. Unlike them, it relies entirely on visual metonymy. Each of the three visual vehicles is linked to its tenor (Nijinsky) by the metonymic principle of functional proximity. Although the importance of this simple structural change is not immediately evident, its ultimate consequences are profound. In particular Nijinsky is defined not in terms of himself, as Junoy's previous subjects are, but in terms of his *function.* What matters is not who he is but how he dances. Instead of the human being, the author chooses to depict the professional Nijinsky, who consists of a series of graceful leaps and turns. Verbally the poem comprises a series of metaphors interrupted by a single objective image. Of course, the connotations of saccharin and menthol have changed over the years. In 1917 these recently invented substances stood for modernity and progress, for human triumph over nature. A symbol of concentrated energy, like the spiral, the artificial sweetener combines with the spearmint flavoring to evoke an intensely pleasurable, refreshing form of dance. Thereafter Junoy singles out Nijinsky's prominent deltoid muscles, which are responsible for much of his grace. Covering the two shoulder joints, these triangular muscles serve to raise the arm away from the side of the body. The final metaphor derives from the shape of these muscles, which suggests the Holy Trinity to Junoy and hence the divine origins of the dancer. The Baudelairean image of "divine mud" is not without Biblical overtones. Combining the spiritual with the sensual, the heavenly with the mundane, Nijinsky personifies a new breed of dancer. As such he is portrayed as the Adam of the ballet world.

In October Junoy published two visual poems—one in *Troços*, the other in *Iberia*, which had a much larger circulation. Dated August 1917, "ja de bona hora" ("before long") consists of a single sentence arranged in a vertical zigzag pattern: ("before long there will be a rain of rose/petals and pergolas with triangles of muscat/grapes, but my pain does not melt away in the sunlight"). At each angle there is a circular cluster of dots representing a shower of blossoms. Although at first glance the poem's design appears to be abstract, which would make it a visual

Aesthetics of visual poetry

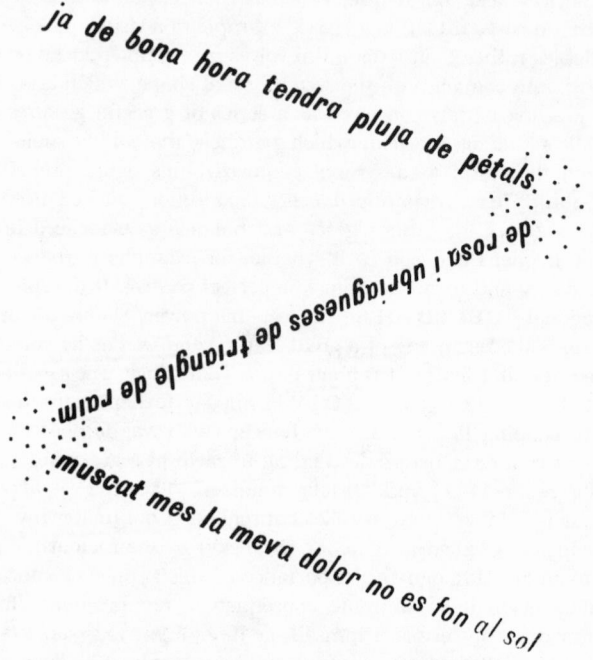

Figure 26. Josep-Maria Junoy, "Ja de bona hora tendra pluja de pétals"

analogy, it is actually an outlined form. Retitled "Zig-Zag" in 1920, the poem traces the downward path of a rose petal that has become detached from a bush. Since the angle of descent remains constant from one line to the next and since the (visual) length of the lines is uniform, this event clearly takes place on a windless day. From these clues we deduce a highly specific image. Seesawing back and forth in the still air, a single petal settles gently to the ground. In addition to the latter image, the two triangles introduce a subtle delta motif that suggests the triangular bunches of grapes on the pergola.

At the verbal level Junoy utilizes parataxis and condensation to create a remarkable density of allusion. From the initial images we know that the time must be early autumn. Soon the leaves will begin to fall, and the trees will hang heavy with fruit. The key to the poem, however, lies in the image of the sun, which does not appear until the very end. Evoked in connection with the author's pain, it presides over the entire composition, which is divided into three parts visually and verbally. Progressing from the rose to the grape to himself, Junoy draws implicit parallels and creates implicit contrasts. These revolve about the central concept of dissolution that ties the sections together. The key verb is *fondre-se* ("to dissolve or melt"), which, like the sun, is postponed until the end. Just as the rose dissolves in a shower of petals and the grape melts in the mouth, Junoy waits expectantly for the

Josep-Maria Junoy

dissolution of his pain. Although the nature of the latter is never specified, following a common poetic convention the reader is free to identify it with the pangs of unrequited love. This symmetry extends to the visual images as well, which follow a fluid downward course. The falling rose petals lead to the branches sagging with grapes (whose juice runs down our throats), which suggest an image of a sobbing speaker. Whether he is actually shedding tears is unimportant. What matters are our expectations, which cause us to envisage that possibility. In this manner the three vertical images are linked together by horizontal metaphor.

At this point the reader encounters an important structural contrast whose effect depends on the implicit parallels we have just examined and whose agent is the sun. Although the sun is plainly responsible for the biological destiny of the rose and the grapes, evoked at the beginning, it has no effect whatsoever on Junoy. The images of maturation and resolution in the first two lines contrast with the implicit sterility of the final line. Nowhere is the basic opposition more evident than in the author's water imagery. In contrast to the freely falling "rain" with which the poem opens, the speaker's pain is represented as a block of ice that will not melt. This metaphor suggests that he is unable to cry and that tears are associated with the dissolution of his pain. Although the poem opens and closes with contrasting metaphors, verbally it is largely metonymic. Most of the images conform to the conventional picture of an autumn landscape that exploits physical proximity. Visually "ja de bona hora" is a tautological composition. The verbal image is simply translated to the visual plane, where it undergoes objectification. On one level the poem represents a fairly traditional amorous lament expressing the lover's pain in the face of rejection. On another it embodies a yearning for an organic existence. From a Christian point of view – Junoy was a devout Catholic – this amounts to longing for a return to a state of natural grace in which the individual is reunited with the environment.

Dated 1917 and included in *Poemes i cal·ligrames*, "Eufòria" was probably composed in the summer or late spring of that year. Visually the work consists of five lines radiating out from a common center. In each case the reader must begin in the middle and work his way toward the periphery. The visual configuration itself hesitates between outlined form and visual analogy. The underlying principle seems to be that of a release of energy, in keeping with the title, which describes a highly emotional state. If the visual image is ambiguous, the radiating pattern conjures up images of nuclear fission, radio waves, or a star. To decipher the poem we must begin at one o'clock on the dial and proceed in a clockwise direction: "cos nu al sol/mentol al cor/espiral de rialles/una rosa color de rosa/decisions sinòptiques" ("nude body in the sun/menthol in the heart/spiral of laughs/a rose-colored rose/synoptic decisions"). The process here is closely related to that in "Pierre Ynglada" and elsewhere. Each of the first four lines serves as an example of euphoria, which is perceived as a shared characteristic. They are not synoptic decisions so much as synoptic *equivalents* linked together by the principle of horizontal metaphor. Verbally the poem consists of a single tenor (euphoria) linked to multiple vehicles. Taken together these constitute a landscape portrait. One is reminded of Manet's *Déjeuner sur l'herbe* or Renoir's *Jeune Femme au soleil*. Despite the semantic incompatibility of the last two words ("decisions sinòptiques") their meaning is

97

Aesthetics of visual poetry

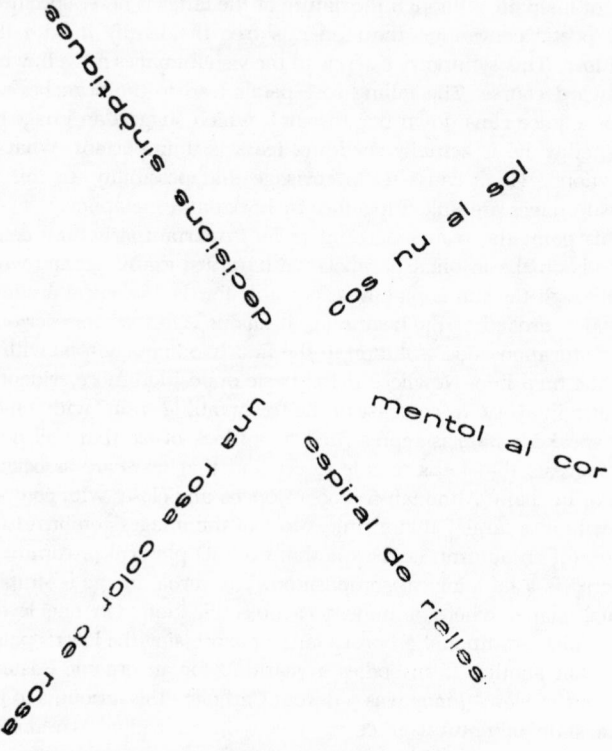

Figure 27. Josep-Maria Junoy, "Eufòria"

clear. Like Marinetti's *tavole sinottiche di valori lirici* ("synoptic tables of lyric values"), the previous lines summarize the salient points of a larger situation, which explains their telegraphic style. It is up to the reader to supply the missing context and to complete the picture.

Interestingly, the verbal structures reflect the visual configuration on two different levels. For one thing Junoy proceeds from the inside out, from subjective feelings to objective phenomena. Thus the sensation of well-being attached to sunbathing gives way to the sound of laughter. Inner joy ("mentol al cor") leads to the voluptuous rose. For another thing, each of the first four lines contains an image that conforms to the visual pattern. The first of these allows us to identify the visual configuration. Although this fluctuates in the course of the poem, it is still possible to point to a primary image that dominates the composition. Like "ja de bona hora," "Eufòria" is motivated by the powerful rays of the *sun*. In the next line the visual pattern is repeated by the palpitating heart, which transmits blood and sound waves in every direction. Although it is possible to reconcile the spiral in line 3 with the radial model, in fact it refers to another visual characteristic. In reading the poem we must rotate the text 360 degrees in order to decipher its lines. From a visual standpoint these three images are thoroughly dynamic. Returning to the radial pattern in the fourth line, the rose introduces a static note that slows the poem's momentum. Visually the composition comprises a series of tautologies geared to successive lines. Sun, heart, spiral, rose – each consists of a verbal image that has been raised to the visual level.

Junoy's masterpiece "Guynemer" is the only one of his visual poems to achieve international recognition. It is also the only example of this genre cited by name in the literary histories of Catalonia.[10] Published in *Iberia* on October 6, 1917, "Guynemer" was translated into French and issued as a pamphlet about March 1, 1918.[11] The poem's title refers to the French aviation ace Georges Guynemer, who disappeared over Pool-Capelle, Belgium, during an aerial dual that would have been his fifty-fourth victory. Apollinaire, who immediately grasped the visual principle at work, described the composition as follows:

> Sur une page de japon, en points représentant les constellations, on peut lire *Ciel de France* tandis que la chute de l'avion du grand aviateur est figurée par une courbe qui se lit de bas en haut pour indiquer la remontée au firmament de l'âme du héros.

> On a single page, in dots representing constellations, are the words "Sky of France," while the plunging airplane of the great aviator is depicted by a curve that reads from bottom to top, indicating the path of the hero's soul on its way to heaven.[12]

The economy of line in this composition is unprecedented in the history of visual poetry. To have designed a simple curve that would depict two opposite motions (and notions) was a stroke of genius. Apollinaire neglects to add that the curve is tapered toward the top to give the illusion of distance. This is the only visual poem in Catalonia to incorporate a three-dimensional perspective. In addition the first two words are larger and darker than the rest, suggesting the doomed aircraft as it plunges through space. The visual and verbal messages are actually congruent here, since the poem begins with a metaphor for the airplane, "en l'estel" ("in the star"). Threading its way through the words "CEL DE FRANÇA" ("SKY OVER FRANCE"), the curve reads "en l'estel mortalment ferit per l'espai hi brunceig encara el lluent cor del motor mes l'ánima viva del adolescent heroï vola ja vers les constelacións" ("In the mortally wounded star the motor's glowing heart still buzzes through space, but the intrepid soul of the young aerial hero already soars toward the constellations").[13] A note at the bottom informs the reader that Junoy has petitioned the French minister of public instruction and the president of the Société Astronomique to name a constellation after Guynemer.

In terms of visual composition "Guynemer" juxtaposes two sorts of shaped writing. Like "ja de bona hora," the central curve retraces the path of an actual object and consists of an outlined form. However, the alphabetical constellations are like nothing we have seen before and do not seem to correspond to our typology. Careful consideration of the various categories reveals that they are a unique type of visual analogy based on the technique of distorted letters. The latter are not bent into unusual shapes but decomposed into a series of dots to suggest individual stars.

99

GUYNEMER

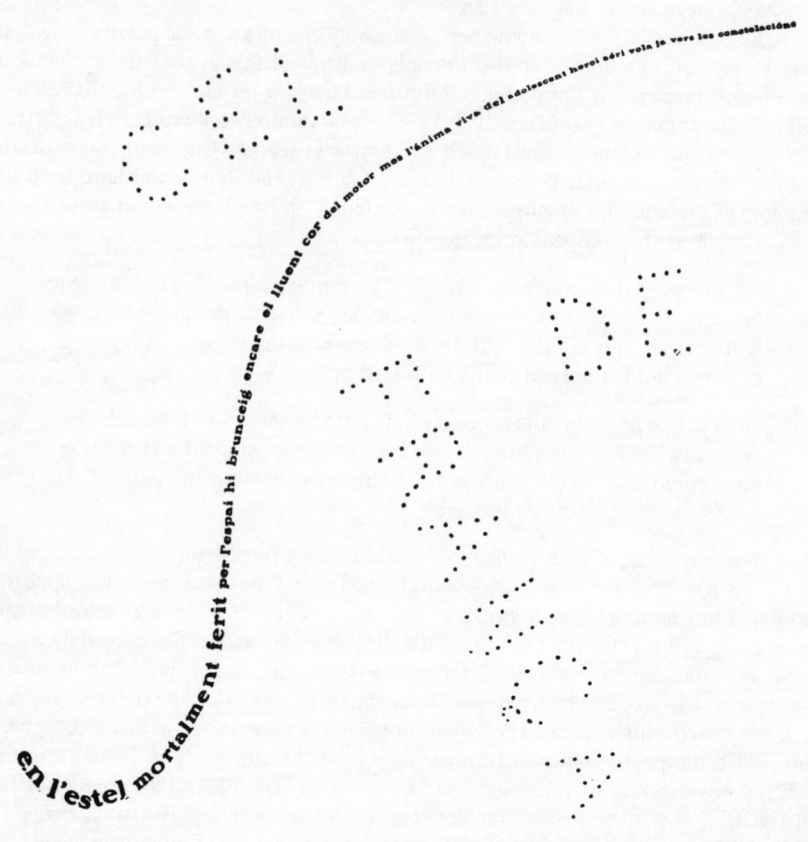

Figure 28. Josep-Maria Junoy

100

Josep-Maria Junoy

Despite their dematerialized state, they spell out their subject at the same time that they enact it. Pursuing the implications inherent in this process, we can identify "CEL DE FRANÇA" as a visual metonym based on the principle of physical proximity. The latter depends not on the letters' shapes but on their peculiar texture. Juxtaposed with the verbal message "night sky," the visual response is to project images of stars. The relation between the two messages is thus that of part to whole. The verbal tenor is both dispersed and perpetuated by its visual vehicle in a synecdochic exchange. That the sinuous curve exploits tautological structures is more readily apparent. Indeed it functions as a *double* visual tautology. This is in keeping with the dual metonymic focus of the verbal text, which superimposes one narrative episode on another. On the one hand, the plunging airplane is related to Guynemer through functional proximity. On the other, the relation of the ascending soul to the aviator is that of part to whole. Both trajectories are realized at the visual level.

Like most of Junoy's works, the poem depends on a series of oppositions: up versus down, heaven versus earth, soul versus body, life versus death, and so forth. Although we have encountered these before in "Estela angular," they are presented here visually as well as verbally. Each of the verbal oppositions is inscribed in the polarity of the visual text. Interestingly, no direct mention is made of Guynemer's death. Instead his physical fate is transferred to the airplane, which is personified as a human being. Even here the distancing process continues, for the final image – now twice removed – is that of a *star*. In this way Junoy uses displacement and metaphor to minimize the actual loss. The "mortally wounded star" seems incongruous at first, which may explain why it was deleted in later versions. The existence of constellations spelling "CEL DE FRANÇA," however, makes it clear that the action takes place at night. This means that the airplane's "glowing heart" – an anthropomorphic metaphor for its flaming engine – is highly visible. As the craft plunges to the ground its arc resembles that of a meteor or falling star. Indeed the star is the most important image in the poem. That "Guynemer" begins and ends with this image gives the composition a deliberate symmetry. In addition the visual progression star ⟶ glowing heart ⟶ constellations, which follows an upward path, balances the verbal falling-star metaphor, which plummets in the opposite direction. Visually and verbally the poem ends on a positive note. On both levels we witness Guynemer's apotheosis. At this point something very interesting happens: The poetic frame expands to include the reader and brings us back to the real, that is, nonpoetic, world. Proceeding from fantasy to fact, Junoy seeks to project his poetic vision on reality. In asking that a star or constellation bear the aviator's name he is seeking to revive an ancient tradition. The heroes of Greek mythology, among others, were often metamorphosed into stars to commemorate an important event. By transferring his name to a constellation Guynemer would acquire a mythic dimension in life (or death) rivaling the mythos of Junoy's poem. The tragic image of the falling star would be obliterated forever by the glory of the rising star, which would mark his final triumph.[14]

"Guynemer" not only represents the high point of Junoy's visual career; it marks the end of his experimentation with this genre. Following its widespread success he was apparently unwilling to risk his reputation on other works, which could not fail to be inferior. For all practical purposes he had exhausted the potential of visual poetry as he understood it. The October 1917 issue of *Troços* contained a poem entitled "C_2H_2" which inaugurated a new series of works written in *vers libres*. Though relatively brief, Junoy's visual period awakened other Catalan poets to the possibilities of visual form. Among those who followed in his footsteps were Vicenç Solé de Sojo, Joan Salvat-Papasseit, Joaquim Folguera, and Carles Sindreu i Pons. Although their works are extremely interesting, visually they are not as appealing as Junoy's. Junoy was an accomplished artist who possessed a sophisticated sense of design. Keenly aware of the nuances of visual language, he extracted a maximum of meaning from the shape of his poetry. Oscillating between outlined form and visual analogy (which he favored), he experimented with a wide variety of visual effects. Although his works exhibit a definite preference for visual metonymy, visual tautology is also a favorite device. Since it is a more demanding form, visual metaphor is used sparingly. As much as anything Junoy's final significance derives from his dual training in art and literature. One of the few visual poets with genuine artistic gifts, he was able to accommodate the demands of the verbal sign to the nature of visual signification with great success.

6

Modes of visual analogy in Catalonia

Time and tennis

In Chapter 5 we examined Junoy's pioneering role in the Catalan visual poetry movement. The next two chapters explore the visual poetry of those who came after him, especially that of Joan Salvat-Papasseit, who will be studied separately from the others. During the decade following the publication of "Guynemer" the genre enjoyed a certain vogue and underwent a number of transformations. With the exception of Carles Sindreu i Pons, Junoy's immediate successors were colleagues and friends who continued to draw on French and Italian sources. Among the first to follow Junoy's lead was Vicenç Solé de Sojo, whom he once characterized as "una rosa en whiskey."[1] Although Solé's commitment to visual poetry was limited to two poems, these reveal considerable originality and talent. If anything they are even more geometric, more abstract than Junoy's compositions. The first poem, "Sonet," which appeared in *Iberia* on April 20, 1918, is a sonnet in name only. The title refers not to its verbal properties but to its visual configuration, which consists of three outlined forms arranged one above the other. An example of visual wit, "Sonet" translates the traditional sonnet structure into plastic terms: The two quatrains are rendered as rectangles and the two tercets as triangles. Since the verbal text follows no consistent pattern, the basic 4–4–3–3 model is preserved at the geometric level. The poem in translation reads as follows:

> Whirling shells in the Spring air above the land-
> scape of the Ile de France.
> Flights of airplanes in the starless night and the sou-
> nd of bugles.
>
> Moving triangles that scrutinize space and carve
> into the shadow.
> Disabled veterans wearing medals on their chests. And in their eyes
> a dazzling brightness.
>
> Still warm ashes of those who died for France. (In
> the Invalides the marble Sepulchre is grown red-
> der.) And the name of another casualty: Galliéni.

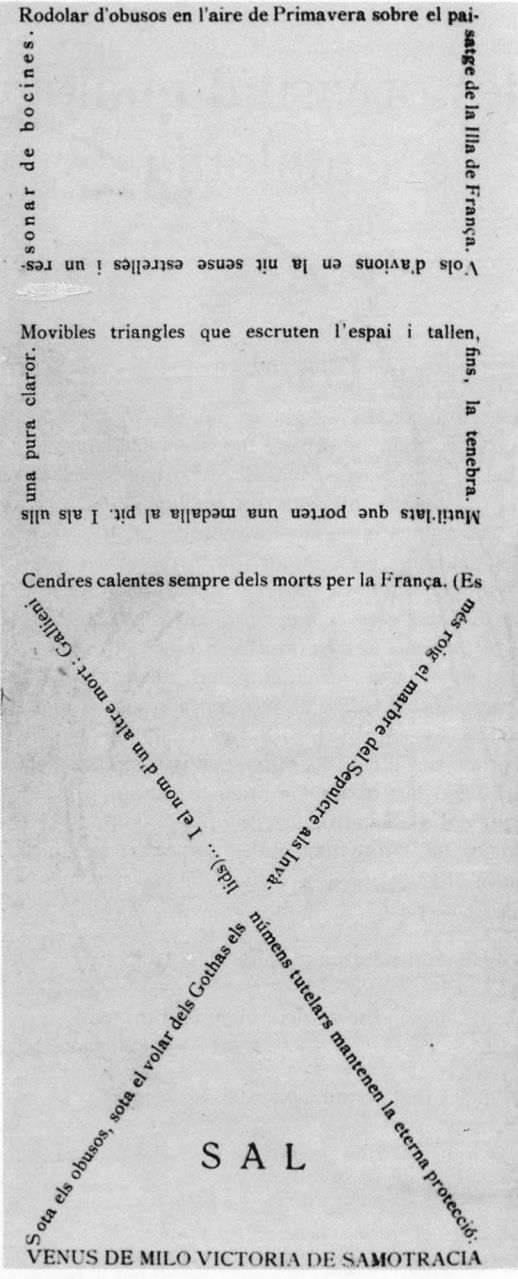

Rodolar d'obusos en l'aire de Primavera sobre el paisatge de la Illa de França. Vols d'avions en la nit sense estrelles i un ressonar de bocines.

Movibles triangles que escruten l'espai i tallen, fins, la tenebra. Mutil·lats que porten una medalla al pit. I als ulls una pura claror.

Cendres calentes sempre dels morts per la França. (Es més roig el marbre del Sepulcre als Invàlids)... I el nom d'un altre mort: Gallieni. Sota els obusos, sota el volar dels Gothas els númens tutelars mantenen la eterna protecció.

SAL

VENUS DE MILO VICTORIA DE SAMOTRACIA

Figure 29. Vicenç Solé de Sojo

104

Modes of visual analogy in Catalonia

Beneath the shells, beneath the flight of the Gothas, the
titular divinities continue their eternal protection:
VENUS DE MILO VICTORY OF SAMOTHRACE
GRACE

At first glance the poem seems to be totally descriptive. The illusion of objectivity stems from a series of rapid vignettes representing various aspects of the war, which give it the character of a newsreel or documentary. Linearity and sequentiality are linked to the principle of *vraisemblance*, which determines the author's textual strategy. This explains why the work is almost totally devoid of metaphor. The latter is a disruptive trope, a discontinuous structure that persistently calls attention to itself. Metonymy, on the other hand, seeks to disguise its presence and to preserve the status quo. Rooted in the objective world, it reassures the reader and helps him to naturalize the text. Linked together by horizontal metonymy, the verbal images in "Sonet" illustrate different facets of wartime existence and stress the "reality" of Solé's portrait. In a similar vein the author refuses to betray his presence by commenting on the action or by addressing his audience. In fact, however, "Sonet" is a resolutely personal poem that implies much more than it states. Buried just beneath the surface, Solé's feelings are easily divined. The composition itself describes a nighttime bombing raid over the French capital. Since the Gothas (a type of German bomber) entered the war only toward the end, concentrating on Paris, we can situate the actual attack during the spring ("primavera") of 1918. Whether Solé was an eyewitness or whether he relied on newspaper accounts, the subject obviously had great immediacy. Throughout the poem there is a dichotomy between attacker and victim that extends beyond the air raid to encompass the entire history of the war. General (later Maréchal) Galliéni, for example, was one of the heroes of the Battle of the Marne in 1914. His death in 1916 was a national tragedy. In general the personal suffering of the French soldiers is contrasted with the impersonal enemy, who wages war by (flying) machine. Whereas the French are near at hand, the Germans are somewhere high above in the clouds.

"Sonet" begins in the air with the image of antiaircraft fire directed at the oncoming planes. Although in theory the field of action includes the entire Ile de France region, it quickly zeros in on Paris. As the capital the city is a sort of "island" in the midst of France. While the bugles are sounding the alert below (and directing the gunners), searchlights crisscross the sky in triangular patterns that repeat the geometric design of the tercets. The enemy has chosen a starless (i.e., cloudy) night in hope of approaching undetected. From this scene the author cuts to the disabled soldiers on the ground whom the war appears to have blinded. Severe as it is, their fate pales beside those who have actually lost their lives. The subject of these lines is thus the misfortunes of France. The section itself constitutes a lament on this theme, the importance of which is indicated by its central position in the poem. Since the focus is on French military losses, Solé invokes Galliéni and the Hôtel des Invalides as metonymic signs. The former symbolizes the casualties of the present war, whereas the latter was the central hospital for disabled veterans. Equally important, it is the last resting place of Napoleon – French militarism personified – whose catafalque and multiple coffins resemble the poem's visual configuration. Masquerading

Aesthetics of visual poetry

O I R L

Paisatge de glicines en floració

emmirallant-se en l'aire blau

a través del filat de la raqueta.

CLAPES DE SOL

Agil corre sobre la court de set capes.

Onades intermitents de «Canadian's Popy»

VELA LLISTADA BLANOA I VERDA

Triangles

la nuca

MEL

sobre

de seda

CIRERES. CIRERES. CIRERES.

Dolly, ja és tard...

V. Solé de Sojo

Figure 30. Vicenç Solé de Sojo

as a witty commentary on sonnet structure, the latter turns out to be a realistic picture and a visual tautology. Not only does Solé evoke the sarcophagus; he depicts it as well. In this manner the verbal realism of the text is continued at the visual level. Nor is the image of the blood-red tomb as arbitrary as it seems. Composed of red prophyry, the outer sarcophagus easily serves as a (metaphoric) symbol of military bloodshed. Returning to the air raid in the last tercet, the author invokes the protection of two sculptures belonging to the Louvre: the *Venus de Milo* and the *Nike*, or *Winged Victory of Samothrace*. As goddesses they will rescue France from her predicament.

At another level a different drama is being enacted around the juxtaposition of airplanes and statues. Symbolizing German aspirations, the Gothas (the etymology of which is symptomatic) threaten to destroy French culture, which is personified by the

106

Modes of visual analogy in Catalonia

masterpieces in the Louvre. Whereas the French recognize the importance of preserving artistic treasures, their adversaries have no qualms about dropping bombs on them. The analogy to the fate of the Rheims Cathedral is clear. Moreover, the repercussions of this act go far beyond the immediate situation. As the epitome of classical antiquity the two statues represent the origins of civilized life as we know it. Once again the barbarian hordes are sweeping down from the North and threatening to obliterate civilization. Solé's last comment – "**SAL**" – is revealing. Although its literal meaning is "salt," its figurative meanings include grace, elegance, wit, intelligence, and perhaps even wisdom. Some of these attributes describe the *Venus* and the *Nike*, but *all* of them describe French culture. These are the qualities that have made France great and that will see her through the war. Despite its tragic subject matter "Sonet" ends on an optimistic note. Thematically the poem can be divided into three movements corresponding to evocation, lament, and celebration. A final glance reveals an additional visual message centered on the word "**SAL**." At this point, following a series of visual cues, the term asserts its literal meaning. Reviewing the picture for the last time, the reader realizes that the triangular tercets depict not only a catafalque but an *hourglass* with a solid base consisting of capitals. The large pile of "SALT" in the lower half indicates that Germany's time has just about run out. France's *salvation* is just around the corner. Thus the poem closes with a striking visual metaphor that complements the ealier visual tautology and prefigures Germany's defeat. If the catafalque stresses human mortality, the hourglass symbolizes the irrevocable passage of time. Together they illustrate the vanity of human ambitions.

Solé's second visual poem is totally different.[2] Not only is it nongeometric, it is situated in Barcelona and devoted to another favorite male pastime (besides war) – girlwatching. Nor is the work exclusively visual, since it includes numerous nonplastic elements. Published in *Trossos* in April 1918, it consists of eight lines of poetry arranged in traditional fashion that are interrupted by a brief visual interlude. Because the design is abstract, one cannot identify it before reading the poem. The title itself is not immediately helpful: "**CIRL**." Since this period antedates the codification of Catalan spelling, Solé may be thinking of the word *serrell*, a fringe of string or beads on the edge of a dress. From internal evidence, however, the title almost certainly contains a typographical error and should actually read "**GIRL**." The significance of using the English word rather than its Catalan equivalent will become clear from this translation:

> Landscape of flowering wisteria
> reflected in the blue air
> through the mesh of the tennis racket.
> **SPLASHES OF SUN**
> She runs agilely across the hard clay court.
> Intermittent waves of Canadian Poppy
> **HONEY**
> Silk triangles
> on the nape of her neck
> GREEN AND WHITE STRIPED AWNING
> **CHERRIES.   CHERRIES.   CHERRIES.**
> "Dolly, it's getting late . . . "

Aesthetics of visual poetry

This composition is organized around the principle of landscape portraiture. Like "Sonet," it consists of a series of verbal metonyms horizontally structured to conform to a particular physical setting. Inserted into this structure at regular intervals, three metaphors sparkle like jewels set in a belt: "**CLAPES DE SOL,**" "**MEL,**" and "**CIRERES.**" Solé highlights these images by printing them in boldface capitals and by isolating them from the rest of the text. Unlike "Sonet," which is a cityscape, "CIRL" is situated in the countryside. From the fact that the wisteria is in bloom and the sky is blue we know it is a beautiful spring day. These indications plus the "**CLAPES DE SOL**" ("**SPLASHES OF SUN**") coming through the trees provide the poem with a leafy setting. Within this framework the action takes place on the grounds of the Barcelona Racquet Club. As in the earlier composition Solé utilizes an objective narrative technique. Like "Sonet" the poem is an impassioned commentary masquerading as pure description. Whereas the former is populated by a great many characters, the latter restricts these to two. One is on stage, the other standing in the wings. The star, of course, is the pretty "**GIRL**" of the title whom we see playing tennis. The "silk triangles" at the nape of her neck indicate that she is wearing a scarf, and the emphatic "**MEL**" ("**HONEY**") describes the color of her hair. From this brief description the reader begins to understand her special attraction for Solé. In Spain she is something of a rarity – a woman with silky blond tresses. Not only is she attractive; she is athletic.

The second character is the author himself, who is inscribed in the work as an implicit observer. From our vantage point in the foreground we glimpse him sitting on the terrace under a striped awning with a drink in his hand. The awning itself is represented visually by a single diagonal line. To the right an X-shaped design represents the silk scarf and suggests that we are viewing the scene through the mesh of a tennis racket. In this manner the central drama of the poem is raised to the visual level and objectified. Framed by the verbal text, the two characters confront each other in the center of the page. To be sure their identity is not immediately evident. To discover the subject of this section it is necessary to peel back several layers of allusion. Although the figures are plainly labeled "awning" and "triangles," their relation to each other is uncertain. Despite their existence as concrete verbal objects, visually the figures are barely recognizable. Both objects are rendered as visual analogies according to the principle of abstraction. Both consist of dislocated phrases whose authority derives from their orientation on the page. Like the figure on the left the figure on the right is a visual tautology. Having reconstructed the outlines of the awning and the scarf, the reader must bridge the gap between these objects and the characters associated with them. Whether he succeeds depends on how well he understands Solé's metonymic code.

At the time this poem was written it was fashionable in Barcelona to spend the afternoon at the Racquet Club talking with friends and drinking imported whiskey. Judging from the evidence before us, the author's favorite brand was Canadian Poppy, occasional whiffs of which are wafted to him by a slight breeze. Conceivably, the refrain "**CIRERES. CIRERES. CIRERES.**"

108

Modes of visual analogy in Catalonia

("**CHERRIES. CHERRIES. CHERRIES.**") could refer to a fruit garnish in his drink, perhaps a Manhattan or an Old-Fashioned. Like its English equivalent, however, the Catalan term involves a salacious double-entendre. Watching the attractive girl and her friends, Solé is overcome with the desire to put an end to their virginity. That the last line is in italics means that it is spoken aloud. "Dolly, it's getting late," one girl observes, implying that it is time to go home. Through her we finally learn the name of the captivating tennis player, which provides an additional clue to her identity. At this point the pieces begin to fall into place. The girl's name, her blond hair, her athletic ability, the poem's English title – these traits distinguish her as an Anglo-Saxon tourist who is enjoying a Spanish holiday. We even have a clue as to her country of origin. For if we assume that Dolly comes from Canada, she is clearly the most intoxicating "Canadian poppy" at the club.

From here to eternity

Joaquim Folguera was an important intermediary between France and Catalonia. Although he was occasionally tempted by Futurism,[3] his translations of modern French poetry introduced the latest experiments to his friends in Barcelona. Like Junoy he admired Apollinaire and even corresponded with him. As early as April 1, 1917, Folguera published a translation of the calligram "Il pleut" in *La Revista*, which led him to experiment with this genre himself.[4] Like much of his work this appeared posthumously, first in the memorial issue of *Un Enemic del Poble* (*An Enemy of the People*) (March 1919), then in *Traduccions i fragments* (1921). His first attempt, "Vetlla de desembre plujós" ("A Rainy December Evening"), was only partially visual but succeeded in capturing the rainy melancholy of "Il pleut." In both works rain and music intermingle on the thematic level, whereas the rain's vertical trajectory (deflected by the wind) is depicted visually. Apollinaire's composition represents a series of raindrops trickling down a windowpane. In "Vetlla" the visual effects are more rudimentary. Although most of the poem is traditional in appearance, Folguera introduces two visual analogies at different points. The first of these consists of the word "**ROSEC**" ("**REMORSE**") printed in boldface and arranged vertically on the page. Recurring every few lines, it features a tapered silhouette in which each letter is in a progressively smaller font. In general the vertical trajectory of the rain is counterbalanced by the horizontal thrust of the wind, which spatializes the work still further. On three occasions one encounters a second visual analogy based on the word "vent" ("wind"), which is repeated in a horizontal series. Each time the size (font) of the word increases or decreases with each repetition, for example, **vent vent vent**.This crescendo or decrescendo effect corresponds to a rise or fall in the wind.

The two remaining poems are modeled on Apollinaire's calligrams. The first, entitled "Musics cecs de carrer" ("Blind Street Musicians"), is even dedicated to Apollinaire:

109

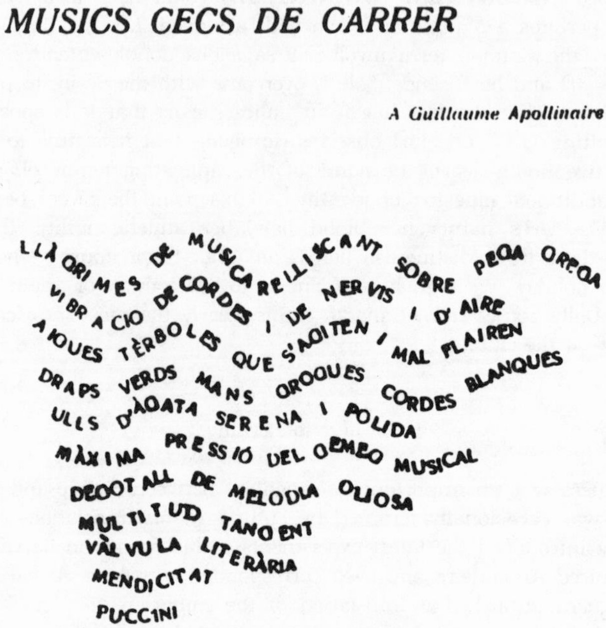

Aesthetics of visual poetry

MUSICS CECS DE CARRER

A Guillaume Apollinaire

LLÀGRIMES DE MUSICA REILLISCANT SOBRE PEÇA ORÇGA
VIBRACIO DE CORDES I DE NERVIS I D'AIRE
AIGUES TÈRBOLES QUE S'AGITEN I MAL FLAIREN
DRAPS VERDS MANS GROGUES CORDES BLANQUES
ULLS D'ÀGATA SERENA I POLIDA
MÀXIMA PRESSIÓ DEL GEMEC MUSICAL
DEGOTALL DE MELODIA OLIOSA
MULTITUD TANGENT
VÀLVULA LITERÀRIA
MENDICITAT
PUCCINI

Figure 31. Joaquim Folguera

Tears of music gliding on resin
Vibration of strings and nerves and air
Turbid, turbulent waters that have a foul smell
Green cloth yellow hands white strings
Eyes of serene and polished agate
Maximum pressure of the musical moan
Gutter of oily melody
Tangent multitude
Literary valve
Beggary
Puccini

At the verbal level "Musics" represents a group portrait. Evoking a group of blind musicians, it is divided fairly evenly between metaphor and metonymy. The task of the latter trope is to describe the musicians and their physical setting. The former's function is largely interpretive, allowing the author to comment on the scene itself. Once again we encounter the characteristic mixture of water, music, and melancholy. The only example of solid form to appear in Catalonia, Folguera's poem has

110

Modes of visual analogy in Catalonia

essentially the same visual configuration as "Il pleut" – with one difference. Comprising eleven wavy lines extending horizontally instead of vertically, it represents both sound waves and water. Although one critic claims that the visual image depicts the ocean,[5] there is nothing in the work to support this interpretation. On the contrary, the dominant water imagery is linear rather than cyclical. The action is bracketed between the "tears" in the first line and the flowing gutter in the seventh. Moreover, "tèrboles" ("turbid") suggests that the water is muddy, which together with its foul odor rules out large bodies of salt water. From the context it is clear that the design represents not the ocean but a stream of dirty, smelly water rushing through the streets.

Seen in this perspective the design constitutes a visual tautology. At the same time, however, the image has an additional function that transcends mere description. Mirroring the competition between metaphor and metonymy in the verbal text, it can also be interpreted metaphorically as waves of music. More precisely, the picture's dual focus corresponds to the equation established in the text between the putrid water and the beggars' repulsive music. Although it seems at first to represent a visual metaphor, like the first image it is actually a visual tautology. The verbal equation is simply duplicated at the visual level. Although the overflowing gutters undoubtedly exist, they serve as the central metaphor of the poem. Like water, music is normally associated with purity and life. Contaminated by an unhealthy environment, they both become disgusting. Where these images diverge is in their function. If polluted water is the principal metaphor, polluted music is the central symbol, representing the musicians' pathetic lifestyle. The reader is left at the end with a disturbing picture of dirty, blind beggars playing a Puccini aria on their violins and possibly singing. Standing in the "tangent multitude" gathered around them on the street corner, Folguera is repulsed first by their horrible music, then by their appearance, and finally by their hopelessly squalid existence.

Folguera's second visual poem depicts an airplane in flight. Entitled "En avió," it is a classic exercise in outlined form. Although its subject matter is reminiscent of "Guynemer" (Figure 28, Chapter 5) the poem's careful figuration places it in the tradition of Apollinaire. Whereas Junoy's airplane is plunging earthward out of control, Folguera's is climbing vertically like a rocket. Eliminating perspective like the Cubists, he confines the graphic elements to a single visual plane, but unlike the Cubists he respects their original sequence. Although the airplane is flattened and schematized in the process, the final portrait is still recognizable. With a little effort the reader can make out the fuselage, the wings, and the tail of an early biplane. Deciphering the poem takes a bit longer, for with one exception the lines are either upside down or vertical. Not the least of the problems is deciding *how* to read. Which lines do we read first and in what order? How do we reconcile the different perspectives, and what is their relationship to one another? One solution is to submit the text to a series of operations dictated by literary and artistic convention. This approach assumes that the poet wanted the lines to be read in a certain order. It also assumes the existence of an implicit reader (thus inscribing the reader in the text) who is familiar with these conventions. Following the visual convention that circular forms progress in a clockwise direction, the latter must rotate the poem to

111

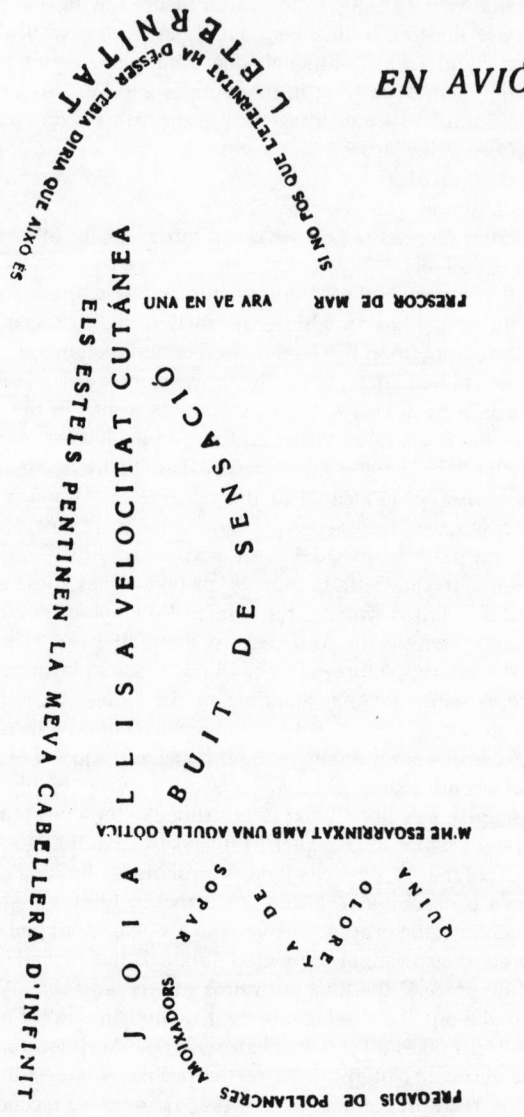

Figure 32. Joaquim Folguera

the right in three 90 degree movements. In each of the four reading positions, he must read all the lines he can according to two additional conventions. Each time he must read from top to bottom and from left to right. This procedure gives the following results:

112

Modes of visual analogy in Catalonia

Una en ve ara
J O I A L L I S A VELOCITAT CUTÁNEA
BUIT DE SENSACIÓ
Fregadis de pollancres amoixadors
Quina oloreta de sopar
M'he esgarrinxat amb una agulla gótica
Frescor de mar
Si no fos que l'eternitat ha d'esser tèbia diria que això és
L'ETERNITAT
ELS ESTELS PENTINEN LA MEVA CABELLERA D'INFINIT

Here we go/S M O O T H J O Y CUTANEOUS VELOCITY / LACK
OF FEELING / Rustling of caressing poplars / Quintet slight odor of sup-
per / I have scratched myself on a Gothic needle / Refreshing sea / If
eternity didn't have to be so dull I would say that this is / ETERNITY /
THE STARS PAINT MY HAIR WITH INFINITY

Despite its typographical complexity "En avió" is fairly straightforward. The
poem begins on a personal note with Folguera trying to describe what it feels like to
fly. That his experience is largely indescribable compounds the problem and forces
him to adopt several metaphoric strategies as a result. These allow him to escape
the confines of narrative discourse and to approximate his experience analogically.
The first two lines are in capitals and form the most substantial part of the airplane: its body. More than anything they testify to the poet's feeling of exhilaration
as he soars through space. The words "J O I A L L I S A" are subject to several
interpretations, all of which are valid. For one thing, *joia* means both "joy" and
"jewel." For another, *llisa* denotes smoothness, simplicity, or evenness depending on
the context. The fact that both terms are subject to ambiguity encourages the reader
to explore their various combinations and permutations. This operation produces a
cluster of metaphors centered around two different readings. At one level the image
evokes the airplane's beauty and simplicity of line, which are compared to that of a
jewel. Both are precious objects reserved for special occasions. At another level the
image evokes Folguera's delight as a passenger. "Smooth joy" is probably the best
translation here, for it suggests the smoothness of the flight as well as the author's
constant emotion. That Folguera wishes to stress smoothness rather than simplicity
is evident from the increased spacing between the letters, which retards the reading
process. Paralleling the airplane's steady progress, the latter is conceived as a slow,
deliberate operation. This device, which depends on dislocated letters, is yet another
instance of visual analogy.

From this it is clear that Folguera's "lack of feeling" is not an absence of
emotion but a lack of physical sensation ("sensació"). Although he is aware of
events around him, including the airplane's speed and the wind whistling through
the cockpit ("VELOCITAT CUTÁNEA"), his attention is directed *inward*. During
his flight, in which he attains a state of nirvana, the author mechanically records
the sights, smells, and sounds within his sphere of perception. That these are
juxtaposed with his mental operations to form a psychovisual collage means that

Aesthetics of visual poetry

"En avió" functions as a *poème simultané*. Consistent with the aesthetics of the latter genre, the poem takes shape around a metonymic structure corresponding to its physical setting. In addition to numerous metonymic objects, whose relation to one another will become clear in a moment, Folguera introduces a series of interpretive metaphors in the guise of thoughts. The visual configuration is neither metaphoric nor metonymic but tautological. Depicting the airplane specified in the title, it simply makes the verbal anchor manifest.

The orderly progression of the verbal images themselves corresponds to the vertical ascent of the airplane. This fact validates the reading strategy adopted earlier, which is predicated upon the discovery of just such structures. From this point of view the value of a particular reading depends on the interpretive coherence it elicits. Rising above the poplar trees, through an open window Folguera glimpses five people eating dinner in their apartment. This is the first indication that the action is situated in (or above) a city and that it takes place at night. Continuing upward the airplane grazes the Gothic spire of a building, which involves a play on words. Since *agulla* means "needle" as well as "spire," Folguera pretends to prick himself as he passes by. The edifice in question is probably Gaudi's famous Sagrada Familia, the spires of which dominate much of Barcelona. This impression is reinforced when we learn that the anonymous city is near the sea: It must be the capital of Catalonia. Finally, as he leaves the last vestige of civilization behind, the poet appears to merge with the infinite. Freed from earthly cares and with the scent of the sea in his nostrils, Folguera participates in his own apotheosis. His ascent to heaven recalls the central episode of Apollinaire's "Zone" in which angels accompany an airplane on its way to Paradise (*Po*, p. 40). Whereas Apollinaire focuses on the airplane itself, which symbolizes modern inspiration, Folguera concentrates on his personal experience. The title is symptomatic: "En avió."

The author's emphasis on process here suggests that more is at stake than a simple airplane ride. What, after all, is the purpose of this ride? And why does it end with Folguera's apotheosis? To answer these questions we must transcend the text itself and consider it from the standpoint of implicit structure. It is also useful to recall one of the fundamental rules of poetics: "Poems are significant if they can be read as reflections on or explorations of the problem of poetry itself."[6] The present composition is concerned not with poetry per se but with the poetic process. More precisely, Folguera is interested in the phenomenon of poetic inspiration during which the poet experiences divinity. This explains the work's trajectory and its conclusion. It also explains the phallic shape of the airplane. Paralleling the increasing tension preceding the act of inspiration, the latter's vertical flight serves as a sexual metaphor. The final moment of orgasmic release corresponds to Folguera's possession by the god. It is this act that constitutes his final apotheosis and that is the ultimate subject of the poem. As a vehicle for poetic inspiration, moreover, the airplane serves as a modern-day Pegasus. The author chooses the airplane as his emblem in order to stress the power and the modernity of his inspiration. Since this equation is established verbally and projected onto the visual plane, the picture is a double visual tautology.

114

Modes of visual analogy in Catalonia

Irony and contemplation

According to Guillermo Díaz-Plaja, the publication of Sebastià Sánchez-Juan's *Fluid, poemes* (Barcelona: Nova Cultura, 1924) marks the end of visual poetry in Catalonia.[7] Except for an occasional bent or vertical line, however, visually this slim volume is entirely traditional. The last examples of this genre actually occur four years later in *Radiacions i poemes* by Carles Sindreu i Pons.[8] The latter work takes as its epigraph two lines from Apollinaire's "Les Fenêtres": "La fenêtre s'ouvre comme une orange / Le beau fruit de la lumière" ("The window opens like an orange / The beautiful fruit of light"). These lines serve as the model for the "radiations" of the title, which are short, pithy aphorisms and/or flights of metaphor. Visually the most successful poem is the example entitled "Futbol" ("Soccer"), which combines both framed and shaped writing. Framed at the top and on the left by a heavy dark line, the text consists of multiple outlined forms depicting a small circle flanked by two parallel curves. These are directed toward the angle of the frame. From its position between them, at the top of the arc, it is clear that the small circle represents a ball soaring through the air. The parallel curves indicate its trajectory. Although it is tempting to identify the right-angle frame as a soccer goal, this is almost certainly not the case. According to this interpretation the design would depict a successful attempt to score a goal, whereas the text describes a futile attempt. At the last second the goalie has managed to block the crucial kick: "amb el llavi esquinçat / ara un home ha blocat / l'ironia" ("with a torn lip / now a man has blocked / [the] irony"). From this it is evident that the frame is symbolic rather than realistic. It represents not a piece of equipment but the block itself; the effectiveness of the block is underscored by the heaviness of the lines, which are clearly impenetrable.

Once this is understood we are free to return to the text, which at first does not make a great deal of sense. The key lies in recognizing that *blocar* is used intransitively. Rather than blocking irony, whatever that means, the man is simply performing a blocking action and its relation to irony is unspecified. That there is a pause after this gesture is indicated by the end rhymes "esquinçat"/"blocat." Taken together the first two lines form a perfect Spanish alexandrine. Although it is possible to reconstruct the poem on the basis of prosody and visual phrasing, much of the confusion could have been avoided with the proper punctuation. In the absence of punctuation – a Cubo-Futurist trait found throughout the volume – the reader must supply a colon at the end of the second line. The revised translation reads as follows: "with a torn lip / now a man has executed a block: / irony." At last the reader is in a position to appreciate Sindreu's accomplishment. Judging from Apollinaire's epigraph, for example, "Futbol" was conceived as a *radiació* rather than as a *poema*. Its pictorial version exemplifies the principles of the genre at both the visual and the verbal levels. Although the poem appears to be a simple description of a soccer play, in reality it is a definition of a rhetorical trope. Equating the latter game with the game of life, the poet defines irony metaphorically in terms of soccer. Irony is a defense mechanism, he implies, the function of which is to protect the emotionally wounded from further injury. Like the battered goalie the ironist seeks to block any attempt to penetrate his personal territory.

Aesthetics of visual poetry

FUTBOL

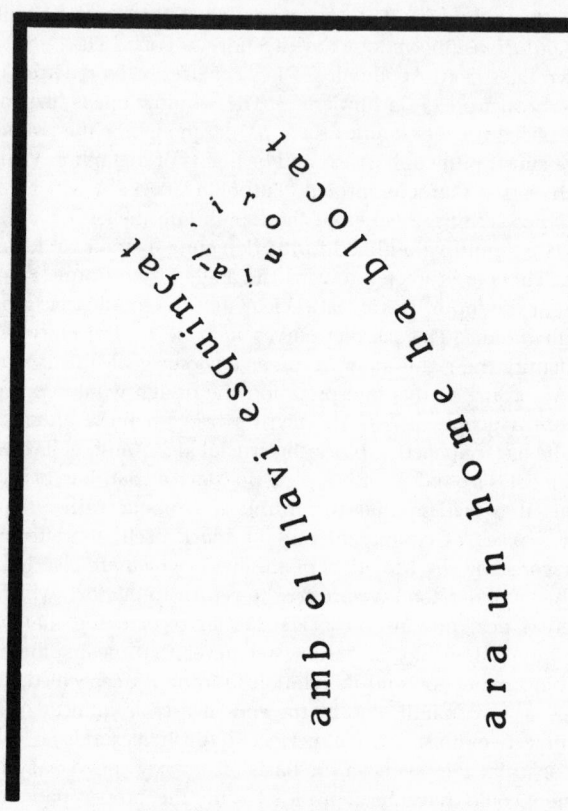

Figure 33. Carles Sindreu i Pons

In this manner the player's torn lip represents his physical condition through metonymy (synecdoche) and his emotional state through metaphor. To uncover its third function we must investigate the etymology of an extreme form of irony: *sarcasm*. Significantly, the term derives from a Greek verb meaning "to bite one's lips in rage." From this we can infer that the ironist-goalie is both hurting and angry. Irony is conceived as a hostile act the reflexive nature of which is evident in the image of the bitten lip. In a sense the ironist is his own victim. Concisely phrased and with attention to stylistic detail, Sindreu's definition is both perceptive and witty. Verbally the poem consists of a metonymic fragment (whose metaphoric

116

Modes of visual analogy in Catalonia

EL VOL DE L'ORENETA

Un mateix so
— Si bemoll — pianíssim
És dins el vent
UNA ALA LLISA
FRISA
Frisa
Arran de terra el frisa -
Ment
L'aigua clara és TIVANTA
El bec tan fi
La ferida li
Allarga
LA LLUM LI OBRE EL CAMÍ
Oh les plomes agudes! — Metall i alè diví —
El gran safareig irradia en ondes extra-
Curtes
«Jeux d'eau» de Debussy
El vol de l'oreneta

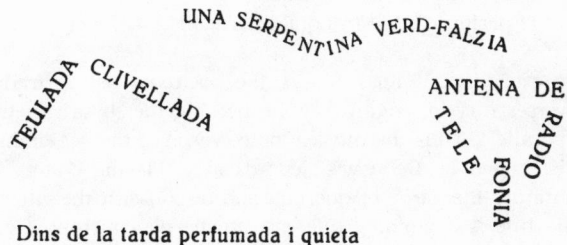

Dins de la tarda perfumada i quieta

Figure 34. Carles Sindreu i Pons

function has been noted) juxtaposed with a simple metaphor: irony = block. This equation is based on the principle of functional similarity. When it comes to representing the latter visually, the author's options are fairly limited. To depict the goal, its defender, his antagonist, other teammates, and so on is technically feasible but artistically forbidding. Sindreau's solution is to portray part of the total scene by showing the path of the ball as it encounters the block. Linked to the vehicle of the verbal metaphor (the block), the design thus functions as a visual metonym.

In many ways "Futbol" is Sindreu's best visual poem. Visually and verbally it combines economy of statement with maximum expressiveness. Despite its brevity there is a certain unity of purpose and style that is lacking in the other two works. The first of these is entitled "El vol de l'oreneta" ("The Flight of the Swallow"):

117

Aesthetics of visual poetry

A single note
– G flat – pianissimo
Is in the wind
A SUPPLE WING
SKIMS
Skims
The landscape at ground
level
The clear water is TAUT
The sharp beak
Enlarges
Its wound
THE LIGHT THE BUILDINGS THE ROAD
Oh what graceful feathers! – metal and divine breath –
The large pond radiates extra-short
Waves
"Jeux d'eau" by Debussy
The flight of the swallow
SERPENTINE THE COLOR OF MAIDENHAIR FERN
FISSURED TILE ROOFTOP
RADIO-TELEPHONE ANTENNA
In the perfumed and tranquil afternoon

With the exception of lines 19–21 the poem is cast in traditional form. Although the verses vary in length, they are tied together by a variety of syntactic and thematic parallels. Thus the musical note evoked at the beginning – uttered by the swallow – is echoed by Debussy's "Jeux d'eau" ("Playing Waters") toward the end, which continues the game of question and response. If the latter is a musical composition, its title is a punning reference to the pond's ripples, caused by the swallow swooping down to snatch a drink in midflight. This at least appears to be the sense of lines 9–12, in which the bird pierces the pond's skin with its beak. Following this metaphor to its logical conclusion, Sindreu describes the widening ripples as a "wound" that the swallow enlarges. Underlying both metaphors is the image of the latter's sharp beak, which is compared to a surgeon's scalpel. Like the first image it is an example of implicit metaphor. In both instances a concrete tenor is paired with an invisible vehicle. Both the pond's skin and the equation beak = scalpel must be deduced from the context. The convergence of text and reader brings each metaphor into existence. Since the same process governs the literary work in general, the one represents a microcosm of the other.

Continuing the game of statement and counterstatement, the water's ripples mirror the concentric radio waves being transmitted by the antenna at the lower right. The fact that these are sensed rather than seen makes no difference. That the author intends us to make such a comparison is clear from his terminology. On the one hand, the poem incorporates a short-wave radio (radio telephone); on the other, a disturbance in the water produces "extra-short waves." The concentric circles are also implicit in the swallow's song, which radiates outward in every direction. From

118

Modes of visual analogy in Catalonia

its position in the middle of these congruent patterns, the swallow dominates the landscape, as it does the poem. We are at the symbolic center of Sindreu's universe, in which beauty and grace represent the supreme aesthetic virtues. For better or worse this configuration is purely verbal. Conceived as a landscape, "El vol de l'oreneta" is overwhelmingly metonymic. With the exception of a few scattered metaphors, Sindreu takes a series of objects and strews them across the poem. For the most part these objects *are* the poem. In keeping with the latter's descriptive premises the author employs a telegraphic style. This device not only permits him to maintain an illusion of objectivity, but stresses the isolation of the individual elements. Typically, one encounters very few active verbs. Many phrases have none at all. Nowhere is Sindreu's love of metonymy more apparent than in his approach to the swallow, which is depicted through a series of tightly focused lenses. Seen first as a disembodied song, then as a supple wing and a sharp beak, the bird exists as a collection of attributes that are enumerated one by one. Although we see "the flight of the swallow," we never see the swallow flying.

At the visual level Sindreu abandons his preoccupation with structure in favor of pictorial illustration. Whereas the words in capitals introduce the swallow and set the scene, the pictorial elements provide a visual synopsis. Interestingly, the transition from the verbal to the visual section is facilitated by a sort of interdisciplinary parallelism. The linear notation "El vol de l'oreneta" is followed by an undulating line designed to mimic the swallow's flight: "UNA SERPENTINA VERD-FAL-ZIA." To be sure the words are highly metaphoric, but their mimetic function is never in doubt. By evoking "SERPENTINE THE COLOR OF MAIDENHAIR FERN" Sindreu may be referring to the dark green mineral of the same name, to festive streamers thrown at parties, or even to a garter snake. All of these are verbal metaphors that do not figure in the visual design. Positioned above the schematic rooftop on the left and the antenna on the right, the trajectory itself belongs to the green-backed swallow. The antenna continues this trajectory and suggests the bird swooping down toward the water. Relegated to the end of the poem, the visual sequence summarizes the preceding lines and leaves us with a vivid picture. The figures themselves are visual analogies, their shapes illustrating various types of dislocation. Like the antenna and the tiled roof, the swallow's trajectory represents a visual tautology. A pictographic device *par excellence*, the design may be substituted for the words and vice versa.

Although we encounter the sinuous trajectory again in "Pleniluni" ("Full Moon"), where it has an analogous function, the latter poem has little in common with its predecessor. Certainly the tone in both is peaceful and serene, and both works take place out of doors. "Pleniluni," however, is a meditation rather than a celebration. It rejects the descriptive bias of "El vol de l'oreneta" in favor of suggestion and insinuation. Curiously, the visual component embodies a different aesthetic than the verbal. Although the former is resolutely cubo-futurist, the latter recalls the earlier achievements of the Symbolists. Not the least of our problems is determining the nature of the verbal–visual link, which seems to be rather tenuous. Among other things, we must decide whether the visual element is abstract or representational. Despite the fact that the entire poem is cast in visual form, there is little that is immediately recognizable:

119

Aesthetics of visual poetry

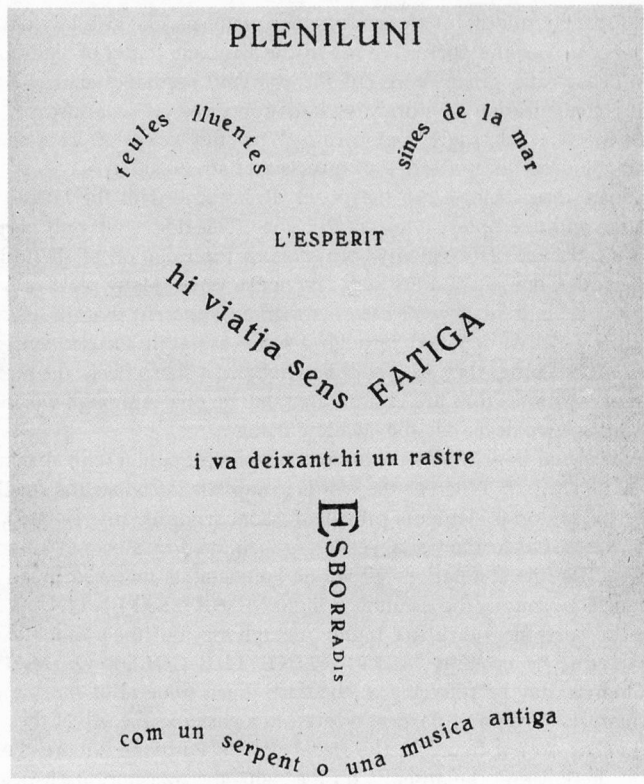

Figure 35. Carles Sindreu i Pons

shining roof tiles   breasts of the sea

ONE'S SPIRIT

travels there without FATIGUE
and leaves a trail that is

BLURRED
like a serpent or an ancient tune

In spite of its avant-garde appearance, "Pleniluni" is a fairly conservative poem. If we rearrange the lines according to their natural sense units, they form a quatrain with rhyming second and fourth verses: "fatiga" / "antiga." Although its message is ambiguous, there is nothing very startling about it. Dazzled by the beauty of the moonlit scene, Sindreu falls into revery. The discrepancy between his present situation and the one he is imagining is expressed in spatial terms by the metaphor of a spiritual "voyage." Since he refuses to specify his destination, that is, the subject of his revery, we assume that this is a private and highly personal

Modes of visual analogy in Catalonia

domain. Although the fact that Sindreu leaves few traces of his passage ("a blurry trail") says something about the nature of the imagination, it also prevents us from following in his footsteps. In the last analysis, of course, the trail is the text itself, which records the author's imaginary voyage. If at the verbal level it is deliberately obscure, enough visual traces remain to permit us to identify Sindreu's objective. Verbally it is conceivable that this is the seashore evoked in the first line – the dream of a landlocked poet – in which case there would be no problem to begin with. It is even possible that, like that of countless others before him, Sindreu's destination is the *moon*. We cannot tell since the syntax is ambiguous. Visually, however, these interpretations are impossible. The seashore clearly represents the point of departure, the moon a silent witness.

Positioned side by side, the first two phrases are mirror images of each other: "teules lluentes"/"sines de la mar" ("shining roof tiles"/"breasts of the sea"). Not only do they have the same number of syllables; each one forms the upper half of a circle. Given their shape and symmetry, they obviously represent two breasts – normally depicted as the *lower* halves of two circles. If the halves are inverted here, it is because they represent the breasts of the sea, which we can visualize as the crests of the waves. Coincidentally, this shape is also that of the roof tiles seen in cross section. At this point the verbal images become equivalent and interchangeable, like the visual images. Each is a metaphor for the other. We are left with the image of an expanse of undulating tile superimposed on the undulating surface of the sea. Thematically and stylistically this procedure recalls Paul Valéry's *Le Cimetière marin* (*Cemetery by the Sea*), in which doves on a roof top become sailboats on the water. Visually each of Sindreu's images conforms to the description of a visual analogy. Whether tiles or waves or breasts, they are essentially abstract forms. And since they reproduce a verbal image, they are also visual tautologies. The translation from waves to breasts is effected at the verbal, not the visual, level, where it provides another example of implicit metaphor.

The first word of the next line, "l'esperit hi viatja sens FATIGA" ("ONE'S SPIRIT voyages there without FATIGUE"), forms a trough between the two semicircles. The rest of the phrase appears below it in a V-configuration. Although the emphasis on the last word is puzzling, the reader finally glimpses the subject of Sindreu's meditation. Visually the two lines of poetry combine to form a perfect heart with "L'ESPERIT" in the middle. Clearly the poet's revery is romatic, as befits a young man on a moonlit night, and is directed toward an unnamed woman. The progression appears to be the following:

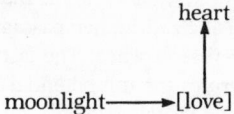

At the verbal level the full moon of the title leads the poet to think of love. Although it is never mentioned by name, love is present as an implicit metonymic vehicle. The proof of its existence lies in the outlined form of the heart, whose source is precisely this emotion. The latter image completes the metonymic series and becomes a vehicle itself. As the traditional locus of love, the heart is connected to this emotion

121

by the principle of physical proximity. As such it represents an implicit visual metonym. The remainder of the poem is anticlimactic. The third line is centered beneath the heart, except for the visual analogy "ESBORRADIS" ("blurred"), which hangs below it vertically like a sword. Each letter is smaller than the one before, so that the word appears to vanish as the reader proceeds, like the blurred trail in the poem. This is an autoillustrative form as well as a visual analogy. The same is true of the sinuous final line, which represents a snake moving from left to right: "com un serpent o una musica antiga" ("like a serpent or an ancient tune"). The verbal metaphor is simply translated to the visual level. In general Sindreu's visual technique is highly ideogrammatic. Breasts, heart, path, snake – each image represents a different phase of the poem, a different movement. Evolving in a linear manner, they constitute a sort of visual shorthand. The author is thus able to transmit a visual message closely paralleling his verbal message.

It remains to indicate the possibility of another, complementary approach to the visual imagery. With a little effort we can detect the outlines of a woman's body. The first line depicts her breasts, the V-figure represents her waist, the next line her hips, and the tapering "ESBORRADIS" her legs, which are pressed together. If we assume that she has her hands clasped in front of her, the V would depict her arms rather than her waist. Up to this point Sindreu appears to have a corpse on his hands, for the body has no head. Fortunately, the situation can be remedied by incorporating the title "Pleniluni." Translated to the visual plane, the verbal moon provides the circular shape we need in precisely the right location. Presenting a frontal view of a nude female body, the poem suggests that Sindreu's revery is carnally inspired. Although it is tempting to identify the anonymous female as a moon goddess, the snake at her feet recalls the myth of Adam and Eve. Beyond a doubt we are in the presence of Eve the Temptress, whose seductive shape beckons in the distance. Since she symbolizes womankind in general, Sindreu's revery is probably not directed toward any one individual. Alone on a romantic evening without a girlfriend, he fantasizes an erotic encounter with an attractive woman. The poem's tone and diction lend dignity to his dream, and the heart establishes a romantic context.

Interestingly, the woman exists only at the visual level, where her origins are shrouded in mystery. Verbally, however, the poem consists of a metonymic sequence in which she plays an important part. If it begins with the progression from moonlight to love, the latter emotion generates two visual images that illustrate it in more detail: the heart and the woman (love object). In turn the outlines of the woman's body lead back to the verbal level, where they generate the metaphor "breasts of the sea." Indeed the entire landscape is eroticized by her passage. Present as a visual metonym, she is conspicuous by her verbal absence. The last of the Catalan visual poets (until recently), Sindreu demonstrates the full potential of the genre. Like Solé and Folguera he mixes outlined forms and visual analogies (which he favors). Unlike Folguera, who relies exclusively on visual tautology, he also cultivates visual metonymy. Whereas Solé experiments with visual metaphor and Folguera with solid form, Sindreu prefers simple visual statements and uncomplicated forms.

122

7

Joan Salvat-Papasseit

Among the various visual poets in Catalonia, Joan Salvat-Papasseit is in many ways the most interesting. Certainly he was the most energetic member of the avant-garde, and his writings reveal a keen sensitivity coupled with a sense of passionate conviction. One critic has even called him "el poeta catalán más interesante de la primera mitad del siglo veinte" ("the most interesting Catalan poet in the first half of the twentieth century").[1] Paradoxically, Salvat's poetry underwent a long period of neglect after his death, and only recently has he begun to receive the attention he deserves.[2] Born into an impoverished family, Salvat lost his father at the age of seven and spent the next six years in an orphanage. Thereafter he worked as a night watchman for the Port of Barcelona, was apprenticed to a religious sculptor, and eventually managed the book department of the Galeries Laietanes. Along the way he developed a passion for anarchism – traditionally a strong political force in Catalonia – and became involved in the struggle for social justice. In 1917 he founded the first of several journals, *Un Enemic del Poble: fulla de subversió espiritual* (*An Enemy of the People: A Review of Intellectual Subversion*), the title of which is revealing. Emulating Ibsen's doctor-hero on a political level, Salvat sought to diagnose the ills of society and to prescribe a cure. In the realm of poetry his revolutionary ardor is confined largely to aesthetics. In general his poems are directed toward the general reading public rather than the educated elite. As Josep Batlló remarks, he was the "primer poeta proletario de la lengua catalana" ("the first proletarian poet in the Catalan language").[3]

The Futurist Adventure

Without a doubt the dominant influence on Salvat's work was that of Italian Futurism, whose inflammatory rhetoric appealed to him. Among other things, his 1920 manifesto *Contra els Poetes amb minúscula* (*Against Lower-Case Poets*) is subtitled *primer manifest català futurista* (*The First Catalan Futurist Manaifesto*).[4] Witness also the title of his 1918 review *Arc Voltaic* (*Electric Arc*)and his first book, *Poemes en ondes hertzianes* (*Wireless Poems* – 1919). It is easy to see why one of his contemporaries called him "el Marinetti Català."[5] As his manifesto proclaims, Salvat valued enthusiasm most of all. Here, as elsewhere, the emphasis is on modernity, novelty, the present, the future, struggle, and youth. "Vivim sempre de Nou," he cries. "El demà és més bell sempre que el passat." ("Let us cultivate the New. Tomorrow is

Aesthetics of visual poetry

always more beautiful than the past.") Elsewhere, citing Walt Whitman, he defines the modern poet in terms of a capacity for energetic activity: "El Poeta serà, doncs, l'home entusiasta" ("The Poet must be enthusiastic!").[6]

Although Salvat, like the rest of his contemporaries, borrowed the term *cal·ligrama* from Apollinaire, he gave it a different meaning. Content with a looser definition, he used it to describe any poem with a visual element. Salvat's "calligrams" themselves vary from the highly verbal to the highly visual. Despite one or two protests to the contrary, they have few common denominators. While Salvat claims in one place that his visual poetry can be reduced to classical alexandrines, for example, nothing could be farther from the truth.[7] Here, as elsewhere, he is probably emphasizing the role of classical discipline in his poetry. Similarly, his statement that they are "cal·ligrames del viure social a la nostra ciutat" ("calligrams of social life in our city") is only partially true.[8] Many have no social focus at all. Writing in 1925, Agustí Esclasans attempted to find a unifying principle based on verbal form rather than subject matter. Again his conclusion that each calligram represents "una pura anècdota" – by which he presumably means a descriptive episode – is only partially correct.[9] Most of the visual poems, however, belong to one category or the other (or to both). With one or two exceptions (such as the prayer "Jaculatòria"), they either are brief vignettes or are concerned with social life in Barcelona.

Salvat's first visual poem appeared in *Arc Voltaic* in February 1918. Entitled "Plànol" ("Map," pp.16 – 17), it is scattered all over the page and resembles a schematic diagram. Normally, the reader would progress from left to right and from top to bottom following two literary conventions. In visual poetry, however, a certain tension exists between the visual and the verbal. There is always a chance that a pictorial convention may intervene and direct one's attention elsewhere. This is true of the present work, for example, which relies on visual coordinates to structure the reading process. Here the literary rules are offset by the observation that the text descends the page in an S-shaped curve. Beginning at the upper left, it swerves to the right before returning to the left at the bottom. Since the poem possesses very little verbal continuity, the reader succumbs to the visual flow of the words instead. This operation produces the following reading:

> **MONT AVENTÍ**
> DECADÈNCIA
> ESGLÉSIES
> XALETS
> ARISTOCRÀCIA   VICI
> IRONIA EN EL CRIM
> SUBURBIS
> RAMÈRES POBRES
> LA GALERA
> HONRADESA   FAM
> HOSPITAL
> El sol ho encén tot
>
> – Però no ho consum

124

PLÀNOL

A J. M. de Sucre

MONT AVENTÍ

D
E
C
A
D
È
N
C
I
A

ESGLÉSIES

XALETS

ARISTOCRÀCIA   VICI

IRONIA EN EL CRIM

S
U
B
U
R
B
I
S

RAMERES POBRES

HOSPITAL   LA GALERA

HONRADESA   FAM

El sol ho encén tot

—Però no ho consum

Figure 36. Joan Salvat-Papasseit

125

Aesthetics of visual poetry

MOUNT AVENTINO / DECADENCE / CHURCHES / CHALETS /
ARISTOCRACY   VICE / IRONY OF THE CRIME / SUBURBS /
POOR STREETWALKERS / THE GALLEY SHIP / HONESTY
HUNGER / HOSPITAL / The sun inflames everything / – But does not consume it

Having reached the bottom, the reader pauses to interrogate the text, which resists any attempt to impose an interpretation. At the verbal level, where it is characterized by fragmentation and ambiguity, "Plànol" verges on incoherence. For the most part it consists of a catalogue of isolated nouns whose relation to one another is unclear. In the almost total absence of verbs there is nothing to indicate the subject of the poem, nor is there any sign of action. The absence of visual clues is equally frustrating. Despite Salvat's preoccupation with visual symmetry the poem appears to be entirely abstract. To be sure "DECADÈNCIA" and "SUBURBIS" are aligned vertically and "ESGLÉSIES" and "HOSPITAL" are both curved. In each case, however, their shape is divorced from their status as linguistic signs. Although their visual aspect recalls the *analogia disegnata* developed by the Futurists, the two forms are worlds apart. Unlike the principle of visual analogy, which decrees that a word's shape should evoke the object or the activity it denotes, these examples have no connection with reality. Their dislocated letters exist purely as visual gestures.

Fortunately, the reference to Mount Aventino at the beginning provides a clue to Salvat's intentions. One of the seven hills of Rome, the sacred mountain served as a refuge for the plebeians who in 494 B.C. revolted against the patricians. Refusing to cooperate with the Roman nobility, they returned to the city only after their demands had been met. Traces of this momentous event survive in all the Romance tongues, where the expression "to withdraw to Mount Aventino" describes a policy of isolation and noncooperation. In view of Salvat's anarchist convictions, he is undoubtedly advocating a similar policy here. More important, the poem compares the two classes and comments on their relations from classical antiquity to the present. Each is represented by a cluster of metonymic attributes carefully selected by the author. For once there is not a single metaphor in the poem. Salvat is concerned with concrete reality, not flights of poetic imagination. Historically, the vice-ridden aristocrats at the top are depicted as the villains, whereas the poor people at the bottom are the heroes. The "DECADÈNCIA" of the former, who own sumptuous chalets and control the Church, contrasts with the integrity ("HONRADESA") of the latter, who suffer from hunger, illness, and oppression. Their plight is symbolized by the images of the hospital and the galley ship, which represent their destinies. If they do not succumb to disease, they are bound to die from forced labor. What vices the plebeians have, such as prostitution and theft, stem from their poverty, whereas those of the patricians are deliberately cultivated. For the poor it is a question not of self-indulgence but of survival. Seen in this perspective the composition serves as a map of the social and political hierarchy.

At this point one begins to wonder about the poem's visual topography. From all indications, for example, the S-shaped curve is more than an abstract form. In the context of the struggle between pleb and patrician it seems to depict a spiral

126

Joan Salvat-Papasseit

road climbing to the top of Mount Aventino. As such it uses outlined form to create a visual metonym. But if this interpretation is correct, what are the plebeians doing at the *bottom* of the hill? Although the reference to galley slaves establishes a classical context, the positions of the historical participants are reversed. The explanation seems to be that Salvat has superimposed two different systems of reference (topographic and hierarchical) in a context that is simultaneously classical and modern. Whereas in 494 B.C. the plebs were at the top of the heap literally and figuratively, at present they are at the very bottom. A poignant symbol of their fate, Mount Aventino is covered today with convents and churches ruled by modern-day patricians, whereas the poor are relegated to the suburbs. Paradoxically, the hill has come to symbolize the very decadence against which the plebeians revolted. What is particularly vexing, Salvat implies, is the injustice of the present social system in which virtue is punished and vice rewarded. More than anything else, "Plànol" represents the author's indignation at this situation and his determination to expose what he calls "THE IRONY OF THIS CRIME."

From 1918 to 1920 Salvat abandoned the visual poem in favor of poetry in *vers libres*. The only exception is a work entitled "**54045**" (p. 22), published in *Un Enemic del Poble* in May 1919, which describes a brief encounter on a streetcar. Except for the boldface title and a few words in capitals, visual effects are limited to the phrase "**ARC DE TRIOMF**," which spans the page like a rainbow. The latter represents a definite advance over the semicircular forms of "Plànol" in terms of visual mimesis and qualifies as a bona fide visual analogy. The next poem to incorporate visual effects appeared in 1921 in *L'irradiador del port i les gavines* (*The Harbor Lighthouse and the Seagulls*). Once again the major mimetic device is a visual analogy shaped like an arch. This time it reads "**ARC-VOLTAIC**" ("**ELECTRIC ARC**") and depicts an arc lamp. Entitled "Drama en el port" (pp. 12–13), the work contains two additional visual analogies. One of these consists of the word "**TRÀNGOL**" ("**SWELL**"), the dislocated letters of which oscillate up and down like the swell of the waves. The other involves the word "**DRAGA**" ("**DREDGE**"), which slants upward diagonally like the arm of a dredge. Since the visual and verbal signs are congruent in the first two figures. they are visual tautologies. The third figure, which depicts only part of the dredge, serves as a visual metonym. Otherwise the poem is fairly regular and presents no special problems:

```
GULP OF OCEAN
              IN THE NIGHT
(ADORNED WITH MAN-MADE BRILLIANCE
                                  ELECTRIC ARC)
AT MY FEET
        WHITE
              GREEN
                   RED LIGHTS
THE MASCULINE              OCEANLINER
SCREAMING
THE SIRENS DO NOT KNOW IT
                         BUT SCREECH
```

DRAMA EN EL PORT

A Lluís Escobet

GLOP D'OCEÀ
        EN LA NIT

(ABILLAT AMB LA CLAROR DELS HOMES

                            ARC-VOLTAIC)

ALS MEUS PEUS
        LLUMS BLANQUES
                    VERDES
                        ROGES

EL MASCLE   T R A N S A T L À N T I C

UDOLANT

LES SIRENES NO HO SABEN
                PERÒ XISCLEN

ELS EMIGRANTS S'EMPENYEN   D R A G A
    PASSO RAN DE LA
                        QUE ÉS FOSCA I CREIX

LA BOIA INQUIETA
            T À G L
        R   N   O

ARA LES ONES CANTEN EL DESIG D'ENGOLIR

EL TRO   AL LLUNY
                SOSPIR DE LES TENEBRES
JO EM VEIG EN L'HORITZÓ

FORA EL PORT LES GAVINES REPOSEN

Figure 37. Joan Salvat-Papasseit

128

Joan Salvat-Papasseit

```
    THE EMIGRANTS PUSH FORWARD
              I PASS NEAR THE    DREDGE
                                 THAT IS DARK AND
    THE BUOY GROWS ANXIOUS   S   E   L
                          W       L
    NOW THE WAVES SING THEIR DESIRE TO ENGULF
    THE THUNDER        IN THE DISTANCE
                                    SIGH OF THE SHADOWS
    I SEE MYSELF ON THE HORIZON
    OUTSIDE THE HARBOR THE SEAGULLS REST
```

Structurally the poem consists of a single extended metonym, which is generated by the image of the port. From the sound of the ocean in the first line to the perching seagulls in the last, everything conspires to delimit the scene. If anything, the work is overdetermined with respect to its imagery. In addition to its basic commitment to metonymy, "Drama en el port" is heavily metaphoric as well. From the image of the narrator's feet positioned by the running lights to the sight of himself in the distance, Salvat invests the poem with his presence. As a result the setting undergoes personification and assumes elements of his personality. Incorporating a string of anthropomorphic metaphors into his metonymic structure, the author evokes a harbor scene peopled by strangely human voices. The sound of the ocean "gulping" is interrrupted at one point by the impatient screams of an ocean-liner preparing to depart. Thereafter we hear the shrill piping of a buoy dancing on the crest of the waves ("LA BOIA INQUIETA"), then the waves themselves, whose persistent song blends with the shadows' gentle sighs. Salvat not only emphasizes the poem's auditory dimensions; he personalizes it at the same time. In direct contrast to "Plánol," in which inanimate objects bake slowly in the noonday sun, the objects in "Drama en el port" are animated by the night. Indeed they are not objects so much as *characters* whose personalities reflect their various functions.

Salvat's final portrait is both more tangible and more intimate than that in "Plànol." The scene acquires a life of its own, for example, that stresses the organic unity of its various elements. On another level the theme of mutual interdependence opens to include the image of the spectator, who embodies both the author and the reader. Like the objects around him he is part of the larger marine environment, part of a larger structure whose purpose encompasses and eludes him. In keeping with the identification between the harbor scene and Salvat, the former pulses with a nervous energy paralleling the uneven rhythm of the poet's emotions. The screeching sirens, the hurried emigrants, the anxious buoy, the surging waves – therein lies the drama announced in the title. As much as anything, these testify to the author's restlessness as he performs his duties as night watchman for the Port of Barcelona. Envying the departing emigrants who are poised on the threshold of adventure, he longs to accompany them on their journey ("JO EM VEIG EN L'HORITZÓ"). In addition to the themes of energy, adventure, and struggle invoked here, the theme of modern technology heightens the Futurist tone still further. Verbally and visually the arc lamp, the oceanliner, and the dredge loom over the rest of the poem, reducing the human characters to the status of pawns. In a very real sense the heroes of this

Aesthetics of visual poetry

work are the machines – especially the virile oceanliner (*mascle* shares the intensity of the Castilian *macho*) – which symbolize both power and speed.

In the lengthy poem "Marxa nupcial" ("Wedding March"), published in the same volume, Salvat refines the technique of the *analogia disegnata* and adds several touches of his own (see pp. 39–41). Linking the real world to the realm of the circus and the cinema – the repository of modern aesthetics – he uses boldface capitals as before to isolate certain images. These are divided into props, performers, and costumes. The poem begins with the image of a spotlight ("**IRRA-DIADOR**"), which is trained first on a group of clowns ("**PALLASSO**") and then on a pretty circus performer dressed in tights ("**MALLOT**"). Unlike the previous poetry, "Marxa nupcial" focuses on three visual images set off from the text. Utilizing heavy dark lines and boldface letters, these are far more emphatic than any of the visual effects encountered before. The first consists of a slogan separated from the text by a heavy black border above and below: "**Escopiu a la closca/ pelada dels cretins**" ("**Spit on the hairless/heads of the cretins**"). Although it is isolated on the page, this astonishing pronouncement is preceded by the phrase "he llegit un anunci a la pantalla" ("I read an announcement on the screen"), which provides an interpretive context. An example of framed writing, the figure represents a commercial advertisement projected onto a movie screen while the audience is waiting for the film to begin. As such it functions as a visual tautology. The heavy borders may be part of the advertisement, or they may be the edge of the slide used to project it. At the verbal level the advertisement is obviously a piece of futurist propaganda. Equating the older generation with baldness, Salvat denounces the stupidity of the established critics with a gesture that condemns their entire age group. As he remarks in another place, "Caldrà que els vells s'aprestin a obeir" ("The old people will have to learn to take orders").[10] That their generation is hopelessly behind the times is evident from the word "closca," which also designates the leathery carapace of a tortoise. Lumbering along at a snail's pace, the so-called experts will never be able to catch up to the avant-garde.

The next image resembles the first visual analogy ever invented. There are four important differences, however, between Cangiullo's "ꜰᴜᴜᴜᴜ**MARE**" and Salvat's "**EDISSON**" For one thing, the letters are not continuous in the latter but composed of a series of dots. For another, they are superimposed on a megaphone-shaped background that emphasizes their progressive expansion. Curiously, the figure is both a visual analogy and an example of framed writing. Furthermore, the image itself is negative as opposed to the positive print favored by the Futurists. The dots are white and the background solid black, suggesting a piece of film stock with perforations. From the context, however, it is clear that the image represents the beam of a movie projector projecting the humorous "advertisement" seen previously. As the inventor of this apparatus, Thomas A. Edison (whose name here conforms to Catalan spelling) is naturally identified with it. This brings us to the fourth difference. Whereas in Cangiullo's example the verbal signifier and the visual signified are identical (*fumare=fumare*), here they are not (Edison ≠ beam/film). Rejecting the tautological relationship of the former, Salvat introduces a double visual metonym. The latter's dual focus reinforces the verbal–visual link and renders the figure

130

MARXA NUPCIAL

Llum de l'**IRRADIADOR** camaleònic damunt
l'estrella del <u>Circ</u> encara hexagonal

Exit! Exit!! Exit!!!

CLOWNS equilàters líders romàntics
Això és sa i en les constel·lacions de quatre barrets
cònics

La terra només gira perquè jo sóc aquí i jo sóc un
PALLASSO qui agonitza

Margot amb el **MALLOT** i els cabells pintats
rojos sembla un ciri que cremi
Només crema per mi:
Davant dels cent centaures que fan faixa a la Pista
<u>DAURADA D'EMOCIÓ</u>

Margot ara m'esguarda fit a fit i en caient del
<u>Trapezi</u> he llegit un anunci a la pantalla:

Figure 38. Joan Salvat-Papasseit

131

Escopiu a la closca pelada
dels cretins

Aquest home que diu:
—La música de Circ és tan definitiva com no la va conèixer
Richard Wagner —— tanmateix un pompier!

La sombra dels comparses en el sol de les taules
Moure's   i projectar-se   no existir:
La **VIDA** al Dinamisme

Jo protesto que això degeneri també
—Perquè ara el «domador» vol fer jocs malabars
i els cavalls   amb les potes

Més m'estimo l'

Joan Salvat-Papasseit

i en CHA**RL**ᴏᴛ que s'han tornat bessons per

tal d'entrar en sèrio a la glòria del cel

(car ells són ignorants de que venim d'ahir
d'abans d'ahir   de l'altre abans d'ahir
          i més d'abans encara)

L'Esfera del rellotge a les DOTZE fecunda les hores
que vindran   que són :

una	dues	tres	quatre
cinc	sis	set	vuit
nou	deu	onze	

i després el

—i així seré immortal perquè d'aquí ha nascut el meu
JO dins el **TOT**

unusually expressive. Although these four refinements are not absolutely necessary, they should not be dismissed as mere decoration. As we have seen they create a broader context for the image and give it a solidity and specificity lacking in Cangiullo's version. Each addition represents a significant improvement over the original model.

The third visual image constitutes an even greater departure from this model, for the visual and verbal elements seem to be totally unrelated. What are we to make of a large circle intersected vertically by the letters "**C** **NNUʙɪ**"? The last

133

five letters are enclosed by the circle itself, the rim of which fills the gap between **C** and **N,** and extend all the way to its center. Perched on top of the circle, only the first letter extends beyond its circumference. If Salvat had chosen the word "CLOWN" here, it would be easy to picture a circus figure riding on a gigantic unicycle – and indeed this possibility cannot be completely dismissed. Judging from the verbal context, however, the figure is supposed to depict a clock striking twelve. Among other things, this would make it a visual tautology. The text itself is quite explicit: "L'Esfera del rellotge a les **DOTZE** fecunda les hores" ("At **TWELVE** o'clock the clock's face gives birth to the hours"). This notation is followed by the numbers one through eleven, leaving the figure to depict the last stroke visually. Although this interpretation provides a satisfactory explanation of the visual configuration, it is of no help in deciphering the verbal component. To be sure *connubi* ("marriage") recalls the wedding march of the title, but one is at a loss to explain its connection with the timepiece. At this juncture the word "fecunda" suggests a promising path to explore, for marriage and having children are linked together. Reviewing the figure for the last time, one recognizes in its schematic outlines the universal symbol for sexual intercourse. Like the previous figure it functions as a double visual metonym in which the act of procreation is associated with marriage and with giving birth. Like the latter it combines framed writing with visual analogy. Whether the clock is a metaphor for the sexual act or whether the latter is a metaphor for the clock is uncertain. Whatever the explanation, we are left at the end of the poem with the image of the poet giving birth to himself through the medium of the written text. In the last line he congratulates himself on his newfound immortality; " – i així seré immortal perquè d'aquí ha nascut el meu **JO** dins el **TOT**" (" – and thus I will be immortal because from this was born my **I** in **EVERYTHING**").

Neopopularist themes

Although we have previously observed a reaction against abstraction in Salvat's work, the years between 1921 and 1924 saw the triumph of visual realism and the adoption of a neopopularist stance. Of the five visual compositions from this period, four are figurative and one is abstract. In all of them the structural complexity of the earlier works gives way to a calculated simplicity that is typical of the later compositions. The first of these, which appeared in *Proa* in January 1921, uses outlined form to construct a visual tautology. Entitled "Les formigues" ("The Ants"), it consists of a single line that winds its way across the page like a column of ants: "camí de sol – per les rutes amigues – unes formigues" ("path of sun – on the friendly roads – some ants") (p.55). Within the tautological limits of his composition the author could have portrayed the ants in a number of different attitudes. He might have shown them gathered around a morsel of food, for example, or issuing from their underground nest. Instead he has chosen to picture the insects filing across the landscape one by one. Stretching from the upper left to the lower right, their path is delimited by a flower at one end and a starfish at the other. At first glance its gently winding curves suggest that the ants are following one of the "friendly roads" mentioned in the poem. After a moment, however, one realizes

Joan Salvat-Papasseit

LES FORMIGUES

A Josep Lleonart

camí de sol - per les rutes amigues - unes formigues

Figure 39. Joan Salvat-Papasseit

that they must be crossing the road rather than paralleling it. If we assume that the metonymic flower represents the land and that the starfish stands for the seashore, which seems likely, Salvat's ants must be passing from the former realm into the latter. Paralleling the coastline, the road marks the border between these two areas and separates each from the other. In defiance of this arbitrary division the column of ants unites the two and provides a sense of continuity. The fact that their destination is the seashore suggests an amusing thought. Normally extremely hard workers, the ants have taken advantage of a sunny day to spend some time at the beach. In keeping with its general whimsicality "Les formigues" proves to be a portrait of ants on a holiday.

Although a sense of humor had long been discernible in Salvat's poetry, it tended to be peripheral and tinged with bitterness. In "Les formigues" humor is an important ingredient, and the author manages to be thoroughly charming. On the verbal level the sprung rhythm, the asymmetrical couplet, and the comic rhymes are perfectly attuned to the insignificance of the subject. Without the title the ending would come as a complete surprise. Except that it is one syllable short the poem could pass for a haiku – a form on which it may be modeled. Like the Japanese genre it has a tripartite structure and an emphatic ending. Like the latter it depicts a natural scene, in vivid terms, viewed at a particular season (summer) and time of day (noon). Unpretentious in scope, intimate in tone, the poem delights the reader with its casual precision.

Published in 1923, *La rosa als llavis* (*The Rose with Lips*) contains two more visual poems. The first is entitled "Jaculatòria" ("Ejaculatory Orison,") (p. 137) and reverts to the abstract forms of the earliest poetry. The reader's attention is drawn initially to the heavy black bar supporting the title. From there it descends to the four lines below and then gravitates to the upper left-hand corner, where the poem would normally begin. Thereafter the reader performs two parallel operations. Once he has deciphered the column on the left, he submits the right-hand column to the same process:

ROSE THE ROSE AND I AM PRAYING
PETAL THAT EXPIRED TREMBLING
GIVING THE STILL-BURNING KISS
–AND AWAITING ANOTHER PETAL

OH ABSOLUTE BEAUTY
AND I SHALL WEAR **FOREVER** OVER MY HEART
AND I SHALL **DREAM** AT NIGHT
the icon is of gold

DROPS OF BLOOD
THORNS OF LOVER'S-SNARE
WOUND MY FLESH

Although the author may have modeled his poem on an actual object, the likeness – if it exists – is too elusive for the reader to identify. Despite Salvat's use of outlined form, the only pictorial touch in the entire composition is provided by the visual analogy "GOTES DE SANG" ("DROPS OF BLOOD"), the letters of which drip down the right-hand margin. Expressive typography is limited to a few words in boldface capitals, a line in italics, and the initial quatrain in small capitals. Among other things, "Jaculatòria" deserves to be recognized as one of the few modern examples of religious visual poetry. To my knowledge it is the only visual poem in the twentieth century conceived as a prayer.[11] As its name implies, an ejaculatory orison is a type of prayer characterized by brevity and fervor – qualities well in evidence here. In particular Salvat has underlined the title with a solid bar to indicate the intensity of his emotion. The poem's insistent rhythm, redundant rhyme, and elaborate imagery are taken from the Catholic liturgy. Its mystic fervor

Joan Salvat-Papasseit

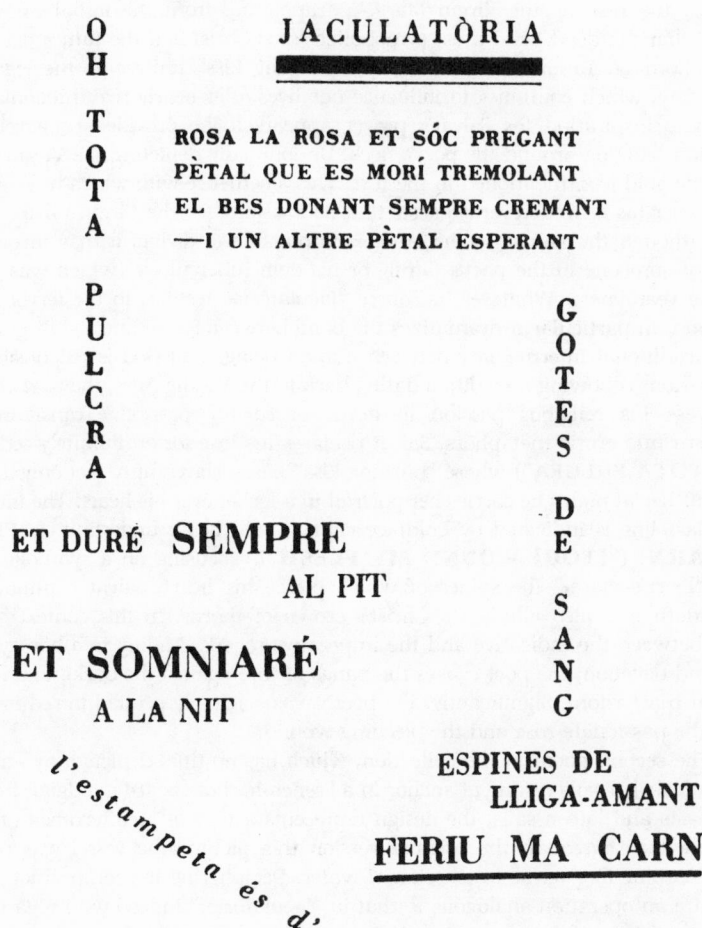

O
H
T
O
T
A

P
U
L
C
R
A

JACULATÒRIA

ROSA LA ROSA ET SÓC PREGANT
PÈTAL QUE ES MORÍ TREMOLANT
EL BES DONANT SEMPRE CREMANT
—I UN ALTRE PÈTAL ESPERANT

ET DURÉ **SEMPRE**
AL PIT

ET SOMNIARÉ
A LA NIT

l'estampeta és d'or

G
O
T
E
S

D
E

S
A
N
G

ESPINES DE
LLIGA-AMANT
FERIU MA CARN

Figure 40. Joan Salvat-Papasseit

and macabre images, however, are peculiarly Spanish and recall any number of medieval paintings on the theme of martyrdom.

The poem itself is almost entirely metaphoric, which makes it difficult to identify its underlying structure. At most it contains a few metonymic references tied to the narrator's continual presence and his religious ecstasy. The first four lines illustrate Salvat's method perfectly. Consisting of a single extended metaphor, they invoke an ethereal rose and two of its petals—one fallen, the other not yet sprouted. To complicate matters the first petal is somehow associated with a passionate kiss. Interestingly, this mixed metaphor functions rather well in the (mystic) context of the poem. Drawing on his knowledge of the Catholic liturgy, the reader quickly

137

Aesthetics of visual poetry

identifies the rose as the Virgin Mary. Extrapolating from the initial image, he realizes that the dead petal must symbolize Jesus Christ and the future petal, the Second Coming. In this context the "still-burning kiss" represents the legacy of Christianity, which continues to influence our lives after nearly two millennia. The immediate inspiration for Salvat's prayer appears to be provided by a religious medallion hanging around the poet's neck. Undoubtedly depicting the Virgin Mary, this is the gold icon mentioned in the text. The vehemence with which he swears to wear it over his heart forever suggests that he is asking for the Virgin's help.

Although the nature of the latter is impossible to divine, it may involve the health of someone in the poet's family or his own tuberculosis (which was to kill him one year later). Whatever its source "Jaculatòria" testifies to the fervor of his conviction. In particular it dramatizes the bond between Salvat and the Virgin, who as the traditional intermediary between human beings and God is responsible for his salvation. Following a tradition dating back to the Middle Ages, the poet chooses to express his religious passion in terms of *earthly* passion. Translating his mysticism into erotic metaphors, Salvat declares his love for an infinitely seductive lady ("TOTA PULCRA") whose "burning kiss" has enslaved him. Not only does he dream of her at night; he carries her portrait in a locket over his heart. The intensity of the last line is indicated by boldface capitals and heavy underlining: "**FERIU MA CARN**" ("**[YOU] WOUND MY FLESH**"). Focusing on a symbolic plant called "lover's-snare," the spines of which pierce his heart, Salvat continues the erotic motif and also alludes to Christ's crown of thorns. In this context "feriu" hovers between the indicative and the imperative moods. Ending in a paroxysm of ardor and devotion, the poet evokes the pangs of love against the background of his personal martyrdom. Significantly, the poem was originally printed in red in homage to the passionate rose and the bleeding wound.

The second poem in the collection, which has no title, depicts a two-masted boat with furled sails resting at anchor in a French harbor (p. 181). Judging from its twin masts and lateen sails, the design represents a type of Mediterranean fishing boat called a *felucca*. In the original version this picturesque vessel was printed entirely in blue to give the impression of water. Deciphering the composition seems to require an operation analogous to that in "Jaculatòria." Indeed with regard both to form and to reading process it represents an inverted version of the latter poem. The reader's eye is attracted not to the top but to the bottom by the heavy black bars supporting the first two lines. Thereafter it moves upward along each of the masts, beginning on the left. Descending diagonally in a final sweep of the sails, it returns to its point of departure.

MARSEILLE PORT D'AMOUR
NOTRE DAME DE LA GARDE PRIEZ POUR NOUS
RESA UNA NOIA EN MON BATELL:

"oh viens tout près de moi

puis pose avec émoi

tes lèvres sur ma bouche

– dans un baiser farouche

je serai toute à toi!"

138

Com sé que es besa
la besaré

SOTA LES VELES LA CAPTINDRÉ

NOTRE DAME DE LA GARDE PRIEZ POUR NOUS

MARSEILLE PORT D'AMOUR

corsari ve i li pren l'aimia—

corsari ve i li pren l'amor

qui no vigila—

oh viens tout près de moi
puis pose avec émoi
tes lèvres sur ma bouche
—dans un baiser farouche
je serai toute à toi!

RESA UNA NOIA EN MON BATELL;

marineret

si no li duia cap cançó—

139

Aesthetics of visual poetry

SOTA LES VELES LA CAPTINDRÉ
Com sé que es besa
la besaré
marineret qui no vigila – corsari ve i li pren l'aimia
si no li duia cap cançó – corsari ve i li pren l'amor

**MARSEILLE PORT OF LOVE / OUR LADY OF THE GARDE
PRAY FOR US** / A GIRL ON MY BOAT RECITES: / "oh come close to
me / then with great emotion press / your lips against mine / – with a
feverish kiss / I will be entirely yours!" / I WILL LEAD HER UNDER
THE SAILS / Since I know she likes to kiss / I will kiss her / The sailor-
boy who is not vigilant – pirates come and take his sweetheart / if he
never brought her a song – pirates come and take her love

The first thing one notices is that the poem is totally symmetrical on the visual
plane. Every line is echoed by a visual parallel somewhere in the poem that is
usually nearby. The symmetry even extends to the typography, which remains
uniform from one parallel to the other. Thus the two passages in small print
represent pennants flying from the masts – which are both composed of capitals.
Similarly, the two lower-case lines slant diagonally across the left mast, forming
the lateen sails. This leaves the pair of lines in boldface capitals at the bottom,
which describe two parallel curves. From their weight and concave shape they are
clearly the upper and lower edges of the hull. The entire boat rests on two heavy
horizontal lines that anchor the composition and represent the calm water of the
harbor. In this way Salvat utilizes outlined form to construct a visual tautology. As
the reader begins to process the poem he discovers that its visual symmetry is
justified by the text, in which one encounters pairs of lovers. Unexpectedly, the
principle of pairing is continued at the verbal level. Salvat chose to situate his
marine romance in Marseille because it was the favorite destination of Spanish
sailors. Of all the distractions offered by the Mediterranean port, their favorite
pastime was trying to pick up French girls. Here the narrator has clearly met with
success. He has not only brought the girl back to his boat; he is about to seduce
her. The lower edge of the hull confirms his amorous intentions and provides an
ironic commentary. **"NOTRE DAME OF THE GARDE PRAY FOR US,"**
Salvat exclaims, because we are about to commit a sin. Borrowed from the church
of the same name in Marseilles, where it is surrounded by *ex voto* plaques, the
phrase scarcely succeeds in concealing his enthusiasm.

Imagining a romantic love affair in a picturesque setting, Salvat mixes passion
with prudence, sophistication with simplicity. These conflicting attitudes toward
love represent opposite sides of the same coin. As much as anything the contrast is
evident in two songs that are incorporated into the poem. Sung by the girl, the
French lyrics describe a woman who is about to give herself to a man and who
invites him to possess her. Applying a widespread metonymic convention, the reader
transfers these emotions to the girl herself, who is behaving quite flirtatiously. Sung
by Salvat's narrator, the Catalan lyrics describe a sailor who is about to lose his
girlfriend to a pirate. The pattern of dominance is reversed here, for she may run off
with another man whenever she wants. Thus women are characterized in the poem

Joan Salvat-Papasseit

ROMÀNTICA

el clar de lluna és un lladruc de gos
quelcom que compromet

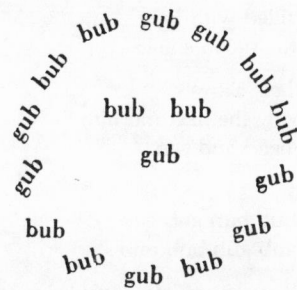

—com una arcova amb llum
la ciutat quan fa lluna

—quan és feta d'una ungla
l'endemà al matí tots els gats s'han fet sang:
al cap i a les orelles s'han fet sang

—i la mar fa

bub bub gub gub bub bub gub gub

gub gub bub bub

Figure 42. Joan Salvat-Papasseit

as alternately passionate and fickle, submissive and demanding. As originally conceived the Catalan folksong serves as a wry commentary on the female sex. Given woman's inherent fickleness, it implies, the wise husband will keep an eye on his wife and will also keep her amused. Salvat gives an ironic twist to the song by introducing it into an ambiguous setting. Assuming that the narrator identifies with the sailor, the reader interprets these lines as good advice. Salvat seems to want to amuse the girl so she will not abandon him. Only after considerable reflection does one realize that the poet identifies with the other male character in the song. Like the pirate, he plans to steal the French girl away from her boyfriend, who has made the mistake of letting her out of his sight. His predictable success will confirm the wisdom of the simple Catalan song.

The last two visual poems belong to *Óssa menor* (*Little Bear*), which appeared posthumously in 1925. Although they have a common interest in folklore and use the rhythms and vocabulary of everyday speech, they differ radically in tone. In the case of "Romàntica" (p. 219) – the title of which is ironic – Salvat evokes the frighten-

141

ing power of the full moon. Rebelling against the romantic conventions associated with moonlight, he creates an atmosphere of Gothic horror:

> moonlight is a dog's howl
> something threatening

gub bub bub gub gub bub bub gub bub bub gub bub gub gub bub bub gub

> – like a bedroom filled with light
> the city when the moon shines

> – when they use their claws
> the cats are all bloody the next morning:
> bleeding from the head and ears

> – and the sea goes
> bub bub gub gub bub bub gub gub
> gub gub bub bub

At the verbal level "Romàntica" is overwhelmingly metonymic. One could even argue that it is *entirely* metonymic, for its three metaphors refuse to behave like metaphors. In theory the first two lines establish the following equations: moonlight = dog's howl and moonlight = something threatening. In each case, however, tenor and vehicle are so far apart as to make the metaphor virtually meaningless. At best they are interesting attempts at synesthesia. In the absence of a tangible image, moreover, the reader's mind tends to decompose the metaphor into its constituent parts. It is no longer a question of equivalence but of sequence. Thus the reader renders the first line mentally as "moonlight makes the dogs howl," which presupposes a relationship of cause and effect. The second line becomes a statement like "There is something about moonlight that is threatening." From independent object to inherent property the change is crucial. Masquerading as metaphors, both images actually function as metonyms. A similar phenomenon occurs with regard to the third equation: moonlit city = bright bedroom. Although this metaphor is much easier to visualize, the reader still tends to dissociate the two images, regarding the vehicle as a limited instance of the tenor rather than equivalent to it. Proceeding on the basis of part to whole, the reader visualizes moonlight streaming through a bedroom window in the middle of a moonlit city. Each element in the poem is thus related to the moon through vertical metonymy and to every other element through horizontal metonymy. As such "Romàntica" functions both as a portrait and as a general landscape.

Without exception the verbal imagery is eery and threatening. If the sound of howling dogs is calculated to set our nerves on edge, the image of bleeding cats is positively repulsive. Even the seemingly innocuous bedroom contains a disturbing element. Whereas darkness is soothing and conducive to sleep, the bright light shining through the windows (like the howling dogs) is probably preventing its occupants from sleeping. Although the visual effects are limited to bursts of onomatopoeia, there is a certain simplicity about them that is appealing. The various "bubs" and "gubs" in the second line, for example, are arranged to form a circle

Joan Salvat-Papasseit

BATZEC

A Joan Garriga Manich

o! aquell encavallar-se
la cadena del pou

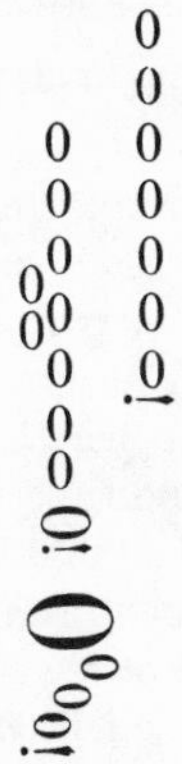

i l'esglai del desprendre's

—la Carme
de treure aigua
va tenir una nena amb el llavi partit

Figure 43. Joan Salvat-Papasseit

representing the moon. A simple outlined form exploiting physical resemblance, it constitutes a visual tautology. This is the only indication in the entire poem that the moon is full–traditionally a time of mysterious events. Although the connection between the verbal onomatopoeia and the visual moon is puzzling at first, the final line reveals that these syllables represent the gurgling of the sea. Conceived as a visual analogy, the line imitates the waves as they oscillate up and down. From this it is clear that the moon is juxtaposed with the water, but more than physical proximity is involved. Since the figure of the moon is composed of actual elements of the sea, it must represent the moon's *reflection* on the water. To see the moon itself as it rises over the Mediterranean the reader must withdraw from the verbal frame and regard the visual text. Positioned above the undulating sea, the moon fills the landscape with its unearthly radiance.

Although "Batzec" ("Heartbeat," p. 245) is an unpretentious little poem, it represents an experiment with a totally new genre–the dramatic monologue. Wishing to avoid the heaviness associated with Browning and others, Salvat provides only a glimpse of his fictional persona:

143

Aesthetics of visual poetry

oh! how tangled
          the well chain is
OOOOOOO!   OOOOOOOO O!   **O** OOO
and how frightening to undo it

– Because Carmen
          went to the well so often
          her baby was born with a harelip.

The protagonist of this charming vignette is a young woman who has come to fetch water from a well. From her general attitude and naive trust in folk beliefs we can tell that she belongs to the common people. Indeed her source of water suggests that the poem is situated in the countryside. According to all indications she is either a peasant girl or the inhabitant of a small village. Judging from the reference to her friend Carmen, moreover, she may also be pregnant. Arriving at the well in any case, she discovers to her dismay that there is a large knot in the chain. Before she can complete her chore she must undo the tangle – a task that frightens her since she risks pinching her fingers. The fact that Salvat obviously sympathizes with her makes the portrait even more touching. Visually the two columns of O's represent the chain, which passes over a pulley at the top (not shown). One must pull on the right in order to raise the bucket on the left. However, since there is a tangle in the middle of the left-hand section – represented by two additional O's – the chain will not pass through the pulley. The bucket itself is depicted as a large horizontal O near the bottom. Beneath it other horizontal O's represent splashes on the surface of the water. Although this section is dominated by visual signs, Salvat places an exclamation mark in each column to remind the reader of their verbal origin. Although the strings of O's function as links of chain at one level, they echo the girl's initial "Oh!" at another. Once we recognize that the links are dislocated phonemes, we can identify the chain as a visual analogy. The poem actually comprises a whole series of exclamations, only one of which is stated verbally. As the unfortunate young woman struggles to free the chain, her repeated cries testify to her fright. At the same time they remind the reader of her palpitating heart, evoked initially in the poem's title.

Although Salvat's visual poetry possesses great diversity of inspiration and execution, it is marked by several constants. At the verbal level his work is remarkable for its vitality, optimism, and explicit emotion. Stung by a long list of social inequities that he knew only too well, Salvat chose to celebrate life rather than to condemn it. To a considerable extent his poetry serves as an autobiographical record of his encounters with humanity. Certainly there is an intensely personal note to most of the poems and an impressive range of emotions. If "Marxa nupcial" is an angry work, "Marseille port d'amour" shows the poet in love, and "Jaculatòria" reveals his religious side. Salvat is sometimes harsh, but he is also capable of humor and of great tenderness. Although his works are noteworthy for their intense passion, they reveal great sensitivity as well. One's final impression is of a man intensely alive, totally receptive to life, and perpetually amazed by existence. These qualities carry over onto the visual level, where the poet's vitality expresses itself in continual experimentation. Varying his designs from one poem to the next, he

144

Joan Salvat-Papasseit

explores idea after idea in an attempt to determine the parameters of visual signification. Although Salvat eventually abandoned Futurism, he continued to observe Marinetti's cult of energy as long as he lived. He also maintained the latter's fondness for visual analogy, although as time wore on he began to use more and more outlined forms. In general his compositions depend heavily on visual tautology. Here and there one finds a visual metonym or two, but Salvat prefers to anchor his images to a solid verbal base. This gives his visual imagery considerable autonomy. The relation of verbal tenor to visual vehicle is not an equation so much as a statement of identity. Visually most of the poems are not concerned with actions or relationships but with themselves. Looming above the verbal text, the visual sign constantly reiterates its presence.

8

The advent of Ultra

The Spanish Ultraist movement flourished from 1919 to 1923 under the guidance of Rafael Cansinos-Asséns and Guillermo de Torre.[1] Writing in June 1919 Cansinos summarized its goals as follows: "Este movimiento aspira a que en él se manifiesten todas las escuelas. El *Ultra* es ante todo una voluntad de renovaciones." ("This movement aspires to embrace all other schools. Above all Ultra represents a desire for renewal.").[2] Ironically, as several critics have remarked, what differentiates Ultraism from its competitors is its lack of specific focus. Although much has been written about the movement's cultivation of novelty and striking metaphor, its dominant characteristic was its unparalleled eclecticism.[3] In their avid search for new principles to replace the *modernista* aesthetic of the previous century the *ultraístas* borrowed from everyone around them. Since they imitated the Italian Futurists as often as they imitated Apollinaire, some of their works are figurative, and others incorporate scattered visual elements. Typically, these utilize expressive typography to create some sort of *analogia disegnata*. In general the most important visual experiments date from a seven-month period between June and December 1919. As we shall see in the next chapter only Guillermo de Torre continued to write visual poetry after this date, culminating in *Hélices* (*Propellers*) in 1923. Although visual poetry per se was restricted to the second half of 1919 (except for Torre), visual elements continued to appear well into 1921. Still, the Castilian experience was much briefer than the Catalan, which covered the period from 1916 to 1928.

The rise of visual poetry

The first true visual poem was Juan Larrea's "ESTANQUE," which appeared in *Cervantes* in June 1919. One of a series of poems chosen to illustrate an article on Ultra by Cansinos, it represents a brilliant exercise in visual and verbal imagery:

Two black wings cover the cygnets
Who are pecking open their shells
What fisherman threw the two fishhooks
Among the golden fishes?
In one of the fountains' branches
A fish jumps suspiciously

146

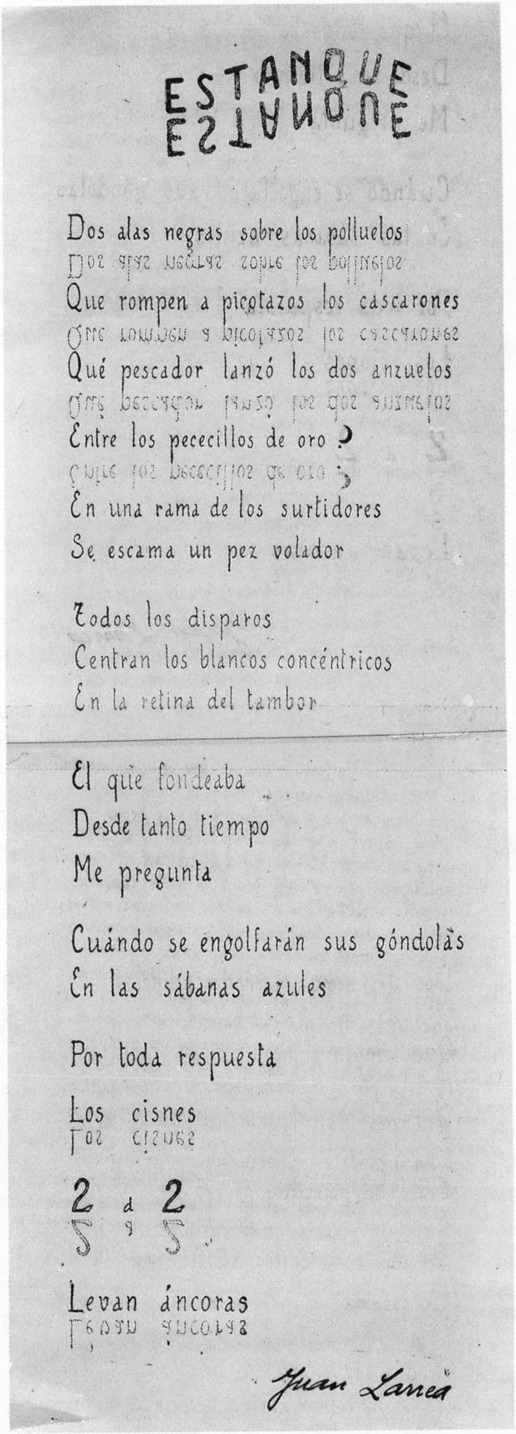

ESTANQUE

Dos alas negras sobre los polluelos

Que rompen a picotazos los cascarones

Qué pescador lanzó los dos anzuelos

Entre los pececillos de oro ?

En una rama de los surtidores

Se escama un pez volador

Todos los disparos
Centran los blancos concéntricos
En la retina del tambor

El que fondeaba

Desde tanto tiempo

Me pregunta

Cuándo se engolfarán sus góndolas

En las sábanas azules

Por toda respuesta

Los cisnes

2   d   2

Levan áncoras

Juan Larrea

Figure 44. Juan Larrea

147

Aesthetics of visual poetry

All the shots
Center the concentric targets
In the cylinder's retina

He who had been anchoring
For such a long time
Asks me

When their gondolas will be engulfed
In the azure sheets

In reply

The swans

Lift anchor

2 by 2

Although a certain Symbolist influence is evident in the poem's diction and choice of subject matter, visually "ESTANQUE" is totally without precedent. Neither the Futurists nor the literary cubists experimented with mirror imagery, which Larrea seems to have invented independently and which he uses to good advantage. Not only does he describe the pond setting in detail; he depicts it visually. The sinuous title, for example, represents a curved Japanese bridge reflected in the water below. Combined with the ornamental carp ("pececillos de oro") swimming lazily in the sun, it imparts a delicate Oriental flavor to the poem. Like the title, seven verses are reflected in the surface of the text, where they are inverted and reversed from left to right. That their mirror image is perfectly legible testifies to the stillness of the pond, whose surface is like glass. No breeze disturbs the flock of narcissistic swans admiring themselves in the center of the lake. The reader's eye is attracted initially by Larrea's title – "ESTANQUE" – whose undulating shape and bilateral symmetry preside over the rest of the poem. Representing a double visual analogy, it exploits functionality and contiguity to produce an image of extraordinary density. Like the word "**EDISSON**" in Salvat's "Marxa nupcial" (Figure 38, Chapter 7), the title depends on multiple visual–verbal links. In its role as a quadruple sign it can be divided into two parts governed by (1) the real image and (2) its virtual companion. Portraying the Japanese bridge, the upper half is related to the pond by the principle of functional proximity. Although its presence is partly ornamental, its purpose is clearly to span the body of water beneath it. The lower half, which consists of the bridge's reflection, is more subtle and more complex. Linked to the bridge by physical proximity, it mediates between the latter structure and the pond. Signifying that the bridge crosses the pond and that the pond contains water, the reflection points in two directions at once. It is literally a floating signifier. In keeping with the poem's status as a landscape, the figure's ultimate goal is scenic. Using two-dimensional cues it encourages the reader to bridge the gaps between the text and the author's three-dimensional experience.

Introduced by the title, the theme of visual doubling is echoed by the first four verses and restated at the end. The poem itself begins and concludes with a double

148

visual analogy. Like the bridge, the swans are attended by their reflections on the water. The former consists of dislocated letters freed from the restrictions of the horizontal. The latter consist of distorted numerals that defy the normal rules of reading. Although the swans sail across the page verbally from left to right, visually their course proceeds in the opposite direction. Superimposing directional polarities, the visual image subverts the authority of the verbal text. Unlike the title, which represents a double visual metonym, it combines visual metonymy and visual tautology. The numerals portray the swans themselves, whereas their reflection evokes the surface of the pond through physical contiguity. Between the two visual extremes the crescent boldface question mark refers to the fishhooks dropped by a careless fisherman. Like the stylized 2's its distorted shape presents a tautological visual analogy. If the poem comprises a series of visual reflections, the same process governs its verbal relations. Structurally the text is an essay in dialectical form in which each level mirrors the other. The graceful curves of the birds' necks, the Arabic numeral 2, the fishhooks lying at the pond's bottom, the crescent question mark, the undulating title, the swan-necked gondolas – all these refer back and forth in an endless series of *correspondances*. The theme of doubling embodied in the numeral 2 is reflected not only in the twin fishhooks, but in the pairs of swans. It is present as well in the jumping fish, whose leap parallels the fountain's jet, and in the fountain, which surges upward only to fall back on itself. Introduced at the beginning by the two black wings sheltering the cygnets, this theme is repeated throughout the poem. Toward the end we encounter two anchorings, those of the humans and those of the swans, in which the author draws a parallel between the birds and his boat. So too the departure of the swans in the final stanza mirrors their birth in the first stanza.

To be sure "polluelos" may also be chickens, so that the initial scene could conceivably portray chicks hatching out of their eggs instead of cygnets (*polluelos de cisne*). Chickens are inappropriate to the aquatic setting, however, and they usually come in two colors – brown or white. From this we deduce that the birds in "**ESTANQUE**," both cygnets and adults, are black swans. Their rare coloration and sumptuous plumage add to the underlying *japonisme* of the poem. After the birth of the swans the poet describes their environment. Besides the fishhooks there are several fountains and a strange image: "Se escama un pez volador." Since this is obviously a freshwater pond the "pez volador" must not be a flying fish, as the dictionaries insist, but simply a fish that jumps into the air. *Escamarse*, "to become wary or suspicious," presents a problem until we realize what Larrea is implying. In his view the fish has a suspicious nature, and thus it leaps out of the water to take a look around. There is also a play on words here, "escama" (scale) evoking the play of light on the fish's scales as it cavorts in the fountain. From all appearances it is probably one of the ornamental carp.

The following stanza is even more difficult but seems to describe the fountains themselves. The poet likens each jet of water to a pistol shot, except that unlike the latter the (vertical) jet returns on itself. This explains why the "target" is at the base of the fountain. The water shoots out of the tube ("tambor"), falls back on itself, and creates a series of concentric ripples centered on the tube's opening, which is compared to an eye ("retina"). Again there is a certain amount of word-

Aesthetics of visual poetry

SED.

Un grito después
        degollará el crepúsculo
      En el instante cúbico
Tus niñas precoces
          que hacen llorar a los pájaros
El paisaje   Como yo
vaciado   con una paja
            sorbo esta estrella herida
En las copas de los árboles ajenjo.

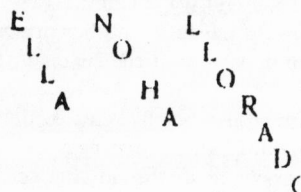

JUAN LARREA.

Figure 45. Juan Larrea

play. "Tambor" not only suggests the revolver's cylinder; it evokes the drumming of the water – like rain – on the pond's surface. And if the primary meaning of "blanco" is target, it also alludes to the white of the eye surrounding the retina. The next two stanzas are deliberately ambiguous. The poet and a nameless companion occupy a rowboat anchored within sight of the swans. His companion wonders when "sus góndolas" will become engulfed in the water. If we assume that the latter is Larrea's son, he may be asking how long it will take his toy boats floating in the pond to sink. The most likely explanation, however, is that the gondolas refer to the birds themselves, which are explicitly compared to boats later on. In reply to the question about their departure, the swans "lift anchor" and sail off into the distance.

"ESTANQUE" was accompanied by a handwritten poem, "Tormenta" ("Storm"), also by Larrea, in which the lines curve sharply downward as if they

150

The advent of Ultra

were being buffeted by a storm. On August 10, 1919, he published a third visual poem in *Grecia*, entitled "SED" ("THIRST"):

Afterwards a shout
$\qquad$ will decapitate the twilight
$\qquad$ In the cubic moment
Your precocious daughters
$\qquad$ who make the birds cry
The emptied $\qquad\qquad\qquad$ As I
landscape $\qquad\qquad\qquad$ sip this wounded star
$\qquad\qquad\qquad\qquad$ with a straw

In the trees' goblets absinth.

It is in vain
It is in vain
It is in vain

SHE HAS NOT CRIED

Although Creationist influence is readily apparent, in its tortured imagery and twisted syntax "SED" anticipates the Generation of '27's experiments with Surrealism. The poem is deliberately refractory, resolutely opaque. None of the characters are identified, and no explanations are given for their actions, which follow one another without apparent reason. Syntactically each phrase is isolated from the others and consumed by a sort of paratactic paralysis. The reader feels lost in a maze in which every verse represents a dead end. Clearly, the poet is not interested in telling a story. Nor does he care whether he is understood. Instead all his effort is directed toward the "cubic moment" of the poem's emotional impact – cubic because it fuses the heterogeneous elements to produce a simultaneous impression. Although this process derives from collage, Larrea is alluding to his mentors Pierre Reverdy and Vicente Huidobro and their experiments with literary cubism.[4] In addition the poet seeks to create a strange, unforgettable experience analogous to what André Breton was to call the "marvelous." At the core of both aesthetics is an emphasis on convulsive beauty that is guaranteed to send shivers down one's back.

$\qquad$ The poem itself exploits the two meanings of *sed*: "thirst" and "drought." The speaker is thirsty precisely because the desolate landscape is suffering from a drought – both physical and spiritual. The first line establishes the tone of perversity and the sense of dislocation that runs through the poem: "Un grito después / degollará el crepúsculo" ("Afterwards a shout / will decapitate the twilight"). Although this is the beginning of the poem, Larrea appears to be telling us what will happen once it is finished. But who will utter the mysterious shout, and for what reason? And how can it possibly decapitate the twilight? The explanation revolves around the image of the guillotine, which is present here as an implicit metaphor. What the author is saying is that a mysterious captain – who can only be God – will shout the order for the twilight to be executed. Metaphorically the death of the prisoner will parallel the end of daylight, which will parallel the end of the poem. Ultimately, of course, the mysterious captain is Larrea himself, who as the author controls all three events. The decollation of the sun, a common theme in *fin de siècle*

151

Aesthetics of visual poetry

poetry, prefigures the wounded star and the girls who are tormenting the hapless birds. These images involve suffering, injury, and even dismemberment. As much as anything they are responsible for the tone of anguish pervading the poem. On another level "Tus niñas precoces / que hacen llorar a los pájaros" suggests that a hostile spectator is present whose glance (*niñas de los ojos*) makes the birds cry. From menace to tears to the denial of these in the final line, the poem follows an ocular path that privileges sight as the principle of landscape. Underlying this drama is another, more familiar scene: a flock of birds chattering in the trees at sunset. Surrounded by thousands of stars, which gleam like eyes in the dark, the birds are signaling the end of day in their customary manner. The fact that the stars are "precoces" confirms our impression that the scene takes place at twilight. As before, the mysterious spectator can only be God, who is invoked here in his capacity as all-seeing deity. Judging from this line and the previous one, he is a harsh deity who is to be feared more than loved.

This brings us to the dialogue between thirst and its alleviation, between emptiness and fulfillment, that is central to the poet's concerns. The birds' tears – an eerie image in themselves – contrast with the drought and desolation, which contrast with the cold drink in the speaker's hand. From one perspective the speaker appears to be sipping absinth through a straw, or perhaps this is merely a recurring fantasy. From another perspective this action becomes a metaphor for his absorption with the wounded star that he sees through the branches of the trees. The operative word here is "copas," which exploits the semantic opposition: treetops/ goblets. Larrea naturalizes this extravagant pun, the terminal position of which makes it even more unexpected, by introducing paraphernalia associated with drinking. The reader completes the operation by noting that absinth is greenish yellow, like the leaves of certain trees, and that the latter's shade can be as cooling as a cold drink. In this manner, despite its purely linguistic motivation, the comparison is transformed into a concrete metaphor.

To understand why the star is wounded we have to examine the last four lines. The figure in this section – a gigantic E with three phrases extending to the right – may have been inspired by a 1917 Futurist text that features three words radiating from a huge S in the same direction.[5] Although the latter represent rays of sunshine, this can hardly be true of Larrea's poem, in which the sun has already set. Although the figure is not immediately recognizable, upon reflection it seems to represent the wounded star. For the first time we are able to identify this object as either a comet or a meteor – most likely the former. Because it has a "tail" the poet compares the comet to a wounded bird like those the girls are torturing. Streaking across the heavens (and the page) from east to west, it leaves a bloody trail behind it.

That "SED" is concerned with a serious problem has been implicit from the beginning. This section, with its triple lament on the theme "Es en vano" ("It is in vain"), stresses that there will be no relief. The very last line, which actually belongs at the beginning, finally states the problem: "ELLA NO HA LLORADO" ("SHE [or IT] HAS NOT CRIED"). This statement probably refers to the star, which, unlike the birds encountered previously, has shed no tears. What it actually means is indicated visually. If, on the one hand, it testifies to the courage of the wounded star/bird who refuses to reveal her pain, the words themselves stream down the page like tears – or raindrops. Present here as a visual analogy, this device is borrowed from Apollinaire's magnificent poem "Il pleut" ("It's Raining") (*Po*, p. 203), where it appears as an outlined form. Visually, then, the final line returns to the problem implied by the poem's title. The anonymous country is in desperate need of rain, but not a drop has fallen. Instead of bringing rain the comet has confirmed its reputation as a portent of disaster. Like the Fisher King, the speaker is left to brood over a dry land and a barren landscape.

What is particularly striking about these two poems is that they were published less than three months apart – "ESTANQUE" in June and "SED" in August 1919. To a considerable extent the former summarizes the preceding Symbolist period, juxtaposing exoticism and opulence, ornamentation and sensation. A dominant pose of aestheticism governs the poet's rendition of the scene and the reader's perception of the poem. Harmony and beauty occupy privileged positions in the text, which seeks to impose a superior order on nature and to defeat the forces of chaos. Stripped of its pictorial elements, "ESTANQUE" remains a highly visual work. Obviously modeled on painting, it functions as a Symbolist landscape in which the page constitutes the frame. This explains why the poem remains resolutely rectilinear. Within these fixed boundaries it confounds reality with physical reflection according to the laws of traditional perspective. Here, as elsewhere, the work of art is conceived as a mirror. From a structural point of view "ESTANQUE" is predominantly metonymic. Larrea evokes the pond setting by means of a linear series of synedochic elements. Images such as the swans, the fishhooks, the carp, and the bridge are linked vertically, like vertebrae, with occasional metaphors branching off horizontally.

If "ESTANQUE" represents the end of an era, "SED" predicts the birth of a whole new aesthetic. Fiercely apocalyptic, the poem depicts an arid landscape from which beauty and harmony have been explicitly excluded. Not only is there no attempt to impose order; the natural chaos of the world is magnified until it assumes a primary role. Here everything is deformed – the landscape, its inhabitants, even the poet's language. The scene itself is peopled with strange characters whose enigmatic actions underscore the pessimistic premise of the poem: "Es en vano/Es en vano/Es en vano." This time reality is conveyed through intentional distortion. Photographic realism no longer suffices since it ignores human passions and subjective impressions. Unlike "ESTANQUE," "SED" is difficult to visualize. There is no coherent frame to order the images, each of which threatens to eclipse the others. Form cannot be imposed from without but must be sought from within. Logic must give way to intuition and feeling. If the first poem is predominantly metonymic, the second work relies heavily on metaphor. Visually the latter features two verbal metaphors that are projected tautologically at the visual level. To be sure the implicit verbal comet is a metonymic symbol of disaster. But the crying rain, the decapitated twilight, the wounded star – these and other images rely on similarity rather than contiguity. Clearly, the poet's imagination has shifted radically from one poem to the next. Abandoning the enumerative technique evident in "ESTANQUE," Larrea proposes a more expressive view of the world in which objects assume a life of their own. Seen in this light, the significance of "SED" is twofold. It

153

Aesthetics of visual poetry

testifies to the poet's desire to (1) revolutionize the written word by (2) restructuring imagination itself.

Night and day

On August 31, 1919, a different sort of visual poem appeared in *Grecia*. Composed by Pedro Raida and entitled "En las noches" ("In the Nights"), it was the first Castilian work to use solid forms, which were generally eschewed by the Ultraists. Raida preferred this style to all others and used it exclusively in his visual poetry:

> *En las noches* ......
>   diáfanas
> de los silencios más claros,
>   cuando solo el viento
>   se encubre y divaga,
> en las sombras sútiles,
> oigo siempre la sonata,
> soberbia y trágica
>   de aquel ARBOL coloso
>   erguido en prócera altanería
>   sobre sus tentáculos sávicos,
>   que pletóricamente muerden
> las entrañas genitales
> de su madre la parda bolchevista.
> Yo no sé si clama; yo no sé si ríe
> en la violenta sacudida
>   de sus ramas potentes,
>   porque siempre me sorprenden
>   con modulaciones y acentos
>   de cadencias fébriles,
>   humildes y místicas
>   y con el
>   rugido
>   paternal
>   del grito
>   ubérrimo
>   de todo
>   hermoso,
>   salvaje
>   amor
>   de la
>   fecunda,
>   atlántica
>   naturaleza.

In the diaphanous/nights/of the clearest silences,/when the lonely wind/conceals itself and wanders,/in the subtle shadows,/I always

The advent of Ultra

hear the sonata,/haughty and tragic,/of that colossal TREE/raised in lofty pride,/on its resinous tentacles,/which repeatedly bite/the genital organs/of its mother the brown Bolshevist./I don't know if it cries out; I don't know if it laughs/in the violent agitation/of its powerful branches,/because they always surprise me/with modulations and accents/of feverish rhythms,/humble and mystical/and with the/ paternal/roar/of the extremely fertile/cry/of all/beautiful,/savage/ love/of/fecund,/Atlantic/nature.

This is a startling poem, to say the least. Among other things, there is nothing about it that is particularly Ultraistic. A meditation on nature in a mode popular at the turn of the century, it is linked to Ultra only insofar as it reflects the cult of energy underlying the movement. The diaphanous nights, the wandering wind, the subtle shadows, the unearthly sonata – these are all themes closely linked to the Symbolist aesthetic that surfaced in Spain as *modernismo*. The leading authority on Ultraism dismisses Raida with the observation "No tenía cualidades poéticas" ("He was not poetically inclined").[6] Certainly there is much in this poem to justify her claim. It is heavily descriptive, for instance, whereas the Ultraists preferred an oblique approach to their subject matter, evoking physical details without naming them. And when the author tires of description he switches to colorless abstractions, ranging from love and beauty to fertility and nature. "En las noches" is also hopelessly bombastic. The entire work consists of two sentences divided into endless dependent clauses and prepositional phrases. Indeed Raida's syntax is so twisted in the final thirteen lines that his conclusion verges on incoherence.

By contrast the text's structure and rhetorical strategies are relatively clear. True to the principle of landscape portraiture, "En las noches" is structured around a series of metonyms associated with the concept "tree." Despite its metonymic backbone it is highly metaphoric. For one thing, each of its "vertebrae" is paired with one or more metaphors whose emotional charge tends to offset its descriptive function. This can be seen in the initial sequence

$$\frac{\text{noches}}{\text{diáfanas}} \longrightarrow \frac{\text{silencios}}{\text{claros}} \longrightarrow \frac{\text{viento}}{\text{solo}} \longrightarrow \frac{\text{sombras}}{\text{sútiles}}$$

and so on. This systematic synesthesia evokes a mental rather than a physical landscape. For another thing, Raida's love of personification leads him to create several extended metaphors and secondary metaphors. Resolved to translate natural phenomena into human terms, the poet begins with a portrait of the wind prowling the landscape like a homeless vagabond. Thereafter he introduces the reader to the principal character – the proud tree – who laughs and shouts as the wind whistles through his branches. The third personification involves the tree's mother, "la parda bolchevista" ("the brown Bolshevist"), whom we glimpse briefly before her son returns in the final section. A number of contextual clues lead the reader to identify this character with the earth, in which the tree is firmly rooted. Although this explains why her skin is brown, it does not account for her radical politics. Rather than an entity devoted to revolutionary change, the earth represents a stabilizing force with a supportive function. This observation suggests that "bolchevista"

Aesthetics of visual poetry

is used metaphorically to describe someone who indulges in unconventional behavior. Engaged in an incestuous relationship with her son, the earth is portrayed as an advocate of free love and bohemian behavior in general.

As bizarre as it may seem, their relationship represents the logical outcome of two stylistic operations adopted in the course of the poem: personification and (implicit) wordplay. The fact that the tree springs from the earth, for example, leads the poet to personify them as mother and son. Noting that their only point of contact is the tree's roots, he searches for a metaphor that will express this relationship and continue the personification. Thinking perhaps of a baby suckling a breast, he chooses to depict a son biting his mother. Extrapolating from these and other requirements, Raida settles on a disturbing image: "sus tentáculos sávicos/ . . . pletóricamente muerden/las entrañas genitales/de su madre" ("his resinous tentacles/ . . . repeatedly bite/the genital organs/of his mother"). The operative word here is "entrañas," translated as "organs," which bridges the gap between the physical phenomenon and its poetic transformation. At the origin of this grotesque image is a linguistic commonplace: "las entrañas de la tierra" ("the bowels of the earth"). Playing on the dual sense of *entraña*, the poet imagines an incestuous act that is logical but entirely implausible and thus succumbs to his own rhetoric. One is tempted to conclude with Ruskin that the pathetic fallacy is an inherently morbid device. The difficulty is compounded, moreover, by the semantic incompatibility between tentacles and biting.

To add to the problems confronting the reader, the final section portrays the tree not as a son but as a father. Wishing to suggest the latter's potency, Raida describes the actual act of incest. Depicting the tree in the throes of sexual ecstasy, the work ends "con el/rugido/paternal/del grito/ubérrimo" ("with the/paternal/roar/of the extremely fertile/cry"). The poem's climax thus coincides with the release of sexual energy. Despite the flaws noted above, "En las noches" remains an interesting attempt at visual poetry. Visually, of course, its solid form is quite appealing. Clustered about the term "ARBOL" ("TREE"), the textual elements depict a solid, leafy tree with a sturdy trunk. Since the picture is a projection of its verbal anchor, it represents a visual tautology. Judging from its regular silhouette, however, this particular tree is motionless. Instead of the wind-whipped specimen described in the poem, Raida evokes the abstract concept "tree." For better or for worse this is an idealized portrait.

On November 20, 1919, Federico de Iribarne published a charming visual poem called "Amanecer desde el tejado" ("Daybreak from the Tile Roof"). Appearing in *Grecia*, as its predecessors had, it was dedicated "A Guillermo de Torre, velívolo en su descomunal avión de diamante" ("To Guillermo de Torre, sailing in his enormous diamond airplane"):

> Before beginning, the curtain
> rises. The star became
> a fountain.
> ORION HAS COLLAPSED
> THE GREAT BEAR KNOCKED OVER THE CART FILLED WITH RUBBLE

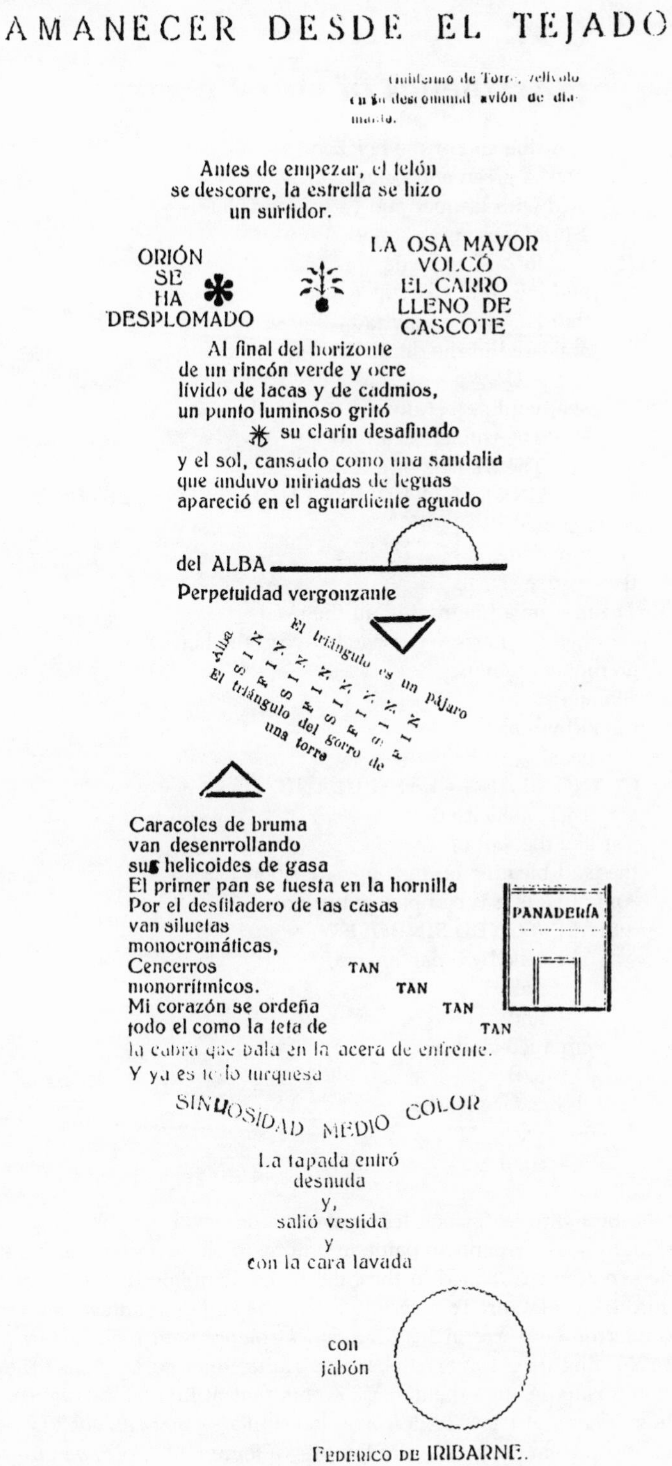

Guillermo de Torre, zclivolo
en un descomunal avión de diamante.

Antes de empezar, el telón
se descorre, la estrella se hizo
un surtidor.

ORIÓN   LA OSA MAYOR
SE   ✳   ✴   VOLCÓ
HA   EL CARRO
DESPLOMADO   LLENO DE
                  CASCOTE

Al final del horizonte
de un rincón verde y ocre
lívido de lacas y de cadmios,
un punto luminoso gritó
    ✴ su clarín desafinado

y el sol, cansado como una sandalia
que anduvo miriadas de leguas
apareció en el aguardiente aguado

del ALBA

Perpetuidad vergonzante

El triángulo es un pájaro
El triángulo del gorro de una torre
SIN FIN SIN FIN SIN FIN
El Alba

Caracoles de bruma
van desenrollando
sus helicoides de gasa
El primer pan se tuesta en la hornilla
Por el desfiladero de las casas
van siluetas
monocromáticas,
Cencerros   TAN
monorrítmicos.   TAN
Mi corazón se ordeña   TAN
todo el como la teta de   TAN
la cabra que bala en la acera de enfrente.
Y ya es te lo turquesa

PANADERÍA

SINUOSIDAD MEDIO COLOR

La tapada entró
desnuda
y,
salió vestida
y
con la cara lavada

con
jabón

FEDERICO DE IRIBARNE.

Figure 46. Federico de Iribarne

Aesthetics of visual poetry

At the end of the horizon,
from a green and ochre corner
livid with lacquer and cadmium colors,
a luminous speck sounded
   its off-key bugle
and the sun, weary as a sandal
that has walked myriad leagues,
appeared in the diluted brandy
of the DAWN
Shameful perpetuity
   The triangle is a bird
   The triangle of a tower's cap
   ENDLESS ENDLESS ENDLESS ENDLESS Dawn
Misty snails
are unwinding
their gauze spirals
The first bread is toasting in the oven
Through the narrow passage between the houses
go monochromatic
silhouettes,
monorhythmic
Cowbells.
CLANG CLANG CLANG CLANG
My heart milks itself
just like the teat of
the goat bleating on the opposite sidewalk.
And already it is completely turquoise
   HALF-TONED SINUOSITY
   The veiled woman entered
      naked
      and
     emerged clothed
      and
   with her face washed
     with
     soap

In the best Ultraist fashion Iribarne combines vivid metaphors, syntactic dislocations, and visual elements to paint an unforgettable portrait of daybreak. Seated on the tiled rooftop mentioned in the title, he contemplates the dawn as the town beneath him begins to stir. To a certain extent the author's vantage point resembles that of Guillermo de Torre in his diamond airplane. Both men occupy privileged positions reflecting their status as observers rather than participants. The preliminary section juxtaposes two metaphoric events that at first appear to be unrelated: "Antes de empezar, el telón / se descorre, la estrella se hizo / un surtidor." ("Before beginning, the curtain / rises. The star became / a fountain.") Borrowed from theatrical vocabulary, the initial metaphor sets the stage for the events to come and establishes a dramatic context. In particular it prepares the reader for the entry of several dramatis personae, headed by the sun, whose appearance will forward the action of the poem. At the literal level the image describes the lightening of the eastern sky that serves as a prelude to the sunrise. The second metaphor is not as easy to explain. The mysterious star does not seem to be the sun, for example, which is called by its proper name elsewhere, *el sol*. Nor is there any explanation of why or how it suddenly becomes a fountain. Following the example of Larrea's "SED," we are free to imagine it not as a comet but as a shooting star. Like the eastern glow it heralds the approach of dawn. Complementing the verbal description, the stellar metamorphosis is depicted visually between the constellation of Orion and that of the Great Bear. This is the meaning of the twin visual signs that represent the beginning and end of the process, progressing from left to right.

With two notable exceptions the juxtaposition of visual and verbal here is typical of the rest of the poem. Inspired perhaps by the illuminated-manuscript tradition, Iribarne inserts a series of illustrations at strategic points in the text. Since these exclude verbal elements and thus escape the typology developed earlier, it can be argued that "Amanecer desde el tejado" is not properly a visual poem. Since the iconic elements clearly participate in the verbal text, however, they can also be seen as variations on framed writing in which the linguistic message is placed beside the pictorial frame rather than inside it. The constellations themselves are suggested only vaguely through the use of capital letters. More interesting from the reader's point of view is the observation that they are behaving rather strangely. Orion the mighty hunter has fallen to the ground, and the Great Bear (the Big Dipper) has knocked over a cart filled with rubble. The significance of these unexplained actions is related to the fact that the constellations seem to be sinking below the horizon – whence their apparent proximity to the earth. Why Orion collapses is difficult to say, but judging from the author's jocular attitude in this section, the son of Poseidon may have been out drinking all night. Whereas the image of Orion stumbling home in the wee hours of the morning taxes our powers of deduction, the reason for the Great Bear's behavior is perfectly evident. Touching the ground on his way past the horizon, Iribarne jokes, the Bear pauses to rummage through a cartload of garbage, which – like his brothers everywhere – he soon manages to upset. The line may also refer to the constellation's shape, which in fact resembles a cart, suggesting that the Big Dipper has "dumped its load." Like the stellar metamorphosis the last two events are in the past tense. Together with the raising of the curtain, they form a prologue to the main drama. In particular the downward path of the constellations balances the upward thrust of the sun. Disappearing over the horizon, they announce his imminent arrival.

Bathed in an opulent array of colors, ranging from irridescent greens to cadmium yellows and oranges, the latter first appears as a "punto luminoso" ("luminous speck"). Restricted to a tiny corner of the sky, the sun is represented visually by a modified asterisk, which figures its radiant energy. In the line adjacent to this symbol the poet indulges in a bit of synesthesia in which he compares the sun's rays to an off-key bugle note. The latter metaphor is particularly appropriate, for if we extrapolate metonymically it suggests an early morning bugle call, such as reveille, used to awaken the troops. Not only does this imply the presence of an army barracks somewhere in the vicinity; the fact that the note is off-key indicates that the bugler is still half asleep. Metaphorically, of course, the image describes the tentative efforts of the sun to penetrate the earth's atmosphere. However, the verb *gritar* ("to shout") complicates things by introducing an additional metaphoric level. Among other things it begins the process of personification that will be continued throughout the poem. In the very next line "cansado" ("tired") furthers this personification, as does the sandal metaphor, which evokes the sun's lengthy journey around the other side of the earth. From this it is evident that the sun's weakness is due to exhaustion, which increases his resemblance to the sleepy bugler. The section culminates in the actual appearance of the sun, which is depicted visually peeking halfway over the horizon. Like the three previous examples the figure functions as a visual tautology. The fact that the horizon is represented by a horizontal line suggests that we are near the sea. This impression is strengthened by the mellifluous "aguardiente aguado" of the dawn. On one level the epithet refers to the sunrise, which is the color of diluted rum or brandy. On another level the double presence of the word *agua* ("water") practically guarantees that the sun is rising over the Mediterranean. The brandy itself provides the ultimate proof. Combining equal parts of fire and water, it describes the sun emerging through the flaming ("ardiente") sea. The water not only reflects the sunrise, so that it appears to be burning; it is actually heated by contact with the sun. The reader is meant to imagine the sea boiling and burning at the same time.

The word "ALBA" ("DAWN") in capitals functions as an intensifier, indicating both the brilliance and the suddenness of the sun's apparition. The next phrase, "perpetuidad vergonzante" ("shameful perpetuity"), is taken from legal terminology and alludes to the cyclical nature of the sunrise. Like a convict condemned to *trabajos forzados a perpetuidad* ("hard labor for life"), the sun is chained to the earth, about which it must circle forever. The repetition of "SIN FIN" in the next section restates this theme. The dawn is "endless" in the sense that it is eternal. Visually the latter section is more difficult to decipher. From a formal standpoint the two triangles balance one another and continue the corner motif established earlier. One represents a bird, the author tells us, whereas the other is the top of a turret. Described as a "gorro" ("cap"), the latter evokes the town's sleeping inhabitants in their nightcaps as well as the military cap worn by the bugler. Judging from these and other visual cues, the structure between the triangles depicts a slanted rooftop with rows of tiles positioned diagonally. Perched on one edge, the bird surveys the tranquil scene. This time the visual design consists of an outlined form. Because it replicates a preexisting verbal image, it too qualifies as a visual tautology.

From the rooftop Iribarne describes the town below as it wakens. Since actual snails would not be visible from that height, the "caracoles de bruma" ("misty snails") seem to be metaphoric constructs. In this context they evoke gauzy clouds of vapor that spiral upward as the town comes to life. One of the first to awaken is the baker, whose shop is represented visually. Technically an example of framed writing, the latter serves as a visual metonym according to the principle of physical proximity. As the smell of baking bread emanates from the bakery, animals pass through the narrow passageways on their way to pasture. Not only is the town near the sea; it is in

The advent of Ultra

a rural environment. Prompted by a neighboring goat, the poet seizes on a startling metaphor to convey the beauty of the scene before him. His heart is gripped by intense emotion, he suggests, like an udder squeezed by a milkman's hand. Among other things this implies that the goat across the street is being milked by its owner. Whereas the following line indicates that the sky has already turned to blue, the next line is fundamentally ambiguous: "SINUOSIDAD MEDIO COLOR" ("HALF-TONED SINUOSITY"). Conceived as a visual analogy, it may describe the muted hues of the sun or the progressive coloration of the hills around the town.

The final section contains another example of metaphorical pyrotechnics. From out of nowhere a mysterious veiled woman appears who is completely nude. After entering a house, she reappears fully clothed and with a freshly washed face. From this fact we realize that she has removed her veil. Structurally the episode is perfectly clear. The binary opposition between nudity and modesty persists from the first set of events to the second, but the elements are reversed. At the heart of this chiasmic structure is the woman herself, who mediates between the two extremes. On a more general level these can be defined as revealment and concealment. The context in which the woman appears leaves little doubt as to her identity. In view of the developments leading up to her appearance she must represent Aurora, goddess of the dawn, who is often portrayed covered with veils. Throwing back her veil at the conclusion of the poem, she emerges radiant and triumphant as the sun climbs above the horizon. Like the town below she is "clothed" in diaphanous light. The work itself concludes on a humorous note. The last image we see is a visual rendition of the sun, shining in the east like a huge bar of soap. Looking back on Iribarne's poem, one notes that it is highly metaphoric at the verbal level but consistently literal with regard to visual phenomena. Conceived as a landscape, the visual text possesses none of the static qualities often associated with this genre. This is because the author has chosen to depict a landscape *in process*. Concentrating in turn on each of the four stages of the sunrise, he manages to capture the temporal element that is missing from most visual poetry. Thus spatial form combines with temporal process to approximate the modes of human consciousness.

Around the zodiac

On December 10, 1919, Luis Mosquera published a visual poem in *Grecia* entitled "Viaje orbicular" ("Circular Voyage"). Utilizing visual analogy and outlined form, it treats a cosmic theme in a humorous light:

> Impassive Chronos is an old man with long, flowing whiskers
> who drives his automobile along the Zodiac's road
> beneath the fruit trees
> stripping petals
> from the constellations'
> b l o o d y
> red roses. . . .

Resembling a giant pinwheel, "Viaje orbicular" revolves about a single amusing conceit. Following the circle of the zodiac from season to season, Chronos

161

Aesthetics of visual poetry

Figure 47. Luis Mosquera

distracts himself by plucking rose petals along the route. Depicted here as Father Time, he is both relentless and remorseless ("impasible") in his passage. His jovial appearance, recalling that of Santa Claus (and Charlemagne), belies the seriousness of his mission, which among other things involves birth and death. Mosquera jocularly modernizes Chronos's image by giving him an automobile – almost certainly a convertible – to drive as he makes his rounds. The zodiac itself resembles a country road as it rambles through orchards and past trellises filled with bright red roses. The latter remind us that Chronos's beard involves an amusing pun. Since "barbas floridas" are literally "flowery whiskers," the old man is perfectly suited to his floral environment. But the term is surely meant to be taken literally as well as metaphorically. As he drives along the road, stopping from time to time to pick a rose, some of the petals raining down on his head stick to his beard, which is thus not only bushy but flowery.

To comprehend the final image, that of blood, the reader must examine the poem visually. Taking the word "sangre," Mosquera creates a visual analogy by

162

The advent of Ultra

carefully spacing the letters and arranging them vertically, a process observed previously in Joan Salvat-Papasseit's "Jaculatòria" (Figure 40, Chapter 7). Here the roses' blood actually seems to drip down the page. The latter metaphor depends on a double correspondence between the two objects. The poet has chosen to compare the rose petals to blood not only because they are red, but because they fall in streams. Instead of a single column, therefore, the reader is meant to imagine a cloud of blood-red petals falling from the sky. And since ultimately the roses serve as metaphors for the stars, arranged according to their constellations, Mosquera appears to be describing a meteor shower. Reviewing the poem, one suddenly realizes why the poet has chosen this particular form. Although the X-configuration initially suggests a pinwheel, upon reflection it proves to depict an hourglass. One can easily make out the two halves of the apparatus as well as the sand remaining in the upper half. If we have seen that the theme of time is central to "Viaje orbicular," the poem now assumes the shape of the traditional device used to measure it. Related to its verbal tenor "Chronos" by functional proximity, the figure represents a visual metonym. In addition it recalls Vicenç Solé de Sojo's "Sonet" (Figure 29, Chapter 6), which features an identical object. In the light of this new information it becomes necessary to reexamine the red stream, for if the falling sand symbolizes the flight of time, the falling blood clearly represents the flight of life. Indeed the second theme is closely tied to the first. Seen in this perspective the poem becomes a self-consuming artifact. Petals, stars, blood, life, sand, and time — all these pass through Chronos's hourglass as he continues on his endless journey.

The next visual poem to appear in *Grecia* was "Signo celeste" ("Celestial Sign"). Published by Adriano del Valle on December 20, 1919, it features two rudimentary visual forms that are framed by the rest of the text:

The star was mine!

Mine . . . !

On the golden staircases the white stars' rosy feet
leave footprints of light,
pilgrims arriving from the barbaric west.
The Moon's axe
bears the blood of a decapitated Sun
who plunged his hair
into the tropical seas
to catch shipwrecked vessels.
ONTO THE ZODIAC'S DISTAFF
Silence's hands
wind the virgin's braids
and the immaculate flax of the Angeluses . . .

Ignoring for the moment the poem's visual aspect, which depicts a night sky, the reader is immediately confronted with the problem of how to interpret the first verse. "¡Mía era la estrella!" the speaker exclaims. "¡Mía . . . !" ("The star was mine! Mine . . . !"). Presumably it is the poet speaking, although one cannot be sure, but why Valle should claim the star for himself is unclear. Nor do we understand the reason for his enthusiasm, which expresses itself through multiple exclamation

163

Aesthetics of visual poetry

SIGNO CELESTE

¡Mía era la estrella!

¡Mía...!

Por
  las
    escalas
      áureas
        dejan
          huellas
            de
              luz
                los
                  pies
                    rosados

de las estrellas blancas
que llegan peregrinas desde un poniente bárbaro.
El hacha de la Luna
tiene sangre de un Sol decapitado
que hundió su cabellera
en los mares del trópico
para apresar a los bajeles náufragos,
Las manos del Silencio

las trenzas de las vírgenes
y el lino inmaculado de los ángelus...

ADRIANO DEL VALLE.

Figure 48. Adriano del Valle

marks and repetitions. The fact that the phrase is in the past tense is undoubtedly significant, since it situates the poem with regard to a single previous event. Other deictic expressions include the possessive adjective *mía*, which personalizes the speaker's relationship to the star and reduces the gap between subject and object. The reader is free to imagine any one of several possibilities. For example, Valle may have made a wish earlier on the first star of the evening – traditionally a lucky star –

164

which he would have thus appropriated for himself. Or again he may be referring to a previous episode in which a particular star served him as a "signo celeste." In the absence of any immediate explanation the line is left dangling while the reader searches for possible connections. At the level of the surface structures his quest is ultimately frustrated. There is nothing in the chain of signifiers that provides an interpretive context.

The next three lines introduce the first of several personifications. A band of stars traverse the sky on a celestial staircase, leaving glowing footprints in their wake. Strictly speaking, the word for "staircase" is *escalera*, not *escala*, which means both "ladder" and "musical scale." In fact Valle is almost certainly playing on the second meaning, for the phrase appears to descend the page note by note, like the musical scale in Vicente Huidobro's "Tour Eiffel," which also doubles as a staircase.[7] This suggests that we are participating in a synesthetic experience akin to the music of the spheres in which light is rendered as sound. Like Huidobro, Valle uses outlined form to construct a visual metaphor based on physical similarity. The first reading of *escala* is more problematic, because the line depicts a staircase rather than a ladder. Since these images appear to contradict each other, one solution is to discard this interpretation altogether. Another is to view the staircase as a visual metaphor related to the ladder through functional similarity. In either case the fact that "escalas" is plural means that there are actually *many* staircases, only one of which is shown. In reality the sky is filled with zigzag patterns of light (and music) extending from horizon to horizon. This is a metaphor for the constellations, the stars of which are joined together (at least on starmaps) by straight lines. Their procession across the sky, on golden stairs, at first appears to result from the earth's rotation. But the heavens move from east to west, whereas Valle's stars come from the "poniente bárbaro" ("barbaric west"). This is confirmed by the visual staircase, which descends from left to right. If we assume that the author is facing the setting sun, he would seem to be describing not sidereal motion but the appearance of more and more stars in the western sky.

Why the west is barbaric quickly becomes apparent – the moon has recently decapitated the sun. Recalling the decapitation of the twilight in Larrea's "SED" the act itself generates a double-edged metaphor. On the one hand, it evokes the "death" of the sun as it sinks below the horizon. On the other, it describes the crimson hue of the moon, which is compared to an axe dripping with blood. Valle is clearly thinking of the traditional moon-shaped executioner's axe with double, curved blades. That it cannot be a scimitar, for example, and thus a lunar crescent, is evident from the circular figure below, which depicts a full moon. An outlined form and a visual tautology, the latter is juxtaposed with the constellation(s) to form a metonymic portrait of the night sky. The sun sinking into the sea is a commonplace, to be sure, but the idea of fishing for sunken ships with the sun's hair is not. Among the various elements of the latter image, including a decapitated head with long, dripping hair, we may discern a reference to John the Baptist. The remaining elements are more elusive. The poet is probably exploiting associations connected with the *redecilla*, or hairnet. Not only was this "little net" worn over the hair; it was often *made* of hair – indeed human hair. Extrapolating from this basic model, Valle transforms the sun's hair into a giant fishing net with which he catches ships.

165

Aesthetics of visual poetry

Returning in the final section to the heavens, the poet introduces a personified abstraction and evokes the constellations. The final, extended metaphor presents Silence seated beside a spinning wheel, winding virgins' braids and flaxen Angeluses onto the zodiac's "rueca." To grasp the significance of this splendid *métaphore filée* fully we have to make one slight correction. The term *rueca* designates a distaff, which holds the raw wool from which the thread is spun. What Valle is obviously thinking of, however, is an *huso*. The latter consists of a horizontal spindle onto which the finished thread is wound. Reflecting a widespread confusion between the two terms, the author substitutes one for the other. The implications of this correction are considerable. It quickly becomes apparent, for example, that the circular figure represents not only the moon but the spindle as well, viewed here along its horizontal axis. Whereas Valle's staircase has numerous antecedents, like the moon, his revolving spindle is a unique contribution to visual poetry. So too is the circular image of the zodiac, which is superimposed on the latter two forms. Although the zodiac figures in Luis Mosquera's "Viaje orbicular," as we have seen, it is restricted to the verbal plane, where its circularity is merely implicit. Like the figure of the moon discussed earlier, the spindle and zodiac are both visual tautologies. Among other things, the image of the Silent Spinner would seem to refer to the three Fates, who spin out human destiny in exactly the same manner. It is they who have determined the fate of the "vírgenes," for instance, who are incorporated into the zodiac in the guise of the constellation Virgo. If Valle is thinking of a specific anecdote here, such as the parable of the Wise and Foolish Virgins or the martyrdom of eleven thousand virgins at Cologne, his subjects remain anonymous. All that matters is their virginity.

Only when the reader reaches the last line does he begin to understand that there is more to the poem than meets the eye. At the moment of its ostensible closure the text opens outward to reveal a whole new level of signification. This is the meaning of the *points de suspension*, which signal the author's refusal to terminate the poem and point to a continuing dialogue with the reader. In order to follow this dialogue to its conclusion the latter must reorder his structural assumptions. In order to finally understand the first verse he must scrutinize the final verse. Among other things, the ringing of the Angelus confirms our impression that the time is shortly after sunset. And its winding onto the zodiac, which mingles music with light, parallels the synesthesia of the musical staircase. However, an unexpected surprise is provided by the word "inmaculado," which, situated between the virgins and the Angeluses, immediately suggests the Immaculate Conception. Remembering that the poem was published during the Christmas season, the reader suddenly perceives that its subject is not Virgo but rather the Virgin Mary. More precisely, it celebrates (and re-enacts) the Annunciation. Like the Angelus, which evokes the heavenly messenger sent to Mary, the "celestial sign" of the title refers to this miraculous event. Reviewing the first verse in the light of this new information, one becomes aware of its astonishing resonance: "¡Mía era la estrella!" In the context of the Annunciation the speaker appears first to be the Virgin Mary recounting *filée* blessed event. The exclamation marks seem to betray her excitement, whereas the emphatic "mía" stresses her personal relationship to the messenger. Seen in this light the "estrella" would designate the Angel, whose heavenly radiance resembles

166

The advent of Ultra

that of a star. However, since much of the work is obviously spoken by the poet and since the speaker appears to be continuous throughout, the first line is probably uttered by Valle. Again the theme of the Annunciation suggests an interpretation connected with Mary. In her role as a "star among women," the author may be saying, she serves him as a guiding light. Remembering that the text appeared during the Christmas season, however, one thinks of another celestial sign – the star followed by the Wise Men to Bethlehem. Accordingly, Valle may be referring to Jesus rather than to Mary. Viewed in this perspective the exclamation would testify to Valle's religious convictions and to his belief in a personal God. In the last analysis it makes little difference which explanation one adopts, for the Annunciation and the Nativity are linked in the Christian imagination in such a way that each celestial sign inevitably evokes the other.

Beginning with the image of the star in the first verse, the shadow of the Annunciation radiates outward to encompass the remaining imagery. Once one identifies the central drama it becomes evident that the visual staircase, for example, represents the path taken by the Angel on his way to Mary. In other words the stairs extend from heaven all the way down to earth. In this respect they recall numerous other contacts between the two realms, exemplified by the story of Jacob's ladder. This also explains why the stairs are made of gold. The precious metal serves not as a symbol of wealth but as an index of the importance of the Angel's mission. If formerly we have observed the personification of the stars descending the staircase, the reason behind this finally emerges. Seen in the context of the Annunciation, each of the stars represents an angel – like the "signo celeste" itself. This explains why Valle calls them "peregrinas" ("pilgrims"): They have come on a religious mission to pay homage to the Virgin Mary. In addition the fact that the angels' feet are "rosados" ("rosy") permits us to identify them as cherubs, who figure prominently in numerous paintings of the Annunciation. Finally, the equivalence of stars and angels suggests yet another interpretation of the liminary verse "Mía era la estrella." The proprietary interest the author exhibits in this object can be attributed not to the star itself but to the Angel of the Annunciation (Gabriel), whom it symbolizes. Thus the verse may very well serve as an invocation to Valle's patron saint, who would seem to be San Gabriel. "It was my personal angel," he appears to be saying, "who was responsible for the Annunciation!"

The last days

On February 29, 1920, a composition entitled "Poema ultraísta" appeared in *Grecia* with the signature Ángel Cándiz. A product of the fertile imagination of Dámaso Alonso, who chose to write under a pseudonym, it consists of an example of framed writing centered on the page between two otherwise unremarkable passages. According to one authority Alonso was seeking to parody Ultraist experiments with visual poetry,[8] which would explain why he preferred not to sign his name. Although other reasons are not difficult to imagine, it is worth noting that his pseudonym has certain connotations. Thus the surname Cándiz appears to be a contraction of *candidez*, which denotes, candor, simplicity, and whiteness. Coupled with the name Ángel, it suggests a number of possibilities. Although Alonso could be attacking the

167

POEMA ULTRAÌSTA

(Y has de encontrar —una mañana pura—
amarrada tu barca a otra ribera.)

A. M.

Solo, hidrópico, solo
estaba porque todos—los unos y los otros—
huyeron. Como a perro sarnoso,
huyeron.　　　　Me dejaron una ventana abietra.
Era la noche:

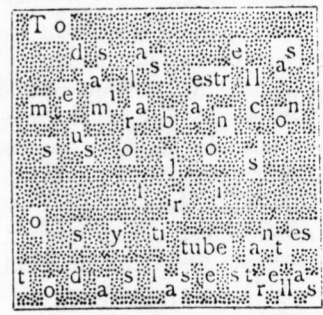

Se habian condensado en mi ventana.
La, la luna, pasó un momento
¡monóculo impertinente!

　　　　　　　　　Ya
　　　　　　　　　se
　　　　　　　　　fué.
Yo estaba solo y grasiento de la última pomada
　　　　　　　　　inútil.
Las tres hermanas vinieron
　　　　　　　　　en silencio.
La mayor me trajo el oléo.
La mediana el sudario.
La más pequeña me besó en la boca.
Las estrellas se fueron, ovejas, a pastar porque
las llamó la sirena del pastor de la fábrica.
　　　　　　　Y me las encontré en el
　　　　　　　　　otro valle.

　　　　　　　　　ANGEL CANDIZ.

Figure 49. Ángel Cándiz (Dámaso Alonso)

The advent of Ultra

simple-mindedness of the Ultraist canon, for example, he could also be stressing the "angelic simplicity" of his own text, perhaps in contrast to the Ultraist aesthetic. And though the text could possibly represent a "candid" assessment of *ultraísmo*, the pseudonym may simply repeat two of Alonso motifs. Not only does his speaker become an angel in the course of the poem, for instance; the latter is flooded with images of whiteness. In short, the evidence is inconclusive. The most that can be said is that the pseudonym contains an element of playfulness. Despite the latter, as Gloria Videla notes, the editors of *Grecia* took the poem very seriously. Among other things they were undoubtedly impressed by the dignified epigraph, taken from the great *modernista* poet Antonio Machado: "And one pure morning you will find/ your boat moored on another shore." Alonso's poem plays on related themes:

> I was alone, hydropic, alone
> because everyone – all of them –
> had fled. As if from a mangy dog,
> they fled,   They left me an open window.
> It was night:
> > All the stars
> > looked at me with
> > their cold
> > wavering eyes
> > all the stars
> Had condensed on my window.
> The moon briefly passed by,
> impertinent monocle!   Now
>   it's
>   gone.
>
> I was alone and greasy with the last useless
>   ointment.
> The three sisters came
>   in silence.
> The biggest one brought me the oil.
> The middle one, the shroud.
> The smallest kissed me on the mouth.
> Sheep, the stars went off to graze,
> called by the shepherd's siren from the factory.
>   And I came across them in the
>   other valley.

It is not difficult to see why the editors of *Grecia* liked this work. If "Poema ultraísta" was intended to be a parody, it is indistinguishable from the real thing. This in itself casts considerable doubt on the author's parodic intentions. And though the title seems to promise a commentary on Ultraist poetics, there is nothing in the text to justify this expectation. Alonso – an important author in his own right but not an *ultraísta* – has created a sharply etched drama and a brilliant visual analogy. In several respects the poem recalls Mallarmé's "Les Fenêtres" ("The Windows"), in which "tièdes carreaux d'or" ("tepid panes of gold") frame a similar

Aesthetics of visual poetry

scene. Like the latter the Spanish composition consists of an interior monologue delivered from a sickbed, possibly in a hospital, by a moribund persona. In both works the speaker is subjected to what Mallarmé calls "l'horreur des saintes huiles" ("the horror of the holy oils") amid competing images of whiteness. Abandoned by everyone, for reasons that are unclear, Alonso's subject describes the night sky seen through a single open window. Like the moon, the shape of which suggests a monocle, the stars are portrayed as spectators peering through the window. Their cold, wavering eyes evoke the stars' twinkling in the cool night air.

The next two lines contain the most beautiful image in the poem, but they also pose a problem: "todas las estrellas / Se habian condensado en mi ventana" ("all the stars / Had condensed on my window"). The metaphor itself seems clear enough: The twinkling stars are transformed into drops of dew on the window. It is a question of poetic metamorphosis. But exactly how is one supposed to understand this process? The poet at first appears to imply either that the dew on the window resembles the stars or that it has finally obscured (replaced) them. But since the window is *open* it cannot possibly be covered with dew. In order to resolve this apparent contradiction the reader must reverse his rhetorical perspective, for upon reflection one realizes that the stars are the tenor, not the vehicle, of the metaphor. Framed by the open window, Alonso is saying, the stars in their crystalline purity resemble dew sparkling on a pane of glass. Like the scintillating constellation in Mallarmé's "Ses Purs Ongles" ("Its Pure Nails") they seem almost to invade the room. Illustrating his metaphor visually, the author fills a square with small dots punctuated by dislocated letters and syllables. The latter represent the stars peering through the window. The former are more ambiguous, in keeping with the reversible metaphor, and can be read as either night sky or dew. The final visual tautology subjects the verbal message to a fourfold framing process. Directed inward, the principle of the visual square is reflected verbally by the parallel structure: "Todas las estrellas" // "todas las estrellas." Directed outward it is mirrored first by the surrounding text, then by the page itself.

The dew metaphor and the fact that the moon has disappeared suggest that dawn is approaching. In the last section Alonso returns to the theme of sickness: "Yo estaba solo y grasiento de la última pomada / inútil" ("I was alone and greasy with the last useless / ointment"). Juxtaposed with "inútil" ("useless"), which is heavily stressed by its position, "última" ("last") indicates how the drama will end. The patient is no longer on his sickbed but rather on his deathbed. His isolation at this moment may reflect the human condition in general. Carrying ominous objects – oil for the last rites, a shroud for his funeral – the three Fates enter silently. Approaching the head of the bed the youngest gives him the Kiss of Death. The last lines consist of three interlocking metaphors. First, the stars change into sheep, which answer their shepherd's call and go off to graze. Among other things this is a metaphor for the dawn, which obliterates the stars. The shepherd's song itself is a metaphor for the factory siren in the next verse, which not only announces the dawn but calls humanity to work. Finally, in the last line, the speaker himself follows the sheep to "el otro valle," which can only be the Valley of Death. As a new day dawns his soul soars through the open window – in answer to a mysterious call – to join the stars in heaven. Like Machado's boat he has passed to the Other Side. Again the

The advent of Ultra

resemblance to "Ses Purs Ongles" is striking. In both poems the occupant's soul seems to exit through a window and become part of a constellation. In both a window serves as the boundary between life and death. Despite its Symbolist thematics, however, Alonso's poem conforms to the Ultraist program by virtue of its metaphoric intensity (and density). The three interlocking metaphors, for example, recall Gerardo Diego's cultivation of the "imagen múltiple" as well as Guillermo de Torre's "imagen polipétala" ("multipetaled image").[9] Parody or not, "Poema ultraísta" is arguably one of the most successful visual poems to come out of the movement.

Although Pedro Raida and Adriano del Valle are obvious exceptions, in general the *ultraístas* preferred to work with visual analogies. Rather than the solid forms of the former or the outlined forms of the latter, they liked to use dislocated and occasionally distorted letters. Interestingly, one encounters relatively few examples of visual metaphor and metonymy. Instead there is a widespread reliance on tautological structures in which the verbal image is replicated and raised to the visual level. Except for Guillermo de Torre, who is the subject of the next chapter, the Castilian poets abandoned visual effects altogether after May 1921. Until the emergence some forty years later of concrete poetry, the roots of which lay in the experiments of the earlier period, visual poetry remained dormant.[10] One strange exception to this observation appeared in book form in 1927. Authored by "Gecé," a pseudonym of Ernesto Giménez Caballero, *Carteles* was published in Madrid by Espasa-Calpe. As its name indicates it was devoted to posters, but posters unlike any seen before. Following guidelines established earlier by the Ultraists, Giménez had recently invented the critical poster, which reduced the traditional book review to a simple chart. *Carteles* itself consists of twenty-five reviews that summarize each book and the reviewer's reactions via a schematic diagram or picture. The latter, many of which are in color (an idea invented by Apollinaire), include a bouquet of flowers and an artist's pallet leaning against a canvas. Although this brief experiment in visual criticism was destined not to bear fruit, it provides an interesting epilogue to the Ultraist adventure.

9

Guillermo de Torre

Although Guillermo de Torre was an interesting poet in his own right, he is known to posterity as the founder of *ultraísmo*. The previous chapter examined some of the ways in which the Ultraists drew on experiments in France and Italy and paved the way for the Generation of '27. Although Torre was Apollinaire's foremost disciple in Spain,[1] he was also a great admirer of Marinetti. Intellectually he belonged to the French literary tradition epitomized by the former, but temperamentally he resembled the latter. This conflict is evident in much of his poetry, which reflects the tension between intellectual and emotional responses. Although the French influence eventually prevailed, Futurism continued to make its presence felt throughout the Ultraist period and thereafter. Thus exclamation marks abound, testifying to the author's enthusiasm, as do references to airplanes, automobiles, telegraphy, turbines, electric arcs, trains, oceanliners, and other dynamic symbols of modern life. Nowhere is Torre's debt to Futurism more evident than in his poem "Aviograma" (1919), an excellent imitation of *parole in libertà* with an epigraph by Marinetti.[2] Significantly, one section of his collection of poetry *Hélices*, which spans the period 1918–22, is entitled "Palabras en libertad" ("Free Words").

Modes of visual analogy

Torre's first experiments with visual effects, inspired by the Futurists, are rather conservative. Dating from early 1919, they are limited to expressive typography and assume three different forms. The first consists of isolated words or phrases reproduced in boldface type and/or capital letters, the function of which is purely emphatic. The second, usually relegated to the left- or right-hand margin, consists of one or more words printed diagonally instead of horizontally. Thus in his *Manifiesto ultraísta vertical* (November 1920) the words "Dirección nórdica" ("Northern direction") and "Cumbre Artica" ("Arctic Summit") are set off diagonally from the rest of the text.[3] Once again the purpose of this device seems merely to provide emphasis. The diagonal orientation, the fact that one group is ascending and the other descending, is entirely gratuitous. The third category is more interesting. As before, words or phrases interrupt the horizontal flow of the text, but this time their semantic value is related to their physical appearance. In other words they represent bona fide visual analogies. The latter may evoke an abstract concept, a specific act, or a concrete object. In the 1920 manifesto, for example, the word "VERTICAL"

Guillermo de Torre

conveys the notion of verticality by bisecting the page perpendicularly. And in Torre's "Epiceyo a Apollinaire" ("Elegy for Apollinaire"), which in spite of its subject was inspired by a Futurist model, the word "AMANECER" ("DAWN") is arranged to form the top of a circle, where it represents the sun peeking over the horizon.[4] Torre repeated this device nearly two years later in "Arco iris" ("Rainbow"), where the title and the words "Arco Iris Inaugural" are each curved like a rainbow. Similarly, the title of a companion poem, "Torreiffel," is designed to evoke the Eiffel Tower.[5] The first word, "TORRE," descends vertically on the page, whereas the second word, "EIFFEL," begins with the terminal letter of the first and extends horzontally. In addition each letter of "TORRE" is larger than its predecessor, so that the word mimics the monument's triangular shape. Elsewhere in the poem the line "ya estoy arriba" ("I'm up here now"), which meanders across the page in an upward direction, reproduces the poet's route through his poetic landscape.

Although visual elements abound in Torre's works, visual poetry per se is fairly scarce. There are really only four poems that fit this description; these are collected in *Hélices* as examples of "Palabras en libertad." Published originally in *Grecia* on October 12, 1919, "Paisaje plástico" ("Plastic Landscape") is an ambitious attempt to integrate a variety of visual devices into a harmonious whole.[6] It is also the most futurist of the four. Although a linear rendition does considerable violence to its visual dimension, the poem can be translated as follows:

Scorching midday in the vortex of the summer countryside
 Darting solar flares cleave Like a swollen apple
 the earth's convex belly the ripe Sun
 perpendicularly sweats hot piercing drops
 The landscape is magnified onto curved torsos
 in the sun-filled noon
SUMMER (God must be accumulating SUN
 trillions of calories
 on the thermal distributor Who has erased all the shadows?
  in his cockpit)
The heat withers dynamic desires
The enervated bodies
   bent over the plain
SIESTA crackle in a glowing orgasm
The solstice weighs on the intoxicated atmosphere
The north wind reaps the blond wheat fields in blue waves
The gigantic ears striate
   the horizon's dermic sapphire AZURE
Questioning sickles placate the
  standing stalks' avidity
The olives contort their trunks split by Phoebus's scythe
 Bunches of verjuice grapes evoke plentiful harvests
 A rustic song floats over golden corn on a threshing floor
 and intersects a voluptuous feminine smile

173

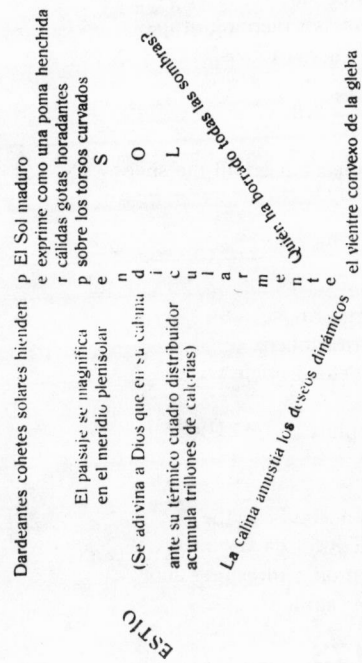

PAISAJE PLÁSTICO

MEDIODÍA igniscente en el vórtice de la campiña estival

Dardeantes cohetes solares hienden

  p El Sol maduro
  e exprime como una poma henchida
  r cálidas gotas horadantes
  p sobre los torsos curvados
  e S
  n O
  d L
  i c
  u
  l
  a
  r
  m
  e
  n
  t
  e

El paisaje se magnifica
en el meridio plenisolar

(Se adivina a Dios que en su calma
ante su térmico cuadro distribuidor
acumula trillones de calorías)

La calina amustia los discos dinámicos

¿Quién ha borrado todas las sombras?

el vientre convexo de la gleba

Los cuerpos enervados
    tendidos sobre el agro
       crepitan en un orgasmo de ardentías

En la atmósfera embriagada gravita el solsticio

A
Z U L I N
      I
        D
          A
            D

Olas de cierzo azul siegan los blondos trigales

Las espigas gigantes estrían
el zafiro dérmico del horizonte

Interrogantes hoces aplacan la
avidez de los tallos erectos

Los olivos contorsionan sus troncos hendidos por el dall febeo

ESTÍO

SIESTA

Racimos agraces evocan las vendimias saciadoras

Sobre la parva gualda de una era flota una copla campesina

que se entrecruza con una ...mínea sonrisa voluptuosa

ESPEJISMO

LA SED

de pulpas acuosas

estrangula las gargantas

HORCAS
BIELDOS
SOLLOS

Los trillos resbalan con modorra sobre las mieses incendiadas.

Campesinos jadeantes en su fervor agreste
  reciben en la hostia solar la eucaristía triptolémica

El río exi guo vi da su cau ce

Las ranas estridulantes de la alberca
  modulan una cansina monodia

Las espigadoras encorvadas sobre los rastrojos

se confunden con los sarmientos de las carrascas

HAY UNA CONSTELACIÓN DE GAVILLAS SOBRE LOS PERDIOS RASURADOS
Los barbechos dormitan   Bancales huérfanos   Zahones abandonados
En la alucinación sensorial
        bajo la caída meridia   advienen:

ESCUADRILLAS DE AVIONES
QUE AGAVILLAN CON SUS HÉLICES
      LAS COSECHAS INFLAMADAS.
Y rítmicamente los élitros sonoros de las cigarras ebrias
      polarizan la harmonía estival

Guillermo de Torre

<table>
<tr><td>

THIRST
chokes the throats

</td><td>

MIRAGE
of juicy pulp

</td></tr>
</table>

EARTHENWARE PITCHERS
PITCHFORKS
WINNOWING FORKS
The threshing machines glide drowsily over the burning grain
Peasants panting in rustic fervor
     receive the Triptolemean Eucharist in the solar host
        Chirping frogs in a pool
        modulate a weary monody
   The tiny river forgets its way
The gleaners bent over the stubble
blend with the vines on the oaks
THERE IS A CONSTELLATION OF SHEAVES ON THE SHAVEN FIELDS
The fallow sections doze   Ruddy gardens   Abandoned chaps
In the sensorial hallucination
       under the aegis of midday
                       arrive:
SQUADRONS OF AIRPLANES
   THAT BIND THE FLAMING HARVEST
      INTO SHEAVES WITH THEIR PROPELLERS.
And the sonorous elytrums of the drunken cicadas rhythmically
   polarize the summer harmony

Although the verbal text presents a sleepy noonday scene dominated by the enervating power of the sun, visually the poem is surprisingly dynamic. Bold lines dart off in every direction, while words and phrases in capitals provide emphatic counterpoint. The latter permit the reader to grasp the import of the poem at a single glance. Thus the first four examples indicate that the scene takes place in "SUMMER," that it contains "SUN" and "AZURE" sky, and that it is "SIESTA" time. The following section stresses the sun's heat by placing "THIRST" and "MIRAGES" in opposition to "PITCHERS" of water and situates the scene in the countryside (a *paisaje* can be either a landscape or a cityscape). The "PITCHFORKS" and the "SHEAVES" of wheat in the fields reveal that it is harvest time. The last section provides a glimpse of the fantasy ending – a modern *deus ex machina* – in which a "SQUADRON OF AIRPLANES" completes the "HARVEST." Only after reading the poem does the reader discover that God is one of the pilots ("Dios . . . en su cabina") and that the episode represents divine intervention. The airplanes themselves are archetypal Futurist symbols and may have been suggested by the buzzing cicadas with whom they are juxtaposed. Certainly their relation to one another is far from from accidental, so that the last five lines appear to represent a simile. The cicadas are so noisy, Torre seems to be saying, that they sound like a squadron of airplanes.

Although "Paisaje plástico" is a highly visual composition, compared with, say, Apollinaire's "Paysage" (Figure 15, Chapter 3), it is extremely abstract. Most of

Aesthetics of visual poetry

the visual effects appear to be gratuitous, and even the vertical alignment of "perpendicularmente" conveys little concrete information. Although the three intersecting lines converging on "perpendicularmente" could conceivably represent a visual analogy – some sort of machinery perhaps – this remains to be identified. On the other hand, the second half of the poem contains a whole series of visual analogies. Thus the X-shaped configuration at the top of the next page depicts the intersection of the "copla campesina" ("rustic song") and the "sonrisa voluptuosa" ("voluptuous smile"). Similarly, recalling analogous figures in the "Epiceyo a Apollinaire" and "Arco iris," the curved line toward the bottom represents the "espigadoras" ("gleaners") bent over their task. However, the circle-and-triangle combination in the center presents several problems: "Los trillos resbalan con modorra sobre las mieses incendiadas / BOTIJOS / HORCAS / BIELDOS" ("The threshing machines glide drowsily over the burning grain / EARTHENWARE PITCHERS / PITCHFORKS / WINNOWING FORKS"). A comparison between this figure and the circular form in Adriano del Valle's "Signo celeste" (Figure 48, Chapter 8) is instructive. Whereas the latter depicts a whole series of objects (moon, spindle, zodiac, etc.), the former seems to have nothing to do with the rest of the poem. Possibly it represents a wheel from one of the threshing machines or their circular path, although normally the machines move in a straight line. In either case the picture would qualify as a visual metonym. There is simply no way of knowing, however, which interpretation (if any) is correct. In the absence of any clues as to the figure's identity the latter appears to be completely arbitrary. At most it illustrates the principle of circularity, which makes it a visual analogy.

The most charming example of all is the tiny river that appears to flow between the threshing machines and the gleaners: "El río exiguo olvida su cauce" ("The tiny river forgets its way"). Here again a comparison between this figure and its counterpart – the staircase – in "Signo celeste" is instructive. Whereas Valle displaces each element of his sentence vertically, for example, he does not disturb its horizontal relationship with its neighbors. Each follows on the heels of its predecessor. In "Paisaje plástico," however, Torre displaces his elements horizontally as well as vertically. The fact that one proceeds word by word and the other, syllable by syllable is of no consequence. What is crucial is the difference in spacing, which produces a stepped figure in the first instance and a diagonal line in the second. This means that Valle's sentence represents an outlined form, while Torre's qualifies as a visual analogy. What prevents the latter from becoming an outlined form is the discrepancy between verbal description and visual representation. Whereas the tiny river is supposed to meander across the landscape ("olvida su cauce"), in fact its course is perfectly straight. Unlike the figures in Apollinaire's "Paysage," which are integrated into a conceptual whole according to the conventions of landscape painting, those in "Paisaje plástico" are meant to be viewed sequentially. If it is theoretically possible to imagine a scene with gleaners in the foreground, a threshing floor in the background, and threshers and a river in between, such an interpretation runs counter to the analogical mode of the imagery. Rather than specific objects or persons, the visual text evokes abstract qualities: linear motion is juxtaposed with circular motion, curvature with intersection.

176

Guillermo de Torre

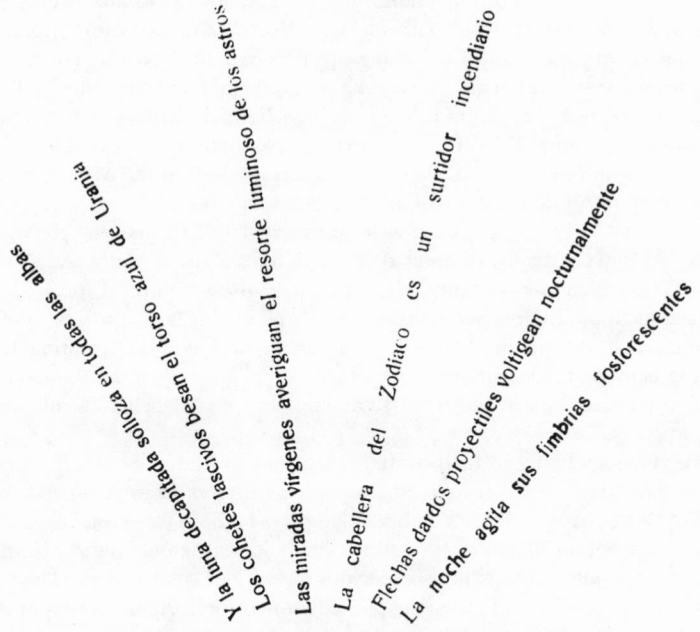

Figure 51. Guillermo de Torre, "Cabellera"

An object lesson

The three remaining works from *Hélices* represent experiments with a different kind of visual poetry. For one thing, the fact that they are much shorter gives them greater unity and visual coherence. For another, though traces of his earlier experiments remain, Torre abandons visual analogy in favor of realistic representation. In keeping with his poetic evolution in general, he begins to distance himself from Futurism and to ally himself with Apollinaire. Each of the three poems portrays a single object. The first example, entitled "Cabellera" ("Head of Hair"), is relatively straightforward. Consisting of six lines radiating upward and outward from a common center, it seems to represent someone's hair standing on end, perhaps from fear or from an electric shock:

> And the decapitated moon sobs in every dawn
> The lecherous rockets kiss Urania's blue torso
> Virgin glances examine the stars' luminous mechanism
> The Zodiac's hair is an incendiary fountain
> Arrows darts missiles sail back and forth nocturnally
> The night shakes its phosphorescent fringes

Aesthetics of visual poetry

Although the lines are of uneven length, they follow an approximate rhyme scheme that divides them into couplets. While Torre's usual scientific jargon (which he associated with modernity) is lacking, his penchant for recondite terms is apparent in the choice of "voltigear" ("to sail back and forth") and "fimbrias" ("fringes"). The key to the poem lies in its title, "Cabellera," which denotes both human *hair* and the tail of a *comet*. That it is intended to evoke both images is evident from the physical appearance of the text. Before one can begin to read the work, for example, it is necessary to rotate it clockwise 90 degrees. Turned on its side, the figure clearly depicts a comet streaking across the sky from right to left. Like the comet in Juan Larrea's "SED" (Figure 45, Chapter 8) it constitutes a visual tautology. Unlike Larrea's version, which is essentially schematic, it is also an outlined form. By linking visual signification to the act of reading, Torre manages to preserve the verbal paronomasia at the pictorial level. A simple physical gesture (rotating the text) suffices to activate the latent visual structure. Although every author depends on the reader's complicity to complete the signifying process, "Cabellera" calls for active participation.

The analogy between the celestial object and its human counterpart is not as arbitrary as it may seem, for *comet* (or *cometa*) derives from a Greek expression signifying "long-haired." Torre's composition plays on both these meanings by juxtaposing an astronomical landscape with a mythological female figure, Urania. The two semantic chains cross when she decides to visit our solar system. The image of "la luna decapitada" recalls the decapitated suns of both Apollinaire and Adriano del Valle as well as Larrea's guillotined twilight. Like its predecessors it may evoke a blood-red globe or perhaps a crescent moon resembling a scimitar. The fact that the moon is sobbing, however, suggests an alternative interpretation. Torre may be comparing the lunar disc to a severed head (rather than a neck) according to the model made famous by Gustave Moreau's painting of Salomé. Whatever the explanation the atmosphere is certainly eerie. The second verse introduces a human figure whose relation to the text is largely implicit. As the Muse of Astronomy, Urania personifies the comet and its trajectory across the sky. Not only does she share its characteristic blue tint; her long hair streams behind her like the comet's tail. At both levels of signification she is portrayed as a "heavenly body." The "cohetes lascivos" ("lecherous rockets") present a problem until one identifies their source. From all appearances they represent yet another reading of the visual text in which the vertical "hair" suggests six skyrockets in flight. Like the arrows, darts, and missiles of a subsequent line, they are attracted to the comet by their similarity of form. Their relation to one another is thus metaphorical.

The "miradas vírgenes" ("virgin glances") in the next line that probe the stars' interiors could conceivably belong to astronomers viewing the comet for the first time. However, they are almost certainly synecdochic references to Urania, whose cosmic trajectory allows her to investigate stellar objects at first hand. The term *virgen* refers to her maidenhood and to the fact that this is her first encounter with our solar system. The following line contains a fourth interpretation of the poem's visual aspect, which this time suggests a "surtidor incendiario" ("incendiary fountain"). The image of the fountain corresponds to the comet's physical appearance, whereas its incendiary properties refer to the (supposedly) fiery gasses in its tail. However, the metaphor is considerably more complicated. Torre is comparing the comet not to a fountain per se but to a special kind of firework resembling a miniature volcano (known in English as a "cone"). This means that the comparison represents a second-generation metaphor, that is, a metaphor of a metaphor. Since all four interpretations are congruent, moreover, they suppose a relationship based on equivalence. If the visual progression is hair $\longrightarrow$ comet $\longrightarrow$ rockets $\longrightarrow$ fountain/firework, the operation is completely reversible. Inevitably, then, the incendiary fountain also describes Urania's flaming tresses.

At the heart of this structure is the Ultraists' fascination with multiple metaphor. Structurally the poem can be diagrammed as a cube the top and bottom of which reproduce the visual and verbal planes. Although the latter are bounded by horizontal metaphor, they are linked to one another by vertical tautology. The reference to fireworks in the fourth verse recalls the rockets encountered previously and prefigures similar devices in the following verse. Among other things, these images suggest that the comet's passage may be mirrored by a pyrotechnic display on the ground. This impression is strengthened by the last verse, in which "la noche agita sus fimbrias fosforescentes" ("night shakes its phosphorescent fringes"). At one level this refers to the contours of the comet, which are outlined by a luminous fringe. At another level there is an implicit comparison between the comet and a woman (Urania) skaking out her long blond hair. At yet a third level the expression evokes the viewer's position on the ground surrounded by displays that light up the night. In this manner celestial and terrestrial fireworks merge into one.

The next poem, which continues this theme, is entitled "Girándula" ("Pinwheel"). An outlined form composed of four intersecting lines, it seems to whirl around and around like a pinwheel on the Fourth of July. It should be added that this configuration is also the international astronomical sign for a fixed star. Once again Torre demands that the reader participate actively in the signifying process. Once again his reading strategy is inscribed in the work's visual structure. As in "Cabellera," we must physically manipulate the text in order to realize the potential implicit in its title. It is up to us to set the poem in motion. Before we can begin to decipher the composition, for example, we must rotate the page counterclockwise 90 degrees. And as soon as we finish the first verse, we must turn it clockwise 45 degrees before we can read the second. To complete the poem this operation must be repeated twice more, so that the act of reading reproduces the whirling motion of the pinwheel itself.

> Un sol de repetición arroja 10.000 proyectiles por minuto.
> Una constelación pluricolor y efímera tapiza el cielo estival.
> El ventilador pirotécnico multiplica sus aspas deshilachadas.
> Los cohetes braman sirenas sobre la ciudad y el mar copulados.

> A repeating sun hurls 10,000 missiles a minute.
> An ephemeral and multicolored constellation carpets the summer sky.
> The pyrotechnic ventilator multiplies its frayed arms.
> The rockets roar sirens above the copulating town and sea.

179

Aesthetics of visual poetry

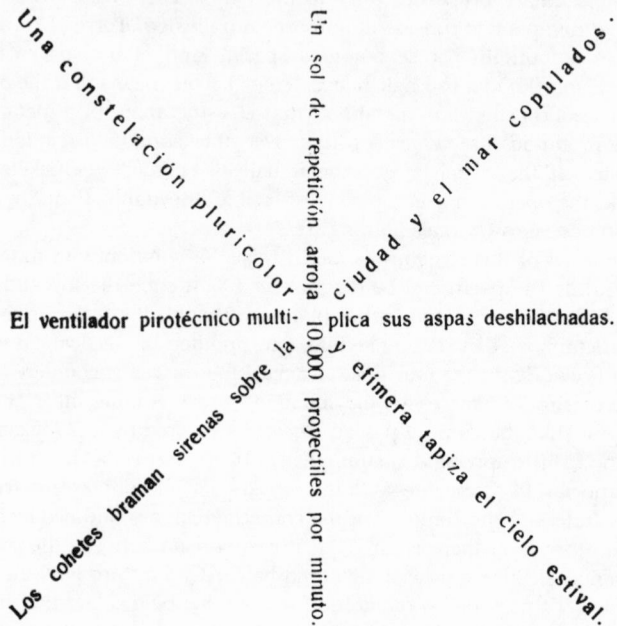

Figure 52. Guillermo de Torre, "Girándula"

The situation is similar, if not identical, to that in the previous poem. "Girándula" evokes a public fireworks display during the summer somewhere on the Spanish coast. Each line revolves about a single verbal metaphor that is projected onto the visual level. This explains the rather strange image in the first verse of the "sol de repetición" ("repeating sun"), which is modeled on that of a repeating rifle. The flash of the gun that launches the fireworks, Torre seems to be saying, resembles the sun, whose celestial fireworks are far superior to any human creation. Launching sunbeams at an incredible rate, it goes on and on forever. The "constelación" in the next verse describes the display itself, the beauty of which rivals that of the heavens. In one respect it even surpasses the latter, for the carpet of artificial stars is both multicolored and ephemeral, like flowers carpeting a meadow.

The third verse focuses on a single firework: the pinwheel of the title. Like the blades of a "ventilador" ("ventilating fan") the pinwheel revolves so rapidly that its arms can no longer be seen. This is what the author means by "aspas deshilachadas" ("frayed arms"). The X-shaped *aspas* turn so fast that they seem to disintegrate. The final verse focuses on another type of firework, namely rockets, which scream like sirens as they soar into the night sky. Bathed in the phosphorescent light of the display, the town and the sea take on a life of their own and fuse together in an intimate embrace ("copulados"). The whirling motion of the pinwheel itself is

180

Guillermo de Torre

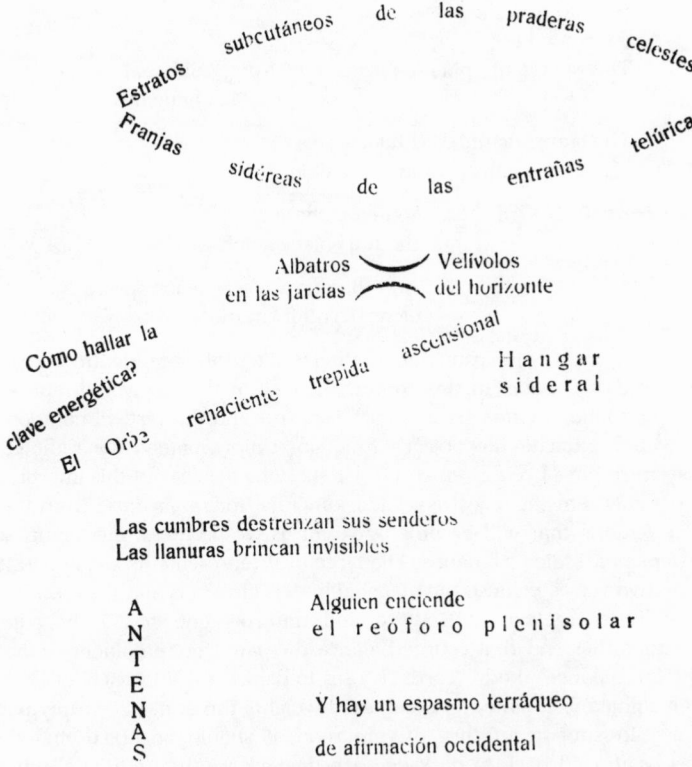

Figure 53. Guillermo de Torre, "Sinopsis"

transferred to the sirens, which spin around furiously to produce their shrill sound. Beginning with the title the visual progression is the following: pinwheel ⟶ sun ⟶ constellation/star ⟶ fan ⟶ siren. The last four images repeat the pinwheel's structure and stress particular aspects of the firework. Like the previous poem, "Girándula" testifies to the author's love of multiple metaphor. In view of its floral shape Torre's own term, "imagen polipétala" ("multipetaled image"), seems particularly appropriate.[7] As before, the poem's horizontal structures are metaphoric, and its vertical structures are tautological.

The final poem, which is entitled "Sinopsis," is by far the most ambitious.[8] Like its two predecessors it consists of a single outlined form with essentially representational premises:

> Subcutaneous strata of the celestial prairies
> Sidereal borders of the terrestrial bowels
> A Sailing Albatross
> in the horizon's rigging

181

Aesthetics of visual poetry

How to find the
energetic key?

The renascent Sphere vibrates upward   Sidereal
                                              hangar

The summits unbraid their paths
The plains gambol about invisible

ANTENNAS   Someone flicks
                  the full solar switch

                  And there is a terraqueous spasm
                  of western affirmation

In view of the poem's cosmic orientation it is tempting to identify the pictorial subject as a radiotelescope. In this context the oval at the top would represent the telescope's parabolic antenna (seen in perspective), and the vertical notation "ANTENAS" would indicate the object's function. Unfortunately, the radiotelescope does not seem to have been invented until 1942, which rules out this interpretation. Nor is it possible that the object is a radar antenna, for radar dates from the same period. For reasons that will become apparent as we progress, the picture almost certainly depicts a scale or balance. The large oval represents its single pan (which rests on the two verses below), the diagonal line its crossbar, and the phrase "Cómo hallar la/clave energética?" ("How to find the/energetic key?") the adjustable weights at the other end that counterbalance the pan. The remainder of the poem constitutes the balance's body. Torre chooses to depict a frontal view of the instrument in an unbalanced state, its unadjusted weights thrusting the empty pan high into the air. In support of this interpretation, it should be noted that the two semicircles positioned back to back beneath the pan are the traditional symbol for the constellation Libra (the balance).

At the verbal level the poem is a dense tangle of scientific jargon, erudite allusions, and deliberate obscurantism. If "Paisaje plástico" ended with the sound of the cicadas' buzzing elytrums (hardened forewings forming a protective covering for the hindwings), in "Sinopsis" one encounters such terms as "subcutáneos," "sidéreas" ("sidereal"), and "telúricas" ("terrestrial") – not to mention the "reóforo" ("rheophore" – an outmoded word for "switch") and the marvelous "Albatros Velívolos" (literally "albatross in full sail"), whose melodious name matches its graceful flight. The first half of the poem is of little help in determining Torre's subject. Not until we reach the phrase "El Orbe renaciente trepida ascensional" ("The renascent Sphere vibrates upward") do we begin to suspect that it describes a sunrise. Equipped with this hypothesis, which provides a focus for our efforts, we look to the rest of the poem for confirmation. Seen in this light the first two lines lend themselves to several interpretations: "Estratos subcutáneos de las praderas celestes/Franjas sidéreas de las entrañas telúricas" ("Subcutaneous strata of the celestial prairies/Sidereal borders of the terrestrial bowels"). The "subcutaneous strata" of the sky, for instance, may refer to striated clouds illuminated by the approaching dawn. Similarly, the "sidereal [i.e., astral] borders" may describe mountains and other natural objects that are outlined against the rising sun. What-

Guillermo de Torre

ever the exact explanation, the line appears to focus on the border separating earth and sky. Or again, in view of the (implicit) reference to Libra immediately below, the lines may evoke the zodiac. Encircling the earth, the twelve constellations in effect form a border between it and the rest of the universe. According to this interpretation the oval figure would reproduce the celestial belt as well as the contours of the balance pan. It is also possible that it represents the (apparent) path of the sun around the earth.

The following section prefigures the dawn itself. The most memorable image is that of the albatross juxtaposed in midflight against a ship's rigging on the eastern horizon: "Albatross Velívolos / en las jarcias del horizonte." This is the first indication that the poem takes place in a marine environment, almost certainly the Mediterranean coast. Although there is no mistaking the immediacy of Torre's image, which is rendered with admirable economy and precision, ultimately its function is metaphorical. This is to say that the lines can be read both literally and figuratively. If at one level the image helps the reader to visualize the setting, at another it represents a striking metaphor for the sun peeking through the branches of a tree. The two images are not mutually exclusive but rather exist simultaneously. Neither has priority over the other. The next two lines pose the question of how to find the key to the sun's energy ("la clave energética") so that it can be released at daybreak. However, the first overt reference to the rising sun does not occur until the following line. Emerging from behind the earth, the "Orbe renaciente" slowly begins its climb. The fact that its hiding place serves as a "hangar sideral" points to an implicit verbal metaphor and an additional reading of the visual text. In the aeronautical context provided by this term the sun is clearly portrayed as a zeppelin making a vertical ascent. This impression is confirmed, moreover, at the visual level, where one suddenly perceives the airship rising toward the top of the page. Thus the oval figure depicts the zeppelin's elongated body, whereas the two horizontal lines below represent its cabin.

The final section describes the actual sunrise. As the sun's first rays strike the mountaintops they reveal a network of alpine paths, but the plains themselves remain concealed in shadow ("llanuras invisibles"). At this point Torre introduces the visual analogy "ANTENAS," the letters of which are aligned vertically on the page. The word itself is delightfully ambiguous. Translated as "LATEEN SAILS" it reinforces the marine imagery encountered previously and evokes a fleet of Mediterranean fishing boats (*feluccas*). Translated as "ANTENNAS" it links sky and earth and prepares the reader for the transmission of energy. Immediately thereafter "Alguien" ("Someone") – who can only be God – "enciende / el reóforo plenisolar" ("flicks the full solar switch") and illuminates all of western Europe. The poem ends with the conclusion of the sunrise and a collective gasp greeting the new day. The "espasmo terráqueo" ("terraqueous spasm") does not refer to the earth and the sea so much as to the general biological response. With the coming of daylight animals (and people) begin to move about, flowers open once again, and plants resume their interrupted growth. In the last analysis, then, the oval figure also refers to the rising sun. Seen in this perspective, the entire poem serves as a visual metaphor for dawn in which the ascent of the balance pan parallels that of the sun. Like the pan the latter will rise only so high before it is compelled to descend again by forces beyond its control.

183

Aesthetics of visual poetry

Compared with the earlier contortions of "Paisaje plástico," the later poems possess a disarming simplicity. In moving from the relative formlessness of the former to the compact structure of the latter, however, Torre developed a more expressive kind of poetry. Although this corresponds to the shift from abstraction to pictorial representation, it is not limited to the visual plane. If the visual appeal of these works is undeniable, the use of multiple metaphor at the verbal level introduces new complexities and aesthetic possibilities. Much of their apparent simplicity may be attributed to the author's overwhelming preference for outlined forms and visual tautologies. In particular the elementary designs favored by Torre create the illusion of an easy conquest. Not until the reader enters into the verbal labyrinth does he begin to appreciate their complex inspiration. Although Torre abandoned visual poetry after 1923, his experiments with this genre represent an important phase of the Spanish avant-garde. Related to the cult of the image practiced by the Ultraists, they reflect a basic dissatisfaction with the limitations of traditional expression and a new awareness of the structural possibilities of language.

10

Marius de Zayas and abstraction

The history of visual poetry in the United States is closely linked to Marius de Zayas, one of the key figures in the early years of the New York avant-garde. Serving as the director of the review *291* during its brief but eventful existence (March 1915 to February 1916), de Zayas was the first to introduce this new art form to America. Not only was he well versed in the theory of visual poetry; he collaborated on three of the five examples published in *291*. De Zayas himself was an artist who originally came from Mexico and who earned his living as a caricaturist for the *Evening World*.[1] A close associate of Alfred Stieglitz, he collaborated on *Camera Work* and authored two books on modern art. He spent the summer of 1914 in Paris in the company of Apollinaire when the latter was publishing his first calligrams.[2] Significantly, the place of honor in the first issue of *291* was occupied by a reproduction of Apollinaire's "Voyage" (Figure 18, Chapter 4) in which a cloud and a bird are positioned above a magnificent locomotive.

Discourse and discontinuity

The second issue of *291* (April 1915) continued the experiments of the first with a work entitled "Mental Reactions." Combining verbal and visual simultanism, the latter is both a poem and a drawing. Conceived as a *poème simultané*, it includes a meditation by Agnes Ernst Meyer that juxtaposes her reflections with her physical surroundings. Conceived as a pictorial exercise, it includes an abstract composition by de Zayas that illustrates and interprets Meyer's poem. This was the artist's first attempt at visual poetry and his most successful. One can gauge the extent of his originality by the fact that the work is totally without precedent. Like Federico de Iribarne in "Amanecer desde el tejado" (Figure 46, Chapter 8), de Zayas inserts a series of illustrations at strategic points in the text. Unlike the former, however, the visual elements in "Mental Reactions" are largely unrecognizable. Moreover, they consist of solid forms for the most part, whereas those in the Spanish poem tend to be depicted in outline. In view of their enigmatic status, de Zayas's figures are really *potential* illustrations, for their significance remains to be discovered. Nevertheless, the latter play a crucial role in the verbal text, which they shape according to their own dictates. In view of this fact they can be regarded as a variation on framed writing. One thinks in this context of the concept of a "cadre intérieur" developed by Apollinaire in 1913.[3] In Cubist painting, he maintained, each picture is framed not

185

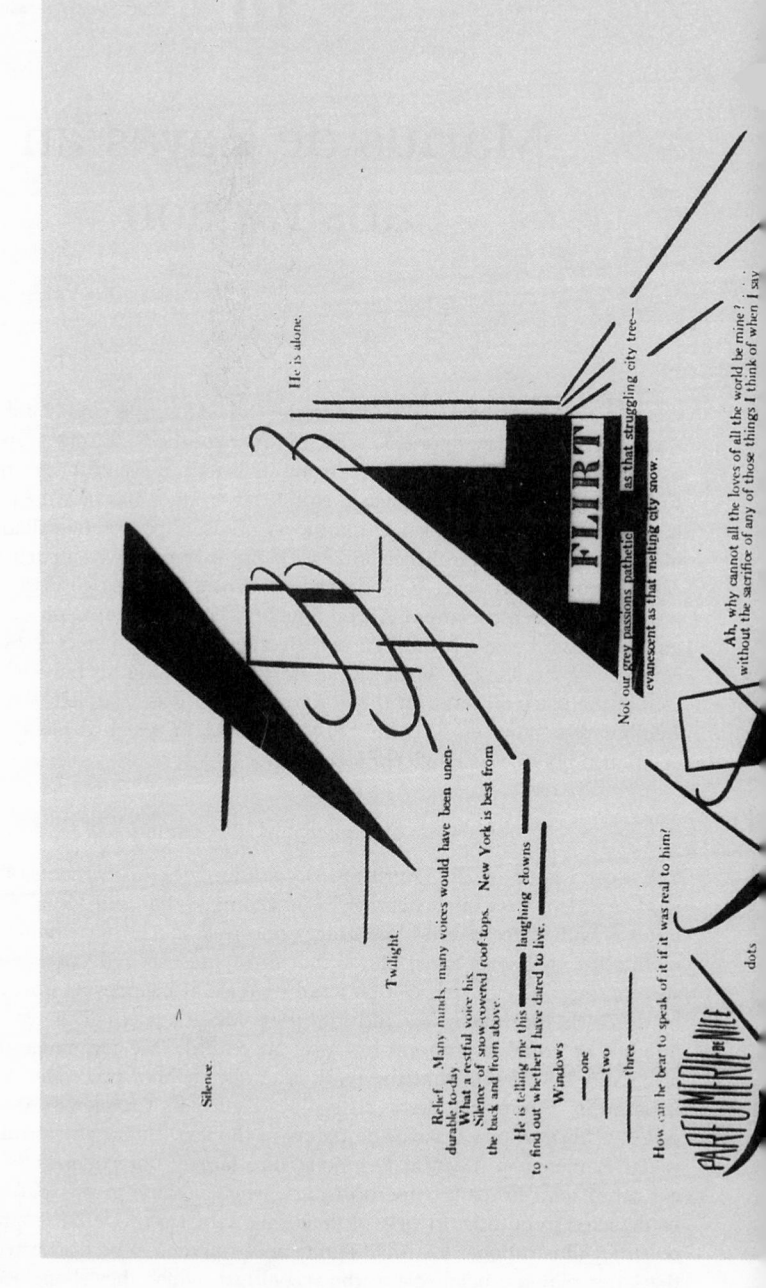

He is alone.

Silence.

Twilight.

Relief. Many minds, many voices would have been unendurable to-day.

What a restful voice his.

Silence of snow-covered roof-tops. New York is best from the back and from above.

He is telling me this ▬▬▬ laughing clowns to find out whether I have dared to live.

Windows

▬ one

▬ two

▬ three

How can he bear to speak of it if it was real to him!

FLIRT

Not our grey passions pathetic   as that struggling city tree—

evanescent as that melting city snow.

Ah, why cannot all the loves of all the world be mine! . . . without the sacrifice of any of those things I think of when I say

PARFUMERIE NILE

dots

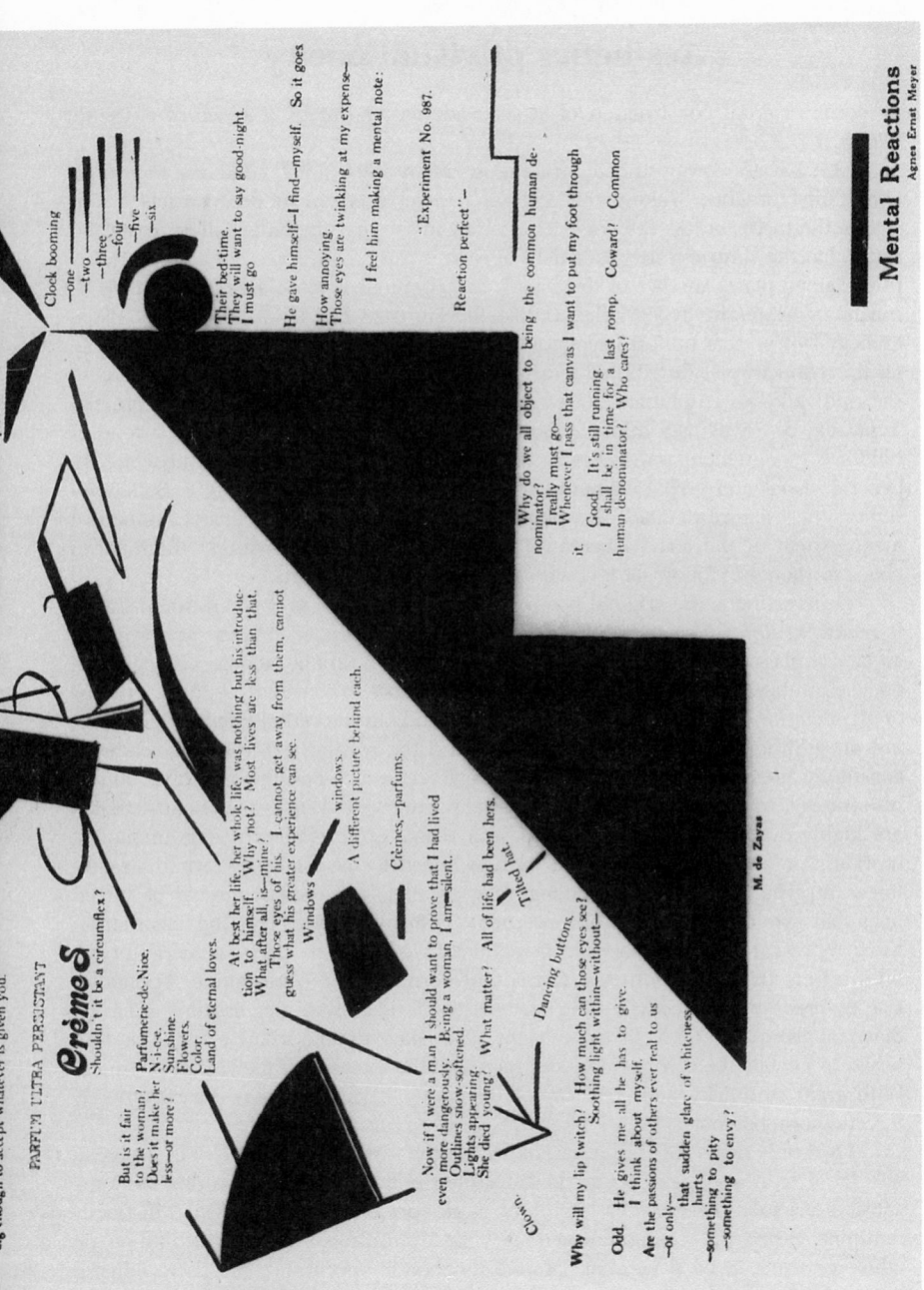

Figure 54. Agnes Ernst Meyer and Marius de Zayas, "Mental Reactions"

Aesthetics of visual poetry

by some external construction of wood and plaster but by a series of elements *within* it.

De Zayas's compositional strategy in "Mental Reactions" conforms to general simultanist practice. Taking the original free-verse poem, he deconstructs it and strews the pieces across the page. This is not to say that the latter follow a random order. On the contrary, the placement of each is carefully worked out according to a preordained plan. Another of the artist's contributions is to isolate certain words by means of expressive typography. Unlike the Futurists he makes little use of visual analogy but prefers uniform typographical effects borrowed from Cubist painting. Of the five examples distributed symmetrically on either side of the page, the two on the right play an emphatic role, whereas the three on the left are purely mimetic. Typically, de Zayas uses a larger font in a different style. In addition he is fond of boldface type, which contributes to the counterpoint between black and white. In general visual and verbal elements are perfectly integrated. As Craig R. Bailey observes, the mixture of lines and planes reflects the "broken, arbitrary, synthetical arrangement of the text."[4] Dickran Tashjian adds that it reproduces "the random chaos of thought" following its own internal logic and rhythm.[5]

Interestingly, the original poem has been spatialized to such an extent that it is relatively static. The verbal discontinuity forces the reader to pause at every turn as he searches for clues as to how to proceed. The ultimate exercise in indeterminacy, simultanist poetry in general subjects the reader to constantly shifting patterns of signification. Here the *visual* discontinuity adds to the verbal effect by introducing an additional element of uncertainty into the reading process. The reader is constantly interrupted by blank spaces that force him to hesitate and to reevaluate his strategy. In order to compensate for the poem's verbal stasis the visual elements are highly dynamic. The composition as a whole exhibits a surprising amount of motion. For one thing, each visual form is linked to the others by several straight lines, implying some sort of exchange. For another, there are a number of curved lines that give the impression of movement. Tashjian suggests that the linear structures represent thought processes in action. In general the nervous energy of the lines offsets the solid geometric forms that dominate the composition. Triangular shapes predominate, contributing an energy of their own and creating a strong diagonal from lower left to upper right. The heavy double triangle at the bottom serves to anchor the composition and increases the intensity of the visual statement. With great simplicity and economy of means de Zayas has created a remarkably forceful composition.

Not only does "Mental Reactions" mark the birth of visual poetry in America; it is the first in a series of poems in *291* authored by women and treating feminine subjects. As such these poems tend to be rather personal and to present a distinctly feminine viewpoint. "Mental Reactions," for example, contains a meditation on what it means to be a woman. Despite its chaotic appearance the poem adheres fairly closely to traditional models. In particular one notes that the words are arranged in two columns. If the "abstract, geometrical shapes that move diagonally integrate the two columns and obliterate their linear logic" (Tashjian), the reading sequence itself is perfectly linear. According to literary convention the reader begins at the upper left and descends vertically to the bottom of the page before subjecting

188

Marius de Zayas and abstraction

the second column to the same operation. There is one important difference from conventional poetry: The title comes at the end. Above all, the reader's initial approach to the poem is dominated by its physical appearance. Although the visual elements are not immediately identifiable, they convey various bits of information. These include such notions as abstraction, force, motion, symmetry, asymmetry, incoherence, and novelty. "Mental Reactions" will obviously be daring and difficult.

The drawing not only establishes the tone of the poem and creates certain expectations; it also announces various themes. The reader-viewer's attention is drawn initially to the heavy double triangle at the bottom. From there it progresses counterclockwise to encompass several forms, including the following words or phrases: "MYSELF," "FLIRT," "PARFUMERIE DE NICE," "PARFUM ULTRA PERSISTANT," and "*CrèmeS.*" Since the last three are in French they connote sophistication, sensuality, and self-indulgence. They also imply that their owner is used to a certain luxury. In fact Agnes Ernst Meyer was married to a very wealthy man, and she traveled in monied circles. Exactly what kind of "crèmes" she has in mind is difficult to say. Given the presence of imported perfume, she may be referring to some sort of facial cream (*crème de beauté, crème démaquillant, crème fond de teint,* etc.). Or again, the reference may be to liqueurs (*crème de banane,* etc.). The fact that the word is plural, however, suggests that it represents a box of chocolates (*crèmes au chocolat*). The style of the lettering, which looks as if it were taken from a box of candy, makes this interpretation all the more likely. The typography of the other two phrases is completely different. Although each of these has its own distinct style, both are imitations of perfume labels. It is not clear whether there are two bottles of perfume or whether both phrases come from the same label.

Printed in large block letters, "MYSELF" specifies the poem's subject and identifies the speaker. "Mental Reactions" is an interior monologue by Agnes Ernst Meyer. Although the events she recounts also involve other people, everything is filtered through her consciousness. As the title indicates, the emphasis is not on the events themselves but on her reflections about them. To understand these one must reconstruct the situation at the center of the poem – a notoriously difficult task. Tashjian concludes that "Mental Reactions" consists of a woman's thoughts (Meyer's) about herself and her husband as she takes in the view from her dressing-room window. However, detailed analysis reveals that the poem records Meyer's reactions to an attractive man at a social gathering. Moreover, the man is certainly not her husband. Toward the top de Zayas summarizes the encounter with an example of framed writing: "**FLIRT.**" This is consistent with what is known about Meyer, who was attractive and quite flirtatious. Thus to a certain extent "Mental Reactions" revolves about two poles. On the one hand, its subject is Meyer's thoughts. On the other, the subject of those thoughts is flirtation. The latter is the pretense for her reflections and the poem's *raison d'être.*

Keeping this discussion in mind, one can finally begin to identify some of the abstract forms. Several critics have noted that the small rhomboid figure at the top and the circle and comma at the lower right resemble eyes. Extrapolating from this, they conclude that the drawing is a fragmented portrait of Agnest Ernst Meyer herself. Whereas Cubist principles are certainly at work here, the latter is actually a picture of Meyer and her gentleman friend in the act of flirting. The lower figure

189

Aesthetics of visual poetry

represents Meyer, and that at the top depicts her companion. That the label "**FLIRT**" belongs to the latter configuration indicates that the man is the instigator. However, the lines connecting them symbolize the personal magnetism of *both* participants. Each is clearly attracted to the other. Since the lower configuration is larger than the upper, it is probably closer to the viewer. As in traditional painting, height and size are a function of distance. From this it would appear that we are looking over Meyer's shoulder in the foreground toward her companion behind her. Since they are seated opposite each other, in actuality one would see her back, not her face. Following Cubist theory, de Zayas translates the scene into two-dimensional terms in which the participants continue to face each other but are displaced vertically. It is clear that Meyer is the bottom figure because this is plainly labeled "MYSELF." The latter depicts her in left profile. The five horizontal lines above her eye/eyebrow fill out her face and indicate the contour of her head. Most likely the viewer is supposed to interpret them as hair. The two converging triangles above the lines may represent a hat, a bow, or Meyer's hair parted in the middle. Below her eye, nine lines of poetry form the lower half of her face. Once again their rounded right edge reproduces the contour of her head. The horizontal zigzag at the bottom represents her chin and neck. This leaves the solid double triangle, which at first suggests a gigantic nose seen in profile. The size and weight of this object, however, suggest that it refers to Meyer's body. Seen from the perspective of her partner, the two triangles can be interpreted as references to her breasts.

Like the first figure, the second is labeled in such a way that it can be identified. At the upper right, immediately next to it, one finds a single, isolated sentence: "He is alone." This confirms that the drawing represents a man and implies that he is available. As before, the portrait presents a profile view of the subject, who is facing toward the right. This time de Zayas introduces a few rectangular shapes to make the composition more masculine. Although it is not as detailed as Meyer's portrait, one can still recognize a number of features. The dark triangle at the top, for instance, appears to be his hair, whereas the solid triangular mass below and to the right represents his body. This means that the open-ended rectangle in between must be his head, which seems to be swiveling back and forth. At least this is the impression given by the two parallel rings encircling the rectangle. The contrast between the man's eye and Meyer's is instructive. Not only is he lacking an eyebrow; their eyes are different shapes. The first discrepancy can be explained by the fact that Meyer is wearing makeup. Her penciled eyebrows are naturally more prominent than his. The second reflects the dichotomy between male and female. Her round eye connotes feminine softness and curves. His rhomboid eye suggests masculine strength and rigidity. Both shapes reflect sexual differentiation.

Abstract caricature

As mentioned previously, de Zayas's representational system is a unique contribution to visual poetry. Although various influences can be discerned, visually "Mental Reactions" represents a continuation of his experiments with modern art. Between 1911 and 1913 de Zayas developed a totally abstract style of painting. Instead of

190

Marius de Zayas and abstraction

depicting the physical appearance of an individual – a superficial process at best – he sought to provide an "analysis." Art was no longer to be rendered as extrinsic impression but as "intrinsic expression."[6] Describing this new form as "abstract caricature," de Zayas outlined his method as follows:

1. The *spirit* of the individual was to be represented by algebraic formulas,
2. his *material self* by "geometric equivalents," and
3. his *initial force* by "trajectories within the rectangle that encloses the plastic expression and represents life."

According to de Zayas, the spirit was composed of (1) Memory (acquired knowledge), (2) Understanding (capability of learning, intelligence), and (3) Volition (the regulation of physical desires, vices, and virtues). By "material self" he meant the human body. Finally, he defined "initial force," which recalls Bergson's concept of *élan vital*, as that which "binds spirit and matter together." In the caricatures it is represented by a line or "trajectory" symbolizing the individual's passage through life. De Zayas distinguished five classes of trajectory based on the positivistic sequence knowledge $\longrightarrow$ progress $\longrightarrow$ conclusion. These categories enable him to relate his subject's life to the general "evolution of humanity."

Interestingly, de Zayas adapted this method to visual poetry. To be sure "Mental Reactions" contains no algebraic formulas, but this is consistent with his general artistic development. By 1915 he had replaced this cumbersome device with a printed phrase or title. The first issue of *291*, for example, featured an abstract portrait of Alfred Stieglitz with the inscription "291 Throws Back Its Forelock." This phrase captures the defiant spirit of "291" – personified by Stieglitz – better than mathematics ever could have. In "Mental Reactions," also a portrait, the verbal element has the same role. Although it is greatly expanded, its function is still to express Meyer's spirit. This is the meaning of the poem's title. De Zayas also seems to depict her "initial force." Thus one can trace an S-shaped curve running from the lower left of her portrait to the top of her head, to the word "**FLIRT**," and ending at "He is alone." This rising curve signifies prosperity and success. Belonging to the fourth category of trajectory, it indicates the acquisition of knowledge and a contribution to progress in general. The fact that Meyer's trajectory stops before reaching the top means that her life is still fruitful, that she still has much to give. The importance of the second principle, that of geometric equivalents, has already been demonstrated. If anything, "Mental Reactions" is more geometric than the abstract caricatures. One has only to contrast it with, say, the biomorphic style of Jean Arp to see how completely this principle governs the poem.

It remains to mention the role of double abstraction in de Zayas's art. His method is twofold: first he chooses an object to symbolize his human subject; then he simplifies it according to Cubist principles until it is unrecognizable. For example, a close analysis of the Stieglitz portrait in *291* reveals that it depicts a camera with an extended bellows. A caricature of Apollinaire, published in *Les Soirées de Paris* in July 1914, portrays the poet as an airplane. As will become apparent, a similar process is at work in "Mental Reactions," which contains *two* object portraits. The key to de Zayas's visual symbolism lies in the upper configura-

191

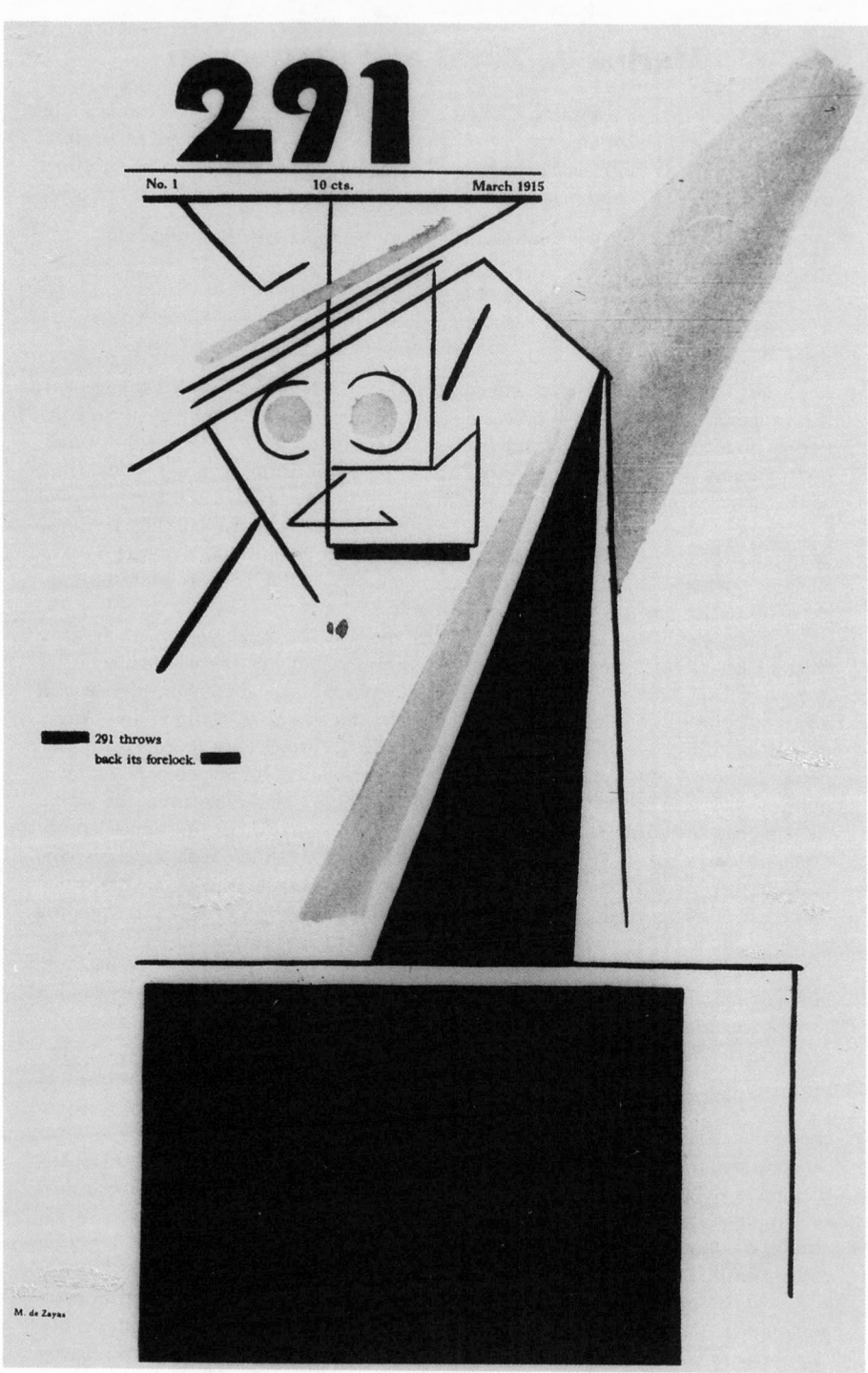

Figure 55. Marius de Zayas, "291 Throws Back Its Forelock"

Marius de Zayas and abstraction

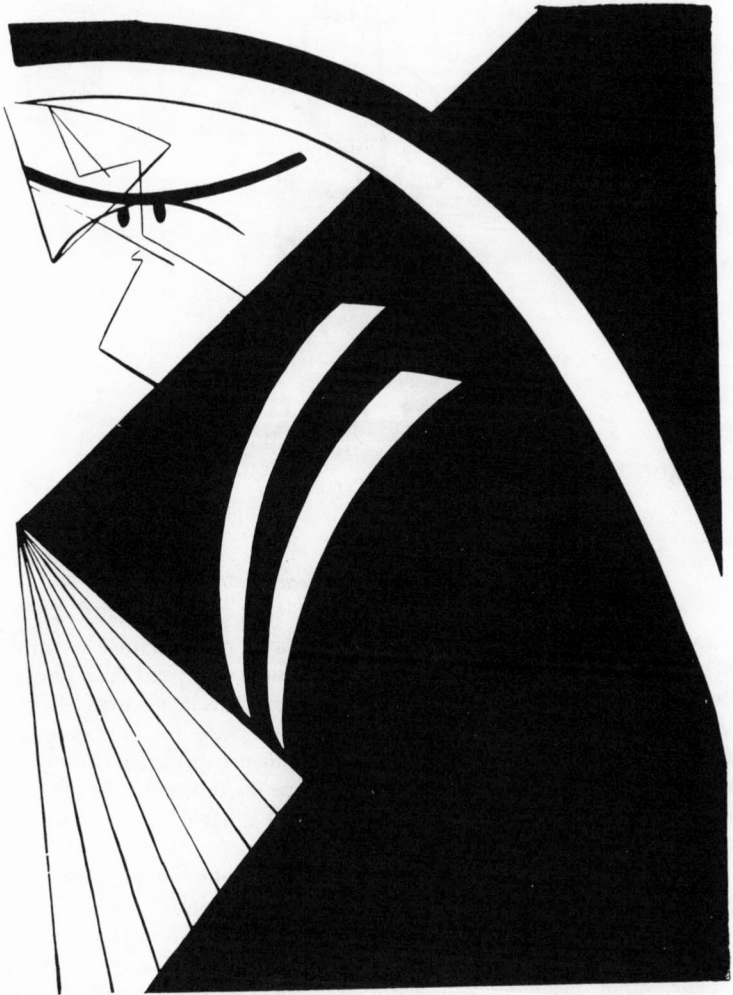

Figure 56. Marius de Zayas, "Guillaume Apollinaire"

tion, the one depicting Meyer's companion. If it is difficult to interpret the solid geometric figures, the central elements provide several clues. In order to identify the design one must look for a tall, rectangular object with an aperture in its side that is subject to rotary motion. Judging from these criteria, the figure almost certainly represents a *lighthouse*. Thus the open-ended rectangle depicts the top of the tower, and the rhomboid eye its beacon. The two parallel rings encircling it indicate that the beacon rotates a full 360 degrees, warning ships in every direction. Given this information, the dark triangular forms at the top and bottom can be interpreted in

193

Aesthetics of visual poetry

Figure 57. Marius de Zayas, "Mental Reactions": the lighthouse

one of two ways. Either they represent cliffs or large rocks, or they constitute the base of the tower. Bearing in mind that the caricatures depend on fragmentation and displacement, the viewer is free to combine the forms in any way. The simplest combination is suggested by their orientation. If one closes the gap between them, aligning their diagonal edges, one obtains an elongated pyramid. To create a recognizable lighthouse the viewer need merely place the beacon on top. The isolated phrase "He is alone" indicates that the lighthouse is situated on a deserted coast or remote island.

The foregoing analysis provides the necessary information to decipher the portrait of Agnes Ernst Meyer. One suspects that it uses fragmentation and displacement and that it is somehow connected with a lighthouse. An inventory reveals the following forms: two large right triangles, two small triangles, a straight line, a circle, a curved line, five tapered lines, and a zigzag. The large triangles are virtually identical, but the small ones differ in size and shape. One of them is an isosceles triangle. In addition the portrait is surrounded by other forms that may or may not have a bearing on it. According to Cubist doctrine de Zayas is free to include elements that have nothing to do with the original object. The purpose of these is aesthetic rather than functional. Similarly, he may choose to duplicate certain elements, a phenomenon corresponding to planar refraction. It is possible, for instance, that the missing object consists of one large triangle instead of two. Given the proximity of the lighthouse, one immediately thinks of a sailboat. Certainly its shape and marine associations are promising. Nevertheless, there are several objections to this interpretation. For one thing, it does not account for any of the auxiliary elements. What is the function of the two small triangles, for example, or the circle?

194

Marius de Zayas and abstraction

Figure 58. Marius de Zayas, "Mental Reactions": the moth

For another, the fact that the beacon is operating means it must be night. It is unlikely that a sailboat would be out on the ocean after dark. In the light of these problems this explanation must finally be rejected in favor of an interpretation centered around the notion of a double triangle.

At this point two observations are in order. It is surely significant (1) that the portrait contains two pairs of triangles and (2) that the right triangles are also equilateral triangles. Proceeding on the assumption that the pairing can be traced back to the original object, one juxtaposes the equilateral triangles in various symmetrical combinations. The solution requires that they be rotated 45 degrees to the left and joined at the apex in such a way that each is a mirror image of the other. Once this is accomplished one perceives that the object is a butterfly. The large triangles are its wings, the circle its head, and the horizontal bar at the lower right (above the title) its body. This means that the smaller triangles are antennae. In reality they are identical – the left is distorted by perspective, indicating that the insect's head is turned. Moreover, the thickness of the antennae indicates that the creature is actually a *moth*. Suddenly everything falls into place. The marine associations of the lighthouse are irrelevant; all that matters is that it is a source of light. At the middle level of signification, between realism and abstraction, the composition depicts a moth fluttering about a lantern, a traditional metaphor for fascination.

Structurally the composition is bounded by horizontal metonymy and vertical metaphor. Like the moth the lighthouse is a visual metaphor that is linked to its verbal anchor through the principle of shared characteristics. Rather than a particular physical quality the latter describes a certain attitude that they have in common,

195

Figure 59. Marius de Zayas, "Mental Reactions" reconstructed

Marius de Zayas and abstraction

a certain stance. In the case of the man and the lighthouse this includes such concepts as visibility, brilliance, and magnetism. With Meyer and the moth it involves such notions as fascination and vulnerability. Horizontally both the verbal and the visual bonds are metonymic. Like the moth and the lighthouse, the human participants are linked by the principle of *stimulus and response* (a variation of cause and effect). Even though the visual bond is metonymic, it comments metaphorically on the verbal relationship because it is tied to two visual metaphors. By virtue of its analogical structure it acts as a simulacrum of the verbal drama. Although the image of the moth fluttering about the beacon symbolizes the general situation, that is, Meyer's attraction to her partner, it refers to one line in particular. "Those eyes of his," she exclaims at one point. "I cannot get away from them." The artist has taken this remark (*A*), translated it into metaphorical terms (*B*), raised these to the visual plane (*B'*), and expressed them according to the rules of Cubism (*C'*). This process can be diagrammed as follows:

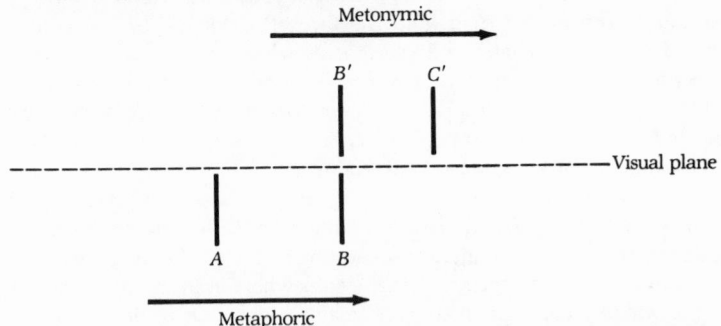

The original subject has thus been subjected to a threefold transformation. Paradoxically, the initial metaphor is finally expressed in metonymic terms, since the lighthouse and moth are represented by a series of synecdoches.

Fragmentation and flirtation

Understanding the visual side of "Mental Reactions" is a necessary prelude to considering its verbal implications. The poem begins as follows:

> Silence.
>   Twilight.
> Relief. Many minds, many voices would have been unendurable today.
> What a restful voice his.
> Silence of snow covered roof tops. New York is best from
> the back and from above.
>   He is telling me this   laughing clowns
> to find out whether I have dared to live.
>   Windows
>   one
>   two
>   three

Aesthetics of visual poetry

How can he bear to speak of it if it was real to him?
PARFUMERIE DE NICE
dots
Red   on
whiteness

The first three words establish the tone (restrained) and the time of day (dusk). The succeeding lines reveal that the scene is situated in New York after a snowfall, which explains the muffled silence that fills the poem. From an apartment at the back of a skyscraper Meyer is able to look down on the rooftops below. As Tashjian remarks, this is the perspective in many of Stieglitz's photographs of the city. Like the rest of the poem the passage combines the speaker's thoughts and sense impressions. At one point the author juxtaposes the unknown man, laughing clowns, and three windows to create an ambiguous situation in which each of the terms is equal to the other two. Thus the windows are simultaneously the windows in the room, the eyes and mouth of the man, and the face of a clown. The last comparison probably refers to their shape and placement, which suggest a crude face. The former focuses on the eyes of Meyer's companion – windows of the soul – which are particularly expressive. This impression is reinforced by the implicit·equivalence between the man and the circus performer. Each of his eyes is in effect a "laughing clown," revealing a sparkling personality and a sense of humor.

To illustrate his mysterious "Red dots on whiteness" de Zayas appends an actual sample (which is colored red). In addition he scatters the words themselves on the page to create a visual analogy suggesting a cluster of dots. From all indications the phrase refers to a polka dot fabric somewhere in the room – either Meyer's dress or the window curtains or even the man's necktie. Or again it may describe the costume of the laughing clowns. The third line places the speaker at some sort of social gathering. Since she is feeling tired, she is pleased that it is smaller than usual due to the weather. Judging from the metonymic perfume label, Meyer and her partner are sitting in her hostess's dressing room, where they are engaged in an intimate conversation. Although she finds his voice restful, the man's words contain a challenge – has she really dared to live? Coupled with this is a meditation on the nature of reality centered on perception versus expression. These themes are developed as the poem progresses:

> Ah, there you go, sitting in judgment again from the personal point of view. He has the ability to give his very self. Be big enough to accept whatever is given you.

PARFUM ULTRA PERSISTANT

CrèmeS
Shouldn't it be a circumflex?

But is it fair
to the woman?   Parfumerie-de-Nice.
Does it make her   N-i-c-e.
less – or more?   Sunshine.
Flowers.

198

Marius de Zayas and abstraction

Color.

Land of eternal loves.

At best her life, her whole life, was nothing but his introduction to himself. Why not? Most lives are less than that. What after all is – mine?

Those eyes of his. I cannot get away from them, cannot guess what his greater experience can see.

Windows

windows.

A different picture behind each.

Crèmes – parfums.

Now if I were a man I should want to prove that I had lived even more dangerously. Being a woman, I am silent.

Outlines snow-softened.

Lights appearing.

She died young? What matter? All of life had been hers.

In the first line Meyer reproaches herself for doubting the reality of the experience. She recognizes that, unlike herself, the man is willing to reveal his innermost feelings. His is the gift of total honesty. One soon discovers that the subject of his conversation is a young woman – possibly his wife – who died at an early age. Although Meyer's response is complex, it centers around the question of what constitutes an authentic life. This is connected in turn with the challenge issued earlier. What does it mean to "really live," she wonders, and how does this apply to women in particular? As she notes, a man would respond aggressively, feeling that he had something to prove. Meyer prefers a more feminine response. On the one hand, she answers the challenge by being flirtatious. On the other, the challenge provokes a personal meditation that causes her to examine her own life. Reviewing the young woman's history, she ponders the traditional male and female roles. It appears that the woman's existence was contingent on the man's, who viewed her as a path to himself. In an earlier (displaced) section Meyer asks whether this makes the woman inferior or superior to the man. Is it fair to the woman? she wonders. The answer is found a few lines later: "Why not?" Subservience does not imply inferiority or unfairness; the relationship depends on the individual man and woman. Meyer's companion is so fascinating that just to be in his presence is enough – whence the visual lighthouse/moth metaphor. Meyer concludes that the woman was lucky to have shared his life ("Most lives are less than that"). Including herself among the less fortunate ("What after all is – mine?"), she ruefully admits that her life has been less than exciting.

As before, the speaker's monologue is interspersed with sense impressions and random thoughts. A number of motifs are repeated – the snow, the windows, and the time of day ("Lights appearing") – which briefly evoke the setting. In addition one encounters the ambiguous "*CrèmeS*" together with the question "Shouldn't it be a circumflex?" The latter can be ascribed either to Meyer's persona or to Meyer herself. It exists simultaneously as a fictional utterance and as an authorial intervention. This passage also develops the perfume motif in some detail. Thus the words

199

Aesthetics of visual poetry

"Crèmes–parfums" support the dressing-room theory by implying that several bottles are present. The label reading "Parfumerie-de-Nice" provokes a series of associations concerning its point of origin. Meyer begins with a *jeu de mots* between the city Nice and its English cognate "nice," which she spells out letter by letter. This word summarizes the associations that follow, which are in fact pleasant. Following in Van Gogh's footsteps, she depicts Provence as a colorful land where love blossoms amid sunshine and flowers. Most of the next section is devoted to her central meditation:

> Clown.　　　Dancing buttons.　　　Tilted hat.
> Why will my lip twitch? How much can those eyes see?
> 　　　　　　　Soothing light within–without–
> Odd. He gives me all he has to give.
> 　　　I think about myself.
> Are the passions of others ever real to us
> –or only–
> 　　　that sudden glare of whiteness
> 　　　hurts
> –something to pity
> –something to envy?
>
> 　　　　　　　　　　　　　　　　　　He is alone

FLIRT

> 　Not our grey passions pathetic　　as that struggling city tree–
> 　evanescent as that melting city snow.
> 　Ah, why cannot all the loves of the world be mine? . . .
> without the sacrifice of any of those things I think of when I say

MYSELF

> Sacrifice? Coward, cheat.
> 　Yes, we women, cowards, cheats all of us who, when our
> kingdom is offered, stop to calculate the price.

The first line continues the window/eyes/clown motif, which is expanded to include dancing buttons and a funny hat. De Zayas introduces a second visual analogy by breaking the line into fragments and slanting these in different directions. Visually and verbally the line evokes a clown dancing about with his hat tilted comically to one side. Inserted into a metonymic context, the buttons are associated with the clown's costume. Viewed metaphorically, they refer to the twinkling eyes of Meyer's companion. As before, the man's penetrating gaze makes her uncomfortable, producing a nervous twitch. Through the window she glimpses a solitary tree partially buried in the snow. The light is generally muted except for a sudden, painful flash that may come from the glare on the snow. It may also represent a flash of insight or a particularly penetrating glance. The first few lines recapitulate previous themes: the man's omniscience, his honesty, and the question of subjective reality. Meyer especially wonders whether the reality of human passion can be communicated and seems to conclude that it cannot. Ordinary ("grey") passions strike the observer as pathetic and evanescent, moving him at most to pity. Al-

Marius de Zayas and abstraction

though extraordinary passions – such as those between the man and the young woman – evoke envy in the observer (in this case Meyer), it is impossible to experience them outside the relationship.

The last lines concern Meyer's own relationship with the man, or rather her response to his challenge, summarized by the word "**FLIRT**." What exactly is the nature of the challenge? What does it really mean "to dare to live?" Besides an element of risk implicit in the word "dare," judging from the man's example it requires total honesty and the gift of self. Complete fulfillment requires complete commitment. By addressing Meyer in this manner he is obviously inviting her to reply in kind. Although she is strongly attracted to him, she is afraid to jeopardize ("sacrifice") her present life by having an affair. Running off with him is even more unthinkable. "Why cannot all the loves of the world be mine?" Meyer laments, wishing to have her cake and eat it too. If her refusal to honor her feelings is cowardly and dishonest, as she admits, it typifies the feminine condition. In her opinion most women are afraid to trade security for a chance to experience paradise. Her solution – flirtation – is a dishonest compromise. At this point the poem changes direction. The final section resolves the immediate issue to Meyer's satisfaction, and the poem ends on a positive note:

> Clock booming
> –one
> –two
>   –three
>   –four
>   –five
>   –six
> Their bed-time.
> They will want to say good-night.
> I must go
> He gave himself – I find – myself. So it goes.
> How annoying.
> Those eyes are twinkling at my expense –
>   I feel him making a mental note:
>   "Experiment No. 987.
>   Reaction perfect"
> Why do we all object to being the common de-
> nominator?
> I really must go –
> Whenever I pass that canvas I want to put my foot through
> it.
>   Good. It's still running.
>   I shall be in time for a last romp. Coward? Common
> human denominator? Who cares?

Suddenly the chiming of a grandfather clock breaks the spell. Each note occupies a separate line and is followed by a dash, indicating that the process is slow and deliberate. The implicit analogy here is with the story of Cinderella. In both cases

201

Aesthetics of visual poetry

this signal forces the heroine to abandon her prince and return to reality. "He gave himself," Meyer remarks, "I find myself." This phrase not only describes her recovery; it summarizes the poem's development. As she notes, the first half is devoted to giving, the second to (re)discovery. Despite their differences both sections are concerned with the assertion of self.

Meyer's immediate pretext for leaving is that it is her hosts' bedtime. At this point her attitude changes abruptly. Although the comment "So it goes" implies resignation, she is quite annoyed. Once she has recovered her bearings, Meyer perceives that the man is merely toying with her. To him she is just another pretty face, another amorous adventure. Though she likes to think of herself as a unique individual, she has responded to his advances exactly as he had predicted. This is what she means by "common human denominator." Her anger is directed not only at the man for deceiving her but at herself for being deceived. If Meyer is tempted to destroy one of her hosts' paintings on the way out, her reasons are psychological rather than aesthetic. She is simply trying to displace some of her anger. Her final solution is practical, psychologically healthy, and immediate. Checking her watch, she decides to attend another party. The joyful atmosphere ("a last romp") will lift her spirits and bury the incident permanently. Thus the poem ends on a defiant note: "Who cares?" Not only does Meyer accept her lot in life; she likes herself just as she is.

Tashjian sees the poem as a meditation on the author's sexual problems, showing her to be "a female Prufrock" incapable of passion. The foregoing analysis, however, reveals the true nature of her problem: She is married to one man and attracted to another. The poem records the development of an adulterous fantasy and its subsequent repression. Seen in this perspective the bottle of French perfume – traditionally associated with sinful passion – becomes the central image. As such it generates a series of associations connected with romantic love, sensuality, and seduction. More than this it is associated with a distinct philosophy of life. This is especially evident in the cluster of images connected with Nice, where the perfume was manufactured:

> Parfumerie-de-Nice.
> N-i-c-e.
> Sunshine.
> Flowers.
> Color.
> Land of eternal loves.

Provence is portrayed as a colorful land blessed with a warm climate in which love flourishes amid the flowers. Interestingly, Meyer systematically negates every one of these attributes in her description of New York. Instead of a sunny locale one sees the city at night in the midst of winter. Not only are there no flowers; the very trees are struggling to survive. Nor is there any color. Like de Zayas's drawing, the metropolis consists of black and white contrasts. And as far as love is concerned, the best that can be found are a few "grey passions." Obviously, New York embodies a different philosophy than Nice. In opposition to the Mediterranean cult of the senses, it embraces the cult of self-denial propagated by the Protestant ethic. There

Marius de Zayas and abstraction

is no doubt that Nice is the more attractive city, as the speaker herself makes clear. The problem is that it does not correspond to Meyer's personal reality, which is tied to New York. Like her partner's promise of "eternal love," the happiness it offers is illusory in her eyes. Reflecting the speaker's dilemma, the poem consists of a dialogue between these two poles, between illusion and reality, which questions the nature of existence.

Although *291* went on to publish other visual poems, "Mental Reactions" remains the best example of this genre. Not only is it a remarkable accomplishment; it is unique in the history of visual poetry.[7] Although Meyer's text follows the simultanist model fairly closely, de Zayas's drawing is very much his own creation. Indeed the theory governing its production antedates the invention of modern visual poetry by at least a year. Among the various factors that distinguish "Mental Reactions" from its predecessors, several deserve to be singled out. For one thing, the composition is the result of a joint collaboration – a situation virtually unheard of in visual poetry. For another, with few exceptions the visual elements are distinct from the verbal elements. De Zayas draws objects and lines in order to illustrate the text. Apollinaire, for example, compresses and reshapes his text in such a way that it illustrates itself. In the calligrams the drawing *is* the text (and vice versa). Even the Futurists, who often introduced graphic elements into their works, take care to make their texts autoillustrative. This is the lesson of the visual analogy, which describes as it depicts and depicts as it describes. Finally, de Zayas draws shapes that are virtually impossible to recognize. Rejecting the representational and analogical principles of his predecessors, he relies on objectification, fragmentation, and dislocation. Without a doubt the application of abstract caricature was de Zayas's original contribution to visual poetry. In "Mental Reactions," through the process of double abstraction he succeeded in creating a work of rare complexity and visual appeal.

Notes

1. Introduction

1. For a history of visual poetry in the West, with special attention to France, see David W. Seaman, *Concrete Poetry in France* (Ann Arbor: UMI Research Press, 1981). Giuseppe Marrochi provides an introduction to modern visual poetry in *Scrittura visuale, ricerche ed esperienze nelle avanguardie letterarie* (Messina and Florence: D'Anna, 1978). See also Giovanni Pozzi, *La parola dipinta* (Milan: Adelphi, 1981), which concentrates on the seventeenth century.

2. For an excellent survey of these conflicting opinions see Wendy Steiner, *The Colors of Rhetoric: Problems in the Relation Between Modern Literature and Painting* (University of Chicago Press, 1982), pp. 1–18.

3. Tamara Karsavina, *Theatre Street* (1931, rev. ed., New York: Dutton, 1961), p. 217.

4. Steiner, in *Colors of Rhetoric*, p. 36, points out that Lessing studied the two media as material artifacts and ignored the cognitive process involved. In fact physiological and psychological experiments reveal that pictorial perception, like literary perception, is a matter of temporal processing (p. 200).

5. Michel Foucault, *Ceci n'est pas une pipe* (Montpellier: Fata Morgana, 1973), pp. 21–2.

6. Pierre Caizergues, *Apollinaire journaliste: les débuts et la formation du journaliste* (Paris: Lettres Modernes, 1981), p. 21.

7. Jacques Derrida, *Marges de la philosophie* (Paris: Minuit, 1972), pp. 3–29.

8. Wolfgang Iser, *The Act of Reading: A Theory of Aesthetic Response* (Baltimore: Johns Hopkins University Press, 1978), pp. 10–19.

9. Stéphane Mallarmé, letter to Henri Cazalis written in October or November 1864, *Correspondance*, ed. Henri Mondor and Jean-Pierre Richard (Paris: Gallimard, 1959), Vol. 1, p. 137.

10. Stéphane Mallarmé, "Préface," *Oeuvres complètes*, ed. Henri Mondor and G. Jean-Aubry (Paris: Gallimard/Pléiade, 1956), p. 455.

11. Gérard Genette, *Figures II* (Paris: Seuil, 1969), p. 150. Genette's immediate source is an observation by Paul Eluard: "Les poèmes ont toujours de grandes marges blanches, de grandes marges de silence" ("Poems always have great white margins, great margins of silence"). Genette adds that the suppression of punctua-

tion in much modern poetry has a similar effect, obliterating grammatical relations and making the poem a "pure verbal constellation" in the tradition of Mallarmé.

12. Paul Claudel, "Les Muses," *Cinq Grandes Odes* (Paris: Gallimard, 1948), p. 16.

13. Ferdinand de Saussure, *Cours de linguistiquè génerale* (1916, Paris: Payot, 1964), p. 57.

14. See, for example, Laszlo Géfin, *Ideogram: History of a Poetic Method* (Austin: University of Texas Press, 1982).

15. Jonathan Culler, *Structuralist Poetics: Structuralism, Linguistics, and the Study of Literature* (Ithaca, N.Y.: Cornell University Press, 1975), p. 162.

16. François Rigolot, "Le Poétique et l'analogique," *Poétique*, No. 35 (September 1978): 258.

17. See Roland Barthes, *Mythologies* (Paris: Seuil, 1957), p. 222.

18. The mechanisms governing the avant-garde are analyzed by Renato Poggioli in *The Theory of the Avant-Garde* (New York: Harper & Row, 1971). See also Matei Calinescu, *Faces of Modernity* (Bloomington: Indiana University Press, 1977), and Peter Bürger, *Theory of the Avant-Garde* (Minneapolis: University of Minnesota Press, 1984).

19. Jacques Derrida, *De la grammatologie* (Paris: Minuit, 1967), p. 428.

20. For a study of Russian visual poetry see Gerald Janacek, *The Look of Russian Literature: Avant-Garde Visual Experiments, 1900–1930* (Princeton, N.J.: Princeton University Press, 1984).

21. For an analysis of Dada's attack on the cultural sign system see Rudolf E. Kuenzli, "The Semiotics of Dada Poetry," in *Dada Spectrum: The Dialectics of Revolt*, ed. Stephen C. Foster and Rudolf E. Kuenzli (Madison, Wis.: Coda; Iowa City: University of Iowa Press, 1979), pp. 52–70.

22. Examples of Futurist collage are examined in Chapters 1 and 2. For a study of Cubist collage see Susan Marcus, "The Typographic Element in Cubism, 1911–1915: Its Formal and Semantic Implications," *Visible Language*, 6, No. 4 (Fall 1972): 321–40. Michel Butor discusses the role of linguistic elements in art in general in *Les Mots dans la peinture* (Geneva and Paris: Skira/Flammarion, 1969).

23. Additional examples are included in *Poesía de la vanguardia española*, ed. Germán Gullón (Madrid: Taurus, 1981).

24. Steiner, *Colors of Rhetoric*, p. 218.

25. Ibid., p. 5.

1. Music of the spheres

1. Carlo Carrà, *La mia vita*, 2nd ed. (Milan: Rizzoli, 1945), p. 184. For a description of the highlights of his Paris trip see the chapter entitled "Apollinaire e Picasso," pp. 184–208.

2. Willard Bohn, "Circular Poem-Paintings by Apollinaire and Carrà," *Comparative Literature*, 31, No. 3 (Summer 1979): 246–71. For a detailed chronology see pp. 253–6.

3. In addition to the article cited in 2 see Alan Windsor, "Apollinaire, Marinetti, and Carrà's 'Dipinto Parolibero,' " *Gazette des Beaux-Arts*, 89 (April 1977): 145–52;

reprinted in French in *Que Vlo-ve?* (Belgium), Nos. 21–2 (July–October 1979): 6–13, paginated separately.

4. See, for example, "A travers l'Europe," published April 15, 1914 (*Oeuvres poétiques*, ed. Marcel Adéma and Michel Décaudin [Paris: Gallimard/Pleiade, 1965], p. 201; cited hereafter in the text and in the notes as *Po*).

5. Gaston Bouatchidzé, Pierre Caizergues, Michel Décaudin, and Pascal Pia, "De Paris à Nîmes, souvenirs et témoignages," *Revue des Lettres Modernes*, Nos. 380–4 (*Guillaume Apollinaire 12*): 31–2. The description is that of Henri Siegler-Pascal, to whom Apollinaire dedicated the copy.

6. This is undoubtedly the "hymne russe de 'La vie pour le tzar' " mentioned by Apollinaire in "Les Pigeons de la Khodinka," ibid., pp. 80–1.

7. Gabriel Arbouin, "Devant l'idéogramme d'Apollinaire," *Les Soirées de Paris*, Nos. 26–7 (July–August 1914): 383–5.

8. See Chapter 3 for the complete text. For the context see Claude Debon, *Apollinaire après* Alcools (Paris: Lettres Modernes, 1981), pp. 62–4.

9. Letter from Apollinaire to André Billy, July 29, 1918, *Oeuvres complètes*, ed. Michel Décaudin (Paris: Balland-Lecat, 1965–6), Vol. 4, p. 778.

10. Daniel Delbreil and Francoise Dininman raise the possibility that Apollinaire may be describing the Seine. See " 'Lettre-Océan,' " *Que Vlo-ve?* Nos. 21–2 (July–October 1979): 31. In fact the verse's triangular shape suggests that we are on a barge crossing Paris.

11. Dininman points out that typographically the original manuscripts are more radical than the printed text. For a detailed comparison see Dininman, pp. 13–15, and also Delbreil, pp. 2–5, both in " 'Lettre–Océan.' "

12. The only truly pictorial Futurist poem is Ardengo Soffici's *Al buffet della stazione* (Figure 5, Chapter 2), but this is a late work.

13. "Bisogna dunque assolutamente evitare ogni preoccupazione decorativa e pittorica" ("Thus it is necessary to avoid every pictorial and decorative preoccupation").

14. Compare, for example, Carrà's collage *Sintesi circolare di oggetti* (Figure 6, Chapter 2), in which the painter's business card and part of a newspaper, dated "Giovedì 30 Aprile [1914]," serve as signature and date. Apollinaire's signature at the end of the poem was omitted subsequently.

15. For a more general discussion see the chapter "Apollinaire et cubisme" in Marie-Jeanne Durry, *Guillaume Apollinaire*, Alcools (Paris: SEDES, 1964), Vol. 2, pp. 175–219. See also Pär Bergman, *"Modernolatria" et "simultaneità"* (Paris: Lettres Modernes, 1962).

16. Delbreil, " 'Lettre-Océan,' " p. 5.

17. Guillaume Apollinaire, *Méditations esthétiques: les peintres cubistes*, ed. L. C. Breunig and J.-C. Chevalier (Paris: Hermann, 1965), p. 67.

18. Durry, *Guillaume Apollinaire*, p. 202.

19. George Schmits, " 'Lettre-Océan,' " *Savoir et Beauté*, Nos. 2–3 (1964): 2691–8.

20. Michel Butor, Préface to *Calligrammes* (Paris: Gallimard/Poésie, 1966), p. 9.

21. Cf. "Zone": "Tu lis les prospectus les catalogues les affiches qui chantent tout haut/Voilà la poésie ce matin et pour la prose il y a les journaux" ("You read handbills catalogues posters that sing at the top of their voices/So much for poetry this morning and for prose there are the newspapers") (*Po*, p. 39).

22. Dininman analyses and charts its formal properties in detail (" 'Lettre-Océan,' " pp. 16–18).

23. Roger Shattuck, *Selected Writings of Guillaume Apollinaire* (New York: New Directions, 1971), p. 20.

24. Cf. Blaise Cendrars, "Lettre-Océan," *Oeuvres complètes* (Paris: Denoël, 1963), Vol. 1, p. 143, which also includes references to Apollinaire's poem.

25. If we read "Bonjour à Nomo et à Nora," the line may refer to girls (Schmits), servants, or pets. Delbreil and Dininman suggest that the words may be Mexican onomatopoeia (" 'Lettre-Océan,' " p. 26).

26. William Weber Johnson, *Heroic Mexico: The Violent Emergence of a Modern Nation* (Garden City, N.Y.: Doubleday, 1968), p. 141.

27. Sent by Albert to Apollinaire on February 19, 1913, it reads: "Les troubles sont terminés depuis hier. Le canon ne résonne plus. Nous y étions habitués. Les mitrailleuses tirent 40 ou 50 coups sans arrêt. Le premier jour j'ai vu tuer des gens des fenêtres de la maison où j'habite." ("The disturbances have been over since yesterday. The cannon no longer sounds. We were beginning to get used to it. The machineguns fire 40 or 50 rounds without stopping. The first day I saw some people killed from the windows in the house where I am staying.") See *Album Apollinaire*, ed. Pierre-Marcel Adéma and Michel Décaudin (Paris: Pléiade, 1971), p. 186. The postcard bears a four-centavo stamp, picturing Juan Aldama, canceled by four wavy lines exactly as in "Lettre-Océan."

28. Letter to Louise Coligny-Chatillon dated February 2, 1915. See Guillaume Apollinaire, *Lettres à Lou*, ed. Michel Décaudin (Paris: Gallimard, 1969), p. 154.

29. Two manuscripts of "Lettre-Océan," given by Apollinaire to Alberto Savinio, are reproduced by Delbreil and Dininman (" 'Lettre-Océan' ") and also by P. A. Jannini, *Le avanguardie letterarie nell'idea critica di Guillaume Apollinaire* (Rome: Bulzoni, 1971), pp. 207–8.

30. Margaret Davies, *Apollinaire* (London: Oliver & Boyd, 1964), p. 240.

31. Scott Bates notes that Apollinaire uses *sirène* and *houhou* elsewhere to mean "prostitute" and that there is probably a pun here (*Petit Glossaire des mots libres d'Apollinaire* [Sewanee, Tenn.: privately printed, 1975], pp. 45 and 95). He interprets the sounds as "le sifflement d'une sirène de bateau" ("the sound of a ship's siren"). The Futurists also make frequent use of sirens (cf. Marinetti in *Zang Tumb Tuuum*), and Apollinaire's *Antitradition futuriste* contains the phrase "**ou ou ou** flûte crapaud naissance des perles apremine."

32. Albert Simonin, *Petit Simonin illustré par l'exemple* (Paris: Gallimard, 1968); Adrien Timmermans, *L'Argot parisien* (Paris: Victorien, 1922).

33. It may also be a sexual reference; see Bates, "Toison d'or," *Petite Glossaire*, pp. 101–02.

34. Basil Woon refers to "those narrow streets in the San José dock area where carmined ladies were wont to tug at your coat-tails as you passed by" (*When It's Cocktail Time in Cuba* [New York: Liveright, 1928], p. 159). Maps in *Terry's Guide to Cuba* (Boston: Houghton Mifflin, 1926) show a Calle San Isidro in the San José wharves area.

35. Willard Bohn, "Orthographe et interprétation des mots étrangers chez Apollinaire," *Que Vlo-ve?* (Belgium), No. 27 (January 1981): 27–30.

36. Philippe Renaud, *Lecture d'Apollinaire* (Lausanne: L'Age d'Homme, 1969), p. 372. Claude Debon reproduces two mystical Hebrew charms with the same shape but notes that there is no evidence that Apollinaire ever saw them (*Apollinaire après Alcools*, pp. 65–8).

37. Jean-Claude Chevalier, *Alcools d'Apollinaire, essai d'analyse des formes poétiques* (Paris: Lettres Modernes, 1970), p. 82; see also pp. 78–87.

38. "Le regard hanté d'imaginaire se porte sur des courbes, puis sur des formes droites ou *vice versa*, les unes semblent appeler les autres" ("The imaginary view focuses on curves, then on straight forms or vice versa, each seeming to attract the other"). In Jean Levaillant, "L'Espace dans *Calligrammes*," *Revue des Lettres Modernes*, Nos. 217–22 (1969) (*Guillaume Apollinaire 8*): 51.

39. According to Roland Barthes this is the monument's most important function: "The Tower is merely the witness, the gaze which discretely fixes, with its slender signal, the whole structure – geographical, historical, and social – of Paris space" (*The Eiffel Tower and Other Mythologies* [New York: Hill & Wang, 1979], p. 13).

40. Apollinaire, *Les Peintres cubistes*, p. 52.

41. Letter from Carlo Carrà to Gino Severini, July 11, 1914, *Archivi del futurismo*, ed. Maria Drudi Gambillo and Teresa Fiori (Rome: DeLuca, 1958), Vol. 1, pp. 340–1.

42. Carrà, *La mia vita*, p. 172. Compare his remarks to Severini (July 11, 1914): "una suggestione di immagini poetiche e colori ottenuti con carte colorate" ("a suggestion of poetic images and colors obtained with colored papers")(*Archivi*, Vol. 1, pp. 340–1).

43. Max Kozloff, *Cubism/Futurism* (New York: Charterhouse, 1973), p. 207; see also pp. 207–13.

44. The first interventionist demonstration by the Futurists did not take place until two months later – in Milan on September 15, 1914, well after the war had begun.

45. At first glance a section in the upper left-hand corner seems to reflect a bellicose attitude: "Zang [T]umb Tuum / [vitto]ria quotidiana di artiglieripensieri / [h]u rrrrrrrrraaaaaaaahhh (penetrante gioioso)" ("Bang Bang Bang / daily victory of artillerymen thoughts / hurrah piercing joyful"). Lifted from Marinetti's *Zang tumb tuuum* (Milan: Poesia, 1914), the onomatopoeia of the title represents artillery fire in the original. Here, however, it functions as a metaphor, as do the "artiglieripensieri" in the following line. Although the sounds may represent fireworks in the context of the celebration (cf. Carrà's reference to "tutti i colori . . . dei fuochi d'artifizio" in *La pittura dei suoni, rumori, odori*), the excerpt as a whole emphasizes its patriotic nature. From this perspective the "artiglieripensieri" are to be interpreted as vigorous, patriotic thoughts reflecting a strong nationalistic posture. They sum up the atmosphere of the crowd (which is "gioioso," not bellicose) as well as the oratory of the political speakers celebrating Italy's sovereign independence. On a more general level Carrà is urging his audience to make patriotism part of their daily life ("vittoria quotidiana"). The difference between warmongering and nationalism, between war and war as metaphor, typifies the different orientations of Marinetti and Carrà in general.

46. The seven sources accounting for 98 percent of the printed papers are Marinetti, "Correzione di bozze + desideri in velocità" (December 1, 1913); Boccioni, "Uomo + vallata + montagna" (February 1, 1914); Carrà, "1900–1913: bilancio" (February

1, 1914); Gustave Fivé, "Sports" (February 1, 1914); Marinetti, "Dune" (February 15, 1914); Soffici, "Passeggiata" (February 15, 1914); and Cangiullo, "Serata in onore di Yvonne" (June 15, 1914). In addition the piece of sheet music is part of a composition by Pratella (*Lacerba*, February 1, 1914).

47. Joshua Taylor, *Futurism* (New York: Museum of Modern Art, 1961), p. 110.

48. Marianne W. Martin, *Futurist Art and Theory 1909–1915* (Oxford: Clarendon Press, 1968), p. 194.

2. The Futurist experience

1. Herbert Marcuse, *Reason and Revolution: Hegel and the Rise of Social Theory* (Boston: Beacon Press, 1960), p. x.

2. Guillaume Apollinaire, *L'Antitradition futuriste: Oeuvres complètes*, ed. Michel Décaudin (Paris: Balland-Lecat, 1965–6), pp. 876a–876c.

3. *Manifesto tecnico della letteratura futurista*, May 11, 1912.

4. See Carlo Carrà, *Disegni*, ed. Franco Russoli and Massimo Carrà (Bologna: Grafis, 1977), pp. 159 and 162.

5. Ibid., p. 160.

6. Ibid., p. 162.

7. Ibid.

8. Ibid., p. 160.

9. I would like to thank Dr. Massimo Carrà, who kindly provided a photographic enlargement of the drawing during the preparation of this study.

10. J. J. Carre, "Ardengo Soffici et Guillaume Apollinaire: au-delà du futurisme," *Revue des Lettres Modernes*, Nos. 183–188 (1968) (*Guillaume Apollinaire 7*): 112.

11. Although the Futurists' headquarters were in Milan, their official journal, *Lacerba*, was published in Florence. Soffici served as co-editor for the two and a half years of its existence, from January 1, 1913, to May 22, 1915.

12. These characteristics probably reflect the influence of Mallarmé, whose poetry Soffici knew well. Compare the sonnet "Ses Purs Ongles" ("Its Pure Nails"), for example, which presents several parallels with "Bicchier d'acqua" and which exemplifies Mallarmé's poetics of stillness and absence.

13. Apollinaire uses the same device in "Côte 146" ("Hill 146"), which dates from 1915 (*Oeuvres poétiques*, ed. Marcel Adéma and Michel Décaudin [Paris: Gallimard/ Pléiade, 1965], p. 613). Like Soffici before him, he repeats the words "à cheval" ("on horseback") four times in smaller and smaller type to evoke a horseman riding off into the distance.

14. Manufactured in Milan, this product was advertised in the *Corriere della Sera* as follows: "Per la cura dei capelli e della barba usate sole *Chinina–Migone*... Una sola applicazione rimuove la forfara e dà ai capelli una morbidezza speciale" ("For the care of your hair and beard use only *Chinina-Migone*... A single application removes dandruff and gives a special softness to your hair").

15. Parigi, o cara, noi lasceremo,
  La vita uniti trascorreremo,
  De' corsi affanni compenso avrai –
  La tua salute rifiorirà.

Sospiro e luce tu mi sarai,
Tutto il futuro ne arriderà. . . .
(*La Traviata*)

16. In 1919 Soffici reprinted the former in *BÏF§ZF + 18* with several important changes. Omitting the right side of the newspaper altogether, he published the left side (much revised) and the coffee machine as separate poems. See Luciano Caruso and Stelio M. Martini, *Tavole parolibere futuriste (1912–1944)*, Naples: Liguori, 1974, Vol.1, pp. 161–2.

3. Apollinaire's plastic imagination

1. Pascal Pia, *Apollinaire par lui-même* (Paris: Seuil, 1954), p. 174; Hubert Fabureau, *Guillaume Apollinaire, son oeuvre* (Paris: Nouvelle Revue Critique, 1932), p. 60; Roger Avermaete, "De l'imprimerie contemporaine," *Le Livre et L'Estampe*, 10 (April 1957): 111.

2. Counterbalancing Soffici's and Arbouin's enthusiastic reviews of "Lettre-Océan," Warnod wrote: "Ce poème (?) est sans doute une manière d'évocation du téléphone et de la télégraphie sans fil mais il n'empêche qu'on regrette de le voir signé par un poète au talent si grand. Ce soir, nous relirons *Alcools*." ("This poem [?] is doubtless a sort of evocation of the telephone and wireless telegraphy, but just the same one regrets seeing it signed by such a talented poet. Tonight I will re-read *Alcools*.") In *Comoedia*, June 22, 1914.

3. Michel Foucault, *Ceci n'est pas une pipe* (Montpellier: Fata Morgana, 1973), pp. 21–2.

4. "Si vous pouviez trouver les numéros de juin et de juillet des *Soirées de Paris*, vous verriez ce que j'ai inventé de plus nouveau pour ce qui touche à l'art poétique" ("If you could find the June and July issues of *Les Soirées de Paris*, you would see the newest thing I have invented in the realm of poetry"). In a letter to Jeanne-Yves Blanc, September 28, 1915 (*Oeuvres complètes*, ed. Michel Décaudin [Paris: Balland-Lecat, 1965–6], Vol. 4, p. 673; hereafter abbreviated *OEC*). In a letter to André Billy dated July 29, 1918, Apollinaire insisted, "[C'est] moi qui ai commencé cette sorte de poésie" ("I am the one who started this kind of poetry") (*OEC*, Vol. 4, p. 778).

5. This discussion is particularly indebted to three studies: Peter Mayer, "Framed and Shaped Writing," *Studio International*, 176, 903 (September 1968): 110–14; Charles Boultenhouse, "Poems in the Shape of Things," *Art News Annual*, 28 (1959): 64–83 and 178; and David W. Seaman, *Concrete Poetry in France* (Ann Arbor, Mich.: UMI Research Press, 1981).

6. Alain-Marie Bassy, "Forme littéraire et forme graphique: les schématogrammes d'Apollinaire," *Scolies*, Nos. 3–4 (1973–4): 165–6.

7. Margaret Davies, "Apollinaire, la peinture et l'image," *Que Vlo-ve?* (Belgium), Nos. 21–2 (July–October 1979): 16.

8. K. R. Dutton, "Apollinaire and Communication," *Australian Journal of French Studies*, 5, No. 3 (September–December 1968): 325–6.

9. Michel Décaudin, "A propos de *Calligrammes*," in *Calligrammes*, by Guillaume Apollinaire (Paris: Club du Meilleur Livre, 1955), p. 181.

10. For an excellent analysis of the role of discontinuity and modern communications in Apollinaire's aesthetic, see Dutton, "Apollinaire and Communication."

11. Wolfgang Iser, *The Act of Reading: A Theory of Aesthetic Response* (Baltimore: Johns Hopkins University Press, 1978), pp. 10–19.

12. See note 5. For a slightly revised version of Mayer's system and a discussion of other typologies, see Mayer's "Some Remarks Concerning the Classification of the Visual in Literature," *Dada/Surrealism*, No. 12 (1983): 5–13. See also Jacques Derrida: "L'histoire de la voix et de son écriture serait comprise entre deux écritures muettes, entre deux pôles d'universalité se rapportant l'un à l'autre comme le naturel et l'artificiel: le pictogramme et l'algèbre" ("The history of the voice and its writing is comprehended between two mute writings, between two poles of universality relating to each other as the natural and the artificial: the pictogram and algebra") (*De la Grammatologie*, [Paris: Minuit, 1967], p. 428). For an illuminating discussion of the development of writing, see the section entitled "Histoire et système des écritures," pp. 397–416.

13. *Oeuvres poétiques*, ed. Marcel Adéma and Michel Décaudin (Paris: Gallimard/ Pléiade, 1965), p. 675; cited hereafter in the text and the notes as *Po*. For a detailed study of this calligram see Willard Bohn, "*Poésie Critique* and *Poésie Visuelle*: Apollinaire's 'Les Lunettes,' " forthcoming.

14. The photograph on which this calligram was modeled reveals that Lou's dress was a solid, dark color. See Guillaume Apollinaire, *Lettres à Lou*, ed. Michel Décaudin (Paris: Gallimard, 1969), plate 10.

15. According to Blaise Cendrars the name was suggested by Apollinaire's neighbor, Dr. Mardrus. See Cendrars's *Blaise Cendrars vous parle* (Paris: Denoël, 1952), p. 244.

16. Gabriel Arbouin, "Devant l'idéogramme d'Apollinaire," *Les Soirées de Paris*, Nos. 26–7 (July–August 1914): 383.

17. Arbouin ("Devant l'idéogramme d'Apollinaire," p. 384) discerns precisely the same mechanism: "Qui n'apercevrait que ce ne peut être qu'un début, et que, par l'effet de la logique déterministe qui entraine l'évolution de tout méchanisme, semblables poèmes doivent finir par présenter un ensemble pictural en rapport avec le sujet traité?" ("Who doesn't perceive that this may only be the beginning and that, following the effects of determinist logic which postulates the evolution of every mechanism, similar poems will eventually present a pictorial whole connected with the subject of the poem?")

18. Ernest Fenollosa, *The Chinese Written Character as a Medium for Poetry* (San Francisco: City Lights, 1969), p. 8.

19. Ibid., p.10.

20. Bassy, "Forme littéraire," pp. 187–8.

21. See Fenollosa, *Chinese Written Character*, p. 33.

22. For the following argument see Bassy, "Forme littéraire," pp. 196–200.

23. Roland Barthes, "Rhétorique de l'image," *Communications*, No. 4 (1964): 40–51; Umberto Eco, "Sémiologie des messages visuels," *Communications*, No. 15 (1970): 11–51.

24. Roland Barthes, "Le Message photographique," *Communications*, No. 1 (1961): 127–38.

25. J. C. Cooper elaborates: "*Salamander.* In Christian Symbolism it represents enduring faith and the righteous man who cannot be consumed by the fires of temptation. In Heraldry it depicts bravery and courage unquenched by the fires of affliction" (*An Illustrated Encyclopedia of Traditional Symbols* [London: Thames & Hudson, 1978]).

26. Compare the following lines from "Les Collines" ("The Hills"): "Sept ans d'incroyables épreuves / L'Homme se divinisera / Plus pur plus vif et plus savant" ("Seven years of incredible trials / Man will become divine / More pure more alive and more knowing") (*Po,* p. 174). "Les Profondeurs" was sent to *La Raccolta,* which appeared from March 15, 1918, to February 15, 1919, but was not published until 1926.

27. Jean Marquès-Rivière, *Amulettes, talismans et pantacles* (Paris: Payot, 1972), p. 328.

28. For a stimulating discussion of the role of words and letters in Cubist painting, see Susan Marcus, "The Typographic Element in Cubism, 1911–1915: Its Formal and Semantic Implications," *Visible Language,* 6, No. 4 (Fall 1972): 321–40.

29. See Stefan Themerson, *Apollinaire's Lyrical Ideograms* (London: Gaberbocchus, 1968), pp. 20–3.

30. Charles Boultenhouse connects the human figure with Eros in "A Note on Apollinaire's Calligram," *Tri-Quarterly,* No. 4 (1965): 41–5. For a detailed analysis of this poem see Willard Bohn, "Landscaping the Visual Sign: Apollinaire's 'Paysage,' " forthcoming.

31. Compare the still life drawing that Juan Gris gave to Apollinaire "vers 1916," which uses the same triangular form (*Les Peintres cubistes,* ed. L. C. Breunig and J.-C. Chevalier [Paris: Hermann, 1965], plate 4).

32. For the first poem see P. A. Jannini, *Le avanguardie letterarie nell'idea critica di Guillaume Apollinaire* (Rome: Bulzoni, 1971), pp. 207–8. Versions of the second poem are reproduced here by the kind permission of the Francis Bacon Library, Claremont, California.

33. The manuscript is reproduced in Pierre Cailler, *Guillaume Apollinaire, documents iconographiques* (Geneva: Cailler, 1965), plate 61.

34. That "Lettre-Océan" is intimately linked to "Simultanisme – Librettisme" can also be seen from the fact that the poem continues the article's polemic against Henri-Martin Barzun.

35. Wolfgang Iser, *The Implied Reader: Patterns of Communication from Bunyan to Beckett* (Baltimore: Johns Hopkins University Press, 1974), p. 288.

36. Bassy, "Forme Littéraire," p. 200. Cf. M.-J. Durry: "Je me sens toujours gênée, devant un calligramme, par le fait qu'il n'apporte qu'une *apparance* de simultanéité" ("Faced with a calligram, I always feel bothered by the fact that it only *appears* to be simultaneous") (during discussion of Jean Levaillant's presentation, *Revue des Lettres Modernes,* Nos. 217–22 [1969] [*Guillaume Apollinaire 8*]:64). Bassy also attacks the notion of simultaneity in general: "Admettons que plusieurs perceptions frappent simultanément nos sens . . . elles n'accèdent pas toutes simultanément à la conscience" ("Admitting for the moment that several perceptions strike our senses simultaneously . . . they do not all reach the conscious mind simultaneously") (p. 202). That he is clearly wrong is demonstrated by Barthes's "Rhétorique de l'image," which analyzes precisely this phenomenon.

37. This is not really as unexpected as it may seem. The same process can be detected in two important precursors of the calligram, both of which are mentioned in "Simultanisme-Librettisme": the poster and Cubist painting. In both cases a simultaneous overview must be delayed until the mind has reviewed the various elements and imposed an interpretation on them.

38. Iser's theory is outlined in *The Implied Reader*, pp. 274–94, and developed in detail in *The Act of Reading*.

4. Toward a calligrammar

1. Roman Jakobson, "Two Aspects of Language and Two Types of Aphasic Disturbances," in *Fundamentals of Language*, by Roman Jakobson and Morris Halle, 2nd ed. (The Hague: Mouton, 1971), pp. 69–96.

2. With three exceptions these can all be found in the *Oeuvres poétiques*, ed. Marcel Adéma and Michel Décaudin (Paris: Pléiade, 1965); cited hereafter in the text and in the notes as *Po.* "Dans les caves" is reproduced in Pierre-Marcel Adéma's *Guillaume Apollinaire* (Paris: Table Ronde, 1968), plate 46. In "De Paris à Nîmes, souvenirs et témoignages," Gaston Bouatchidzé, Pierre Caizergues, Michel Décaudin, and Pascal Pia include a figurative poem featuring a cannon beneath a stylized sun (*Revue des Lettres Modernes*, Nos. 380–84 [1973] [*Guillaume Apollinaire 12*]:32). Finally, the poem "Pablo Picasso" appears in the *Oeuvres complètes*, ed. Michel Décaudin (Paris: Balland-Lecat, 1965–6). In general I have preferred manuscripts and first states to later versions. Thus "Oracles" has been included, and the wire circle reading "mesure du doigt" in "Venu de Dieuze" eliminated. The thirteen calligrams from the Léopold Survage-Irène Lagut catalogue are divided into groups (and hence different poems) as follows: glasses and book; port, clock, and bridge; fabulous beast; horse; woman, fountain, leg, and bouquet; bird and *galette*.

3. "Dans les caves" exists as an independent manuscript but is actually part of another poem, "Du coton dans les oreilles." The calligram in "La Petite Auto" (which dates from January 1915) seems to have existed by itself before the final 1917 version.

4. Only recently has anyone tried to provide a comprehensive analysis. See Alain-Marie Bassy, "Forme littéraire et forme graphique: les schématogrammes d'Apollinaire," *Scolies*, Nos. 3–4 (1973–4): 161–207. See also the eight-fold structuralist typology by Pénélope Sacks, "La Mise en page du calligramme," and Jean-Pierre Goldenstein, "Pour une sémiologie du calligramme," both in *Que Vlo-Ve?* (Belgium), Nos. 29–30 (July–October 1981): 1–17 and 1–8, paginated separately.

5. Charles Boultenhouse, "A Note on Apollinaire's Calligrams," *Tri-Quarterly*, No. 4 (1965): 41.

6. Bassy, "Forme littéraire," p. 172.

7. François Rigolot, "Le Poétique et l'analogique," *Poétique*, No. 35 (September 1978): 257–68.

8. Michel Foucault, *Ceci n'est pas une pipe* (Montpellier: Fata Morgana, 1973), pp. 17–30.

9. Jean Gérard Lapacherie, "Ecriture et lecture du calligramme," *Poétique*, No. 50 (April 1982): pp. 194–206.

10. In the proofs of the ill-fated volume *Et moi aussi je suis peintre*, the syllable *sé* is turned sideways and inserted between *pa* and *mes* to form a rudimentary penis. Thus five different members are affected by the lovers' actions. Charles Boultenhouse detects a reference to Eros, whose classic epithet is "the limb loosener." See Guillaume Apollinaire, *Et moi aussi je suis peintre, idéogrammes lyriques coloriés*, ed. Michel Décaudin (Paris: Sébastien Gryphe, forthcoming), which includes photos of the original proofs.

11. At this point, though consecrated by usage, the term "visual metaphor" becomes problematic. It should probably be reserved for situations in which both the tenor and the vehicle are visual, as opposed to verbal–visual and visual–verbal exchanges.

12. "2ᵉ Cannonier conducteur" (*Po*, p. 214) contains a similar Notre Dame calligram in which the visual metonymy is made explicit: "Souvenirs de Paris avant la guerre ils seront bien plus doux après la victoire" ("Memories of Paris before the war they will be very much sweeter after the victory").

13. These include "Lettre-Océan," "La Mandoline l'oeillet et le bambou," "Le Soleil de la paix," "Je fume en pensant," "2ᵉ Cannonier conducteur," "Premier Cannonier conducteur," "Eventail des saveurs," the woman–fountain–leg–bouquet group for Irène Lagut, "L'Horloge de demain," and "Les Profondeurs."

14. The manuscripts are reproduced in P. A. Jannini, *Le avanguardie letterarie nell'idea critica di Guillaume Apollinaire* (Rome: Bulzoni, 1971), pp. 207–8.

15. Gérard Genette, "Métonymie chez Proust," *Figures III* (Paris: Seuil, 1972), p. 42.

5. Josep-Maria Junoy

1. See, for example, Guillem Díaz-Plaja, *L'avantguardisme a Catalunya i altres notes de critica* (Barcelona: "La Revista," 1932), pp. 17–18.

2. Agustí Esclasans, "L'obra d'En Joan Salvat-Papasseit," *La Revista*, 10, No. 215–16 (1924): 106. For Apollinaire's influence in particular, see Willard Bohn, "Guillaume Apollinaire: Homage from Catalonia," *Symposium*, 33 No. 2 (Summer 1979): 101–17, and Pierre Caizergues, "Apollinaire et l'avant-garde catalane," *Quaderni del Novocento Francese*, No. 1 (1984): 143–70.

3. Although the precise dates are hard to come by, we know that the Dalmau Gallery sponsored an exhibition by Hélène Grunhoff and Serge Charchoune during April and May 1916. For a photograph of the projected cover of the catalogue, with a drawing by Charchoune, see Arturo Schwarz, ed., *Almanacco Dada, Antologia letteraria-artistica, cronologia, repertorio delle riviste* (Milan: Feltrinelli, 1976), p. 579.

4. Diaz-Plaja, *L'avantguardisme a Catalunya*, p. 26.

5. See the *Records i opinions de Pere Ynglada*, ed. Carles Soldevila (Barcelona: Aedos, 1959), especially the chapter entitled "Aquell Josep Maria Junoy," pp. 71–80.

6. See, for example, LeRoy Breunig, "Surrealist Alphabets," *Dada/Surrealism*, No. 7 (1977): 59–65.

7. Roland Barthes, *S/Z* (Paris: Seuil, 1970), p. 74.

8. Françoise Reiss, *La Vie de Nijinsky* (Paris: Plon, 1957), pp. 126–7. In Barcelona Nijinsky danced in both *Narcisse* and *Cléopâtre*.

Notes to pp. 95–115

9. Reproduced in Luciano Caruso and Stelio M. Martini, eds., *Tavole parolibere futuriste (1912–1944)* (Naples: Liguori, 1974) Vol.1, p. 184.

10. Among the critics who mistakenly give 1915 as the date of publication in *Iberia* are Díaz-Plaja (see note 1) and J. J. A. Bertrand, *La Littérature catalane contemporaine 1833–1933* (Paris: Belles Lettres, 1933).

11. "Acaba de sortir," *Trossos*, 2nd ser., No. 4 (March 1, 1918): 2.

12. Published in *L'Europe Nouvelle*, April 6, 1918. See Guillaume Apollinaire, *Oeuvres complètes*, ed. Michel Décaudin (Paris: Balland-Lecat, 1965–6), Vol. 2, pp. 708–10. For a letter from Apollinaire to Junoy (and other relevant information) see Willard Bohn, "Josep-Maria Junoy," *Revue des Lettres Modernes*, Nos. 576–81 (1980): 149–59.

13. The French version reads: "Dans l'appareil mortellement blessé, le moteur, coeur luisant, gronde encore, mais voici que l'âme intrépide du jeune héros vole déjà vers les constellations." The version in *Poemes i cal·ligrammes*, entitled "Oda a Guynemer," contains additional variants: "CIEL DE FRANCE – dins de l'avió mortalment ferit per l'espai hi brunzeix encara el lluent cor del motor mes l'ánima del palid adolescent heroï vola ja vers les constelacions."

14. Junoy's alphabetical constellations recall the calligrammatic sky in Apollinaire's "Voyage" and the constellation mentioned in *Cas du brigadier masqué*, which reads "VIVE LA FRANCE!" The same idea occurs in "Merveille de la guerre," in which Apollinaire imagines a sky filled with flares like the letters in a book. See Guillaume Apollinaire, *Oeuvres poétiques*, ed. Marcel Adéma and Michel Décaudin (Paris: Gallimard/Pléiade, 1965), pp. 198–9 and 270; see also Apollinaire, *Oeuvres en prose*, ed. Michel Décaudin (Paris: Gallimard/Pléiade, 1977), Vol. 1, p. 384.

6. Modes of visual analogy in Catalonia

1. "De la jove poesia catalana," *Troços*, 2nd ser., No. 1 (September 1917): p. 5.

2. The analysis of this poem owes much to discussions with Professor Luis Monguió.

3. See, for example, Folguera's "Ambició," in *Poesies completes*, 2nd ed. (Barcelona: Selecta, 1951), p. 172.

4. Reprinted in *Traduccions i fragments* (Barcelona: La Revista, 1921). See Guillaume Apollinaire, *Oeuvres poétiques*, ed. Marcel Adéma and Michel Décaudin (Paris: Gallimard/Pléiade, 1965), p. 203. Cited hereafter in the text as *Po*.

5. Guillem Díaz-Plaja, *L'avantguardisme a Catalunya i altres notes de critica* (Barcelona: La Revista, 1932), p. 27.

6. Jonathan Culler, *Structuralist Poetics: Structuralism, Linguistics, and the Study of Literature* (Ithaca, N.Y.: Cornell University Press, 1975), p. 177.

7. Díaz-Plaja, *L'Avantguardisme*, p. 17. Despite its promising title Carles Salvador's *Plàstic. Poesies* (Valencia: Pere Peñalver Debón, 1923) contains no visual poetry.

8. Barcelona: Llibreria Calalònia, 1928. After this date the visual movement subsided until the appearance of concrete poetry in the 1950s, which took Spain and the rest of Europe by storm. For an excellent discussion of this development in Catalonia see Miquel Arimany, *L'avantguardisme en la poesia catalana actual* (Barcelona: Pòrtic, 1972), especially pp. 199–223.

Notes to pp. 123–146

7. Joan Salvat-Papasseit

1. Interview with Joan Alavedra by Joan Agut, "El primer poeta anarquista de Catalunya," *Indice*, 21, No. 209 (1966): 36–7.

2. Salvat's six books of poetry have been collected in *Poesies*, ed. Joaquim Molas, 2nd ed. (Barcelona: Ariel, 1978). Page references cited in the text are to this volume. His most important articles can be found in *Mots-propis i altres proses*, ed. J. M. Sobre (Barcelona: Edicions 62, 1975).

3. Preface to Joan Salvat-Papasseit, *Cincuenta poemas*, 2nd ed. (Barcelona: Lumen, 1977), p. 4.

4. Issued as a pamphlet in July 1920, the manifesto is reprinted in *Mots-propis*, pp. 81–3. In March 1922, following Salvat's example, David Cristià (Sebastià Sànchez-Juan) published a second manifesto supporting the latter's campaign to modernize Catalan poetry. Entitled *Contra l'extensió del tifisme en literatura (Against the Spread of Literary Spinelessness)*, it bore the subtitle: "segon manifest català futurista." Ironically, Italian Futurism seems to have taken its name from an earlier movement headed by the Catalan Gabriel Alomar. See, for example, Lily Litvak de Pérez de la Dehesa, "Alomar and Marinetti: Catalan and Italian Futurism," *Revue des Langues Vivantes*, 47, No. 6 (1972): 585–603.

5. Agustí Carreres, "J. Salvat-Papasseit, professió de fe," *Hèlix*, No. 1 (February 1929): 2.

6. "Concepte del Poeta," *Mar Vella*, No. 4 (December 1919). Reprinted in *Hèlix*, (March 1929), and in *Mots-propis*, pp. 79–80.

7. "La ploma d'Aristarc," *La Publicidad*, June 24, 1921. Reprinted in *Mots-propis*, 91–93.

8. "Fragments de lletres girades," *La Revista*, No. 7 (1921): 197–80. Reprinted in *Mots-propis*, pp. 85–86.

9. Agustí Esclasans, "J. Salvat-Papasseit, *Óssa menor*," in *Articles inèdits*, by Joan Salvat-Papasseit (Barcelona: Quatre Coses, 1925), pp. 121–9.

10. *Mots-propis*, p. 24.

11. Although the history of the visual prayer goes back to ancient Greece, the genre has practically become extinct. The Lord's Prayer does appear in Juan Bautista's "Revelación" published in *Grecia*, 2, No. 37 (1919): 15, but the poem as a whole does not function as a prayer.

8. The advent of Ultra

1. See Guillermo de Torre, "Contemporary Spanish Poetry," *Texas Quarterly*, 4, No. 1 (Spring 1961): 60–62.

2. Rafael Cansinos-Asséns, "Los poetas del 'Ultra,'" *Cervantes*, June 1919, p. 86. Cansinos is paraphrasing part of the first Ultraist manifesto, published in *Grecia*, 2, No. 11 (1919): "En nuestro credo cabrán todas las tendencias sin distinción, con tal que expresen un anhelo nuevo" ("Our credo will include all the different trends, provided that they express a yearning for the new").

3. The only book-length study of the movement is Gloria Videla's *El ultraísmo*, 2nd ed. (Madrid: Gredos, 1971). Thorpe Running examines Ultraism in Argentina in

Notes to pp. 146–173

Borges' Ultraist Movement and Its Poets (Lathrup Village, Mich.: International Book Publishers, 1981).

4. For an excellent discussion of Reverdy and Huidobro in the context of Cubist painting see George Yúdice, "Cubist Aesthetics in Painting and Poetry," *Semiotica*, 36, No. 1–2 (1981): 107–33.

5. Neri Nannetti, "Trait-d'union," *L'Italia Futurista*, 2, No. 27 (1917). Reproduced in Luciano Caruso and Stelio M. Martini, eds., *Tavole parolibere futuriste (1912–1944)* (Naples: Liguori, 1974), Vol. 1, p. 198.

6. Videla, *El ultraísmo*, p. 165.

7. Cf. Vicente Huidobro, "Tour Eiffel," *Nord-Sud*, Nos. 6–7 (August–September 1917): 24.

8. Videla, *El ultraísmo*, p. 116. Andrew P. Debicki concurs with Videla and calls the poem "a comic mixture of sentimental expressions, prosaic details, and literary allusions" (*Dámaso Alonso* [New York: Twayne, 1970], p. 30.

9. Gerardo Diego quoted in Videla, *El ultraísmo*, p. 109. Guillermo de Torre, *Hélices, poemas (1918–1922)* (Madrid: Mundo Latino, 1923), p. 86.

10. For the development of concrete poetry in Spain, see José María Montells, "Poesía concreta española," *Insula*, March 27, 1972, p. 13. Fernando Millán and Jesús García Sánchez include numerous Spanish examples in *La escritura en libertad: antología de poesía experimental* (Madrid: Alianza, 1975). See also the special issue of *Poesía* (Madrid) devoted to the calligram (No. 3 [November–December 1978]).

9. Guillermo de Torre

1. For Apollinaire's influence on Torre see Willard Bohn, "Apollinaire's Reign in Spain," *Symposium*, 35, No. 3 (Fall 1981): 186–214.

2. *Cervantes*, September 1919, pp. 27–29. Reprinted in *Grecia*, 3, No. 41 (1920): 7, and in Guillermo de Torre, *Hélices, poemas (1918–1922)* (Madrid: Mundo Latino, 1923), p. 51.

3. This manifesto is reproduced in Gloria Videla, *El ultraísmo*, 2nd ed. (Madrid: Gredos, 1971), plate 2.

4. *Grecia*, 3, No. 38 (January 20, 1920): 13–15. Judging from its subject and from the preface by Isaac del Vando-Villar, the poem was probably written shortly after Apollinaire's death in November 1918. In *Apollinaire y las teorías del cubismo* (Barcelona and Buenos Aires: EDHASA, 1967), p. 26, Torre claims that it was composed "siguiendo la técnica de los caligramas" ("according to calligrammatic technique"), but this is clearly impossible. He may have been thinking of "Paisaje plástico."

5. *Cosmópolis*, 9, No. 34 (October 1921): 200–3. A French version of "Torreiffel" (dated 1920) had appeared in *La Vie des Lettres* in July.

6. The principal variants are the following: In the earlier version "SIESTA" slants downward, the words "SOL VERTICAL" are arranged vertically in the lower left-hand corner, "BIELDOS" and "HORCAS" occupy opposite places, and the phrase "En la alucinación sensorial abajo la égida meridia advienen" occupies a single line. In addition the reference to the "eucaristía triptolémica" is followed by the line "Un intenso y áureo reflejo alucina los ojos" ("An intense golden reflection dazzles the eyes").

7. Torre, *Hélices*, p. 86.

8. "Sinopsis" is a revised version of an earlier work entitled "Ultra-Vibracionismo," which Torre translated into visual terms for *Hélices*. Published in *Grecia* on June 10, 1919, the original poem was dedicated to Miguel Romero and bore an epigraph from Huidobro's *Poemas árticos:* "Palabras puntiagudas en el azul del viento" ("Pointed words in the blue of the wind"). Subtitled "Perspectiva Sinóptica" and modeled on the Futurist *tavole sinottiche di valori lirici*, it reads as follows: "Estratos subterráneos de los confines délicos / Franjas sidéreas de las entrañas telúricas / ALBATROS VELÍVO-LOS / OH HÉLICE REENCARNADA EN EL CORAZÓN CÓSMICO / Cómo hallar el vértice energético / El orbe renaciente trepida ascensional / HANGAR / SIDERAL / Líricas cumbres superatrices. / Lejanas llanuras cotidianistas / TERRÁQUEO ES-PASMO DE OCCIDENTAL AFIRMACIÓN / ANTENAS / PLENI- / SOLAR / REÓFORO / ATERRIZAJE / OH LA FRAGRANTE DEHISCENCIA NOVIDIMENSIONAL."

10. Marius de Zayas and abstraction

1. For a study of his art and its influence on Francis Picabia see Willard Bohn, "The Abstract Vision of Marius de Zayas," *Art Bulletin*, 63, No. 3 (September 1980): 434–52. See also Douglas Hyland, *Marius de Zayas: Conjurer of Souls* (Lawrence, Kansas: Spencer Museum of Art, 1981), which is heavily indebted to the preceding study.

2. For the history of his relations with Apollinaire see Willard Bohn, "Guillaume Apollinaire and the New York Avant-Garde," *Comparative Literature Studies*, 13, No. 1 (March 1976): 40–51.

3. Guillaume Apollinaire, *Les Peintres cubistes*, ed. L. C. Breunig and J.-C. Chevalier (Paris: Hermann, 1965), p. 89.

4. Craig R. Bailey, "The Art of Marius de Zayas," *Arts Magazine*, 53, No. 1 (September 1978): 141.

5. Dickran Tashjian, *Skyscraper Primitives: Dada and the American Avant-Garde 1910–1925* (Middletown, Conn.: Wesleyan University Press, 1975), p. 34.

6. These quotations and the following summary are taken from the preface to his 1913 exhibition at "291." The latter was reprinted in *Camera Work* on two different occasions: first as "Exhibition Marius de Zayas" in Nos. 42–3, (April–July 1913):20–2, then as "Caricature: Absolute and Relative" in No. 46 (April 1914): 19–21.

7. De Zayas later stated, with characteristic modesty, that the *291* poems were based on work by Apollinaire and the Futurists. See "*291* – A New Publication," *Camera Work*, No. 48 (October 1916): 62. He added that they represent experiments in "psychotype, an art which consists in making the typographical characters participate in the expression of the thoughts and in the painting of the states of soul, no more as conventional symbols but as signs having significance in themselves." Both the definition and the term "psychotype" are lifted from an article by Amédée Ozenfant entitled "Psychotypie & typométrique," *L'Elan*, No. 9 (February 1916), inside front cover.

Bibliography

Adéma, Pierre-Marcel. *Guillaume Apollinaire.* Paris: Table Ronde, 1968.

Adéma, Pierre-Marcel, and Michel Décaudin, eds. *Album Apollinaire.* Paris: Gallimard/Pléiade, 1971.

Alavedra, Joan. "El primer poeta anarquista de Catalunya," with Joan Agut. *Indice,* 21, No. 209 (1966): 36–7.

Apollinaire, Guillaume. *Anecdotiques.* Edited by [Pierre-]Marcel Adéma. Paris: Gallimard, 1955.

———. *Et moi aussi je suis peintre, idéogrammes lyriques coloriés.* Edited by Michel Décaudin. Paris: Sébastien Gryphe, forthcoming.

———. Letter to Félicien Fagus. *Paris-Midi,* July 22, 1914. Reprinted in *Points et Contrepoints,* No. 105 (December 1972): 3–4.

———. *Lettres à Lou.* Edited by Michel Décaudin. Paris: Gallimard, 1969.

———. *Méditations esthétiques: les peintres cubistes.* Edited by L. C. Breunig and J.-C. Chevalier. Paris: Hermann, 1965.

———. *Oeuvres complètes.* Edited by Michel Décaudin. 4 vols. Paris: Balland-Lecat, 1965–6.

———. *Oeuvres Poétiques.* Edited by [Pierre-]Marcel Adéma and Michel Décaudin. Paris: Gallimard/Pléiade, 1965.

———. *Oeuvres en prose.* Edited by Michel Décaudin. Vol. 1. Paris: Gallimard/Pléiade, 1977.

Apollonio, Umbro, ed. *Futurist Manifestos.* New York: Viking, 1972.

Aragon, Louis. "Suicide." *Cannibale,* April 25, 1920, p. 4.

Arbouin, Gabriel. "Devant l'idéogramme d'Apollinaire." *Les Soirées de Paris,* Nos. 26–27 (July–August 1914): 383–5.

Arimany, Miquel. *L'avantguardisme en la poesia catalana actual.* Barcelona: Pòrtic, 1972.

Avermaete, Roger. "De l'imprimerie contemporaine." *Le Livre et L'Estampe,* 10 (April 1957): 109–14.

Bailey, Craig R. "The Art of Marius de Zayas." *Arts Magazine,* 53, No. 1 (1978): 136–44.

Barthes, Roland. *The Eiffel Tower and Other Mythologies.* Translated by Richard Howard. New York: Hill & Wang, 1979.

———. "Le Message photographique." *Communications,* No. 1 (1961): 127–38.

———. *Mythologies.* Paris: Seuil, 1957.

219

Bibliography

"Rhétorique de l'image." *Communications*, No. 4 (1964): 40–51.

S/Z. Paris: Seuil, 1970.

Bassy, Alain-Marie. "Forme littéraire et forme graphique: les schématogrammes d'Apollinaire." *Scolies*, Nos. 3–4 (1974–5): 161–207.

Bates, Scott. *Guillaume Apollinaire*. New York: Twayne, 1967.

Petit Glossaire des mots libres d'Apollinaire. Sewanee, Tenn.: privately printed, 1975.

Batlló, Josep. Preface to *Cincuenta poemas*, by Joan Salvat-Papasseit. 2nd ed. Barcelona: Lumen, 1977.

Bautista, Juan. "Revelación." *Grecia*, 2 No. 37 (1919): 15.

Bergman, Pär. *"Modernolatria" et "simultaneità."* Paris: Lettres Modernes, 1962.

Bertrand, J. J. A. *La Littérature catalane contemporaine 1833–1933*. Paris: Belles Lettres, 1933.

Bohn, Willard. "The Abstract Vision of Marius de Zayas." *Art Bulletin*, 63, No. 3 (September 1980): 434–52.

"Apollinaire's Reign in Spain." *Symposium*, 35, No. 3 (Fall 1981): 186–214.

"Circular Poem-Paintings by Apollinaire and Carrà." *Comparative Literature*, 31, No. 3 (Summer 1979): 246–71.

"Guillaume Apollinaire: Homage from Catalonia." *Symposium*, 33, No. 2 (Summer 1979): 101–17.

"Guillaume Apollinaire and the New York Avant-Garde." *Comparative Literature Studies*, 13, No. 1 (March 1976): 40–51.

"Josep-Maria Junoy." *Revue des Lettres Modernes*, Nos. 576–81 (1980) (*Guillaume Apollinaire 15*): 149–59.

"Landscaping the Visual Sign: Apollinaire's 'Paysage.' " Forthcoming.

"Orthographe et interprétation des mots étrangers chez Apollinaire." *Que Vlo-Ve?* (Belgium), No. 27 (January 1981): 27–30.

"Poésie Critique and *Poésie Visuelle:* Apollinaire's 'Les Lunettes.' " Forthcoming.

Bouatchidzé, Gaston, Pierre Caizergues, Michel Décaudin, and Pascal Pia. "De Paris à Nîmes, souvenirs et témoignages." *Revue des Lettres Modernes*, Nos. 380–34 (1973) (*Guillaume Apollinaire 12*): 27–43.

Boultenhouse, Charles. "A Note on Apollinaire's Calligram." *Tri-Quarterly*, No. 4 (1965): 41–45.

"Poems in the Shape of Things." *Art News Annual*, 28 (1959): 64–83; 178.

Bóveda, Xavier, César A. Comet, Fernando Iglesias, Guillermo de Torre, Pedro Iglesias Caballero, Pedro Garfias, J. Rivas Panedas, and J. de Aroca. "Ultra." *Grecia* 2, No. 11 (1919): 11.

Breunig, LeRoy. "Surrealist Alphabets." *Dada/Surrealism*, No. 7 (1977): 59–65.

Buckley, Ramón, and John Crispin, eds. *Los vanguardistas españoles (1925–1935)*. Madrid: Alianza, 1973.

Bürger, Peter. *Theory of the Avant-Garde*. Translated by Michael Shaw. Minneapolis: University of Minnesota Press, 1984.

Butor, Michel. *Les Mots dans la peinture*. Geneva: Skira; Paris: Flammarion, 1969.

Preface to *Calligrammes*, by Guillaume Apollinaire. Paris: Gallimard/Poésie, 1966.

Bibliography

Cailler, Pierre. *Guillaume Apollinaire: documents iconographiques.* Geneva: Cailler, 1965.

Caizergues, Pierre. "Apollinaire et l'avant-garde catalane." *Quaderni del Novocento Francese,* No.1 (1984):143–70.

Apollinaire journaliste: les débuts et la formation du journaliste (1900–1909). Vol. 1. Paris: Lettres Modernes, 1981.

Calinescu, Matei. *Faces of Modernity.* Bloomington: Indiana University Press, 1977.

Cangiullo, Francesco. "Fumatori II." *Lacerba,* 2, No. 1 (1914): 10–11.

Cansinos-Asséns, Rafael. *La evolución de la poesía (1917–1927).* Madrid: Paéz, 1927.

"Los poetas del 'Ultra.' " *Cervantes,* June 1919, pp. 84–6.

Carrà, Carlo. *Disegni.* Edited by Franco Russoli and Massimo Carrà. Bologna: Grafis, 1977.

La mia vita. 2nd ed. Milan: Rizzoli, 1945.

Tutta l'opera pittorica. Edited by Massimo Carrà. 3 vols. Milan: Edizioni dell'Annunciata and Edizioni delle Conchiglia, 1967–8.

Tutti gli scritti. Edited by Massimo Carrà. Milan: Feltrinelli, 1978.

Carre, J. J. "Ardengo Soffici et Guillaume Apollinaire: au-delà du futurisme." *Revue des Lettres Modernes,* Nos. 183–8 (1968) (*Guillaume Apollinaire 7*): 112–24.

Carreres, Agustí. "J. Salvat-Papasseit, professió de fe." *Hèlix,* No 1 (February 1929): 2.

Caruso, Luciano, and Stelio M. Martini. *Tavole parolibere futuriste (1912–1944).* 2 vols. Naples: Liguori, 1974–7.

Cendrars, Blaise. *Blaise Cendrars vous parle.* Paris: Denoël, 1952.

Oeuvres complètes. Vol. 1. Paris: Denoël, 1963.

Chevalier, Jean-Claude. *Alcools d'Apollinaire, essai d'analyse des formes poétiques.* Paris: Lettres Modernes, 1970.

Claudel, Paul. *Cinq Grandes Odes.* Paris: Gallimard, 1948.

Cooper, J. C. *An Illustrated Encyclopedia of Traditional Symbols.* London: Thames & Hudson, 1978.

Cristià, David [Sebastià Sànchez-Juan]. *Contra l'extensió del tifisme en literatura.* Barcelona: privately printed, 1922.

Culler, Jonathan. *Structuralist Poetics: Structuralism, Linguistics, and the Study of Literature.* Ithaca, N.Y.: Cornell University Press, 1975.

Davies, Margaret, *Apollinaire.* London: Oliver & Boyd, 1964.

"Apollinaire, la peinture et l'image." *Que Vlo-Ve?* (Belgium), Nos. 21–2 (July–October 1979): 1–20, paginated separately.

Debicki, Andrew P. *Dámaso Alonso.* New York: Twayne, 1970.

Debon, Claude. *Guillaume Apollinaire après Alcools.* Vol. 1, Calligrammes: *le poète et la guerre.* Paris: Lettres Modernes, 1981.

Décaudin, Michel. "A propos de *Calligrammes.*" In *Calligrammes,* by Guillaume Apollinaire. Paris: Club du Meilleur Livre, 1955, pp. 179–87.

Delbreil, Daniel. " 'Lettre-Océan,' " by Daniel Delbreil, Françoise Dininman, and Alan Windsor. *Que Vlo-Ve?* (Belgium), Nos. 21–2 (July–October 1979): pp. 1–6; 22–38; paginated separately.

Derrida, Jacques. *De la Grammatologie.* Paris. Minuit, 1967.

Marges de la philosophie. Paris: Minuit, 1972.

221

Bibliography

Díaz-Plaja, Guillem. *L'avantguardisme a Catalunya i altres notes de critica.* Barcelona: La Revista, 1932.

Dininman, Françoise. " 'Lettre-Océan,' " by Daniel Delbreil, Françoise Dininman, and Alan Windsor. *Que Vlo-Ve?* (Belgium), Nos. 21–22 (July–October 1979): pp. 13–22; 22–38; paginated separately.

Drudi Gambillo, Maria, and Teresa Fiori, eds. *Archivi del futurismo.* 2 vols. Rome: DeLuca, 1958.

Durry, Marie-Jeanne. *Guillaume Apollinaire,* Alcools. 3 vols. Paris: SEDES, 1956–64.

Dutton, K. R. "Apollinaire and Communication." *Australian Journal of French Studies,* 5, No. 3 (September–December 1968): 303–28.

Eco, Umberto. "Sémiologie des messages visuels." *Communications,* No. 15 (1970): 11–51.

Esclasans, Agustí. "J. Salvat-Papasseit, *Óssa menor.*" In *Articles inèdits,* by Joan Salvat-Papasseit. Barcelona: Quatre Coses, 1925, pp. 121–29.

"L'obra d'En Joan Salvat-Papasseit." *La Revista,* 10, Nos. 215–16 (1924): 105–9.

Fabureau, Hubert. *Guillaume Apollinaire, son oeuvre.* Paris: Nouvelle Revue Critique, 1932.

Fagus, Félicien. "La 'Poésie figurative.' " *Paris-Midi,* July 20, 1914.

Fenollosa, Ernest. *The Chinese Written Character as a Medium for Poetry.* San Francisco: City Lights, 1969.

Folguera, Joaquim. *Poesies completes.* 2nd ed. Barcelona: Selecta, 1951.

Traduccions i fragments. Barcelona: La Revista, 1921.

Foucault, Michel. *Ceci n'est pas une pipe.* Montpellier: Fata Morgana, 1973.

Fuster, Joan. *Literatura catalana contemporànea.* Barcelona: Curial, 1972.

Gecé [Ernesto Giménez Caballero]. *Carteles.* Madrid: Espasa-Calpe, 1927.

Géfin, Laszlo. *Ideogram: History of a Poetic Method.* Austin, University of Texas Press, 1982.

Genette, Gérard. *Figures II.* Paris: Seuil, 1969.

Figures III. Paris Seuil, 1972.

Goldenstein, Jean-Pierre. "Pour une sémiologie du calligramme." *Que Vlo-Ve?* (Belgium), Nos. 29–30 (July–October 1981): pp. 1–8, paginated separately.

Gullón, Germán, ed. *Poesía de la vanguardia española.* Madrid: Taurus, 1981.

Huidobro, Vicente. "Tour Eiffel." *Nord-Sud,* Nos. 6–7 (August–September 1917): 24.

Hyland, Douglas. *Marius de Zayas: Conjuror of Souls.* Lawrence, Kansas: Spencer Museum of Art, 1981.

Ilie, Paul, ed. *Documents of the Spanish Vanguard.* Chapel Hill: University of North Carolina Press, 1969.

Iser, Wolfgang. *The Act of Reading: A Theory of Aesthetic Response.* Baltimore: Johns Hopkins University Press, 1978.

The Implied Reader: Patterns of Communication from Bunyan to Beckett. Baltimore: Johns Hopkins University Press, 1974.

Jakobson, Roman. "Two Aspects of Language and Two Types of Aphasic Disturbances." In *Fundamentals of Language,* by Roman Jakobson and Morris Halle. 2nd ed. The Hague: Mouton, 1971.

Janacek, Gerald. *The Look of Russian Literature: Avant-Garde Visual Experiments, 1900–1930.* Princeton, N.J.: Princeton University Press, 1984.

Bibliography

Jannini, P. A. *Le avanguardie letterarie nell'idea critica di Guillaume Apollinaire.* Rome: Bulzoni, 1971.

Junoy, Josep-Maria. *Guynemer.* Barcelona: Antonio Lopez, 1918.

"De la jove poesia catalana." *Troços,* 2nd ser., No. 1 (September 1917): 5.

Poemes i cal·ligrames. Barcelona: Llibreria Nacional Catalana, 1920.

Karsavina, Tamara. *Theatre Street* (1931). New York: Dutton, 1961.

Kostelanetz, Richard, ed. *Visual Literature Criticism.* Carbondale: Southern Illinois University Press, 1980.

Kozloff, Max. *Cubism/Futurism.* New York: Charterhouse, 1973.

Kuenzli, Rudolf E. "The Semiotics of Dada Poetry." In *Dada Spectrum: The Dialectics of Revolt,* edited by Stephen C. Foster and Rudolf E. Kuenzli. Madison, Wis.: Coda; Iowa City, University of Iowa Press, 1979.

Lapacherie, Jean Gérard. "Ecriture et lecture du calligramme." *Poétique,* No. 5 (April 1982): 194–206.

Lessing, G. E. *Selected Prose Works of G. E. Lessing.* Edited by Edward Bell. Translated by E. C. Beasley and Helen Zimmern. London: G. Bell, 1879.

Levaillant, Jean. "L'Espace dans *Calligrammes.*" *Revue des Lettres Modernes,* Nos. 217–22 (1969) (*Guillaume Apollinaire 8*): 48–63.

Lista, Giovanni. *Futurisme: manifestes, documents, proclamations.* Lausanne: L'Age d'Homme, 1973.

Litvak de Pérez de la Dehesa, Lily. "Alomar and Marinetti: Catalan and Italian Futurism." *Revue des Langues Vivantes.* 47, No. 6 (1972): 585–603.

Mallarmé, Stéphane. *Correspondance.* Edited by Henri Mondor and Jean-Pierre Richard. Vol. 1, Paris: Gallimard, 1959.

Oeuvres complètes. Edited by Henri Mondor and G. Jean-Aubry. Paris: Gallimard/Pléiade, 1956.

Marcus, Susan. "The Typographic Element in Cubism, 1911–1915: Its Formal and Semantic Implications." *Visible Language,* 6, No. 4 (Fall 1972): 321–40.

Marcuse, Herbert. *Reason and Revolution: Hegel and the Rise of Social Theory.* Boston: Beacon Press, 1960.

Marinetti, F. T. "Dopo il verso libero le parole in libertà." *Lacerba,* Vol. 1, No. 22 (1913): 252–4.

Selected Writings. Edited by R. W. Flint. New York: Farrar, Straus, & Giroux, 1972.

Zang tumb tuuum. Milan: Poesia, 1914.

Marinetti, F. T., Umberto Boccioni, Carlo Carrà, and Luigi Russolo. "Programma politico futurista." *Lacerba,* 1, No. 20 (1913): 221–2.

Marquès-Rivière, Jean. *Amulettes, talismans et pantacles.* Paris: Payot, 1972.

Marrochi, Giuseppe. *Scrittura visuale: ricerche ed esperienze nelle avanguardie letterarie.* Messina and Florence: D'Anna, 1978.

Martin, Marianne W. *Futurist Art and Theory 1909–1915.* Oxford: Clarendon, 1969.

Mayer, Peter. "Framed and Shaped Writing." *Studio International,* 176, No. 903 (September 1968): 110–14.

"Some Remarks Concerning the Classification of the Visual in Literature." *Dada/Surrealism,* No. 12 (1983): 5–13.

Millán, Fernando, and Jesús García Sánchez, eds. *La escritura en libertad: antología de poesía experimental.* Madrid: Alianza, 1975.

Bibliography

Montells, José María. "Poesía concreta española." *Insula*, March 27, 1972, p. 13.

Morris, C. B. *A Generation of Spanish Poets 1920–1936*. Cambridge University Press, 1969.

Nogueras Oller, Rafel. *Les tenebroses*. Barcelona: Plaça del Teatre, 1905.

Ozenfant, Amédée. "Psychotypie & typométrique." *L'Elan*, No. 9 (February 1916), inside front cover.

Pia, Pascal. *Apollinaire par lui-même*. Paris: Seuil, 1954.

Pinottini, Marzio. *L'estetica del futurismo, revisioni storiografiche*. Rome: Bulzoni, 1979.

Poesía. Madrid: Ministerio de Cultura. No. 3 (November–December 1978).

Poggioli, Renato. *The Theory of the Avant-Garde*. Translated by Gerald Fitzgerald. New York: Harper & Row, 1971.

Pozzi, Giovanni. *La parola dipinta*. Milan: Adelphi, 1981.

Renaud, Philippe. *Lecture d'Apollinaire*. Lausanne: L'Age d'Homme, 1969.

Rigolot, François. "Le Poétique et l'analogique." *Poétique*, No. 35 (September 1978): 257–68.

Running, Thorpe. *Borges' Ultraist Movement and Its Poets*. Lathrup Village, Mich.: International Book Publishers, 1981.

Sacks, Pénélope. "La Mise en page du calligramme." *Que Vlo-Ve?* (Belgium), Nos. 29–30 (July–October 1981): 1–17, separately paginated.

Salvat-Papasseit, Joan. *Articles inèdits*. Barcelona: Quatre Coses, 1925.

    Mots-propis i altres proses. Edited by J. M. Sobre. Barcelona: Edicions 62, 1975.

    Poesies. Edited by Joaquim Molas. 2nd ed. Barcelona: Ariel, 1978.

Sánchez-Juan, Sebastià. *Fluid, poemes*. Barcelona: Nova Cultura, 1924.

Saussure, Ferdinand de. *Cours de linguistique générale* (1916). Paris: Payot, 1964.

Schmits, George. " 'Lettre-Océan.' " *Savoir et Beauté* (Belgium), Nos. 2–3 (1964): 2691–8.

Schwarz, Arturo, ed. *Almanacco Dada: antologia letteraria-artistica, cronologia, repertorio delle riviste*. Milan: Feltrinelli, 1976.

Seaman, David W. *Concrete Poetry in France*. Ann Arbor, Mich: UMI Research Press, 1981.

Shattuck, Roger. "Apollinaire, Hero-Poet." In *Selected Writings of Guillaume Apollinaire*. Edited and translated by Roger Shattuck. New York: New Directions, 1971.

Sindreu i Pons, Carles. *Radiacions i poemes*. Barcelona: Llibreria Catalònia, 1928.

Soffici, Ardengo. *Ardengo Soffici: l'opera incisa*. Ed. Sigfrido Bartolini. Reggio Emilia: Prandi, 1972.

    BÏFŠZF + 18. Simultaneità e chimismi lirici. Florence: Vallecchi, 1919.

    "Chicchi del grappolo." *Lacerba*, 2, No. 3 (1914): 42–3.

    Cubismo et futurismo. Florence: La Voce, 1914.

    "Il soggetto nella pittura futurista." *Lacerba*, 2, No. 1 (1914): 7–8.

Steiner, Wendy. *The Colors of Rhetoric: Problems in the Relation Between Modern Literature and Painting*. University of Chicago Press, 1982.

Steiner, Wendy, ed. *Image and Code*. Ann Arbor: University of Michigan Press, 1981.

Tashjian, Dickran. *Skyscraper Primitives: Dada and the American Avant-Garde 1910–1925*. Middletown, Conn.: Wesleyan University Press, 1975.

Bibliography

Taylor, Joshua. *Futurism*. New York: Museum of Modern Art, 1961.

Themerson, Stefan. *Apollinaire's Lyrical Ideograms*. London: Gaberbocchus, 1968.

Torre, Guillermo de. *Apollinaire y las teorías del cubismo*. Barcelona and Buenos Aires: EDHASA, 1967.

"Contemporary Spanish Poetry." *Texas Quarterly*, 4, No. 1 (Spring 1961): 55–78.

Hélices, poemas (1918–1922). Madrid: Mundo Latino, 1923.

Historia de las literaturas de vanguardia. Madrid: Guadarrama, 1965.

Videla, Gloria. *El ultraísmo*. 2nd ed. Madrid: Gredos, 1971.

Windsor, Alan. "Apollinaire, Marinetti, and Carrà's 'Dipinto Parolibero.'" *Gazette des Beaux-Arts* 89 (April 1977): 145–52. Reprinted in "'Lettre-Océan.'" Daniel Delbreil, Françoise Dininman, and Alan Windsor, *Que Vlo-Ve?* (Belgium), Nos. 21–2 (July–October 1979): pp. 6–13, paginated separately.

Ynglada, Pere. *Records i opinions de Pere Ynglada*. Edited by Carles Soldevila. Barcelona: Aedos, 1959.

Yúdice, George. "Cubist Aesthetics in Painting and Poetry." *Semiotica*, 36, Nos. 1–2 (1981): 107–33.

Zayas, Marius de. "Exhibition Marius de Zayas." *Camera Work*, Nos. 42–3 (April–July 1913): 20–2. Reprinted as "Caricature: Absolute and Relative" in *Camera Work*, No. 46 (April 1914): 19–21.

"*291* – A New Publication." *Camera Work*, No. 48 (October 1916): 62.

Zayas, Marius de, and Paul B. Haviland. *A Study of the Modern Evolution of Plastic Expression*. New York: 291, 1913.

Index

Adéma, Pierre-Marcel, 47
Alavedra, Joan, 123
Albert-Birot, Pierre, 60
Alomar, Gabriel, 216n4
Alonso, Dámaso, 167–71
Apollinaire, Guillaume, 4, 6, 9
  calligrams for Léopold Survage, 52, 83
  in Castile and Andalusia, 146, 171, 172,
    177
  in Catalonia, 85, 86, 88, 98, 109, 111, 124
  contribution to visual poetry, 49–51, 53–6
  and Marius de Zayas, 185, 188, 191, 193,
    203, 218 n7
  role of Chinese ideogram, 56–8
  use of metaphor and metonymy, 70–84
  visual poetics, 46–68
Apollinaire, Guillaume, works of
  Case d'armons, 76
  "La Clef," 21
  "Coeur couronne et miroir," 56–8, 60, 62,
    63, 64, 65, 73, 80, 81, 82
  "Du coton dans les oreilles," 55
  "Coup d'éventail," 58–9, 60, 62, 78–9, 82
  "La Cravate et la montre," 51, 53, 54, 60,
    62, 75–6, 79
  "2e Cannonier conducteur," 76, 78, 79
  "Les Fenêtres," 18, 22, 64, 115
  "La Figue l'oeillet et la pipe à opium," 51,
    52, 58, 74
  "Fumées," 79
  "L'Horloge de demain," 53
  "Il a contemplé les foules," 52, 83
  "Il pleut," 60, 109, 111, 153
  "Je fume en pensant," 79
  "Lettre-Océan," 9–24, 27–8, 56, 60, 62,
    67, 69–70, 73, 74, 82
  "Lierre herbe de la fidelité," 74
  "Loin du pigeonier," 76–8
  "A Lou, hommage respectueusement
    passionné," 52, 55
  "Lundi rue Christine," 18, 22, 64

  "Madeleine," 53
  "La Mandoline l'oeillet et le bambou," 60,
    62, 64
  "Montparnasse," 60, 74
  "L'Oiseau et le bouquet," 70, 77, 78
  "Pablo Picasso," 79
  "Paysage," 55, 60–2, 74, 83, 175, 176
  Les Peintres cubistes, 17
  "La Petite Auto," 74
  "Poème du 9 février 1915," 53, 74–5
  "Premier Cannonier conducteur," 76, 77,
    78, 79
  "Les Profondeurs," 53, 58
  "Simultanisme-Librettisme," 18–9, 21, 22,
    64–6
  "Survage est le nom qui lui convient," 83
  "De toi depuis longtemps," 73
  "Tour," 23–4
  "Le Troisième Poème secret," 82
  "Visée," 75
  "Voyage," 60, 71–3, 83, 185
  "Zone," 17, 114, 178
Aragon, Louis, 91
Arbouin, Gabriel, 14, 55–56
Arp, Jean, 191

Bailey, Craig R., 188
Ball, Hugo, 7
Barthes, Roland, 5, 58, 93, 208 n39
Barzun, Henri-Martin, 22, 64, 66
Bassy, Alain-Marie, 49, 52, 56, 58, 64, 67,
  70–1
Battló, Josep, 123
Bergson, Henri, 191
Bétuda, 95
Boccioni, Umberto, 85, 91–3
Breton, André, 151
Boultenhouse, Charles, 70
Browning, Robert, 143
Butor, Michel, 18, 19

Index

Cándiz, Ángel, *see* Alonso, Dámaso
Cangiullo, Francesco, 16–17, 51, 130–1
Cansinos-Asséns, Rafael, 146
Carrà, Carlo, 9
  "Cd'hArcOUrFÉ," 43
  Festa patriottica, 9–14, 24–8, 46, 69–70, 208 n45
  "Rapporto di un NOTTAMBULO milanese," 30–6, 46, 69–70
  Sintesi circolare di oggetti, 43, 44–5
Carre, J. J., 36
Carreres, Agustí, 123
Cendrars, Blaise, 64, 66
Charchoune, Serge, 85
Chevalier, Jean-Claude, 23
Chirico, Giorgio de, 52, 87
Claudel, Paul, 4
Cristià, David, *see* Sánchez-Juan, Sebastià
Cubism, 17–18, 36–7, 39–40, 43–5, 70, 84, 88–9, 111, 185–91, 194, 197
  see also literary cubism, simultanism
Culler, Jonathan, 4, 114
cummings, e e, 3

Dada, 7
Davies, Margaret, 21, 49
Debussy, Claude, 118
Décaudin, Michel, 50
Delaunay, Sonia, 64, 66
Delbreil, Daniel, 17, 23
Derrida, Jacques, 3, 6
Díaz-Plaja, Guillermo, 86, 111, 115
Diego, Gerardo, 171
Dininman, Françoise, 23
Durry, Marie-Jeanne, 18, 67

Eco, Umberto, 58
Esclasans, Agustí, 85, 124

Fagus, Félicien, 46
Fenollosa, Ernest, 56
Folguera, Joaquim, 102, 109–14, 122
  "En avió," 111–14
  "Musics cecs de carrer," 109–11
  "Vetlla de desembre plujós," 109
Foucault, Michel, 2, 46, 71
Futurism, 4, 6, 43, 50, 188, 203, 218 n8
  in Castile and Andalusia, 146, 147, 152, 172, 173, 175, 177, 218 n8
  in Catalonia, 85, 86, 89, 91–3, 95, 98, 109, 115, 119, 123–4, 126, 129, 130, 145, 216 n4
  ideological implications, 29–30
  poetics 13–17
  verbal painting, 9–14, 24–8, 29–45
  visual poetry, 9, 15–17, 29–30, 37–45

Gecé, *see* Giménez Caballero, Ernesto
Genette, Gérard, 4, 83–4
Giménez Caballero, Ernesto, 171
Gleizes, Albert, 85
Grunhoff, Hélène, 85, 88–90
Guynemer, Georges, 98

Herbert, George, 48
Horace, 1
Huidobro, Vicente, 51, 165

Iribarne, Federico de, 155–61, 185
Iser, Wolfgang, 3, 50, 66, 67, 68

Jakobson, Roman, 62, 83, 90
  theory of metaphor and metonymy, 69–70
Junoy, Josep-Maria, 7, 85–102, 103, 109
  "Art poètica," 90–1
  "C₂ H₂," 102
  "Estela angular," 91–3, 95, 101
  "Eufòria," 97–9
  "Guynemer," 99–101, 103, 111
  "ja de bona hora," 95–7, 98, 99
  "Jongleurs d'Hélène Grunhoff," 88–90

Kozloff, Max, 24–5

Lapacherie, Jean Gérard, 71
Larrea, Juan
  "ESTANQUE," 146–50, 153
  "SED," 150, 151–4, 165, 177
  "Tormenta," 150–1
Léger, Fernand, 60–2
Lessing, Gotthold Ephraim, 1
Levaillant, Jean, 23
literary cubism, 17–18, 22
  in Castile and Andalusia, 147, 151
  in Catalonia, 85, 113–14, 115, 119
  see also Cubism, simultanism

Machado, Antonio, 169–70
Mallarmé, Stéphane
  "Les Fenêtres," 169–70
  "Ses Purs Ongles," 170–1
  Un Coup de dés jamais n'abolira le hasard, 3–4, 18–19, 49, 50
Manet, Edouard, 97
Marcuse, Herbert, 29
Marinetti, Filippo Tomaso, 14–17, 33, 85, 98, 123, 145, 172
  "Correzione," 25
Martin, Marianne W., 28
Mauron, Charles, 23
Mayer, Peter, 50–1, 53
metaphor and metonymy
  in Apollinaire's calligrams, 62, 70–84
  Jakobson's theory of, 69–70

227

Index

Meyer, Agnes Ernst, 185–203
Moreau, Gustave, 178
Mosquera, Luis, 161–3, 166

Nijinsky, Vaslav, 94–5
Nogueras Oller, Rafel, 85
Nougués, Xavier, 85

Panard, Charles-François, 46–8, 51
Picabia, Francis, 88
Pound Ezra, 4
Puccini, Giacomo, 111

Rabelais, François, 46–8, 51
Raida, Pedro, 154–5, 171
Renaud, Philippe, 23
Renoir, Auguste, 97
Reverdy, Pierre, 151
Rigolot, François, 5, 71
Rousseau, Henri (le Douanier), 58

Salvat-Papasseit, Joan, 102, 103, 123–45
    "Batzec," 143–4
    "54045," 127
    "Drama en el port," 127–30
    "Les formigues," 131–6
    "Jaculatòria," 136–8, 144, 163
    "Marseille port d'amour," 138–40, 144
    "Marxa nupcial," 130–1, 132–4, ,144, 148
    "Plànol," 124–7, 129
    "Romàntica," 140–3
Sánchez-Juan, Sebastià, 115, 216 n4
Saussure, Ferdinand de, 4
Schmits, Georges, 18, 20, 21, 22
Shattuck, Roger, 19
Shklovsky, Victor, 50
Simonides of Keos, 1
simultanism, 17–19, 22–3, 24, 64–8, 113–
    14, 151, 185–8, 203
    see also Cubism, literary cubism
Sindreu i Pons, Carles, 102, 115–23
    "Futbol," 115–17

"Pleniluni," 119–22
"El vol de l'oreneta," 117–19
Soffici, Ardengo
    "Bicchier d'acqua," 37–40, 51, 69–70
    Al buffet della stazione, 40–4, 50, 69–70
    Lines and Volumes of a Street, 36
    "Passeggiata," 25, 40, 36–45
    Simultaneità di Donna Carretto strada, 36,
        37
Solé de Sojo, Vicenç, 102–9, 122, 163
    "CIRL," 106–9
    "Sonet," 102–6, 108
Steiner, Wendy, 8
Stieglitz, Alfred, 185, 191, 192, 198

Tashjian, Dickran, 188–9 198, 203
Taylor, Joshua C., 26
Togores, Josep de, 85
Torre, Guillermo de, 146, 155, 158, 171,
    172–84
    "Arco iris," 173, 176
    "Aviograma," 172
    "Cabellera," 177–9
    "Epiceyo a Apollinaire," 173, 176
    "Giràndula," 179–81
    Manifiesto ultraísta vertical, 172
    "Paisaje plástico," 173–6, 182, 184
    "Sinopsis," 181–3
    "Torreiffel," 173
    "Ultra-Vibracionismo," 218 n8

Valéry, Paul, 121
Valle, Adriano del, 163–7, 171, 176, 178
Van Gogh, Vincent, 200
Verdi, Giuseppe, 42
Videla, Gloria, 155, 167–8

Whitman, Walt, 124

Ynglada, Pierre, 85–8

Zayas, Marius de, 7, 185–203, 218 n7

228